Dear Tina,

This was an incredibly enjoyable research have truly paid off. Thank you for following your heart and listening to the inner voice that guided you, bringing together the historical insights of the Parkers, both Anglo-Comanche and the Mennonites, whose faith kept them going where others would have quit.

Future generations will enjoy the opportunity to experience firsthand the challenges of life endured by these remarkable men and women who persevered in their quests for a better life for themselves and all those to come. Thank you for preserving this story of our ancestors pursuing a better life.

With Gratitude,
PaulaAnn Tahmahkera Phillips, Anglo-Comanche.
Great-great-Granddaughter of Chief Quanah Parker, Anglo-Comanche

In *Post Oak*, Tina Siemens masterfully brings to life the complexities and human stories within the historical context of the Seminole people and the era of "Cowboys versus Indians." This prequel to her first book, *Seminole: Some People Never Give Up*, delves deep into the experiences of the Parker family and Chief Quanah Parker, based on both primary sources and credible historical accounts.

Siemens' dedication to accuracy and balanced storytelling shines through as she navigates through various accounts and narratives. Her commitment to presenting both sides of the argument and acknowledging the messiness of human nature adds depth and nuance to the historical events. The book is not just a recounting of history but a thoughtful exploration of the human spirit amidst conflict.

Readers will appreciate Siemens' thorough research and the way she weaves together different perspectives to create a cohesive and engaging narrative. The book challenges preconceived notions and invites readers to reflect on the complexities of history and the people who lived it.

Overall, *Post Oak* is a commendable addition to historical literature, offering a well-rounded and thought-provoking perspective on a turbulent era. It's a must-read for those interested in history and the human stories behind it.

Mark Woommavovah
Former Chairman of the Comanche Nation

Post Oak

QUANAH PARKER, THE COMANCHE, AND THE MISSION

TINA SIEMENS

BASED ON A TRUE STORY

© 2025 Tina Siemens

All rights reserved. No part of this book may be reproduced or transmitted in any form or by any means whatsoever without express written permission from the author. The scanning, uploading, and distribution of this book via the Internet or via any other means without the author's permission are illegal and punishable by law. For permission requests, reach the author at the following contact information:

Email address: SeminoleTheBook@gmail.com.

Printed in the United States of America.

ISBN 979-8-3042-7864-5

First Trade paperback edition in 2025.

Author Consultant and Editing: Company 614 Enterprises, LLC.
Cover Image: Jon Ren
Cover Design: Diren Yardimli
Text Design and Composition: Rick Soldin

Photos from the Tina Siemens Family Collection are used with permission.

Author Photo: Alejandra Dodge

Scripture taken from the New King James Version®. Copyright © 1982 by Thomas Nelson. Used by permission. All rights reserved.

When purchasing electronic editions, please purchase only *authorized* electronic editions. Do not participate in or encourage electronic piracy of copyrighted materials. Your support of the author's rights is sincerely appreciated.

Post Oak is a work of historical fiction. It has been heavily researched, and information has been used from many sources. This includes reported actions and conversations of most of the historical characters. However, since we weren't there, we can't be sure of how they acted and what they said. Thus, all incidents, dialogue, and characters, with the exception of well-known historical figures, are products of the author's imagination and are not to be construed as real. Where real-life historical persons appear, the situations, incidents, and dialogues concerning those persons are entirely fictional and are not intended to depict actual events or to change the entirely fictional nature of the work. In all other respects, any resemblance to persons, living or dead, is entirely coincidental.

Dedication
HISTORY MATTERS

Those who fail to learn from history are doomed to repeat it.
~ Winston Churchill

To all the gatherers and tellers of history: may you continue to pass down lessons from the past to a younger generation so they can see and repeat the good and learn not to repeat the bad. This is my mission in life—to give to our children and grandchildren this history.
~ Tina Siemens

Table of Contents

Foreword 9
About the Artist Jon Ren 13
Introduction 15

Rachel 18	**Naduah** 152
Chapter One 19	Chapter Fourteen 153
Chapter Two 30	Chapter Fifteen 159
Chapter Three 37	Chapter Sixteen 173
Chapter Four 45	Chapter Seventeen 181
Chapter Five 54	Chapter Eighteen 189
Chapter Six 65	Chapter Nineteen 199
Chapter Seven 81	Chapter Twenty 207
Chapter Eight 89	
Chapter Nine 99	**Quanah** 224
Chapter Ten 109	Chapter Twenty-One . . . 225
Chapter Eleven 119	Chapter Twenty-Two . . . 233
Chapter Twelve 131	Chapter Twenty-Three . . 238
Chapter Thirteen 143	Chapter Twenty-Four . . . 249

Chapter Twenty-Five 261	**Henry** 373
Chapter Twenty-Six 270	Chapter Thirty-Nine 374
Chapter Twenty-Seven ... 274	Chapter Forty 381
Chapter Twenty-Eight ... 284	Chapter Forty-One 393
Chapter Twenty-Nine ... 289	Chapter Forty-Two 403
Chapter Thirty 296	Chapter Forty-Three 411
Chapter Thirty-One 301	Chapter Forty-Four 419
	Chapter Forty-Five 424
Herman 313	
Chapter Thirty-Two 314	**Post Oak Mission** 436
Chapter Thirty-Three ... 324	Chapter Forty-Six 437
Chapter Thirty-Four 333	Chapter Forty-Seven 445
Chapter Thirty-Five 339	Chapter Forty-Eight 454
Chapter Thirty-Six 347	Chapter Forty-Nine 465
Chapter Thirty-Seven ... 354	Chapter Fifty 472
Chapter Thirty-Eight ... 365	Chapter Fifty-One 480

Epilogue 487
Post Oak Photos 503
Bibliography 531
Biography of Tina (Katharina) Siemens 543

Foreword
by Ron Parker

I am the great-grandson of Quanah Parker and a proud, full-blooded citizen of the Comanche Nation of Oklahoma. I am also a founder and director of the Quanah Parker Society and curator of the Quanah Parker Museum in Quanah, Texas.

I have spent nearly fifty years bringing Quanah Parker's legacy to Quanah, Texas, and beyond. Tina Siemen's book will help do that.

My parents were Marquerite (Tahchawwickah) and Baldwin Parker, Jr. My grandfather, Baldwin Parker, Sr., and his wife lived with Quanah when they first got married. Grandfather quickly learned that Quanah was the boss; the Chief did what he wanted to do.

From 1944 to 1957, I attended the Post Oak Mission Church. Established by Henry Kohfeld in 1895, it was the only church on the western range.

When I lived in Parker, Arizona, I met Henry Kohfeld's son in Fresno, California. He told me how the mission was started.

Henry Kohfeld, Reverend Isaak Harms, and Peter Bergman traveled by wagon to the agency office at Fort Sills in Lawton, Oklahoma, to establish a church among the Comanches.

"You've got to go see Quanah Parker," the Indians told him.

They pointed out the direction to Quanah's Star House. Later, Mr. Kohfeld, along with an interpreter, set out. After several attempts, the men found Quanah was not home. They told the family members they would stay down by the creek, so they camped out and waited.

Quanah finally came in with a group of people.

The next morning, Quanah asked, "Who are those people down by the creek?"

"They want to start a church."

"Tell them to come up here," Quanah said.

The missionary, Henry Kohfeld, and his interpreter appeared and told Quanah about his desire to build a church. Quanah went into his house to speak with his tribesmen. When he came back out, Quanah had a hatchet in hand.

Quanah hopped on his horse, told Henry and the interpreter to do the same, and raced two to three miles west before getting off and cutting a V-notch in a large post oak tree. After he pulled the hatchet out, it was like a handshake.

"Here, you can build your Jesus house if you will build a day school as well," Quanah told him.

And the Post Oak Mission Church was built in 1896. The Post Oak Mission School was built in 1948.

I loved the Post Oak Mission Church. It was great the Mennonites came. When I was there, Mrs. Anna Gomez was the nurse. She took us to the hospital if we needed to go. I loved her and the Neufelds and Gerbrandts and many more Mennonite Brethren missionaries who came through the years.

The best thing that happened to us Comanche was the Post Oak Mission Church. That's why I consider myself Mennonite brethren.

At the Post Oak Mission Church, I started out as an usher and a song leader. In plays, I was Joseph and sang bass. Eventually, I became a member of the board but not a deacon.

Quanah had other beliefs even though he preached a sermon at his son Harold's funeral. He had some sons who were preachers. And he never kept the Indians from getting baptized despite not being baptized himself.

Quanah believed in a creator, but his creator was on a mountain and not in a church. He held many peyote ceremonies. My dad said he was healed with the medicine—peyote—which helped with the hallucinations. One time, I was in there for about six hours and drank some tea, but it didn't affect me.

My grandfather was a big peyote man. He used to sing in his back room. My dad claimed there was nothing more beautiful than sitting up on a water drum and watching the sunrise. It was like a hymn to him. Still, I wouldn't drop my religion to sit up on that.

Historians always frame Quanah's coming to the reservation as a surrender, yet I haven't seen any surrender papers. I always say he came to terms with coming in, but he still made the right decision to bring his people in. They would have annihilated him.

According to stories I heard, Quanah met McKenzie at Bowie Creek because Quanah was afraid to come in. Quanah never got off his horse and looked down on McKenzie just in case something happened.

Quanah was a leader. But what makes a leader? I am not a follower, so I don't know if I was born with it. After his mother was captured, he had a reason to be a leader. He had to do what he had to do. Quanah Parker brought his people into the 20th century but preserved the Comanche culture.

I never heard of stories of Quanah scalping people, but he was fierce and a good warrior. And he loved his mom, Cynthia Ann Parker. I'm sure she died of depression.

Quanah's opponents and detractors claim he was a rich man. He was not. He gave things away because he had a big heart. Quanah couldn't even leave money to his daughter to rebuild the Star House. She had to trade it off to get it rebuilt.

Quanah gave everything away. When people arrived, he fed them with some cows he kept. If people came to his house, he gave them what they needed.

Quanah cared a lot for his people, looking after them as best he could while trying to protect their way of life. He died poor, so saying he was rich was a misconception that the Whites put on him.

The schools at Cache thought us Native Americans were dirty and so forth. There were hardly any students in the schools when Quanah came in. He started his own school and was the superintendent of the one-room schoolhouse in Cache, Oklahoma.

Quanah hired his own teacher for his kids. He sent his children off to Carlisle, Pennsylvania. He sent my father to a school in Oklahoma City. We have family members who are medical doctors, Eagle Scouts, teachers, pharmacists, and have PhDs. We don't brag about ourselves, but we are not followers.

Another misconception is that Quanah never had seven wives under one roof at one time. His house wasn't big enough. Instead, he had two or three wives at a time. They didn't have a formal marriage or divorce process. "It's just time for you to leave."

Quanah was active in his civic duties and ambassador roles. The reservation had strict rules, and Quanah's job was to maintain order and compliance with them. They couldn't fight the government.

Going back to my youth, attending the Post Oak Mission Church was the highlight of my week. Then, at twenty-two, I went to war in Vietnam.

I served in the U.S. Army—the First Battalion, 28th Infantry Regiment—for over two years, mostly north of Saigon near the Cambodian border. I was a captain and came out of Vietnam; I still have difficult times today.

"Peace with honor." President Nixon said it, and Secretary of State Kissinger, too. I've seen people die, and there is no peace with honor in any war.

Sometimes I wake up in a cold sweat. A military helicopter from Fort Sill or any shot will scare me. Yet, Quanah would've been proud of me in Vietnam. No other family members went to Vietnam, though my uncle fought in Germany as a Code Talker.

When I came home, I built walls between people to avoid grief. I lost myself in grief.

But there is always the Post Oak Mission church. When folks around the country die, their family will bring them back to Post Oak to be buried.

GOODWILL, GOOD WAY.
  ~ Ron Parker

Author's Note: Ron was interviewed on June 17, 2021. He greatly supported this project and the West Texas Living Heritage Museum in Seminole, Texas. Sadly, he passed away on December 12, 2022, before he could see either this book or the museum completed. He is dearly missed.

About the Artist Jon Ren

The front cover image is an acrylic painting I did of Quanah Parker. It took one full month working 40 to 60 hours a week. There were a lot of ups and downs, especially with the color of the sky. It took me four or five times to get it right.

I've been an artist all my life. When I was very little, I started drawing with pencil before moving up to pen and ink. My dad, Chuck Ren, was an artist, and he nurtured my talent.

Dad started off doing commercial art in Southern California, where I was born and raised. Dad painted all the team posters for the NFL, which were then sold at stadiums back in the '70s and '80s. He also painted several movie posters and memorabilia before entering Native American art. That's where Dad really took off with originals and limited-edition prints. Truly, everything I learned was from him.

I was always scared to start painting because there is so much more involved. In fact, I didn't start painting until I was in high school, where a great art teacher, David Lash, mentored me. Since then, I've always painted with acrylic because it dries fast. You can make mistakes and paint over it or make it look like watercolor or oil. Acrylics are much more forgiving.

I followed a similar route as Dad. I went to the Colorado Institute of Art and graduated in 1990. Dad further tutored me in painting and I did some NFL posters like the Dallas Cowboys and Detroit Lions. Then, I started painting Norman Rockwell-type art.

Dad got sick in 1995 and passed away. He was right in the middle of the Great Indian Chief series. His last painting was Geronimo. The series was going to be released in limited edition prints. His publisher asked me to finish the last three chiefs: Red Cloud, Quanah Parker, and Sitting Bull. So I did. After that, I got into wildlife, my current passion.

Tina Siemens

My wife, Kathleen, three daughters, and I eventually moved to West Virginia, where we bought and restored an old Victorian farmhouse. We bought other properties and restored them, too, becoming an investor/landlord. But I didn't realize how much of my time it would take up.

Now, it's a balancing act to run the real estate and paint. I'm still active in attending festivals and available for commission.

Quanah has always been someone I was fascinated by; he has always been my favorite. That's why I hope you love the front cover image of him and this book as well.

My work can be viewed at JonRen.com. I can be reached at jonrenwv@gmail.com. I hope to hear from you.

~ Jon Ren

Introduction

This book is a prequel to my first book, *Seminole: Some People Never Give Up*. In many ways, it was much tougher to write. First, I met with the surviving Parkers at Quanah Parker Day in Quanah, Texas, and interviewed Ron Parker, great-grandson of Chief Quanah Parker. After listening to his stories, I started researching this book. And let me tell you, there are a lot of books and information out there.

Much of it has been embellished and romanticized to fit the moods and sentiments at the time. Just reading some of the so-called "eyewitness accounts" is hard to stomach for our modern understanding of journalism. For example, 100 years ago, readers could not imagine a young girl would choose to stay with "savages" instead of coming back to family and civilization. Yet credible information shows she did just that.

As I started compiling the stories, I went first to the primary sources. Those were accounts written within a few years of the events, and the authors were kidnapped or involved in the attacks. From there, I read accounts written fifteen to fifty years later, sometimes by someone who knew someone who was there. I have tried to add pieces of the stories that made sense to me.

For example, one account says a single male returned to the fort to see if he could rescue anyone. Another account says he was captured while two or three other men rescued him. In this case, I accepted the one eyewitness to the event who wrote his version three years after the attack versus the other one written decades later. Different authors and researchers will make different decisions.

Despite all this, the main threads are accurate. The primary points and lessons are correct. And the facts I chose don't affect those threads or plot points in any way—at least in my opinion.

Tina Siemens

I hope you sit back and enjoy this book rather than consider whether a captive was put on an Indian's horse and hurried away by one Indian or carried on foot by two other Indians. The main point is she was captured and couldn't be rescued.

If mistakes are made, they are mine. If I receive credible information about a mistake and I agree with it, I can easily update this manuscript. Modern technology makes it possible.

Finally, I've tried to tell both sides of the "Cowboys versus Indians" argument. Both sides committed horrific abuses and were often honorable and caring of the other. Like real life, people are messy; they are sinners. No one is as great as we make them out to be or as horrible as we believe. We just aren't.

Enjoy!

~ Tina Siemens

What is life? It is the flash of a firefly in the night. It is the breath of a buffalo in the wintertime. It is in the little shadow which runs across the grass and loses itself at sunset.

~ Chief Crowfoot (1830–1890)
Blackfoot Tribe

Rachel

Chapter One

May 19, 1836
Near present-day Waco, Texas

Seventeen-year-old Rachel Parker Plummer spotted the Indian sprinting through the open fort doors, coming directly toward her. The face, painted in red, black, and ochre, carried a tomahawk in one hand and a fourteen-foot lance in the other.

Fear gripped Rachel, causing her to freeze. As the man came closer, she tried to will her legs to run, but they refused. Before she could move, he was there.

The Indian thrust the lance into the ground next to her and reached for a sheath strapped to his waist. She watched as he drew out a long knife and brought it to her face. It all happened so slowly. He had her and would do what he wanted. She knew that.

The Indian grinned, then grimaced as he seized Rachel's fiery red hair and jerked her head back. She felt the blade cut into her scalp.

Seconds later, the savage held up her long hair and screamed like a crazy man. Rachel thrashed her arms wildly at the Indian and hit him several times.

"What the—" Luther said, grabbing his wife's arm. "You just hit me!"

Rachel opened her eyes and jolted up in bed, feeling for her scalp. After smoothing back her red hair, she slowed her breathing and relaxed.

"It was so real," she said. "An Indian scalped me."

Luther swung his feet out of bed, the feather-filled mattress shifting underneath him. "Those stories again?"

Rachel's breathing steadied and she felt her stomach. "Yes. I hate it when we have those drills. After we sing hymns, Grandpa starts with the stories, and I know I will have nightmares."

"Don't listen to them. Just walk away."

Rachel shook her head. "It's hard."

A dull gray light filtered through the logs of their cabin as Luther lit a lamp. He pulled up his overalls and stepped into a pair of work boots. "Those stories don't bother me. I'm going to milk the cows. I'll be back."

Rachel was used to this routine. He'd return with a pail of milk. Then, they would have some bread from last night's supper with pieces of cooked bacon wrapped in old butcher paper. It was always the same.

Her routine started by crawling out of bed and waking their eighteen-month-old son, James Pratt Plummer. She'd fuss with him for a few minutes before assembling breakfast.

After breakfast, Luther would trudge out to the fields with the rest of the men while she stayed behind, preparing food for supper.

During midday, one of the adults would return to the fort and grab some food for the ones in the fields. After a short break, the field workers would labor until six or seven before coming in for the night. The routine rarely changed.

Today was Thursday. Everyone worked until Saturday night. Sunday morning, they would hold a Pilgrim Predestinarian Baptist Church service. No one worked again until Monday morning.

"Come on, James Pratt," Rachel said as she lifted him out of the small bed. "Let's get you ready for the day."

The little boy giggled. "M-Momma," he croaked with a thumb stuck in his mouth.

He was just beginning to talk and loved that thumb. Surely, he'd soon grow out of it. Besides, he had the Parker chin, causing John Parker, Rachel's grandfather, to constantly pick up little Pratt and hold him tight. It was always a cute sight.

Like clockwork, Luther returned an hour later with a pail of fresh milk. He sat at the table with his son next to him in a crudely built highchair.

Rachel poured three cups of milk and served the meager breakfast before saying a prayer.

"Dear Heavenly Father, please bless this food so that it nourishes our bodies. Let us spread the Good News of Jesus Christ to the unbeliever. And protect us this day as we toil under your sun while not forgetting Your Son's sacrifice for our sins. Amen."

"Amen," Luther added as he reached for some bacon. "Your grandpa is barely touching the ground. He's so excited about the news."

Two days earlier, James Parker, Rachel's father, returned home. He had been commanding some troops but disbanded them since the war for Texas's independence was over.

James told his father, John, that the defeated General Santa Anna had signed the Treaty of Velasco five days earlier. That meant the Republic of Texas was now its own country.

This was incredible news since the Parkers had not only been instrumental in forming the Texas Rangers but attended the initial meeting to declare independence from Mexico and form the new republic. The Parker clan beamed with pride over their new Republic of Texas.

The door to their cabin opened and a young girl walked in holding a bucket of water. Rachel stood and grabbed the pail.

"Oh, thank you so much, Cynthia Ann. This saves me a trip."

Luther put his hand on the little nine-year-old's shoulder and looked at his wife. "Since you're pregnant again, I asked her to carry your water."

He turned to the girl and held the door open. "Thanks, Cynthia. Tell James I'll be right out. We'll walk to the fields together."

As he followed the little girl outside, he noticed the sun's rays streaming over the twelve-foot-high sharpened-to-a-point cedar posts surrounding their fort. It was an impressive structure, built without nails or iron.

It included defensive features such as a bulletproof double gate and two blockhouses on opposite corners. One of the blockhouses guarded the entrance.

A blockhouse was a tiny two-story building with a larger block sitting on top of a smaller one at ground level. Men would occupy the upper block and shoot through gunports in the walls, even aiming through holes in the floor.

Anyone—Mexicans, Indians, or bandits—would be foolish to attack Parker's Fort, as it was known in the area. Yet all twenty-four adults knew that an attack was a real possibility when they moved here. That's why they built the fort.

The three Plummers were finally dressed, fed, and ready for the day. Luther studied his wife. "How do you stay so clean? There's not a speck of dirt on you."

"That's why you married me. I can be clean even in this rough country."

"Okay, but your bright red hair sealed the deal."

He kissed Rachel, patted the baby growing inside her, and tussled the hair of his only son. Then he picked up a skin of water and left the tiny cabin.

With little Pratt dressed for the day, Rachel put away the food and began preparing for a supper eleven hours away.

Outside the cabin, Luther joined up with James Parker, his father-in-law and former Texas Ranger.

"Ready to hoe some weeds and plant some seeds?" Luther asked.

"I am," James replied. "I just look at the weeds like blocks in our path. Each one I chop down is one less problem we have to deal with later."

"What about the seeds?"

"They're children, growing up tall and strong. If my father can produce eleven children from two wives, I can grow twenty acres of corn with this hoe and some good seed."

Luther chuckled and shook his head at the mention of his grandfather-in-law. John Parker was somewhat of a legend throughout the United States.

A renowned Indian fighter, John Parker turned back the Indians in Georgia and Illinois so settlers could live in peace. Three years earlier, in 1833, Mexico and Stephen F. Austin recruited the seventy-five-year-old Parker to come to Texas to fight Indians and make it safe for folks to work the land.

When John learned of all the free land Mexico would give him per head, he went to his eleven children and convinced six sons and two daughters to come too. With 4,600 acres given to each head of a family, the Parker clan could stake a claim to over 25 square miles.

This was an enormous amount of land. And all without taxes and customs duties for ten years. All they had to do was pledge allegiance to the Mexican government.

That was an easy decision, especially with their innate desire to bring the Good News of Jesus Christ to the different native tribes in this country. Someone had to save them or die trying, though who had to die was a matter of perspective.

Back in September 1833, in Crawford County, Illinois, the Parker clan loaded thirty oxcarts with guns, powder, bullets, food, farm tools, and seed and began the three-month 900-mile journey to Texas. Upon arriving in early November, John met with Mexican officials, swore allegiance, and received his paperwork for the land grants.

In the spring of 1834, John set out to scout a wide swath through Central Texas, including an area known for rolling meadows and fertile black soil. In late 1834, John Parker found what he was looking for: paradise.

It had forests, fields, creeks, and a large river running through it—everything his family needed to create their own world. There was game everywhere, and the fish practically caught themselves.

The land was located in Central Texas, forty miles east of the Wichita Indian tribe known as the Wacos. The Wacos had lived on the Brazos River for thousands of years.

John understood that Indians who stayed put and didn't roam around were like anthills. If he didn't step on one, they wouldn't bite him. And around his new land, he had plenty of anthills.

He met with the local tribes and told them what he was doing. He even paid one tribe $2,000 for 2,300 more acres. It was a good strategy that would provide peace, especially since he was farther west and north of other settlers.

The bare fact was that John Parker wasn't near the western frontier. He *was* the western frontier.

After arriving, the next step was to survey the massive acreage. John divided the land into parcels and distributed it among the family heads.

Once the metal pins were pounded into the ground at the corners of each parcel, John set about drafting maps to show his claims. He would have to file them with the Mexican officials in San Antonio or Nacogdoches.

While he mapped it out, he and his family furiously built a fort on one acre of land in the center of the parcels. John's fort design was genius.

His Indian battles had given him a deep knowledge of what it took to defend a group of people. He also understood that the best battle was one that never happened.

When a fort looked impenetrable, the bad guys went somewhere else. All he and his family had to do was follow a few rules.

First, always keep the gates closed and locked. That prevented easy access by the attackers.

Next, several men had to remain inside the fort with loaded guns at all times. They had to be ready at a moment's notice to climb into the blockhouses and start shooting at anything that moved.

Finally, it was vital to have bags of powder and balls next to one's gun so the shooting could continue. Since a skilled marksman would take at least sixty seconds to reload, they had several loaded guns in the blockhouses. Otherwise, it was one shot and done.

Keeping these three rules was why they constantly drilled. During a typical drill, an alarm would sound, and men would run from the cabins carrying guns, powder, and balls.

They would race into their assigned blockhouse, climb the steep stairs, and pick out targets John had set up outside the fort. The men had contests to see who could hit the most.

Even the women were trained to use firearms.

Each week, they participated in this drill. If there was a nearby threat, they practiced two or three times a week. It became routine for all of them. And it kept them completely safe—so far.

This day in May birthed a beautiful spring morning. At eight o'clock, the sun was full in the sky. Bright green dragonflies flitted around, eating the early mosquitos.

John's two sons lifted the heavy timbers off the supports and opened the double gates, swinging them wide open. John stayed behind and watched as his son, James, walked out carrying a hoe and some water. Luther was next to James.

Eight other men joined the pair, leaving six men to guard the fort. John Parker, the patriarch of the clan, was one of the men who stayed behind.

Instead of closing and locking the gates, John headed back to his cabin. Perhaps he told his son Silas to do it. Or maybe John's other son Benjamin was assigned the duty of closing the gates. Or maybe John never gave the command because with the Treaty of Velasco signed, the Mexican threat was gone and he felt comfortable. Whatever it was, the seventy-seven-year-old John Parker turned his back on the open gate and walked away to prepare for the day.

Besides John Parker, his sons Benjamin and Silas stayed behind with him to guard the fort. Others pulling guard duty were George Dwight, Samuel Frost, and Samuel's son Robert.

Soon, the six of them would walk around the fort carrying their guns, ready for action. If they could do some chores while keeping their guns handy, great. If not, at least they survived another day.

In addition to the six men inside the fort, eight women and nine children worked on preparing supper. A welcome breeze flowed through the open gates into the six cabins, cooling the inhabitants.

Each cabin was set against the spiked walls. Yet today, for some unknown reason, none of the men carried a weapon, and none of the settlers were aware of the nightmare about to hit them.

With the men gone, Rachel and Cynthia Ann picked up two wire baskets to collect eggs from the dozens of chickens running around.

"First one to find Gracie gets to dry the eggs," Rachel said. "Loser washes 'em."

"I'm going to find her first," Cynthia Ann said, referring to their favorite chicken. "You'll see."

"No, you won't," Rachel said, holding Cynthia Ann back as she tried to run away.

Cynthia Ann giggled as she twisted around and escaped her cousin's grip, then sprinted to the favorite spot of their laying hens.

Just after 9 a.m., Benjamin heard a noise and walked through the open gates to check it out. In front of him was a stunningly large band of Indians on horseback.

Benjamin stood still as the mass inched closer to the fort. One of them approached the settler carrying a white flag.

"What do you want?" Benjamin said, eyeing the painted and heavily armed warriors.

Another Indian kicked his horse forward and joined the one carrying the white flag.

"Friends, we make treaty with white man," the second Indian said in broken English. "We want cow and water. Where is water?"

Benjamin studied their horses, some dripping wet. It was obvious they knew where the water was because they'd just crossed a creek.

"You can't have the cow, but we will give you other food. I'll be right back."

He turned and hurried back inside the fort.

Young Cynthia Ann dropped her basket of eggs and stared through the opening, frightened to see so many horses.

"Indians!" she yelled as she turned and ran from the entrance, raising the alarm.

Rachel was nearby and went to the gates to have a better look. Silas, her uncle, jogged up behind her.

"They're Tawakonis, Caddoes, Keechis, and Wacos," Rachel said to Silas, who carried four rifles and several shot pouches. "There's at least eight hundred of them," she added.

The tribes she mentioned were mostly friendly with white settlers, so that was good news to Silas.

Rachel's sister, Sarah Parker Nixon, ran to the small gathering. Sarah was nineteen, two years older than Rachel.

"I'm going to warn the men in the fields!" Sarah said, out of breath.

Before anyone could respond, she took off for the low, narrow door at the rear of the fort.

Benjamin, jogging away from the open gates, was intercepted by Silas and Rachel.

"What do they want?" Silas asked.

"A cow and directions to water. I told them they couldn't have a cow, but I'd give them some food." Then he said matter-of-factly, "They plan to kill us, so I'm going to buy some time for everyone to escape."

By now, Cynthia Ann and Sarah had told everyone inside the fort. The elder John Parker hurried to his sons.

"What's going on?" John said.

Benjamin told him the same story.

"What kind are they?" John asked.

"Comanche, maybe some Kiowas," Benjamin replied, correcting Rachel's misinformation.

John's jaw tightened. He knew about the Comanche. His fort was located on the site of their previous attacks. Yet he also knew the Comanche didn't attack forts. They had lost too many braves and horses. Instead, the Comanche loved to draw soldiers outside and fight them on Comanche terms.

John had no desire to ever fall for that ruse. That's why he had worked so hard stockpiling the fort with plenty of food and ammunition.

There was also a bubbling spring just out the back door to provide lots of fresh water. Rachel called it a "gushing fountain." John had been diligent in keeping several water barrels filled to the brim.

With dried meats and stored food, his thirty-three-person colony had enough supplies to hold out for two weeks against any attack. If it rained and they captured more water, they could hold out for a month.

No Indian tribe would waste more than a day or two to kill whites. It was too big a risk for them. The Texas Rangers or Mexican soldiers might be alerted and come to the rescue, firing rifles at the Indians.

The Comanche's battle strategy was the word "wʉnʉ?yʉ?itʉ," which meant to surprise the enemy, hit hard, and take what they could get before leaving fast. With the fort totally self-contained and secure, no one could touch the Parkers.

It was a simple yet winning strategy. All they had to do was keep the gates closed and locked. It was a principle they had agreed upon and practiced each day—keep the gates closed and we all live.

John stared hard at the gates, swung open as wide as they could go. Then he slapped his forehead.

He glanced at the sky and reminded himself it was May 19, 1836. "This is my final day on Earth," he muttered.

Silas grabbed him. "Dad, let's close the gates and man the blockhouses. We can hold them off."

"They won't let us close the gates," Benjamin said. "Besides, there's too many of them. Even if we got the gates closed, we can't get to blockhouses fast enough. It would take but seconds before they scaled the walls with ropes and killed all of us. Then they'll kill the ones in the fields. This is just like the Alamo. We're going to die right now so we can give the others time to save themselves."

"No!" Silas said. "By God, I'm fighting them." He held up the four rifles, hoping Benjamin would take one.

John Parker slammed a fist into his palm, angry at the lapse in security. "Ben's right. We must save as many as we can. I'll take Sallie and head to the fields. Maybe we can survive and cross the Navasota. We'll probably die too, but I gotta try it."

As John and Rachel turned to go, Silas gripped Rachel's arm. "Stay here and watch the Indians. Let them see you're not panicked so they don't come in too quick. I have to go back to my cabin because I got the wrong shot pouch. They'll kill Ben, then me, but at least I'll get a couple of them savages!"

Rachel followed orders and watched the mass of painted men and horses crawl closer to the main entrance. Behind her, the elder John Parker moved as fast as he could to his cabin and grabbed his rifle. Sallie, his second wife, stood outside, worried and confused.

"Come on, let's go," John said, jerking her arm. "Follow me."

As various members of the Parker clan ran to the rear door, Silas noticed George Dwight, another occupant of the fort.

"Where are you going, George?" Silas asked as George clutched his wife and one-year-old daughter. "Good Lord, you aren't gonna run, are you?"

George shook his head. "No, I'm going to try to hide the women and children in the woods."

Silas moved closer to George and glared. "Stand and fight like a man," he spat out. "If we must die, we will sell our lives as dearly as we can."

Silas ducked inside his cabin to grab his shot pouch. When he reemerged, he saw George hustling his family through the rear door. Silas held two rifles, one of them his favorite Kentucky Long Rifle. He planned to make each one count.

By now, Benjamin had collected a small sack of food and ignored Rachel as he ran past her toward the gates. Rachel's little boy grasped her hand and put his face in her long skirt.

"It's okay, Pratt," she soothed, her voice quavering. She placed a hand over her belly, hoping to calm her unborn baby, too.

Rachel stood utterly still as Benjamin left the fort and approached the two Indians. As he did, the other Indians eased their horses around Benjamin, surrounding him.

Peering between two horses, Benjamin glanced back at Rachel with a horrified expression on his face. Suddenly, a long lance pierced his right shoulder from behind. He grappled at another lance headed for his stomach and pushed it to the side. A third lance pierced his left thigh.

"*AIIEEEEE!*" he screamed to the heavens.

The pain was immense, and this excited the Indians. They released ear-piercing yells and war whoops. The fight for Parker's Fort was on.

Chapter Two

James Parker was bent down and dropped some seed into the black soil. After using his hoe to cover it, he stood upright and wiped the sweat from his brow.

"This Texas soil is rich. We should make a good crop. We might even—"

A man's scream interrupted him. James turned back toward the noise and stared at a forest of trees.

"Something's wrong!" James yelled to the other men, who also stared in the direction of the fort. "Let's get back there!"

Two of the men dropped hoes and picked up their rifles. The others didn't have firearms, so they carried their hoes for protection.

It was a good five-minute walk, so they hustled until they spotted Sarah running toward them and crying.

"What's wrong?" James asked, grabbing his daughter by the shoulders.

"Indians!" she said, out of breath. "Lots of them at the gates."

James pushed her aside and ran hard. He had covered two hundred yards when Patsey, his wife, came running, carrying their baby and with four children in tow.

"There's hundreds of 'em," Patsey said. "I think they killed Ben. Maybe Silas, too."

The other men caught up to James and heard Patsey's words. Lorenzo Nixon grabbed his wife, Sarah, and held her tight as she cried into his chest.

"What do we do?!" Luther pleaded. "My Rachel and little Pratt are still in the fort."

James looked around at the group of panicked settlers. "I'll get the women and children into the woods. We'll hide until the Indians leave. Luther, you run to the Faulkenberry's place and warn them."

James snatched a gun from one of the men and handed it to Lorenzo. "You head to the fort and see what's happening." Lorenzo hesitated. "Go now!"

"Be careful, Lorenzo," Sarah said, releasing her husband. "Please come back to me."

Lorenzo kissed his wife on the lips and took off, checking to see if the rifle was loaded as he ran.

James turned to other men. "Pick up these children and carry them to the river. Run if you can, and don't look back!"

The group followed his orders and soon they were at the banks of the Navasota River. James knew this river well. There were several high sandbars, and he used them to help the women and children cross safely.

He found some dense trees on the other side and organized the survivors into a secure hiding spot. Then he headed back across the river, retracing his steps.

He had not reached the edge of their fields when he spotted George Dwight and his sixteen-year-old wife, Malinda, who carried their child in her arms. Coming up behind George was Samuel Frost's wife, Lizzy, with her children clinging to her.

"Where are the others?" James asked. "Did you see Lorenzo?"

George tried to catch his breath. "Yes. I told him all was lost. They're either killed or captured."

James shook his head in disbelief. It had been such a perfect morning. How could this be happening? That fort was impenetrable.

"Where is Lorenzo now?" James asked.

"He's headed back to the fort to see if he can rescue anyone."

"Did you see my father?"

"No. I didn't see anyone behind me." George paused. "But I don't know how anyone else could've made it out the back. The savages entered the fort so fast we barely escaped."

James rubbed his jaw and considered the options. "All right," he said finally. "Let's get you all across the river and with the others. Run as fast as you can."

Waist-high weeds parted as Lorenzo Nixon cautiously approached the back of the fort, sliding his hand under the rifle, ready for action. Thirty feet away, he dropped to his knees and crawled to the rear door, which was ajar.

Using one eye to peer around the doorjamb, he saw two Indians dragging off Lucy Parker, Silas's wife. Four Indians carried each one of Lucy's children as Lucy struggled and fought from her back. But the two Indians firmly had her legs and she could do nothing but flail helplessly and try to hit her captors.

Lorenzo had no time to think. He ducked through the doorway, shouldered his rifle, and yelled, "Let her go or I'll shoot!"

The six Indians spun around to see a rifle pointed at their faces. Stunned at this turn of events, the two dragging Lucy dropped her legs. As none of them had weapons other than knives tucked into their belts, they turned and ran away.

Lorenzo swung the rifle over to two Indians carrying the children and they dropped them, joining the others sprinting toward the entrance of the fort.

The other Indians used this diversion to duck behind a cabin and yell for help. Several warriors at the entrance, now alarmed by the fleeing Indians, fixed arrows to their bows as they ran.

Lorenzo knew he had only one shot. Once he fired, they would be on him and recapture Lucy and the two children while scalping him. He used the threat of firing the gun to his fullest advantage.

In mere seconds, Lucy got to her feet and picked up her four-month-old daughter. Then she grabbed the hand of her three-year-old son and ran past Lorenzo, who hurriedly backed toward the exit, his rifle trained on the approaching warriors.

Once Lucy was outside, he turned and followed them out, slamming the door shut and jamming a stick in the handle. The stick wouldn't hold long since they could climb into the blockhouse and shoot through the gun ports, but it gave them a chance.

Momentarily free of the fort and Indians, Lorenzo hoisted the little boy onto his shoulders.

"Run to Faulkenberry's place!" he yelled to Lucy as the pair sprinted away. "And run for your life!" he added, waiting for an arrow to pierce his back.

James Parker hurried his new escapees across the muddy Navasota River and found his original party. The expanded group numbered eighteen, with twelve children ranging in age from one to twelve.

"What are we going to do?" one of the men asked.

"Try to make it to Tinnen's settlement on the Old Spanish Road," James responded.

"That's almost ninety miles away!" the man protested.

"Yes, but it's on the Navasota River, so we can't get lost. And we'll always have water. We can cross and recross the river to lose the savages who are most assuredly following us."

"What about Luther? He might reach help and form a militia."

"Yeah, he might," James replied. "Or the help he raises may flee. Or be captured. Or maybe they get killed. Too many ors. We have all these women and children here. Imagine what happens to them if we're wrong."

The group fell silent as they considered his words. They had all heard what Indians did to women and young girls.

James took the opportunity to check the three rifles they carried. Each one was loaded. With just a single shot pouch to last them on the journey, they would have to use stealth to make it. And with no food, it would be toughest on the children. But it was their only choice. They had selected a place so far from civilization that they would probably pay the price—unless they could make it to Tinnen's settlement.

"When do we leave?" someone asked.

"When the moon is out. I'll sneak back to the fort and see what's going on. Maybe I can grab some food."

"No," they said in unison. "You might get caught and the Indians could find their way back here. We'd rather starve than see you go."

James considered all this. "All right. But let's travel only at night and hide by day. I'm going to climb this tall tree and see if I can spot the fort."

James had one of the men give him a leg up and reached for the first branch on an old post oak. He lifted himself up and slowly picked his way to the top.

Once there, he gazed west at the fort. All he could see was the east side and part of the rear. Nothing moved, at least on those two sides.

He climbed down and dusted himself off. "I've changed my mind. Let's take off now. We can make a lot of miles before it's dark. If the sky is clear, we can walk in the dark."

James studied the twelve children. Most were barefoot and wore nothing more than a shirt and undergarment. The briars and thorns would ravage them.

He hesitated momentarily before picking up one of his children and setting her on his shoulders. The five other adults did the same. At least half of the children could ride this way—for a while. It would take a miracle to get out of this alive.

The trail north of the Parker's Fort connecting the Faulkenberry's place was thin but usable. Luther ran faster than he'd even run in his twenty-five years of life. As it was only a half mile away, the trip took six minutes.

One of the Faulkenberrys—Evan—was hanging up washed sheets when he saw Luther running. He froze and waited for him to stop.

"Indians!" Luther croaked out, trying to catch his breath. "Hundreds of them. Where's David?"

"Back at the cabin working on the plow," the young man said, pointing at a simple structure. Luther took off, and Evan followed him.

Luther pushed open the door without knocking and found David Faulkenberry stunned at the sudden visitor. Before David could get to his feet, Luther blurted out everything he knew.

David grabbed his pistol and two rifles. "Evan, run and get old man Lunn, Bates, and anyone else they have. We'll load up and wait for them to get here. Then we'll go take a look."

Fifteen minutes later, David organized his group—fifteen in all. The boys and men loaded up on firearms and shot pouches and took off south down the trail to Parker's Fort.

As they drew near, David stopped the group. "Luther, come with me and let's see what we can see."

With the rest hiding among a stand of sweetgum trees, he and Luther scouted the fort. The pair crawled through the high grass and saw ten to fifteen Indians killing the cattle. They had already tied up the horses and were leading them away. After seeing dozens of Indians everywhere, David tapped Luther on the arm and motioned a retreat.

The two found the others waiting for them, most shaking with fear.

"We can't stay here," David announced. "There's too many of 'em. Let's cross the Navasota and see if we can find the Parkers. They must be hiding in the woods there."

Before they could set off, Lorenzo Nixon came running in their direction, a child on his shoulders and a rifle in his hands. Lucy Parker followed, her baby clinging to her neck.

Since Lorenzo couldn't see the concealed group, Luther stepped out from the trees and waved him over. Relief flooded Lucy's face. She collapsed in the trees, happy to be free with two children but crying for her two captured ones. It was a bittersweet moment.

The men talked among themselves and decided to proceed across the Navasota. Once there, they didn't find James Parker's group.

This wasn't a surprise since they were likely a mile or so north of where James Parker had been headed. With no choice, they hid in the forest and waited.

Several hours later, Lorenzo considered the circumstances. His wife Sarah was with James Parker. Desperate to be back with her, Lorenzo announced that he would work his way down the river and see if he could spot some tracks.

"Maybe I'll find them and we can make a larger force. You all stay here in the woods until I get back."

Luther grabbed his arm. "If you find Rachel, tell her I'm safe and will stay with the Faulkenberrys until we can meet up again."

Lorenzo nodded but didn't tell him that Rachel had likely been captured.

Faulkenberry objected to the idea but there wasn't much he could do. Before he could say more, Lorenzo was off.

It didn't take long for Lorenzo to find the spot where the Parker group had crossed the river. He followed the tracks to their hiding place in the woods, yet nobody was there.

Lorenzo studied the ground and saw the tracks led south, back to the river. He followed them and found broken branches and snapped twigs. Some scraps of clothing attached to briars informed him that the group had crossed back over the river from east to west. This was confusing.

Lorenzo slipped down the riverbank and found the tracks. The children's bare feet were clear, and the depressions in the sand were fresh. Yet now they were headed from west to east and angled north, the exact direction he had come from. This would put them closer to the fort and their pursuers. It made no sense.

Perhaps I missed something, he thought.

For hours, he searched and continually found confusing tracks, sometimes headed away from the fort and others heading toward it. By dusk, his only conclusion was that the Parkers had been captured and his wife, Sarah, taken prisoner. The thought sickened him.

A noise from the west side of the river caught his attention. It sounded like Indians on horseback, possibly searching for him. He had to hide.

Lorenzo decided to wait until dark before heading north to return to David Faulkenberry and his group. Hopefully, they hadn't been captured too.

Chapter Three

Rachel's eyelids fluttered as her foggy brain tried to make sense of everything. She was lying on her stomach when something stabbed her hand. She couldn't understand who would do that.

Breathing in slowly, Rachel forced her eyes open and saw her favorite hen, Gracie, pecking at something on her fingers—ants. As each one stung her, Gracie ate them.

"Good girl," she moaned.

Lifting her head, she turned slightly to the right and saw nine-year-old Cynthia Ann curled up in a ball. Peeking between her arms were Cynthia Ann's blue eyes covered in fear.

Cynthia Ann's five-year-old brother, John Richard, was a few feet away, crying.

It took a good minute until Rachel could roll over on her back. The warm earth caressed her bottom.

It made no sense until she saw her undergarment crumpled up a few feet away. She grabbed the edge of her skirt, now at her midsection, and pulled it back down to her legs, covering her nakedness.

Rachel looked in the other direction and saw Elizabeth Kellogg. She, too, was on her stomach, her face down in the dirt and her body stripped of clothing. Maybe she was dead.

Rachel remembered Elizabeth fleeing but stopping to grab her life's savings—$100 in coins.

Suddenly, it all came back. Rachel had been standing at the entrance, watching Uncle Benjamin. When the Indians stuck lances into him, she tried to move but couldn't. Her legs were frozen, just like in those nightmares.

As if lances weren't enough, some of the savages fired arrows into Benjamin's helpless body.

Two warriors dismounted and clubbed his head. Benjamin fell to his knees, trying to stop the punishment, but there were too many.

As he let loose another scream, one of the Indians took a knife and sliced the scalp from his skull. Blood dripped from the hairy mess. The Indian held it up in the air, causing more war cries. Then they turned their gaze through the open gates and spotted Rachel.

Finally, her legs cooperated. Though four months pregnant and holding eighteen-month-old Pratt, Rachel ran as fast as she could.

Somewhere behind her, Silas let out a bloodcurdling scream as if he captained a thousand men. She heard a gun fire and an Indian cry out in pain. Then another gun fired. Silas must have killed some.

Rachel remembered Silas's wife, Lucy. She had four children with her, and she argued with Silas about leaving, but he refused. Like Rachel, she and her children ran to the rear of the fort, but Lucy had been behind Rachel.

As Rachel drew closer to the small door, she noticed a short, stocky warrior behind her. Lucy and her children drifted over to the side to avoid him as he barreled after Rachel. With every five steps Rachel took, he gained three. It was going to be close.

As Rachel ducked down and exited the fort, she slammed the door shut. She was free, with her son clinging tightly to her neck. Yet the Indian had not given up.

A quick glance behind saw him push through the door and grab a hoe leaning against the wall. He carried the implement in his hand and began swinging the handle. The whistling sound was the last thing she remembered.

Rachel inspected herself. She was a mess. Dirt stained her hands and clothes. In a panic, she felt for her scalp and cried when her long red hair was intact. Yet her hand was full of red. A gash in her scalp dispensed blood freely.

She wiped the blood on the dirt and tried to clean her hands. With that done, she looked for Lucy Parker but didn't see her.

Rachel searched her memory for more. She vaguely recalled young Pratt being ripped from her arms and an Indian dragging her by the hair.

She'd also heard Silas yell, "Huzzah!" It sounded like he was at the rear exit, possibly trying to free Lucy and his children.

Seeing Cynthia Ann and John Richard were also prisoners, Rachel knew the Indians had captured at least two of Silas's children. Maybe Lucy got away with the other two.

Rachel's mind continued to clear. She had been dragged back to the place where Uncle Benjamin was killed. His mutilated body lay twenty feet away, the arrows and lances sticking up and his face unrecognizable.

"M-Momma," she heard from somewhere.

Eyes darting around, Rachel spotted her precious child sitting on a horse, a tall Indian just behind him with arms around the boy.

"James Pratt!" she yelled at him.

"M-Momma!" the boy cried, his little arms waving. "Oh, Momma!"

"Baby!" Rachel yelled again.

This exchange dislodged a squaw who'd been kneeling over something. She got to her feet and approached Rachel as she called out to her son. That's when Rachel saw the whip.

It struck her several times about the head and shoulders. This was followed by an angry face standing over her.

Rachel cried and continued to get whipped. Eventually, Rachel stopped calling for her son and the woman was satisfied, returning to her task.

An Indian brushed past the captives, carrying a stick with scalps hanging from it. Gray hairs on one of them matched John Parker's head.

"Oh, Grandpa," Rachel moaned. "I'm so sorry."

A few minutes later, the captives were moved back inside the fort. Rachel collected her undergarment and slipped it back on when they showed her where to sit.

The cabin doors were open as Indians cut up the beds, the air thick with feathers. Other Indians were busy plundering the fort for weapons, tools, and food.

When they found the medicine bottles, the savages broke most of them. A bottle of white powder interested two of them. They walked over to Rachel and held the bottle in front of her.

The Indian who had talked to Uncle Benjamin came over to interpret. "What is this?" he asked her.

Rachel squinted her eyes and read, "Arsenic." Then she shook her head.

The Indian was dissatisfied and thrust it into her face.

"I don't know!" she said. "Grandma took care of the medicine. Ask her."

The two Indians turned away and called two more over. They took turns pouring some powder into their hands before wetting a finger with saliva and painting their faces and bodies a brilliant white. Once they had used up the entire bottle, the four white peacocks walked among the others, proudly showing off their new paint.

Rachel smirked and muttered, "That will not end well for you."

Two hours later, one of the painted Indians started coughing. He was in distress, his mouth burning.

He ran to a cask and scooped out water, gulping it fast. His painted cohort was bent over, vomiting.

The one at the cask seemed better but walked a few steps and collapsed. He rose to his feet and fell again.

The other two whitened Indians came over and tried to help, but a few minutes later, one of them clutched his throat and dropped to his knees. The last one stood perplexed at this turn of events.

Fifteen minutes later, he ran to the cask and gulped water. This was followed by vomiting.

Of the four painted Indians, three were on the ground writhing in pain, and one was entirely still, likely dead.

The rest of the Indians were everywhere, looting and plundering. Most ignored the four afflicted Indians sprawled out on the ground, assuming they had found the white man's whiskey.

By the time an older Indian, possibly a chief, came over to the four and kicked them, they were dead.

The chief summoned a squaw, the one who had hit Rachel, and she worked at trying to revive one of them. This caused her to rub the paint all over her hands. Several times, she tasted the paint but went back to slapping the dead Indian. She worked on the other three before finally giving up.

When she reported this to the chief, he became concerned. But soon, other Indians appeared and carried the men to a spot where two more Indians were dead, possibly killed by Silas.

Rachel watched as several warriors dabbed at the white paint and put some on their bodies. Again, Rachel smirked. They might not die today, but they would likely be gone within the week.

Good riddance.

It was after midnight when the Indians stopped their activities inside the fort. Rachel continuously scanned the entrance and rear exit, hoping—*praying*—that Luther would come and rescue her and little Pratt. But no one ever came.

The Indians built a large fire in the center of the fort, using dozens of pages from her father's bookshelf to start it.

One of the books was a Bible. Rachel wondered what justice God would inflict on the savages, but she didn't have to wait long. Another Indian, whom she called Helper, had rubbed off some white paint from a dead one. Helper began showing signs of distress, grabbing his throat and coughing. Then he vomited.

Rachel nodded and murmured, "Time to join your buddies."

"Ye ye ye ye ye!" a crazy Indian yelled at her.

Before she knew it, he had pushed her face down to the ground and was busy tying her hands behind her back with a plaited leather thong. The Indian spared no mercy, pulling it tight into her wrists. Then he tied her ankles together, connecting the two thongs so her hands and feet were suspended in the air over her back.

Rachel struggled to breathe as dirt and grass collected in her mouth. She turned her head to the left so she could breathe, unsure how long she could hold out.

Soon, the Indians danced around the fire, raising their scalps and celebrating a great victory. Occasionally, one of them came over and kicked or beat Rachel on the head with their bows.

The wound on her forehead opened and blood streamed down her face. In minutes, it pooled on the hard-packed ground, making it hard to breathe without drawing in the blood. She choked several times, unsure how long she could go on.

An hour into the dance, someone set little Pratt a few feet away on her right side. Because her face was pointed to the left, she couldn't see her son. But she did hear him crying. Then she heard smacks and thuds as the Indians beat him, too.

There she was, bleeding profusely, struggling to breathe, and hearing but not seeing her young son crying for her. It was more than any heart could stand. If she could find a way to kill herself and her son, she would do it.

Just when she had given up hope, Elizabeth Kellogg was placed somewhere nearby.

"Rachel," she said between the Indian's whoops and yelling.

"Elizabeth!" Rachel cried out.

Before the two could say another word, Indians jumped on Rachel, landing on her back and legs, putting their full weight on her. She couldn't tell if they were male or female but was grateful none of her legs snapped. Rachel closed her eyes and passed out.

The morning air was quiet and thick with dew. A light blue sky woke Rachel to find her arms and legs still tied in the same position.

She had no feeling in her wrists or feet, which was a blessing since the pain from the tight bonds had been intense. At least she'd survived to see the sunrise.

The fort soon came alive, with Indians moving across the grounds and loading up horses. Two Indians approached Rachel and cut her free.

Her limp arms and legs dropped to the ground. They kicked her to get up, and she tried but was unable.

Seeing that she couldn't move, one of the warriors carried Rachel to a horse, mounted, and sat her in front of him. Rachel grabbed on to the horse's mane to keep from falling over.

Without ceremony, the Indian kicked the horse forward, and they moved north with hundreds of other riders.

Around noon, they stopped and watered the horses and themselves. A squaw approached Rachel and gave her a half cup of water. She slurped it up all too quickly.

"Food?" she asked, but the woman ignored her.

When they mounted up, she looked for her aunt and son but didn't see them. With each gallop north, she knew any hope of rescue faded. If they made it to Indian country in northwest Texas, she'd never see her family again.

Along the way, Rachel took in the prairie land and timbers. When they came to the Cross Timbers, she knew they were 80 or 90 miles north of Parker's Fort. It was depressing.

The Cross Timbers area had received its name when early settlers had crossed the prairies only to run into walls of dense timbers—blackjacks, post oaks, hickory, and elm—running north to south. Many times, they had to cross and recross these rugged timber stretches, an almost impenetrable barrier for wagons.

One year earlier, Washington Irving had described crossing the Timbers as "struggling through forests of cast iron." If the Indians felt the same way, they didn't show it, for they easily navigated through the area.

As the sun dipped below the horizon on the sixth day of hard riding, the band reached the Grand Prairie and stopped. Rachel watched as two bands of Indians exchanged words and separated.

She spotted Elizabeth Kellogg, who was now dressed in a deerskin, and nodded to her. Elizabeth was with a band of Kichai Indians who reined their horses over and headed west. Rachel's group aimed east, back through the Cross Timbers.

Darkness arrived, and they stopped and dismounted. A squaw brought Pratt to her for breastfeeding and Rachel hugged her little boy tight. He hugged her too, crying, as she kissed all over his head.

The woman grabbed Rachel's blouse and tore it open, motioning her to nurse little Pratt. When Pratt failed to nurse, Rachel signaled with fingers to her mouth that Pratt ate food. Instantly, they grabbed Pratt and pulled him away.

The little boy reached out with bloody hands and cried, "Momma! Momma! Momma!"

Rachel sobbed aloud as the woman took Pratt away. She never saw him again.

Soon, the Indians slammed Rachel down on the ground and retied her hands and legs in the same position as the night before. She cried hard, her heart bursting as she thought about Pratt.

Elizabeth was gone, too. So were Cynthia Ann and little John Richard. She was truly all alone, waiting for the next beating or worse.

Chapter Four

James Parker stopped at the river's edge. The sun was high, casting light on anything that moved.

He didn't want to be exposed like this, but he had no choice. The Indians could appear behind him at any second.

James waited until his small party caught up to him. They were a motley crew, bareheaded and barefooted.

With no food and a wilderness filled with poisonous snakes and man-eating predators, James couldn't plan on making it to Tinnen's settlement without losing anyone. All he could do was his best.

The river bottom was sometimes hard and dry but other times muddy. James thought up a ruse to lose his pursuers.

"Turn around and walk backward across the river," he told his crew. "It might confuse the Indians. It's worked before."

They followed his orders. It was slow going as they needed to watch their footing on the small rocks and debris littering the sandy bottom.

They made it to the other side, but James waited until they reached hard ground before ordering them to turn around and walk forward.

Maybe this will buy us some time, he thought, never dreaming his trick would also fool Lorenzo Nixon.

Lorenzo heard the yelling and screaming from the fort as it drifted on the wind. It was dark, and the moon was not fully visible.

He had been sitting with his back to a large elm, the surrounding brush hiding him from the Indians. The rifle rested on his right leg, waiting for a target he hoped would never come.

Lorenzo had been thinking over the earlier events. Being in the fields when the cries came. Running to the fort. Rescuing Lucy Parker and her two children. The flight north to Faulkenberry's place. Back down the river searching for the Parker clan, yet finding only disappointment. So far, he had seen no one, not even an Indian.

Once he judged it to be past midnight, he stood silently and took in his surroundings. Nothing stirred. The time was right to return to Faulkenberry's group; they wouldn't wait for him forever.

Lorenzo had two choices. The safer direction would be north while staying on the east side of the river. However, due to the large curve around the river, it would take longer.

The other option was to take a straight route north and cross the winding Navasota several times. That would be quicker but put him back on the fort side and closer to the enemy.

Of course, the Indians could be all over the east side of the river looking for him. If he headed straight north, he could angle west and possibly see more survivors from the fort. His last trip had freed Lucy and her two children. Maybe he could rescue the other two.

Lorenzo decided to risk the west side. Soon, he was near the fields they had been working not fifteen hours earlier.

A groan off to the left caused him to take cover. The groan continued. Someone was injured about twenty feet away in the tall grass.

The moon was out, and he could see more easily.

Maybe it's an Indian, he thought.

He reached for his knife and quietly slid it out.

I can finish him off.

Lorenzo crawled on his belly, the rifle in his left hand and a knife in his right. The groan drew closer. He could see some grass pressed down.

As quiet as a ghost, he rose and prepared to strike when a face with long hair caught his eye. It was Sallie Duty Parker, John Parker's wife. He put the knife away and found her lying on her back.

"Granny," he whispered. "It's me, Lorenzo."

Her thoroughly bruised body was stripped of clothes. A large cut across her chest oozed blood, as did holes in her hands and legs. It was clear she'd been staked to the ground and repeatedly molested. The old woman tried to open her eyes.

Lorenzo placed his hand on her head. "Can you get up?" he whispered.

She moaned.

"Come on. I'll help you up."

As he lifted the thin, frail woman, she fainted. Lorenzo lowered her down to the grass.

"I'll be right back."

He hurried to the river and removed his shoes. After washing them in the rushing water, he filled each one and hurried back barefoot through the brambles and burrs to Granny.

Bending over her, he gently pressed a shoe to her lips. She drank some and coughed, taking in all she could. When she was done, he used the rest to wash her face.

He made three trips, filling the seventy-seven-year-old with life-giving water and washing the wounds on her chest, hands, and feet.

As she lay there recovering, Lorenzo scouted around. He quickly found their patriarch, John Parker.

He, too, was stripped bare. An arrow protruded from his chest, and his scalp was gone. So were his private parts. Lorenzo shuddered to think about what order had occurred.

John had been spread out and pinned to the ground with lances too. Ants and other insects busily feasted on the corpse, taking away what they could. He looked away in disgust.

After much effort, Lorenzo managed to get Granny up and swung her arm around his shoulder. With this, they could move, but not very fast.

Yet somehow, the pair managed to reach Faulkenberry's cabin. No one was there, but at least he could wrap and tend to Granny's wounds.

Before daybreak, he pressed the woman with food and water, taking some himself. When she was ready again, he got her up, and they staggered across the river.

As they reached the dense woods, they found the Faulkenberry group still waiting for him.

"Help me with Granny," Lorenzo said.

In the early morning light, two women stepped forward and took her away.

"What did you see?" David Faulkenberry asked.

Lorenzo filled him in.

"Where's Luther?" Lorenzo asked after scanning the area.

"He went off south, along the river, searching for his wife and child. He just couldn't stay here and do nothing."

Lorenzo shook his head. "I found their tracks headed back to the fort. I fear they've been captured."

The two men said nothing for a few minutes until David broke the silence. "In that case, I think we should head east to the settlement near Fort Houston. It's about sixty miles away, but it's our best chance. I don't think the Indians will follow us there."

Lorenzo smoothed back his haggard hair. "Yeah, Fort Houston is the best way to save Granny. They have a doctor there. Let's get moving before they find us."

Just as James feared, the Parker group's journey to Tinnen's settlement was treacherous. Blackberry vines ripped the flesh of every refugee. The only ones wearing shoes or boots were James Parker, his wife Martha, and Lizzy Frost. The other fifteen were barefoot.

It wasn't long before they were a gashed and bloody bunch. The group said very little, instead focusing on putting one foot in front of the other.

Lizzy Frost was inconsolable at leaving behind her husband Samuel and son Robert. She hoped they were still alive but understood how unlikely that was.

It had been five days since fleeing the fort. During that time, James caught two skunks and two turtles, cooked them, and divided the meat among the six adults and twelve children.

Still, they all felt gnawing hunger. After walking countless miles, they lacked the energy to continue.

"I don't think we can go any further," George Dwight said. "Our feet are raw and bleeding."

Post Oak

James inspected the group as most of them fell to the ground. It was clear that another plan was needed.

"We're about thirty-five miles from Tinnen's settlement," James said. "I'll go there alone and bring help. George, wait here until I return. I can make it by morning if I go now and God blesses me with a clear sky and bright moon."

Exhausted, George nodded. "I'd give you some food if I had any, but I don't. Godspeed."

James Parker took off at once. He found a trail on the west bank of the Navasota and followed it all night.

At first light, he spotted smoke rising in the distance. That had to be the settlement.

With increased vigor and energy, James hurried toward the smoke. Upon seeing it was a cabin, he approached cautiously and knocked.

Captain Richard Carter answered. He had fought in the War of 1812 and had recently fled after General Santa Anna brought his army into Texas to quell the rebellion.

Even though the war was over, Captain Carter and his family didn't trust Santa Anna. They were staying put until the ink on the new treaty had dried for more than a few weeks.

As James told the Carters his story, they plied him with food. While James ate, Captain Carter prepared five horses.

Carter recruited a neighbor, Jeremiah Courtney, to join him. The three quickly took off and headed north.

Just after dark, the rescuers arrived to find George Dwight and company waiting for them exactly where James had left them. The Parker group was in tears, so grateful to see the horses and food.

They put the women and children on the horses, and the rest walked. While the group traveled south, they ate the food that had been brought for them. There was no time to stop and fix a meal.

On May 25, six brutal days after the attack on the fort, the Parker group arrived at Tinnen's Settlement. The Carters and others promptly saw to their wounds as James sent off an express pony to Houston for government troops.

Major John W. Moody rode fast and hard and Parker's request was soon answered. Five hundred troops were ordered to Tinnen's settlement.

James Parker celebrated with his family. "We'll get those savages yet!"

"You're not goin' back to the fort, are you?" his wife asked.

"Of course I am, Martha," James replied. "There might be survivors there, waiting for us. We need to save them or, at worst, bury our dead."

"I don't want you to go back," Martha pleaded. "You might be killed."

"I might, but I'll take a few with me."

Martha turned away, distraught and afraid.

While they waited for the troops to arrive, a starving Luther Plummer staggered into the settlement. James rushed to his aid, and they soon revived him.

Luther told them all he knew, having left the Faulkenberry group to search for his wife and son. Hearing Luther's news, which wasn't much, James was even more determined to return to the fort.

As the days ticked by, a dispatch came from Fort Houston. Lorenzo Nixon and Faulkenberry's group had arrived safely at the nearby settlement. And they had Granny, too.

Lorenzo sent word he was making the 150-mile journey to Tinnen's settlement. He wanted to be with his wife, Sarah, and bring James up to date on what had happened.

James was relieved they made it and excited to finally hear some news.

It would be a whole week before Lorenzo arrived. Sarah ran to greet him, holding him tight.

James, impatient to hear what Lorenzo had to say, pried Sarah away and sent the women and children next door. He understood what he was about to hear, and it wasn't meant for them.

In less than an hour, Lorenzo explained everything—the numbers killed, the names of the captives, and the discovery of his dead father and Sallie, also known as Granny. James was crushed but not surprised.

"What about Granny?" James asked. "How is she doing?"

Lorenzo lowered his voice and shook his head. "The doctor at Fort Houston is treating her, but the wounds are infected. They said the Indians coat their lance tips in horse or buffalo manure, anything nasty they can find. Poor Granny was running a high fever when I left. The doctor told me she probably wouldn't make it. I'm sorry to tell you this."

James pounded a fist into his palm, something his dad had always done. His father and two brothers were dead. Now, he would likely lose his stepmother.

He decided right there to move his family farther away from the edge of civilization. It was too big of a risk for them to stay at Captain Carter's cabin right on the frontier. Another raid could come, and they would all be killed.

James jumped up and made arrangements to leave. But first, he had to find Lizzy Frost.

He walked to her cabin and told Lizzy the news. It was highly likely her husband and son were dead. No one had seen them leave the fort.

Of course, she was devastated, but until someone saw their bodies, she kept a sliver of hope tucked away in her heart.

News of the attack on Parker's Fort spread throughout Tinnen's settlement. The deaths and captured children were especially incendiary.

Most were as outraged as the Parkers. After all, if it could happen to the Parkers, it could happen to them.

James borrowed more horses and carts to move his family southeast to the Grimes settlement, farther from the frontier. It took several days but the Parkers finally arrived.

By now, most of Texas had heard the news. Everyone in the new republic wanted to help James Parker in any way they could.

Through the charity of Andrew Montgomery and Jesse Grimes, James procured half a house for his wife Martha and their children. All he could do was promise to pay since he had no money.

James formulated a plan to return to Parker's Fort but the measles took hold of his family. He refused to wait until they healed and left them in the care of the neighbors. Then he received a double blow.

News reached the Texan government that General Santa Anna was claiming he had signed the Treaty of Velasco under duress (since he was a prisoner); thus, it wasn't valid. Supposedly, Santa Anna was turning his army around and preparing to attack Texas again. The 500 soldiers promised to James Parker were reassigned to head off the Mexican army.

It was hard news to swallow, yet he would not be deterred or delayed from returning to his family's settlement. Calling on the charity and kindness of those around him, James arranged horses, supplies, and weapons for his thirteen followers.

They set off one June morning and made the trip in three days. What they found was tragic but not unexpected.

The horses were gone; the crops were destroyed. Some of the cabins had been burned but still stood. Every bit of household furniture was gone.

After seeing the mess, James and his followers became despondent. But the worst part of the trip was finding the bones of their dead.

His brother Benjamin was found first, just outside the fort. Samuel Frost and his son, Robert, were ten feet inside the entrance. Silas was found farther back inside the fort, his arms and legs spread apart, a sure sign of torture.

Finally, the body of their patriarch, John Parker, was found where Lorenzo had discovered him. Nothing was recognizable on any of them since animals and insects had eaten all the flesh.

"What are we gonna do?" Luther Plummer asked, grateful that the bones of his wife and son weren't there.

"Let's collect some lumber and make a box," James ordered. "We will set the bones in that and bury the box." Then he remembered something. "Except Silas. He and I made a promise that whoever survived, the other would not bury him here. We'll take his bones with us."

The process took a full day since many of the group stood around with their rifles pointed in different directions in case the Indians showed back up.

Once the grave was dug, the box was lowered, and James said a prayer. "Dear Heavenly Father, we know our days on this earth are short and numbered. And we know You have prepared a place for us that no one can imagine. Thank You for the lives and impact of Samuel Frost, Robert Frost, John Parker, Benjamin Parker, and Silas Parker."

He hesitated, his voice heavy with emotion and eyes filling with tears.

"And please lead us in the right direction to find our captured relatives: Elizabeth Duty Kellogg, Rachel Plummer, James Pratt Plumber, Cynthia Ann Parker, and little John Richard Parker. In Your eternal mercy and grace, Amen."

Everyone in the group wiped their eyes and began tossing in dirt. It took no more than a minute to fill in the hole.

James pounded a wooden cross into the fresh soil and dismissed them all, but he lingered around the grave.

Before he turned away, he said, "Rest, my father. And rest, my brother—rest. Wish to God I were with you."

Again, James slammed a fist into his palm.

The group spent three days at the fort recovering what coins and money they had secreted. They were pleased to find a few cattle hiding in the tall grass. After rounding them up, the group mounted their horses and headed back.

James rode alongside Luther and said, "When we return, I'll prepare provisions and mounts so we can start the search for the captives."

Luther stared straight ahead. "But how will we know where to find them?"

"The tracks show they headed north. I'm sure they're in Comanchería. We will search every settlement on the frontier and see if they have any news or have seen one of them. But truly, we shall let God show us the way. He knows where they are."

Luther sighed and said nothing. James picked up on his attitude.

"You don't sound too enthusiastic. You do realize it's your wife and son who are missing, right?"

"Of course I do," Luther said, his anger rising. "But there's too many of them and only two of us. Riding around the prairie looking for Indians seems like a good way to be pinned to the ground and scalped—or worse."

"No, there's God. He's worth a thousand Indians, you'll see. We'll find our missing loved ones and bring them home safe."

Luther shook his head and kicked his horse forward. He was done talking to his hardheaded father-in-law. He just wanted to get back and sort things out.

Chapter Five

Rachel Plummer studied the approaching outcrop. It resembled a large root running across the land, much like a massive oak tree back in Illinois.

She had named that tree Billy after her cousin because he was tall, too. Billy had spread its roots over the surface, creating places to hide when she was a child. The rocks and earth she neared seemed like Billy.[1]

Teepees covered a long stretch of land behind the outcropping. Since the teepees were on the south side, Rachel assumed the location protected the village from the brutal north winds that arrived in winter. By now, it was clear to her the Indians knew how to survive in all types of environments.

Rachel had never ridden a horse for so long or so far. With each step, she grew more fatigued. The trip down from Illinois had been mainly in an oxcart, although she had walked a lot, but now, her legs and inner thighs ached from chafing, and her buttocks were numb.

None of this could be good for her unborn baby. Truly, it had been a hard seventeen days since the raid on Parker's Fort, but at least she and her soon-to-arrive baby were alive.

After leaving the Cross Timbers in Texas, her band crossed the Big Red River and stayed for three days. Once fully rested, the band headed northwest.

The land grew bare, the trees gone. Only scrubby timber appeared, certainly not tall enough to shelter behind.

The rivers and water they encountered were clean and fresh. After the Big Red River, though, some of the streams were salty like brine.

---

[1] This camp was in the Snow Mountains in the disputed Mexican Territory or present-day Colorado.

No matter. The land was rich and the game was everywhere, as evidenced by the warriors who brought in deer, antelope, and buffalo to eat.

During her trip, Rachel learned much about her Comanche captors. Whenever they stopped, they motioned to her to collect buffalo dung.

The heavy disks were piled into a circle by the women and lit on fire. The buffalo dung produced enough heat to cook food; a pile lasted days if necessary. In a land without timber, it was a clever substitute.

Another aspect of their way of life was the lack of sanitation. The women collected dung and then prepared meals without cleaning their hands.

They also never bathed in the plentiful water sources unless the lice were too much for them to bear. She found some in her hair, making her sick.

When allowed, Rachel washed her entire body with sand at a river or lake. In the summer heat, the water felt good.

As for her hair, she learned that sand could rid her of most of the lice, but it was hard to rinse it out completely. Still, sand was much better than lice.

The big Indian behind her pulled the reins and the horse stopped. He grunted something and pointed to the ground.

Rachel had picked up parts of their language and knew this phrase meant dismount, jump off, or get down—one of those. Heart pounding, she slid off the horse and smoothed out her skirt as best she could. She knew without a doubt she was about to discover her future life, however short that might be.

As the rest of the band dismounted, women from the camp came running over and hugged their men. A few words were exchanged before the women took the horses' reins and led them to a corral where they would be fed and watered.

Another Indian came to Rachel and grabbed her arm, yanking her in the direction of a teepee on the outer edge of the camp. An old man appeared at the open flap.

The Indian escorting Rachel pushed her toward the man, who grabbed her and said something. It was clear that she had just been given to the old man.

No sooner had this happened than did a squaw appear from inside the teepee and start yelling at her. She battered Rachel with a switch until she lowered her gaze to the ground. A younger girl did the same thing.

The blows stung her as she tried to dodge and block them. It didn't take long to understand that Rachel owed reverence to the woman, who was likely the old man's wife, and the young girl, who was probably the couple's daughter.

Rachel's heart slowed. At least the anxiety of being tortured had faded. They wouldn't be beating her if they planned to kill her.

Perhaps they wanted to ransom her. She could only hope.

Rachel adjusted her buckskin covering and picked up a flat stone. She had a lot of work to do. In the past three months, work was all she'd done.

From birth, Comanche girls and women understood that they were responsible for cutting wood, building fires, taking down and putting up teepees, skinning and butchering game, and turning buffalo hides into soft, supple blankets and robes. The women worked all the time.

"Does it ever end, Mary?" she asked another white captive.

"No," Mary replied. "Never. This is all we are good for—work—and, of course, the other thing."

Rachel knew what that meant. Once or twice a week, the old man took her into the teepee.

Occasionally, she was loaned out to another Indian, always younger than the old man. Each time a buck forced her into a teepee, Rachel assumed it was some form of payment or the collection of a debt. She thought of her growing baby and endured it.

"Who's in charge here?" Rachel asked Mary.

"They have a war chief who makes big decisions when attacks are planned. But any warrior can get his friends together and go on a raid. They don't seem to need anyone's permission. All they do is smoke the sacred war pipe and offer it to other warriors. Any warrior who takes it agrees to go on the raid."

Rachel picked at some fat and continued dragging the flat stone over the buffalo hide. "What about disputes?"

Mary looked around to ensure they were alone. If they got caught talking, they'd be hit with the switch.

"There's a civil chief for the camp who makes all decisions that don't deal with war or raids. He's like a judge and a bank president all in one. He resolves disputes and keeps the peace."

Rachel nodded as she inspected the scraped hide. She had a quota of ten hides each moon, as the Indians called a month. She had heard the beatings were severe for missing it. Thankfully, she had made her quotas—so far.

Tanning hides and skins was hard physical work. Once the men killed the animal, they either carried it back to camp or sent the women out to the carcass.

When she arrived at the dead animal, she used a knife to cut a circle around the ankles of each leg. Then she cut from the tail and followed the backbone through the animal's underside to the neck.

At the neck, she cut another circle around it. After making vertical cuts along the inside of each leg, she slowly peeled off the entire skin.

Often, Rachel had to use a knife to free the skin from the flesh, but with patience and careful work, it eventually came off in one piece.

Now that she had a whole skin, she had to scrape off the fat and flesh. This was accomplished by using a stone tool or blunt bone.

She had to peg the entire skin to the ground or use a long log leaned at an angle between her legs to keep the skin from moving while she worked the tool up and down.

Once the inside layer of hide was clean, she usually removed the fur from the other side unless they told her not to. Just getting past this step took at least a day, if not two.

With the skin clean on both sides, Rachel washed it well. Then, depending on the weather, she dried it in the sun for a day.

Once dry, she collected some deer and buffalo brains, working the mess into the skin to make it soft. Even though this step wasn't as hard as scraping, the constant rubbing and massaging tired her fingers.

She noticed the other women could do this work in half the time it took her. And their hands were as large as a man's, with solid, thick fingers.

The next phase involved stretching and working the skin. The goal was to get it dry and soft.

To do this, the skin was continually stretched and pulled. The more labor applied, the softer the skin.

Finally, the skin was smoked. This process accomplished two things.

If the skin got wet, the softness returned as fast as it dried out. The second result of smoking kept insects from spending time on the skin looking for food. Better smoking brought fewer bugs inside a teepee.

With the skin now soft and pliable, it was given to one of several skilled women in the camp who made clothing or teepees out of it. Sometimes, they made bladders to hold water or food. Smaller skins made pouches for carrying personal items.

It was constant production so the men could trade the surplus skins. At least the women could gossip while doing their work. It was the only time they really could.

"There's a council tonight," Mary said.

"What happens at a council?" Rachel asked.

"They discuss raids, fights, moving to another spot, all while smoking something they call peyote. It gives visions to the medicine man and older ones."

"Are we moving again?"

"I don't know," Mary said. "We'll find out tomorrow morning."

"Why not tonight?"

"Because we aren't allowed to attend councils or ask about it. Just keep your mouth shut if you want to avoid a thorough beating from Kicking Knee."

Kicking Knee was Rachel's owner. Rachel nodded and continued working the buffalo hide.

Since her arrival, they had moved every three to four days. This was even more work for the women as they took down the teepees and packed the three lodge poles on a mule, one pole on its left, another on its right, and a third leaning off its rump, allowing the mule to drag the poles along while being balanced.

Efficient.

That evening, another band arrived. The new warriors dismounted and greeted their hosts. As Rachel collected their horses, she recognized several Indians from the raid on her fort. Instantly, she lowered her eyes and worked her way to the corrals, where she stayed for several more hours.

The next morning, she was back working on the skins with Mary.

"Did you learn anything?" Rachel asked her.

Mary whispered, "I heard that the white man's medicine killed eight of them. Do you know anything about that?"

"Yes," Rachel replied, keeping her emotions in check. "They painted themselves with arsenic. They're fortunate to have lost only eight."

"One of the dead was the wife of a war chief. They mentioned you and wondered if you were also filled with the white man's evil spirit."

"What does that mean?" Rachel said, worried.

"They quickly moved on to something else, so I think you're safe."

"How did you learn all this? I thought we couldn't attend councils."

Mary grinned. "I crept to the teepee and listened through the opening in the bottom. But don't you go doing that. Only I can do that."

"What happens now?"

"We move in two days, and then the men go off to raid white settlements."

Rachel felt her baby kick. "When I have my baby, will they let me keep it?"

Mary lowered her head. "I don't know. If it slows your work, they won't. Just start treating the wife and daughter well. And ask the wife for advice on what you can do to keep your baby because they need more children here. With the women working so hard and riding horses everywhere, they have few babies. Maybe convince them they need another member of the band. If it's a boy, he could become a warrior."

Rachel nodded and grabbed a hunk of deer and buffalo brains, mashing it into the skin. She recalled the words of Jesus: "Behold, I am sending you out as sheep in the midst of wolves, so be wise as serpents and innocent as doves."

Rachel had already broken the innocent part by not telling them about the arsenic. She and her Baptist Parker clan had been charged to save the unbelieving Indians. Instead, she had allowed eight to die.

Now, she needed to be wise and pray God forgave her. Unlike King David and Bathsheba, maybe He would let her keep the baby.

Maybe not.

The labor pains came late one night during a driving rainstorm. Kicking Knee drove her from his teepee so he could sleep. A screaming woman was nothing he wanted to deal with. At his age, he needed a good night's sleep.

The pain was intense, but Rachel had been through it before. She stood in the rain, cold water dripping off her buckskin and drenching her thoroughly.

Out of the darkness and rain, a woman grabbed her arm and led her to another teepee. A fire burned softly in the middle, its light reflecting off the brown skin of another woman shedding a blanket and preparing to help.

The woman who had saved her from the rain was a midwife. She knew Rachel had given birth before as the camp had discussed her son Pratt.

"You are no first-timer," the midwife said, smiling. "This will go easier."

Rachel wasn't so sure as she recalled Pratt's birth. That entire process lasted eighteen hours. After barely two hours, she had decided she wouldn't make it. But she caught a second, third, and fourth wind and somehow gave birth to her first son. If she could survive that, she could make it through this.

The midwife kneeled to check how far Rachel was dilated.

"Before the sun rises," she predicted.

The midwife was right. A few hours later, the tiny body of her son swaddled in Rachel's arms, nursing.

The midwife and woman smiled, patting Rachel's head before crawling under the covers. Rachel leaned back and tried to sleep, too, but she was nervous the men might take him. She had to stay awake to save her baby boy.

The band was back at the same spot when she had first arrived in early June. This was obviously one of their favorite places. And why not? The men could climb up and sit on the outcropping, watching the plains below for buffalo or enemy. With a river not two hundred yards from the teepees and the north wind blocked, it was as good as it got.

Six weeks had passed since giving birth. Rachel and her baby boy, Luther Thomas Martin Plummer, Jr., were doing well. She had been so kind to Kicking Knee's two women that she was sure Luther would make it. And she had mastered the Comanche language along with most of their slang and idioms.

Rachel constantly eavesdropped on conversations outside the teepee, listening for any sign of danger. So far, all was well.

Kicking Knee had even taken her two nights earlier while Luther nursed. It was her first time since giving birth. What that meant, she had no idea.

All she could do was pray that she didn't get pregnant and give birth to a little savage. She could barely imagine her husband taking her back now. Holding a Comanche baby would make it impossible.

Before she'd given birth, Rachel worked extremely hard to meet her quota. As the weather turned colder, she wore nothing more than a thin buckskin. They never offered her anything thicker. To make matters worse, she was always barefoot even though Kicking Knee's women wore moccasins.

In October, the ground was cold at night, making it difficult to keep working. She tried sitting and wrapping her feet in the long buckskin, which helped, but not for long.

When she had to tend the horses, she took her skins to continue working on them but cleverly stood on them for some relief. Surprisingly, the warmth from the horses helped. If she could work herself among them, they blocked the cold, harsh wind, too.

When the temperatures dropped, Rachel returned to the teepee and warmed herself by the fire. Each time she sat there, she was amazed at the ingenuity of the teepee's design.

By now, all settlers and most Americans knew about the danger of lighting fires inside a house. Proper ventilation was a must.

Fireplaces had dampers, flues, and chimneys to direct the harmful exhaust out of the house. Potbellied stoves had a pipe taking the smoke through the back wall or a roof. Yet this teepee had a fire right smack in the middle. It was a death trap, except it wasn't.

The bottom of the teepee was rolled up on the inside, with the extra fabric hanging three to four inches off the ground. Air flowed from under the teepee and fed the fire. The resulting smoke drifted up to the narrow opening between the three lodge poles.

A flap at the top could be adjusted to allow more or less heat to escape. If there was no fire and it rained, the upper flap would be closed to keep everyone dry.

If a snowstorm came, they could unroll the inner fabric on one-half of the teepee and attach it to the ground. This allowed more warmth to collect on that side while the wind whipped under the other side.

Even though Rachel had not endured an entire winter, she could see how the Comanche survived cold weather in teepees as long as the women gathered plenty of wood.

This cold November morning, Rachel rested inside Kicking Knee's teepee, comfortably warm under a thick buffalo hide. She knew she should be up working but she was weak.

Women were fed after the men ate and usually had less to choose from. Rachel, being a captive and slave, ate last. The food was typically cooked but not always.

She had trouble adjusting to the Indians' diet. As such, she lost weight. Add in the backbreaking labor, and she was nothing more than skin and bones.

Sure, she was behind. Mary urged her to work harder and longer. Yet even the cruel Comanche would not punish baby Luther for the sins of his mother. Would they?

Rachel caressed Luther as he dozed in and out of sleep, occasionally nursing. She kissed his tiny head.

Suddenly, the flap opened, allowing the morning light to stream in. Rachel shielded her eyes as five men entered the teepee.

Her heart dropped, and her body started shaking. Instinctively, she turned away from the men and shielded her precious boy.

"Please, I'll get my work done," Rachel cried. "Please!"

One of the men rolled her over, exposing little Luther to the others. Another man grabbed the baby and wrapped his strong fingers around its throat. An intense anger burned on his face as he squeezed the life from the tiny soul.

"No!" Rachel screamed. "Stop!"

She raised up to fight but the others held her back, forcing her to watch her baby's murder.

When the Indian was sure the boy was dead, he tossed it up and let the body fall to the frozen ground. Satisfied, they handed the baby back to Rachel and left.

Rivers of tears flowed down Rachel's cheeks as she clutched her child. Gently rocking the boy, she dared not gaze at his bruised neck. Instead, her tears landed on his face and dripped off. Yet each tear seemed to give the baby life.

After a minute or so, she noticed some movement. Then he drew a breath. Incredibly, little Luther was still alive. Like his mother, he was a survivor!

Rachel took some water and washed the blood from Luther's face. Sure enough, he was breathing again. She held him to her breast and sobbed a prayer of thanks to God for this miracle. Then she focused on nursing him back to life.

Rachel wiped the tears from her cheeks as she fed little Luther. What had started as a horrendous morning had turned into a glorious day.

Rachel smiled at Wild Rose, Kicking Knee's daughter, as the Indian girl entered the teepee. Wild Rose noticed Rachel tending to her baby and left. Minutes later, the five men returned.

Rachel panicked. "No, please!" she begged.

Rachel frantically searched for an escape but it was too late. One of the men ripped the baby from her arms as another punched her to the ground.

The five men went outside and tied a plaited rope around the baby's neck. Rachel, who had recovered from the blow, ran out to get Luther back. The men caught her and held her up so she could do nothing but watch and scream and cry.

The tallest Comanche grabbed the plaited rope and dragged the tiny boy, naked, through large clusters of prickly pear cacti, each one eight to twelve feet high. The little child cried and screamed, his arms flailing at the thorns sticking into his body, but he soon stopped.

The evil spirits controlled the man as he tossed the boy to the top of the cactus and pulled him down, repeating this several times.

Rachel thought about burying her head in her hands, but she had to watch. She needed to remember this cruelty to tell the world about it—*if she survived.*

After the boy had endured the cactus, another man mounted a horse and tied the rope to his saddle. Then he rode around in a large circle, dragging the baby hundreds of yards until he was literally torn to pieces.

When the horse stopped, another man gingerly lifted the baby by the leg, careful to avoid the thorns sticking out of the tiny body, and tossed him into Rachel's lap.

She stared down at her son and knew he was dead. There would be no resurrection this time.

The five men left.

Dazed, Rachel didn't know what to do.

One of Kicking Knee's friends, Falling Rock, came over to her. "You can bury him. We will help you."

Rachel looked up at the broad Indian and nodded. She had learned that offers of help often evaporated if one didn't move fast enough.

As distraught as she was, Rachel wrapped little Luther in a piece of deerskin and carried him to a spot away from camp. Falling Rock and another man followed her with crude shovels. When she pointed to the spot, they started digging. In ten minutes, the hole was open.

Rachel dropped to her knees, kissed her boy one more time, and gently placed tiny Luther in the bottom of the hole. Ever so slowly, she covered him up.

At the small mound before her, she prayed to God for help to endure this deep, heart-wrenching pain.

Her firstborn, young Pratt, was gone. Was he even alive? Now tiny Luther was gone, too. Who knows how many more babies she might have, only to see them killed by these merciless fiends.

Rachel again remembered King David, who had lost his baby boy as a result of David's sin with Bathsheba. David had fasted and prayed for three days, hoping God would revive the child. God did not.

When David finally got up, his servants questioned him for stopping his fast. David replied, "But now he is dead. Why should I fast? Can I bring him back again? I shall go to him, but he will not return to me."

That was how Rachel felt. Her baby was gone. He would not return to her.

Would she see him again in heaven?

Would she ever return to civilization?

Would her young heart not break from the cruelest torture imaginable?

Chapter Six

James W. Parker and his group eventually reached the Grimes settlement. Other than chasing a stray cow that wandered from their small herd, it had been an uneventful trip back from the fort. He mostly avoided his son-in-law, which wasn't hard since Luther rode ahead.

So many thoughts plowed rows of anxiety in his head. But one sprouted crops faster than the others: *I must find Rachel and Pratt. How do I do this with no money or men?*

When the cattle were finally corralled and the horses put up, James made his way to the temporary residence. Before he could enter, a voice called to him.

"James, I must speak to you for a moment." It was Dr. Adams.

"What is it?" James asked, dusting himself off from the long ride. "I just returned and need to see my family. I have a lot to do."

The doctor came close and grabbed his arm. "I know, but step over here, away from the house." Dr. Adams pulled him behind the small barn.

"What's with all the secrecy?" James demanded.

Dr. Adams removed his hat. "We received news your stepmother died at Fort Houston. I'm so sorry to tell you that."

"Oh no, not Granny, too!"

James pounded a fist into his palm.

"How many more will die at the hands of these savages?"

Dr. Adams waited until James had fully absorbed the news before continuing.

"As for your wife… I'm saddened to tell you she's not doing well. She's ill from the measles, and with her horrible time at the fort and her escape, I'm afraid her prognosis is not good. I fear it's beyond my medicine to heal her."

James pulled up his thick hair with both hands and moaned painfully. "Oh God, no. Please, God, don't take my wife. Please!"

Dr. Adams said nothing.

"What can I do?" James asked, desperate and afraid.

"Pray."

James dropped to his knees and clasped his hands to his chest. "Dear merciful God our Father. Please spare my wife and heal her so she might experience the joys of a free Texas. And please direct me to my daughter and grandson. In Christ's precious name, amen."

Dr. Adams patted his back. "That was beautiful, James. Just beautiful."

James got to his feet and dusted himself off.

"Doctor, that prayer gave me a feeling of inner peace. I know my precious Martha will get better. And come hell or wildfire, I'll get Rachel back too."

Dr. Adams tried to hide his frown. "I hope so, James. I truly hope so."

The two men walked to the house and eased back the door. Martha was on a pallet of straw, her body thin and her skin ghostly pale.

Horrorstruck, James covered his mouth with his hand. It was worse than Dr. Adams had said. Her eyes barely registered a dim flame of life.

James had seen plenty of death, even staring into men's eyes right before their souls fled the body. Yet, seeing his wife's eyes, he feared the slightest breeze would blow the flame of life out.

James went to Martha and softly caressed her face with his rough hands. She didn't move or recognize him. Her mind was gone.

Quietly, he studied his two young boys sitting beside her. They were more like corpses than children.

He hugged them and went back outside with Dr. Adams.

Before James could speak, the doctor asked him what happened at the fort. James left nothing out, including discovering his father's and brothers' bones and their burials.

"We couldn't find the route the savages took because the rain and wind covered their tracks. Even if *all* the men had wanted to go, we didn't feel it was safe."

He let that last comment hang there for a moment.

"I need to see General Houston and get a large company of soldiers to tear through these woods and find them. It's the only way to recover our hostages. May I use your medicines on my wife to see if I can heal her myself?"

"Sure, James," Dr. Adams said, nodding. "Whatever you need."

"I would pay you if I had any money. Instead, I'll pray for you and your family's health and prosperity."

Dr. Adams half-smiled. "You do that, James."

The doctor walked away, certain he'd be attending at least one more funeral real soon.

The horses skipped along, excited. Somehow, they sensed the destination was close and fresh feed awaited them.

Atop a brown mare was James Parker. It was a hot August day as he wiped his brow and navigated the road to Nacogdoches, where he hoped to find General Sam Houston.

Next to James was Colonel Nathaniel Robbins, a well-known soldier who had fought with Sam Houston. Both men needed something from the general and hoped to find him in good spirits.

"Do you want me to do the talking or do you want to handle it?" Colonel Robbins asked.

James thought for a moment. He knew Robbins was good friends with Houston. But so was he. After all, James had helped create the Texas Rangers and supported Houston in everything he did.

"No," James replied. "I'll do the talking. You stand there and back me up. When I get the men we need, you can ask for your favor."

"Okay. At least providence is with us."

"How so?"

"It's Saturday," Colonel Robbins said, a smile creeping across his face. "The general loves Saturday nights. It's his favorite time of the week."

James chuckled. "If this doesn't work out, I might be looking for a bar, too."

Two hours later, the men arrived at Nacogdoches, the oldest town in Texas. Sure enough, General Houston was conducting business from a large office on the second floor of a bank. The office had a separate exterior staircase to avoid disrupting the bank's business.

"I love being over all the money," Sam Houston said, greeting the two men. "Makes me feel rich."

James clasped the hand of the new republic's president with both of his. "Good to see you again, General. I could use some of that money as I'm plum out of it."

James immediately shook his head, regretting his comment. Levity had no place here.

"I heard about the attack on your fort," the general said. "Gruesome business. Take a seat, gentlemen, and tell me about it."

Houston used a cane to hobble back to the desk and poured three glasses of bourbon.

"Still recovering?" Robbins asked.

"Yeah. And it's embarrassing being shot in the ankle, of all places."

"There's a lot of dead Mexicans who would trade places with you," Robbins said. "There's no dishonor in being wounded in battle, especially a battle you won."

"And freeing us from Mexico's yoke," James added.

Houston nodded. "How's your family, James?"

"God has seen to my wife's recovery."

James explained how Martha and his children had received a miracle, coming back to life just one week after he returned from the fort. He credited the prayers, not the heavy doses of medicine he'd administered. They were still weak, but the fire of life burned bright in their eyes.

James told Houston he'd sold the cattle and split the proceeds with Luther and the other Parkers. He was upset that Luther kept his share instead of giving it back to James so he could hunt for his wife. Luther seemed more interested in moving on and hoping for the best.

James told how he'd moved his family to Jesse Parker's colony, about 50 miles east of the Grimes settlement. Jesse wasn't related to James, but he was generous with his assets and possessions.

James used the cow sale money to purchase a tract of land and build a temporary camp. After fixing it up and securing his family as best he could, he found Colonel Robbins and convinced him to ride along to Nacogdoches.

James leaned forward and placed his hands on the general's desk. "Sir, I want your permission to raise a company of men to find the savages who have my family. I want to chase them to their hideouts and get our people back. I'll probably find other captives too. Who knows?"

Houston shook his head. "I understand your pain and motivation to go after them, but I know Indians. I've spent many years with them, trading and so forth. I'm convinced the only way to deal with them is through a treaty. We must be friends with them, or at least not enemies."

James tried to hold himself together. "Sir, with all due respect, we must trounce these savages severely. Only then will they take instruction and leave us alone."

Houston took a sip of bourbon and studied the man across from him.

"No, James. Treaty first. Then we'll get your family back. I know that'll work. You need to trust me on this matter."

James shifted his argument. "Sir, I know you think we are likely seeking the glory that such an expedition would bring. However, we are both willing to serve in the ranks. You can name your own officers, and we will follow them to the fiery abyss if need be. The officers and even yourself will reap heavy praise from a successful expedition."

Houston grimaced. "This isn't about my glory or praise. I'm barely holding the Republic of Texas together. I have Santa Anna and his Mexicans just south of me, threatening to turn around and barrel through here again. We have a ragtag army as it is. I can't send men out hunting in the wilderness for captives they may never find. Treaties and ransoms are what we must do. If they break the treaties, then we'll ride down every one of those Indians and kill them."

"No!" James shouted, his face was twisted with rage.

The room became deadly quiet.

Houston leaned back and crept a hand closer to a pistol on his desk. He understood men and knew how insubordination could turn dangerous.

Houston pushed back his chair and used his arms to lift himself up.

"Listen here, Parker!" he growled. "I'm making the decisions and a treaty *will* be made. When we do, they will stop the raids."

The general pounded the desk, stunning the two men.

"When that happens and your family is returned, you can buy me a drink and apologize. Understand?"

James felt his face hot and angry. He was about to lose his composure when Robbins tapped his arm and whispered for him to wait outside.

Fists clenched, James fought every impulse and walked out the door. Once he was down on the street, he paced back and forth, awaiting his traveling partner.

Twenty minutes later, the colonel appeared.

"How did it go?" James asked, calmer but still gritting his teeth.

"He's a stubborn man," Robbins replied. "All he said was treaty, treaty, treaty."

"Did he grant you any favors?"

"He did. He appointed me collector of public property."

James looked sideways at his companion and shook his head. "Well, I guess *you* made out all right."

Colonel Robbins furrowed his brow. "No one likes a tax collector. Don't you know your New Testament and Matthew?"

He waited for a reply, but none came.

"Why don't I buy you a drink? General Houston figured you'd be sore so he recommended Teal's Tavern. It's two streets over. He said to tell Sammy to put our drinks on his tab. Come on, let's run up a tab on the general."

James balled his fists but let it go. He needed to dampen his anger and concentrate on finding his daughter.

The two entered the saloon and found an unoccupied table. It was a bar with all kinds of people and a place where Sam Houston would likely be seen. The bartender came over and asked them what they would like to drink.

"A bottle," Robbins said. "And charge it to General Houston. He said to tell Sammy."

"That's me," the bartender said, straightening up and looking over the pair. "May I ask how you two know him?"

Robbins nodded. "I fought with him at San Jacinto and James here helped form the Texas Rangers. We just left his office over the bank. If we're lying, go ahead and arrest us."

Sammy snorted. "In Nacogdoches, we usually shoot thieves. But I'll buy your story unless I hear otherwise. So you want a bottle?"

Robbins pointed at James. "Parker here needs it more than me. The Indians captured his family. He plans to go after them."

The bartender's eyes widened and he rubbed his chin. "Parker, eh? We had some news come through here about that. So the attack was on your fort?"

"Mine, my brothers' and my father's," James replied.

"Yeah, I read about that. Sorry for your loss. Let me get that bottle right away."

Sammy wasn't gone long. When he returned, a man was with him.

"Gentleman, this here's Bruno de la Huerta. He comes through Nacogdoches twice a year. He's followed the news about the raid on your fort and knows a lot about Indians. I don't want to impose, but if you're going after them, he might be of some help."

An old-looking young man stepped from behind the bartender.

"Bruno de la Huerta at your service."

James and Robbins shook his hand.

"Take a seat," Robbins said. "I see you already have a drink, but feel free to refill it from our bottle."

"Especially if you can help get my family back," James blurted out.

Bruno frowned as he sat down. "I doubt I can do that. But I can tell you what I know."

In the light from a window, James could see the man better.

"You're a Mexican!" James said with contempt. "We just whipped you and your kind. What are you still doing here?"

Bruno was ready for this. "Sir James, I am not a Mexican. I am Spanish. My family is from Spain. I have been educated in the United States."

"Then what are you doing here in Texas, especially now?" James wasn't letting go.

Bruno stayed calm. "As Sammy said, I stop here twice a year on my way to Washington. I sell to Americans and Texans. We make the best blades—sabers and long knives and some personal armor. My family has been in Mexico since the 1500s. De la Huertas had a long, unbroken line of serving the Spanish government until the rebellion. But fortunately, even the Mexicans saw the value of keeping Huerta Arms intact."

"So you sell weapons?" Robbins interjected. "Why are yours so good?"

Bruno flashed a salesman's smile. "We understand how metals can be combined in such a way to provide power and grace in one blade. And we have a great deal of knowledge in strategy and tactics. So, despite the rebellion against Spain, our company has continued to flourish. And our dead competitors have helped."

"You kill your competition?" James said, pointing at the Spaniard. "That sounds no better than the savages who attacked us at the fort."

Bruno held up his hands. "Perhaps I misspoke. You see, when our customer swings our saber against a competitor's cheaper blade, one of them will break. The blade that maintains its form is then thrust into the belly of the other. It is in this way we receive many referrals from our satisfied and *still alive* customers. Of course, our competitors receive no referrals since their customers can no longer speak. Their business literally dies with each broken blade. And it is only when the soon-to-be dead soul sees our blade up close and holds it with both hands that he feels the superb quality slide through his belly. The words 'Huerta Arms' are on his lips just before the redness of life drains from his body. Of course, it is too late for him to become our customer."

"Okay, so your arms are good," Colonel Robbins said. "But we heard you know about Indians. What can you tell us?"

"Yes, I do," Bruno replied. "And I heard that it was mostly Comanche that took your family. Am I correct?"

"There were other tribes, but you can start with the Comanche," James replied impatiently. "I tried to get General Houston to grant me a company of men to go after them and he refused. He says a treaty is the only way. What do you say?"

Bruno swirled the brown liquid in his glass. "The general is a brilliant warrior and tactician. He is even a client. However, a treaty will not work. My family has been in the New World from the beginning, and we have seen how everything developed."

Post Oak

"Well, I have a bottle here, senõr," James said, holding it up. "I'll keep pouring if you'll keep talking."

Bruno's smile returned. "You are quite persuasive, Sir James, so I accept. However, I must warn you that you might not like what I am about to say."

James slapped the table. "I'll be the judge of that. Start talking."

Bruno downed the last drops of whiskey in his glass, smoothed his black hair to the side, and cleared his throat.

"The Spanish landed on this continent in 1502. My family came later, in 1519, and helped defeat the Aztecs. We stayed and helped conquer the Mayans in the 1600s.

"During the 1600s and 1700s, we moved north, easily conquering the smaller native tribes. They were no match for our weapons and tactics. Behind us, we set up military presidios or forts in your language and stocked them with soldiers. When the area was safe, we constructed missions to convert the savages. I must confess we were prideful, confident our armies would advance all the way to the frozen fields of the North Pole if need be."

"What stopped you?" James asked.

"Four years ago, we captured a warrior named He Runs Fast. The Indian was born a Comanche but taken captive by the Apache as an adult. He was going to be tortured. By some miracle, he had a little understanding of herbs and was credited with saving a chief's highly valued wife. The chief spared He Runs Fast and the Comanche prisoner learned the ways of the Apache. Later, we captured him and discovered more about both tribes. We combined his stories with what we knew and came up with an understanding of these brutal but effective savages.

"For many centuries, long before the Spanish arrived, the Indians were torturing and killing each other. Over time, they fractured into hundreds of tribes and thousands of bands within these tribes. Each tribe occupied an area and fended off Indian challengers. Since the land north of the Rio Grande to the North Pole was well-watered and rich with game, all tribes were satisfied. Any attacks they made on each other were born of pride and greed, not hunger or thirst."

"Where do the Comanche fit in?" Robbins asked, growing impatient.

"The lowest of all these tribes were the Comanche. They were beaten and pushed around to a small area 1,000 miles north of here. It was cold and they were not good fighters. But the Apache were. The Apache lived in an area just above the Rio Grande. It included Texas, the New Mexico Territory, and all the land to the Pacific Ocean. Yes, the Apache were excellent fighters but still no match for our soldiers. Then something terrible happened. We did not realize it then, but it killed many of my countrymen."

"Disease?" Robbins said.

"No. Horses. This continent had none. We brought them over from Spain. The ones we chose were well-suited to this climate. Once we started conquering the land, we made sure never to let a savage own a horse because we knew if they got horses, our advantage would be lessened. Besides, seeing our men mounted on horses and glittering in the sun frightened many of them. The horses helped us scare the savages into submission."

"Well, there are horses everywhere," James said. "Somebody must've left the corral gate open."

"Right you are, Sir James. In 1680, we were surprised by a revolt. The Pueblo Indians were constantly attacked by the Apache, who were good with what few horses they possessed. We could not protect the Pueblos as we had promised. They grew angry, and although the Pueblos were not good fighters, they greatly outnumbered us. They forced the Spanish out of the New Mexico Territory and took our horses too, perhaps ten thousand."

"Whew!" Robbins said. "That's quite a big herd to lose."

Bruno nodded. "Yes. Many horses simply escaped and roamed the Great Plains, multiplying in large numbers over the years. The ones the Pueblos captured were traded with other tribes, and soon, the horses multiplied in their care. In a very short time, horses overran the continent."

James tapped the table with his finger. "Hey Bruno, I'm waiting to hear about the lowly Comanche."

Bruno poured himself more whiskey. "Perhaps I am talking slowly so I can drink more."

"You wouldn't be the first," James said as he suppressed a grin. Despite the anger he had come in with, he was starting to like this Spaniard.

Bruno continued. "Somehow, the lowly Comanche got a few horses. According to He Runs Fast, one of their chiefs realized how valuable a horse could be in battle. You see, for most tribes, horses were used for transportation, to carry people and supplies from one place to another. Some learned to hunt game from atop a horse. And other tribes loved the taste of horseflesh so they consumed their supply. Yet this Comanche chief had a vision others did not. By the early 1700s, the Comanche knew how to fight, and it was unlike anything the other tribes had ever seen.

"The Comanche left the north and fought their way south, taking up huge swaths of land. Then they met the Apache. The Apache understood horses, but not like the Comanche. With the Apache now mounted on horses we foolishly supplied, they stopped our advance north. But twenty years ago, we started seeing the Apache disappear. We thought a disease was taking them. But it was the Comanche. They were pushing the Apache toward the ocean. Now, the Comanche rule the Great Plains, not the Spanish, nor Mexicans, nor Americans, and certainly not the Texans."

"How are they different?" James leaned forward, fully engaged.

"They do not fight like Aztecs and Mayans. Those tribes had towns and did not move around.

"We sent our troops to their dwellings and simply overpowered them. But the Comanche do not have towns. They do not stay in one place long. We are unable to find them. Without finding them, there is no killing them. And our armored horses and shining soldiers, once an unstoppable force, were too slow to keep up. The Comanche ran around our soldiers, firing eight arrows from the same bow before the first one struck. Most of the arrows bounced off the metal armor but some killed the horses.

"Then our men were afoot, carrying heavy armor and plodding through the brush. The Comanche crept in at night and killed one or two soldiers while taking some horses. The next morning, more men were afoot. Travel was slow. This kept us in their lands longer.

"Each night, we lost more soldiers. Soon, they finished off the remaining men except those who had already died of thirst or starvation. It was a death by a thousand cuts.

"Like the coyote, they are patient and willing to wait from afar. With our men dead, they came and picked over the corpses, taking the Huerta blades and anything else they wanted."

"That sounds grim," Colonel Robbins said, a dark shadow over his face. "How did you stop losing men?"

"You were our savior, Sir Nathaniel."

"Us? What are you talking about?"

Bruno moved the glasses out of the way so he could use the table.

"This is the Rio Grande," he said, using a joint in the wooden planks, "and this is Mexico. Here is the Republic of Texas. The Spanish and the Mexican governments encouraged Americans to settle here in Texas."

He pointed to a spot near the top edge of the table.

"We needed a buffer against the Indians. After all, you seem to believe it is your destiny to conquer and occupy the entire continent. Our leaders said, 'Let us see how they do against the Comanche.' So, now we wait."

James wore a serious look. "I think I understand you, Senõr Bruno. We were allowed into Texas to be the sheep for the Comanche wolves."

Bruno flashed a wicked grin. "Yes. It is your blood we are willing to sacrifice to save ourselves. Is that so wrong?"

James ignored the question. "What can you tell me about finding my family and killing the Comanche?"

Through clenched teeth, Bruno drew in a deep breath. "He Runs Fast detailed so much for us. He explained the far distances Comanche travel to steal, kill, and destroy. A band might be camped just above the Red River in the Oklahoma Territory and ride south through Texas and cross the Rio Grande, ready to make war on us, and all within a few days. No amount of scouting or picket lines can stop these warriors. They are too fast and too quiet.

"Their horses are the key. Each one is smart and agile, with much stamina. The horses forage the grass of the plains, so there is no need to carry feed. And each horse can travel great distances between watering. By using these beasts—the very ones we let loose—the Comanche can strike our people and disappear. Strike and disappear again.

"If you go after them, they pick you off one at a time until you are no more. I urge you, Sir James, do not go after your family. Instead, send word to trade for them. The Comanche are greedy like the other Indians. Horseflesh and arms, maybe gold can be traded for captives. If you try to find them, you will die, never seeing your family again."

James lowered his head to the table. The bottle was almost empty, and he was no longer listening. For his purposes, the meeting was over.

The next morning, rays of sunshine streamed through the curtains of the second-floor hotel room. Lying in the bed, James Parker rubbed his throbbing temple, a result of the alcohol at Teal's Tavern. He propped up his pillow and thought about his next moves.

In the light of a new day, he had to admit that he'd learned much from Senõr Bruno. He'd gone to sleep, certain he would stop looking for his daughter.

But now that he'd slept it off, his mind was changing. It would be impossible to live with himself without going after Rachel. She might be calling out for him right now.

He'd pursue those savages and risk death trying to find her, but somehow, he'd get his daughter back. Maybe he'd find their campground and lead the army to it. Then they'd be eradicated once and for all, another evil scourge wiped off the face of the earth.

A sudden knock on his door sat him upright.

"Who is it?" James asked.

"It's me—Nathaniel. I have some news. Open up."

James slid into his pants and fixed his suspenders before opening the door.

"Houston agreed to give us troops?" James asked.

"No, something better. Your sister-in-law is here! The one the Indians captured."

The horses ambled along steadily, a blazing sun beating down on the riders. Leading the pack was James Parker. His eyes scanned the horizon, ever on the lookout for problems.

Just behind him on a gray mare was Elizabeth Kellogg, his wife's sister. A day earlier, he had purchased her from some Delaware Indians for $150. They had bought her from a band of Kichai Indians.

Apparently, after the raid on the fort, the different tribes divided up the captives, and the Kichai took Elizabeth. Of course, James didn't have the $150. He didn't have any money.

Stepping in to solve this problem was General Sam Houston. He gladly paid the ransom without asking James to pay it back. It was hard for James to stay mad at a man like that.

After being purchased, Elizabeth was examined by the doctor. Despite an initial cleansing, she looked unlike the woman who had previously occupied that body.

She was healthy but her mind was like Martha's. She just needed some time to recover.

"Maybe she can tell me what happened to Rachel," James told Robbins.

"Don't count on it," Robbins said. "She's in shock. You may have to hold your questions until we return home. Let her acclimate."

After attending to his sister-in-law's needs, James returned to General Houston and again urged him to change his mind. But Houston stood fast. He was sure a treaty was the best way forward and was willing to bet the lives of Texas citizens on it.

Once James realized Houston's mind was made up, he thanked the man and checked out of the hotel.

Franklin Milligan asked to join them as he was traveling in the same direction and didn't want to go alone. James welcomed him along, especially since Franklin had a spare horse to set Elizabeth on.

Around noon, the group set out west, back to James's makeshift house.

So far, the ride had been uneventful. They had camped by a small stream and hardly slept, with Elizabeth's cries and screams keeping them up all night. With only men around, it was hard to comfort the former hostage.

As the riders crested a small hill, they found a man on a horse holding a rifle. James and Nathaniel pulled pistols and cautiously rode up to him.

"What's going on here?" James asked.

"My name's Jace Smith."

He turned and pointed at something in the high prairie grass.

"I caught an Indian stealing my horses and shot him. He's over there in the weeds. I think he's dead."

James kicked his horse over to the grass and aimed his pistol, ready to finish the job. The Indian was still, probably dead, so James dismounted and approached the body.

"He's still breathing!" James yelled back to the men. "The ball grazed his forehead and knocked him out."

The Indian rolled his head, opened one eye, and started mumbling. James grabbed some rope and expertly tied his hands and legs.

Franklin dismounted and helped. Together, the two men carried the Indian back to the road and away from the tall grass where the Indian's friends could've set an ambush.

No sooner did the Indian's body touch the road did Elizabeth start crying.

"What's the matter?" James said, grabbing the reins of her horse and patting her leg. "He's not going to hurt you."

"He—" she blurted out.

"He *what*?" James asked.

"He shot and scalped your father. I remember the scars on each arm."

James ran back to the Indian and held up his arms. A twelve-inch knife scar tracked across each arm. James dropped the Indian's arms and stood up, face red and hot.

"You no good—"

"We aren't taking him with us, are we?" Elizabeth cried, her head in her hands.

Hearing Elizabeth's voice, the Indian raised his head. He seemed to recognize her, yet he was stunned at how this could be. Then he fell back and pretended to be dead.

Filled with evil-spirited wrath, James went to his saddlebag and removed a long knife. After finding a dead branch from a nearby post oak tree, he cut it into four pegs, pounding each one into the ground. With that done, he tied the Indian's arms and legs to the pegs. Using his knife, he cut the dirty loincloth, making sure not to nick the Indian.

Naked and exposed, the Indian opened his eyes and stared at James. At first, it seemed like contempt. But then James understood what it was—fear.

James licked his lips in anticipation and tested the edge of the long knife.

Tina Siemens

"An eye for an eye. A tooth for a tooth. And other parts of your body too. Hold him steady, boys. I think he's hungry so let's give him a taste of his own medicine."

A single scream pierced the hot August fields, traveling for miles in the light breeze. Then another scream, this one louder than the first. After several long minutes, it stopped.

Chapter Seven

Two months had passed since baby Luther was killed, yet Rachel had little time to mourn. Between fighting the cold weather and working every minute, any additional energy she possessed was put into surviving. She had to tell the world about these savage people.

Like usual, the men lay around the fire at night, telling stories, staying up late, and singing about their brave exploits. The women had to serve the men water so they didn't have to move.

Rachel gritted her teeth as she brought cups of water to one of the men who had killed her baby. She prayed to God for forgiveness while fighting the bitter rage of revenge and wishing that she had some arsenic to put in his drink.

For the men, it was mostly the same during the day. They sat around inspecting the bindings of their arrowheads and sharpening the edges.

Sometimes they went hunting. Other times they slept or coupled with their wives. Surrounding them at all times and working ceaselessly were the women of the tribe.

Rachel's work quota and other chores helped take her mind off her suffering. That was the only good thing about it.

By now, she had accepted her situation. Mary told her it would take some time, but eventually the Comanche life would seep inside her, blotting out the life she'd had before.

At first, she didn't believe it. But as each day passed with no rescue or ransom in sight, she could feel it happening.

Another chore Rachel had was looking for firewood and other materials to burn. Often, she trekked miles to find it. Sometimes, during these trips, she discovered caves set into the mountain nearest the camp.

One she found interesting had unique rocks at its entrance. With no one around, she stepped inside the opening. The sun's angle allowed her to see a hundred feet into the mountain.

She didn't have a torch, so she dared not go past the illuminated area. Still, the urge to explore compelled her; something drew her to it.

She didn't fully understand this but knew she had to satisfy this yearning.

As she loaded the horse with firewood and rode back to the camp, Rachel formulated a plan. It started with finding a rare tender moment with Fist On Chest, Kicking Knee's wife.

"Would you allow me to explore the cave just over the ridge?" she asked, staring at her feet with head bowed before Fist On Chest.

Fist On Chest smiled and shook her head. "No."

Rachel turned and went back to her chores, but she continued asking every chance she got.

One day in late January, she learned that the band would be moving in a few days.

"The buffalo are coming," Kicking Knee told her as he pointed to the east. "We must find them on the plains."

Their winter stores of food were almost gone. These Comanche preferred to wait until March before moving from the mountain, but their raids on the white settlements late in 1836 kept the men from hunting buffalo.

Sure, they had returned with hundreds of horses, and they could eat horseflesh if necessary. But Comanche saw the horse as a vital part of their warfare, along with their bows, arrows, and lances.

Without horses, they would have to fight on foot. A dismounted battle would eliminate their advantage over the other tribes, not to mention the white soldiers.

Eating a horse was a final desperate measure, something only for emergencies. With the buffalo coming, they could replenish their stores in days while gorging themselves on fresh meat. That's why the buffalo was everything to the Comanche.

Rachel pleaded with Fist On Chest, practically begging her. She even enlisted Wild Rose's help, telling her they might find valuable jewelry she could wear.

"Jewelry is vital for attracting a mate," Rachel told her.

Wild Rose was getting older. By her age, most of the other girls were married and had at least one child.

"The bloom is off the wild rose," Rachel had whispered to Mary as they carried water from the river. The pair had shamelessly chuckled at that.

Rachel's clever words soon affected Wild Rose. The two women went to feed the horses, and Wild Rose agreed to go with Rachel.

Once back in the teepee, they made their plea to Fist On Chest. The stubborn woman felt Rachel's thin buckskin.

Rachel could read Fist On Chest's thoughts: *She can't escape dressed in this. She'd freeze to death before she could find help.*

"You may go with Wild Rose," she said.

Rachel's soul soared. Finally, her deep hunger for adventure would be satisfied.

Early the next morning, Rachel procured some buffalo tallow. The white substance was like candlewax but more malleable. And it burned bright without a wick. She packed an ample amount since running out of light in a cave would mean death.

Along with tallow, she packed food and a flint stone.

"Let's take some firewood and small twigs to start a fire when we take a break," she told Wild Rose. "That will help conserve our tallow."

They gathered everything they needed and stuffed it into bags. When the bags were tied onto their horses, the women took off for the mountain without fanfare from anyone in the camp.

Rachel was almost as skilled at Comanche life as Wild Rose. She knew how to hobble a horse and instructed Wild Rose to help the young Comanche master it. With the horses tied up, the pair unpacked the bags and entered the cave. They walked as far as they dared in the available light. When they reached a deep blackness, Rachel kneeled and started a small fire. From that, she lit a tallow candle for each of them. She put out the fire and collected the unburned twigs for later use.

"Let's go," she said, holding her candle above her head. "We have about ten hours before they get mad we're not back."

Rachel led the expedition, the women ducking here and there as the cave's ceiling required. After walking for twenty minutes, the cave narrowed.

Rachel turned sideways and eased into a large opening. Wild Rose did the same, yet something was wrong.

"I'm not going any farther," Wild Rose declared. "I'm afraid."

"There's nothing to be afraid of," Rachel soothed. "I'm here and I'll go first."

"No. This is as far as I go."

Rachel tried to persuade her to continue but Wild Rose refused.

"All right, I'll go by myself," Rachel said. "You stay here and wait for my return. Then we'll go back together."

Rachel turned her back to Wild Rose, but the Comanche girl grabbed her arm. "You must come back with me."

Rachel wrestled herself free. "I'm not going back! I told you that you didn't have to go with me. Now, don't try to stop me."

Wild Rose anticipated this response. Behind her back, she held a piece of firewood and swung it at Rachel.

Rachel saw it just in time and leaned away from the blow. The wooden stick grazed her right shoulder.

Rachel's left hand grabbed a piece of firewood and surprised Wild Rose, knocking her to the ground. Rachel dropped her candle and jumped on top of the girl, beating her about the face.

Wild Rose screamed for help but they both knew it wouldn't come. They were too far from camp and too deep inside the mountain. Not even their horses tied up at the entrance could hear the screaming.

Rachel let months of anger pour out on Wild Rose.

When Wild Rose stopped fighting, Rachel leaned close to her face. "I will kill you right here if you try to stop me. Do you understand?"

Wild Rose's eyes widened at something above Rachel.

Thinking it was a ruse to gain an advantage, Rachel pinned her attacker's arms with her legs and twisted around. What she saw took her breath away.

A sky of stars and planets had been drawn on the ceiling, the flicker of the candles illuminating everything. Even a new moon was there.

Neither woman had ever seen anything like it. As if supernaturally, they had been carried by their horses to another universe.

Rachel collected her breath and returned her attention to Wild Rose.

"I will let you up and take you back to the entrance. But you must stay by the horses and wait for my return."

Wild Rose fearfully nodded.

Rachel collected the pieces of wood and let her up. Wild Rose found her candle and other supplies and led them back out of the cave as Rachel would only walk behind the crafty Comanche.

True to her word, Wild Rose was happy to tend the horses outside the cave. She promised again to wait for Rachel, leaving Rachel to hope she didn't have to make the long walk back to camp.

With her companion gone, Rachel soon reached the spot of the scuffle. There, she held up the candle and studied the magnificent scene, more spectacular than before.

She saw an entirely new planetary system, a thousand times more glorious and beautiful than the one encompassing the earth. As she moved closer to the stars, Rachel realized the light from the candle was reflected off clear pieces of angular glass rock. She stood there, too amazed to move.

Eventually, she glanced around and took in the rest of the room. The ceiling was twelve feet high. Its sides were coated with the same unique rocks, some jutting out almost three feet. The entire room was one hundred feet wide, its floor smooth.

Rachel walked around the room, unable to measure its length because it bent around into the darkness. If she wanted to see how long it was, she'd have to keep moving.

Before she left, she discovered sections of the floor as transparent as the clearest glass. She tried hard to capture these images in her brain, hoping to recall them in times of stress and unhappiness.

She wanted to stay longer but had to keep moving if she hoped to finish the adventure in one day.

For many hours, she journeyed three to four miles deep down in the cave. It continually narrowed and widened but always allowed her to pass. Yet, nothing excited her like the Star Room, as she now called the place she'd left behind.

Rachel thought about turning back but the thrill of discovering another Star Room kept her moving forward. Soon, her efforts were rewarded when she came to a fork in the cave. The left side dipped into darkness while the right displayed bars from floor to ceiling.

Rachel moved closer to the right side and found a room ten feet high and six feet wide. Though transparent, each bar was solid and thick enough to prevent her from passing.

The bars fascinated Rachel and she drew closer, holding a candle between two of them. With her head turned, she could see beyond the bars. The view easily surpassed the Star Room. She had to get inside it.

Rachel sat on the floor and ate some food, devising a plan. A quick check of the tallow convinced her she had enough to get back to the cave's entrance. But if she kept going forward, she might burn it all out. That would mean certain death since there was no way to feel her way back to the entrance in complete darkness.

To save the remaining tallow and buy some time, Rachel started a fire on the floor and relaxed just a bit, drinking her water and taking in her surroundings. Wisps of wind carried the smoke through the bars and disappeared, another sign that she should move in that direction.

Rachel snuffed out the fire and relit a tallow candle. She moved to one of the bars and used a piece of firewood to break it at the top and bottom. The bar cracked easily.

She examined the unique material and set it aside. Then she squeezed through the narrow opening and entered the most splendid and spacious room she'd ever seen.

The walls, ceiling, and floor were completely transparent, making it feel like she was walking on glass. The room was nearly circular, one hundred feet in diameter and ten feet high.

On one side were three rows of benches, like a house of worship. The other side presented a beautiful stream of water. The river was so clear that she could see the tiniest of objects on the bottom. No imagination on Earth could have dreamed up such a place.

Rachel guessed the river was 150 feet wide. Sticking a leg in, she found it varied from one to two feet deep.

After marveling at this incredible space, she crossed the hidden river and traveled down it for a mile or more. Suddenly, she heard a terrible roar.

Rachel headed toward the strange sound, fearing it could mean danger, but that didn't stop her. Finally, she reached the edge of a precipice.

The main channel of the river raced over the edge, crashing somewhere below. How far down, she had no idea as the light disappeared one hundred feet below her.

The sound was deafening, so she stepped back and found a dry place to recover. She could plainly see she'd come to the end of her journey, and then fatigue overcame her.

As she leaned back, she fell into a deep sleep. Yet mixed in with the water's roar were the dying screams of her baby, Luther. She tried but couldn't tell where they came from.

Rachel thought about her home—her *real* home—and her friends far away, people she'd never see again. For some reason, she thought that her wounded body was bleeding again, sending her mind back to the cruelties inflicted by her Comanche captors.

Out of this strange place came a man who held a bottle with some kind of liquid inside it. He knelt and lovingly bathed her wounds. In seconds, her pain disappeared for good.

She had not woken up yet but was awake because she could touch the man. He consoled Rachel with kind words that she would remember to her death.

Was it possible He was the one who comforted the afflicted and gave strength to the weak? Did God, in His bountiful mercy, extend His hand to a poor wretch like Rachel while she was buried deep in the earth?

Rachel relit her tallow and got up. After taking one last look for the man who had disappeared, she turned and retraced her steps. However, she found the distance much greater.

When she reached the Star Room, she found evidence of Indians searching for her.

Back outside the cave, she discovered that Wild Rose and the two horses were gone. She would have to make the long walk home alone.

With the sun setting, she hurried to make it before darkness overtook her. Otherwise, the wolves and mountain lions would end her journey right there.

Rachel finally returned to camp and walked among the fires. The Indians were astonished to see her.

Falling Rock came up and grabbed her arms, studying Rachel to ensure she was real and not a ghost.

"What's wrong?" Rachel asked.

"We saw the Star Room and thought the spirits had taken you," he replied. "When you didn't return, we were certain you had died."

"I told Fist On Chest we'd be gone all day. And I'm back just as the sun sets. Why worry?"

"You have been gone *two* days. We gave up last night and returned to camp without you. And last night, the wind howled with the cries of your infant. Later, we heard your screams and searched at sunrise but did not find you."

Rachel stepped back, stunned. "Two days?" she said. "That's impossible!"

Leaving Falling Rock, Rachel wandered around the camp, thinking about his words. There was so much to this adventure that she would never understand.

All she could guess was that God had given it to her like a loving gift to ease her pain. She hoped to savor the memories until she died or returned to her family. Which it would be; she had no idea.

Chapter Eight

James Parker covered dozens of miles. How many, he had no idea.

The search for his daughter was much tougher than he'd thought or planned for. With each adversity, he pushed any doubts out of his mind, refusing to think about giving up.

The searcher reached down and pulled up his trousers again. His belt had several new holes punched in it, pulled tighter around his rapidly thinning frame. The rope running through the same loops made sure the belt did its job.

James walked directly into the sinking sun, which was almost below the horizon. It was time to find a place to rest.

Shifting a load of brush and kindling from one arm to the other, he couldn't wait to drop it. He'd been carrying the load for two hours. If he didn't start picking up flammable debris early and before it got too dark to see, there'd never be enough by the time he stopped.

James studied his load. Thank God he had enough to burn. The mistake of no foresight and a man could easily die out here.

As he walked, James thought about how far he'd come. After bringing Elizabeth Kellogg back to his temporary home, Martha came running to greet her. It was an emotional reunion between the two sisters.

Martha didn't realize James hadn't told Elizabeth her mother Sallie, or "Granny" as they called her, had died at Fort Houston. Of course, Elizabeth also had no idea that her stepfather, John Parker, had been pinned down, tortured, and killed. James figured there was no sense in telling her any of that now; she'd find out about it later.

Of all the losses a person could rack up, Elizabeth had seen her share. Her husband had died ten years earlier, making her a widow. That was why she'd joined her mother at the fort. She had nowhere else to go.

James noticed that Elizabeth's spirits immediately improved with Martha by her side. So, one evening, he approached Elizabeth and asked about the raid.

He learned the Indians had divided up the captives before they left the fort, and Rachel and Pratt were taken by Comanches. That was the last she saw of them and all she knew.

A week later, while James was tending to the horse, Elizabeth confided to Martha how she'd foolishly returned to her cabin to retrieve $100 in coins and been quickly caught by the Indians. She skimmed over details of what the male Indians did after stripping her naked at the fort.

She did tell Martha, "Rachel and Pratt were on my left and right sides, no doubt watching everything they did to me. And I watched them abuse Rachel, too." Her eyes filled with tears as the former captive added, "It's difficult to imagine hell will be worse than what we went through."

The next day, Elizabeth told Martha she dreaded thinking about what was still happening to Rachel and Pratt. She hated sleeping at night because "It's going to take a lifetime of nightmares to forget it all. Maybe I can just disappear somewhere, where no one knows what happened to me."

Sadly, Elizabeth would "disappear" less than two years later when she died at age 49.

During a private moment, Martha told James everything Elizabeth had told her. This lit his fuse again.

His simmering rage at hearing the details pushed him to leave his wife and family on September 15, 1836, and set out to find his daughter and bring her home safely.

James talked with Luther, but like the last trip to Nacogdoches, Luther refused to come. Nor would he give or even lend James any money.

Twenty days later, James clenched his jaw and walked away from Luther. Then he mounted up, heading north to Comanche country and an unknown fate.

James kept to his tried-and-true method of collecting brush as he traveled. He found a spot, organized his kindling, and started a fire.

With a blaze going, he situated his pack to get comfortable on the prairie grass and took a long drink from his canteen. With no food, this water was his supper.

He pulled out his journal to make a new entry. The stars were not yet visible, so the only illumination was the fire, which was barely enough to read and write by.

James studied some past entries and realized how far he'd come. He had moved fast and arrived at the Red River on September 27—twelve hard days in the saddle.

Within an hour, he located Jonesborough, the first Anglo-American settlement in Texas. There, he met two men, Major Tinnin and Colonel Fowler. When they heard the story and learned of his mission, both men tried to lend James money, but he refused to take it.

"I have no use for money where I'm going," he told them. "But I could use a new horse. This one is plumb wore out."

The two men referred James to Otis Johnson, who took his tired horse and gave him another one. Otis also fed James and gave him a bed for the night.

When James awoke the next morning, he was refreshed and ready to get back on the road to Coffee's trading post on the Red River. He knew Holland Coffee was a skilled negotiator with all kinds of Indians and a good man for trading money and goods for captured whites. Coffee's post was the first place James thought of going for information on his family and perhaps finding help to accompany him.

While on the path to Coffee's, James ran across a trader who mentioned a white girl had been recovered at Captain Pace's on the Blue River, a tributary feeding into the Red River from the Oklahoma Territory side. James guessed it was another 80 miles and continued along the Red River until he needed to cross it and head north to the Blue River. The water was too deep for a horse to cross.

With no choice, he left the creature with a man named Fitzgerald.

"If I'm not back to your house in ten days, let my family know I'm dead," James told him.

Fitzgerald agreed, and his wife gave James some bread and meat for the trail.

The following day, James struggled to make his way through the swamps and thickets of the Red River bottom. Using his compass as a guide, he walked as far as possible before collapsing into the scratchy prairie grass.

After he removed his mud-caked boots, he discovered massive, painful blisters covering his feet. There was nothing he could do about them, so he went to sleep.

In the morning, James woke with renewed energy. Despite the blisters, he put his boots back on and started walking.

When it was evening, he stopped and set up camp. Once he was next to a crackling fire, he made his daily journal entry.

October 5, 1836 – Walked at least 40 miles today without food and starving. I hope to reach Pace's tomorrow.

James put up his journal and leaned back against his pack. Before he could take two breaths, he fell asleep.

It wasn't long before Rachel approached the fire with Pratt by her side. James tried to touch her, but she refused to come closer. Then, an explosion woke him up.

A wind from the south brought the smell of dirt. With thunder and lightning exploding in the distance, he knew a storm was coming.

James quickly wrapped two pistols under his shirt to keep them dry, just in time to see lightning like Bruno de la Huerta's sabers. It illuminated the prairie around him.

During one flash, he caught a glimpse of an Indian fifty yards away with a tomahawk in his hand. Then it went dark.

At the next flash, he saw the same Indian a few yards closer, this time holding a spear, ready to throw it. James pulled out a pistol and aimed it in the dark.

When the next flash came, he saw nothing. Spinning in a circle, he tried to find the Indian again but couldn't.

Did I imagine that? he thought.

Heavy drops pelted his face. In no time, two feet of water covered the prairie.

James strapped on his pack and got to his feet. His boots filled up with cold water.

With each lightning flash, he saw the prairie was one massive lake. The thunder crashed around his ears like war drums from a Comanche band. He was living a nightmare. Then it got worse.

The wind shifted from the north, and in less than an hour, his clothes froze. He knew he would die soon, so he walked around a small circle through the cold water, desperately trying to stay warm.

Just when he thought it couldn't get worse, it began to snow. The flakes melted in the water but just barely.

Through prayer and God's providence, James was alive to see the sunrise. No longer was it raining or snowing.

With numb fingers, he pulled out his compass and started walking north through the frozen and matted prairie grass. It was difficult to step through it without tripping.

Within two hours, he crested a rise and spotted a forest to the southeast, away from his destination. He had no choice but to head to it.

When he reached the wooded area, he sat down on a stump. His hands and feet were frozen.

James wanted to sleep but knew that meant death. He tried to get up but couldn't. His life was on a razor's edge.

Scooting to one side of the stump, James stretched his arm and grabbed a small tree, using it like a crutch to stand. He was so frozen he couldn't walk. If he let go of the tree and fell, he would be a dead man since he wouldn't have the strength to get up.

He saw a rotted log fifty yards away.

I must get to that, he thought.

James let go of the tree and forced himself to walk. As he reached the log, he collapsed in a heap.

After taking some time to recover, he cut strips from his undershirt and pulled out a pistol. Arranging the cotton strips in the hollowed log, he fired his pistol with gunpowder only and, to his amazement, started a fire.

As his hands and feet unfroze, stinging pain shot through his arms and legs. He could feel them again, and the pain was intense.

The fire roared, and he added more wood to keep it blazing. By staying close to it, he slowly thawed out and dried his clothes. Hardly any moisture remained.

By early afternoon, he decided to start walking north again.

I can't last much longer on this prairie, especially if another snowstorm comes. I must get to Pace's trading post.

A noise startled James. He opened his eyes and stared at the rough-hewn timbers above him. He felt a blanket over his chest and a pillow under his head. It was warm.

He searched his mind and recalled that he'd fallen asleep on the prairie before hearing a calf bleating. He didn't remember what happened next, yet he was here in this place—*alive*.

James lay there for a time and finally stumbled out of bed. To his surprise, he found Mrs. Pace holding a cup of coffee for him.

"This might help revive you," she said.

His words did not come, so he nodded and downed the dark liquid. She took his cup and refilled it. That, too, went down fast.

The smell of bacon, beans, and biscuits stirred a deep hunger. He took a seat at the table and could barely wait for Captain Pace's prayer to be finished before he attacked the plate in front of him. Like the cup, it was replenished with food, and that went down too.

It took a few hours before James felt anything close to normal.

"What are you doing here walking all alone?" Captain Pace asked his guest.

James spoke slowly and explained his quest. With each step in the tale, the Paces listened, captivated and spellbound.

"I'm here because I heard a woman had been recovered and hoped she might be my precious Rachel."

Captain Pace blinked several times and processed James's story. Then he frowned. "I'm sorry to tell you this but the girl belonged to Yorkins. We already sent her to Samuel Marshall's place. The husband is headed there to meet her and take her home."

"Oh no," James lamented. "That hope kept me going through the freezing cold."

Captain Pace rubbed his hands together. "I'm afraid the news gets worse. Some traders from Coffee's were here five days ago. They said your daughter was being held by a band of Indians 60 miles from here. Unfortunately, they killed your daughter's child."

"Oh God!" James cried, clapping his hands to his face. "Poor little Pratt is dead!"

He was unaware this death referred to his baby grandson and not Pratt.

"Stay here another day and let this cold weather blow through," Captain Pace said. "When the wind shifts, you can hurry to their camp. Do you only have two pistols on you?"

"Yes," James replied, downcast and sullen. "Along the way I gave my rifle to a man who set out to engage some Shawnee scouts. I've not been back to see if he was successful."

Captain Pace stood and grabbed a chair. "Why don't you move closer to the fire and rest? I need to go out and check the traps. My wife will take good care of you, James. And let her sew up those holes in your clothes. It's the least we can do."

James wiped away some tears as his voice cracked. "I can't thank you enough for your kindness."

The captain scowled. "We'd do it for anyone in your shoes, 'cept them savages."

On October 19, 1936, five months after the attack on Parker's Fort, James left Pace's trading post. The weather was favorable.

The morning of his departure, Mrs. Pace gave him some venison and bread wrapped in cloth. It was late afternoon when James stopped to eat it.

Sitting on the grass, he took off the cloth and found the gift was barely enough for a few mouthfuls. Still, he couldn't be upset with all they'd done for him. He owed them a lot.

After leaving Pace's post, James assumed he could catch some game. But as he drew closer to his destination, he dared not fire his pistols for fear of alerting the Indians. If that happened, he'd become just another set of bones pinned to the prairie.

By now, James had trudged through the damp prairie grass of the Oklahoma Territory for four days. He was starving again.

He spotted an area by the Blue River that was cleared out. Recent campfires and other broken pieces of flint and bone told him the Indians had been there, just where Captain Pace had told him they would be.

Cautiously, he inspected the grounds, looking for any discarded pieces of food he might consume. There was none.

There were, however, deep ruts in black prairie dirt from horses dragging poles behind them. The hundreds of hoofprints told James there were plenty of Indians to deal with.

He took out his compass and found the tracks pointed southwest toward the Red River. He wasn't an experienced tracker but figured the Comanche band had a two-day head start.

Although he was weak from lack of food and tired from walking nearly forty miles every day, he couldn't give up, especially now that Rachel was so close.

For two days, James stumbled through the prairie grass until he reached the Red River. He could see the spot where the Indians had crossed.

Sitting on the bank, he thought about his situation. Normally, he would swim across the river. But in his weakened condition, he would surely drown.

On this day, the Red River wasn't a source of water for the thirsty but prison bars keeping him from his daughter.

Depressed and unwilling to move on, he knelt and prayed. He would need to find a place to die as he could not possibly go on.

James got off his knees and noticed a stand of trees down the river. Using all his strength, he stumbled over to them and found a log to sit on.

It wasn't five minutes later that a skunk came along, rooting under some leaves and debris for anything to eat. The skunk never heard the branch that crashed down on its neck as it was soon being roasted over a fire.

James was so hungry he couldn't wait for it to be fully cooked. He picked off the meat as it was done and savored the taste until he'd stripped the carcass clean.

It had been six days since his last meal—the meager provisions from Mrs. Pace. He knew that because his journal showed he left the Pace's on October 15. His journal was all he had to remind him of the passage of time and where he'd traveled.

After eating the skunk, James stoked up the fire and made himself comfortable. Then he drifted off and dreamed of finding Rachel.

The sun's rays streamed through the forest and hit James's face. He opened his eyes and found himself a new man. The food and sleep had revived him.

He rolled over and got to his knees, thanking God Almighty. Once again, God had provided.

As James stood, he saw several fallen trees around him. With no saw or way to cut them, he set the logs over the fire and burned each in half.

Once he had eight logs of about the same length, he hunted up some wild grapevine. Fashioning the vines into rope, he tied the logs together using pieces of bark to hold the vines in place. Then he christened the contraption the Parker Raft.

It was early afternoon when James dragged the raft to the river and hopped on. He sat in the middle, clutching the grapevine to keep from sliding side to side.

Using a crude paddle, he steered himself to Fitzgerald's place just as the sun dipped below the horizon. A stunned Fitzgerald found him climbing onto the dock.

"James Parker, is that you?"

"It is," James said. "Can I tie this raft to your dock? I may need it again."

"Sure. Let me help you."

The two men secured the raft, and Fitzgerald led James up the bank to his house.

"It's been what, twenty days? Did you send that letter to my family telling them I'm dead?"

Fitzgerald shook his head. "I drafted one and sealed up the envelope, but no. It's been waiting for a trader to come by and take it to the post office. I'll give it back to you."

"Thank you!" James said, clapping his hands. "Another blessing from God."

"Did you locate your daughter?"

"No. Captain Pace heard about a woman and it was not Rachel. But I did find their camp and realized they had crossed the Red River. I was too weak to pursue them, though."

"What are you going to do?"

"I'm going to rest up a day or two if I could oblige you," James replied. "Eat some food if it wouldn't be too much to bear. Then I'm going to head home."

"Okay, James," Fitzgerald said, slapping him on the back. "At least I still have your horse. That should help."

"That and some of your wife's cornbread."

Fitzgerald grinned. "Come on in and let's get you better."

Chapter Nine

The first warm breeze of the coming spring excited Rachel. She guessed it was mid-March and wiggled her toes in celebration that the cold would soon be gone. Her horse felt it, too, and he trotted a step faster. Hints of greens in the prairie grass meant life was returning to the plains.

Rachel would have loved to wear moccasins but her owner would not provide them. As she had no money or property to trade, she remained barefoot. And she dared not complain about her condition or the two women would beat her, and if necessary, Kicking Knee would as well.

Her horse approached the dead buffalo and stopped. Rachel surveyed the scene.

At least fifty buffalo had been killed. Teams of women were busy skinning and butchering the massive beasts. The one in front of her had five arrows and one lance sticking out of its carcass.

She dismounted and tied the reins to a stone. This allowed the horse to graze on the early grass while she worked on the buffalo.

"Let's cut the liver and gall out for Kicking Knee," Rachel said to Mary. "He'll be here in a minute and expect it."

The two women expertly made three cuts and removed the desired organs just as the Comanche arrived. He said nothing as he leaned over and collected the prize.

Sitting atop his mare, Kicking Knee squeezed the gall over the fresh liver and took a bite. A bloody smile appeared on his face, and juice dripped onto his buckskin breeches and horse. Flies buzzed around his face, but he didn't care. He kept eating, his white teeth red and dark eyes happy before prodding his horse away from the women and trotting back to camp.

Rachel and Mary worked hard for two hours. When the hide and meat had been loaded on a travois, they tied it to Rachel's horse and headed back to camp, traveling slowly to avoid dumping their work on the prairie.

All around them were dead carcasses, most of which the other women had already cleaned since they had more experience and worked faster.

"I think buffalo is the best meat I've ever tasted," Rachel said. "It's better than steak or tenderloin."

"I agree," Mary replied. "I think the hide somehow keeps the meat tender. How often have you seen an arrow enter one side and exit out the other? That wouldn't happen with a cow, I don't think."

Mary was right. Many times, the Comanche rode alongside a buffalo and shot an arrow so hard it went all the way through the beast. The women figured the meat was so tender that the buffalo's body couldn't stop it. Only the thick hide offered any resistance.

The two captives let their horses amble into camp. Near the teepee of one of the chiefs was a gathering. Three lodge poles were tied against each other and buried two feet into the ground. Rachel pulled her horse to a stop and glanced at Mary.

The civil chief, arms folded, stood by while two men ran a rope over the top of the poles and fashioned a noose. Once they were satisfied with the work, two other men dragged a screaming Comanche woman to the noose. She refused to stand so one of the men slapped her hard, knocking her woozy.

Taking advantage of her condition, they held her up while another man fashioned the rope around her neck. Without any words or warning, the loose end pulled tight and the woman was lifted a few inches off the ground. This brought her back to consciousness.

With her hands free, she dug her fingers into the noose, trying to gain some slack or free herself. The woman's legs kicked frantically, hoping to find some footing so she could loosen the rope and breathe. But she was unsuccessful.

Rachel and Mary watched as the woman choked and struggled for several minutes. It was a horrific scene.

When her legs stopped kicking and her body sagged, a young man stuck a lance in her side. The woman didn't flinch as blood leaked out. She was dead, and the man with the lance yelled excitedly, happy with this result.

Rachel and Mary said nothing and proceeded to their teepee.

Four women helped remove the buffalo meat from the travois and roasted it over open spits. Rachel untied the sled and took her horse to the corral. Mary joined her.

"Why was that woman killed?" Rachel asked a female Comanche watering the horses.

She stopped and turned to Rachel. "The woman refused to get her son feathers for his arrows when he commanded her."

"A son had his mother killed over feathers?" Rachel said, unsure if she had translated the words correctly.

The Comanche nodded.

"Did the son approve of that man sticking a lance in his mother's side?" Rachel asked.

"He was the one with the lance. So yes, he celebrated her death. It's a lesson to others."

Rachel grimaced and glanced at Mary. The two captives shook their heads in disgust and started back to camp.

When Rachel saw they were alone, she said, "They know no such thing as mercy. They might ask for it but never grant it to others. This is what you get when you set a godless heathen people free to roam the land. To restore peace and order, God flooded the earth once and killed everyone but Noah's family. After that, He destroyed Sodom and Gomorrah. It never ends."

Kicking Knee confronted them upon their return to camp. "A great council will be held in four days. All the tribes will be represented. You are to stop working the hides and only work to prepare meats and foods. Fist On Chest will tell you what to prepare. You will not dishonor us in any way."

"I understand," Rachel said, bowing and staring at her feet.

As he walked away, Rachel grew excited. Maybe another tribe would purchase her for ransom.

She said a prayer for it, even though it meant more dirty and hungry men would take her in dim, smoky teepees. She could endure it if only to be returned home.

Four days into the council, it was everything Kicking Knee had predicted. There were tribes from the north, east, and west. Even the Comanches' hated enemy, the Apache, appeared.

In a large rectangular tent sat dozens of war and civil chiefs. Some tribes appeared to have one chief for everything. Many interpreters dotted the room, listening and whispering to their superiors. There was even a Comanche chief called Buffalo Hump.

Rachel climbed a horse to see the tribes' encampments. To her amazement, the teepees were more numerous than the buffalo herds she'd seen, with each as close to each other as possible. The line extended so far she could not see an end to them. This war council, as she now understood it was, had to be the largest gathering of Indians in history.

Rachel wanted to listen in but Comanche law was clear. No women were allowed to attend a council. They couldn't even enter to serve water. Instead, pots were placed around the tent for the attendees to serve themselves.

Despite all this, Rachel was determined to know what was being said. Each night, she crept to the edge of the tent and listened in. Several times, she was beaten by another woman or a male teen. She always apologized and slinked away, only to return later.

By the fourth night, she had gathered important intelligence yet had no way to send it to the government.

"What do they plan to do?" Mary asked.

"They intend to invade and take possession of Texas. All whites will be killed or driven from the land. Then, the Texan farms will be given to the tribes who like to raise corn, and the prairie Indians will control all the prairies. In times of attack, each tribe will defend the other."

"Oh no. Anything else?"

Rachel nodded. "The corn-growing Indians must raise a large crop on the Texas farms to feed them. When that happens, all the tribes will attack Mexico. Many Mexicans who are unhappy with the government will join the Indians."

"So they will take over Texas and Mexico?" Mary said, incredulous. "That sounds impossible."

"Well, they aim to try it. And with that accomplished, they plan to attack the United States."

Mary's jaw dropped. "Attack America?"

"Yes. They said the whites have driven the tribes from the east to the west, so they must drive the whites out of the country. They are deeply worried since the whites have almost surrounded them. They fear the whites will soon be so numerous the Indians will be driven to the great waters to the west and everyone killed."

"When are they doing all this?"

"They couldn't agree, but best I could tell, Texas will be attacked in the spring of 1838. Yet others said the spring of 1839. The northern tribes said they would have their own council and determine when they could be assembled to travel the great distance to Texas. They plan to tell the Comanche chiefs and fix a date."

Mary edged her horse closer and whispered, "We should tell someone."

"I agree," Rachel whispered back. "When you have a solid plan, please let me know."

"I'm sure one will emerge."

Rachel wasn't so sure. They were captives in the middle of nowhere. How could they get a message out?

After several days of elaborate ceremonies, the war council broke up. Rachel felt the day was likely March 22, her birthday. She planned to celebrate her new age of eighteen with Mary once it turned dark and there were shadows to hide in.

It was afternoon on the prairie, and Rachel was carrying water from the river. As she neared the camp, a foreign Indian approached her. He wanted something, and she knew what it was. So she stopped and set the pots down, hoping to make it quick.

"I am Yellow Bird," the Indian said. "I am a Bidai and live by the San Jacinto River. Our people attended the Great War Council. I promise you that we will make servants of the white people."

Rachel sensed his anger rising.

"We will take back the land and kill many whites!" he yelled.

To Rachel's astonishment, he cursed her in English. It was the only English word she had heard an Indian mutter since she left the fort.

Rachel stared at the ground and nodded, ensuring he felt both important and right. Eventually, he yelled himself out and left. Rachel picked up the water and hurried back to tell Mary of this interaction.

Many visiting Indians had talked to Rachel, fascinated at her white skin and fiery red hair. But before she could reach Mary, Fist On Chest hit her about the head for taking too long. Rachel gritted her teeth and took the beating.

"Go to the prairie and help Wild Rose," Fist On Chest ordered. "She is digging up roots."

Exhausted from days upon days of work, Rachel sighed loudly and leisurely turned to leave.

Rachel assumed Fist On Chest was jealous of the attention she had received. Yet the Comanche woman took her heavy sigh and slow movements as insolence and swatted Rachel's shoulders with a stiff quirt. It hurt Rachel, and she jumped a few feet before heading toward Wild Rose.

Along the way, she passed men and boys practicing with their bows and arrows. They stared at her.

Since the cave adventure, the men were different somehow. Rachel couldn't tell if it was fear, respect, lust, or something else. Regardless, the distance from Fist On Chest allowed Rachel to cool her boiling temper.

"How can I help you?" Rachel asked Wild Rose, who was bent over digging for roots.

"Go back and fetch the shovel," the girl ordered.

After the fight in the cave, Wild Rose had been careful not to antagonize Rachel. But for some reason, perhaps with the war council over and the men distracted, the two Comanche women had decided it was time for revenge. It was apparent they had coordinated their oppression attempt.

Rachel took in another deep breath and tried to relax. She knew this game. It was like being ordered to dig a hole by one person before another came along and demanded the digger cover it up. This trip back and forth to camp could continue for hours. Rachel was tired and refused to participate.

"You must run back to camp and get the shovel now!" Wild Rose barked. "Stop standing there and move!"

In bare seconds, Rachel decided that telling the government about the impending war council was no longer critical. Instead, she decided life was no longer worth living under such pain and oppression. She would do whatever it took to get the Comanches to kill her. Then she could go to heaven and meet her two boys.

Wild Rose stood up and approached Rachel. "Go now!" Wild Rose screamed inches away from her face.

"I won't go back and play your silly games," Rachel told her, stepping away and turning her left side to face Wild Rose.

Savage screams erupted from Wild Rose as she ran toward Rachel. Rachel stepped to the right and pushed Wild Rose down to the ground as she went past.

Rachel had seen this all before. Without hesitation, she jumped on the Comanche and kept her from getting up.

Wild Rose screamed like a warrior attacking a white settlement. She remembered the beating Rachel had previously inflicted and wasn't going to go through that again.

Thrashing left and right in a desperate attempt to free herself, Wild Rose reached for a large buffalo bone. Rachel beat her to it.

Raising the bone above her head, Rachel struck her tormentor repeatedly. In seconds, the head of Wild Rose gushed blood onto the prairie and over the bones of a long-dead buffalo. Rachel didn't stop.

As she continued the blows, Rachel heard the warriors surround her. At any moment, a lance would be thrust through her back, ending her life on Earth.

Even when the men started yelling, she didn't care. If she were going out, Wild Rose would die too, or at least be crippled for life.

To Rachel's surprise, the warriors didn't touch the combatants despite their bloodcurdling yells.

Wild Rose, unconscious and barely breathing, somehow muttered a plea for mercy.

Rachel leaned back and wiped her own face. Blood and sweat filled her palm. Only the sweat belonged to Rachel.

Rachel breathed hard and forced herself to slow down. Her body finally relaxed.

She got off Wild Rose and couldn't believe the men didn't arrest her. Nor did they touch Wild Rose.

Rachel stood over her enemy and looked down on the girl. With the fight over, Rachel grabbed her arms and helped her up. Then she carried the wounded Comanche to camp.

Rachel leaned her up against a woodpile and brought over a nearby water pot. Another girl handed Rachel a rag and she used it to clean the Comanche's face. Men simply stood around the pair and watched.

One of the big chiefs eventually called Rachel over.

"You are brave to fight and good to a fallen enemy. The Great Spirit directs you. Indians do not have pity on a fallen enemy. By our law, you are clear. It is contrary to our law to show foul play. She began with you, and you had a right to kill her. Yet your noble spirit forbids you. When Indians fight, the conqueror takes the life of his antagonist and seldom spares them."

This was balm to Rachel's soul. She knew the men now respected her and approved of her actions. She couldn't believe how she had been prepared for death but now was rewarded for handing out a beating.

Still, it wasn't all good news. Fist On Chest burned with rage. This white woman had beaten her daughter twice—out of sight in the cave and this time in her presence.

"Get a large bundle of straw!" she ordered Rachel.

Rachel found one and brought it to the angry woman.

The woman spread the straw on the ground around Rachel and stuck some of it in her buckskin. Rachel could see she meant to set her on fire.

Rachel just stood there, knowing the warriors had supported her when she played fair with Wild Rose. She would play fair here while she fingered a hidden knife in her pocket.

"Cross your hands," she ordered Rachel, holding out a leather thong to tie Rachel's hands.

"I will not let you tie me up," Rachel said defiantly.

"Are you willing to be burned to death without being tied?"

Rachel said nothing.

Fist On Chest grabbed a bundle of straw, caught it on fire from a pit and threw it at her. To Rachel's surprise, the bundle ignited and burned her. Blisters formed as Rachel brushed off the painful fire.

Fist On Chest lit another bundle but Rachel held up a hand. "I will fight you if you try to burn me again."

Like her daughter, Fist On Chest was filled with intense rage, letting loose an unholy scream. She threw the lit bundle at Rachel, who charged the woman and pushed her into the pit.

Fire licked the Comanche's back and legs. The pain caused her to hop up, only to find Rachel pushing her back into the fire. This time, Rachel held her down, allowing the fire to burn the woman's skin and hair.

Seeing that she would burn to death, Fist On Chest grabbed a club and hit Rachel in the shoulder and head. Dazed, Rachel snatched the club from her and hit Fist On Chest several times.

By now, Fist On Chest was severely burned. Yet she managed to roll to the side and escape from Rachel.

As she staggered to her feet, Rachel tackled her into a teepee, snapping a lodgepole in half.

Fist On Chest continued swinging her fists while Rachel dodged them. Rachel easily handled the older woman. She was not as fierce as her daughter; perhaps years of toiling in brutal conditions had taken its toll.

The two women brawled into the main path between the teepees while Rachel delivered blow after blow. Seeing her older tormentor tiring and dropping her arms, Rachel rushed her and landed on top. Then Rachel proceeded to beat her senseless.

Like before, the men crowded around and yelled but didn't interfere.

Fist On Chest either refused to ask for mercy or could not. She barely moved her eyelids.

Rachel stopped the beating and, again, collected herself. Then she brought some water over and tended to the woman.

With Wild Rose recovered and on her feet, Rachel turned to her and asked for help to get her mother back to the teepee. Wild Rose refused.

Somehow, Rachel managed to get the woman home. Once she had been attended to, Rachel went to the damaged teepee and repaired it.

The following day, twelve of the chiefs assembled at the Council House. Men came to fetch Rachel, Wild Rose, and Fist On Chest.

They brought the women into the large tent and told them to sit. When the trial began, the place was as quiet and solemn as a church service.

Fist On Chest told her story. Rachel was shocked that the woman had not embellished the tiniest of facts.

"Are these facts true?" the big chief asked Rachel.

"Yes," Rachel replied.

The big chief asked Wild Rose the same question.

"Yes," Wild Rose answered.

"Do you have anything else to add?" he asked all three.

The two Comanche women said no. Rachel, however, got to her feet and spoke up.

"You have mistreated me," she said, referring to the Comanche tribe. "You did not take me honorably but used a white flag to deceive us. Then you killed my friends. Once I arrived here, I was faithful to you. I have served you from fear of death. I would now rather die than be treated as I have been."

Rachel pointed to the sky. "The Great Spirit will reward you for your treachery and abuse to me."

With that, she sat down.

The twelve chiefs whispered among themselves. Finally, the big chief delivered the verdict.

"You must get a new pole for the one you broke in the fight," he said, pointing to Rachel.

Rachel blinked several times. "I will abide by your sentence on one condition."

The chiefs frowned and shifted in their chairs. "What is it?"

"Wild Rose must help me get the new pole."

Again, the chiefs glanced at each other and nodded.

"Let it be," the big chief said. "And from this day on, you shall be known as The Fighting Squaw."

Rachel nodded and walked out of the trial, a grin threatening to appear on her weathered face.

As Wild Rose and Fist On Chest passed by, Rachel studied their eyes. She saw fear or respect, or perhaps a combination of the two.

Whatever it was, she had no more problems with either one again. And the beatings stopped. It was a blessed relief.

Now, if she could only get free of this madness.

Chapter Ten

James Parker guided the horse through another swollen stream. With each bump, he pressed a hand against his cheek.

"Damn tooth!" he said to no one.

His tooth had bothered him since he'd left Natchitoches eight days earlier. It was always something.

The past five months had mostly been unproductive. After returning home from the Red River, James found his family intact and surviving without him.

In November, the Republic of Texas Congress convened at Columbia, and he rode there to ask the government once again for help finding his daughter. He met with General Thomas Jefferson Rusk, an important soldier and leader in winning independence for Texas. General Rusk had just returned from following Santa Anna's Mexican army across the Rio Grande and back into Mexico.

James was excited to talk to Rusk because now that the Mexicans were no longer a threat, he was sure Rusk would give him the men he needed. But General Rusk said he could do nothing unless Congress acted.

James tried Major J.W. Burton but he deferred to Congress too.

He then approached Colonel Richard Sparks again. James had spoken to Sparks in Nacogdoches when he tried Sam Houston's patience.

Sparks was very sympathetic but had no authority to grant him anything. After all, he was just a colonel, more ceremonial than anything.

Before James left Columbia, he dropped off a letter for General Houston, pleading for men. Out of options, he mounted his horse and went back home, where he stayed for two months.

On February 25, 1837, James took off alone for Natchitoches. He asked Luther one more time to come with him or at least provide support, yet he received a no—*again.*

Luther pointed to the futility of the mission. Many of Luther's friends and plenty of James's companions urged James not to go.

"You're just giving them Indians another head to scalp," they said. "Stay and make money, support your family. With the money, you can buy Rachel back."

For most Texans, the advice made sense. With the war over and the Mexicans gone, Texas exploded with work. Opportunity was everywhere as the well-watered fertile land produced bumper crops. Men were getting rich. Why not him?

James, no stranger to hard work, money, and success, turned it all down. He could hardly sleep knowing his daughter was out there with those savages, being brutalized and likely worked to death. He simply had to do something or die trying.

Upon reaching Natchitoches, he offered a $300 reward for "every prisoner among the Indians that might be brought in."

Natchitoches was well-known to traders who often drifted over from Texas and the Oklahoma Territory.

After hearing his story, Mr. D.P. Despelier paid for a local newspaper ad explaining James's story and reward. Since James had little money, it was all he could hope for.

On March 10, 1837, he left Natchitoches. His journey to Monroe slowed considerably due to recent rains.

Then there was the toothache. If it had acted up in Natchitoches, he would have seen a dentist to remove it. Now, he was out here all alone.

At noon, James stopped to eat some food. As he dismounted, he felt for his pocketbook.

"What?!" he yelled frantically.

Looking all around his horse, he found nothing. Before he had eaten a bite, James mounted his horse and started back to Natchitoches. He had to find his pocketbook.

The candy-striped pole twirled around outside the dentist's office, the only one in Monroe, Louisiana. Inside, James leaned back in a chair and gripped the armrests.

"One. Two. Three!" the dentist yelled as he yanked out a tooth. "There you are," he said, holding a bloody mess between two pliers.

"Oh, my mouth!" James whined. "Do you have anything for the pain?"

The dentist unzipped a pouch and pulled out a stash of leaves.

"Take one or two and shove them in that side of your mouth until the hole closes. It'll help."

James studied the pale green leaves. "What are they?"

"The Spanish used to bring them here from the Aztecs or Mayans. One of them, I forget which. Now I have a Mexican trader who brings the stuff up the river. The leaves will give you more energy and some pep while alleviating some of the pain."

"Okay, Doc," James said, pulling out his dirty pocketbook. He shook it off, still angry he had to retrace his steps for twenty miles to find it. But thanks be to God, he had found it on the ground and not in some bandit's hand.

"Where are you going next?" the dentist asked, taking the money from James.

"I have a man who owes me some money here. I aim to collect it and return to the Red River to continue searching for Rachel. Her son Pratt was killed by them savages and I'd like to run into them with a company of men if I can raise one."

"Well, Godspeed to you, sir," he said as he put the bills away.

James left the dentist and rode to the house of his good friend Alfred Ludwig. There, he was treated to an extravagant meal. With his tooth and the pain both gone, he found he could eat more than usual, and he did.

The next day, he located the man who owed him money and they went to the bank to complete the transaction. With a good deal of money in his pocketbook and a few leaves in his cheek, James returned to Ludwig's house and stayed three more nights.

For the first time in almost an entire year, James enjoyed himself. He almost forgot about his quest and the family he'd left behind.

Almost.

But then it was time to go.

"Best of luck to you, James," Ludwig said, handing James a large sack of provisions.

James hugged the man. "God bless you, sir. I hope to send you word of my success. Pray for me."

And with that, James was off again.

James rode up to Marshall's Trading House on the Blue River and dismounted. After tying off his horse, he tapped on the door and found it was open.

"Come on in," a voice said. "We're open for business."

James walked inside and saw all kinds of items for sale.

"I'm James Parker. I'm headed to Comanche country to find my daughter Rachel."

Samuel Marshall set some papers down. "Well, I'll be. We've heard about you, but I didn't think I'd ever meet you."

He came from behind the counter. "Let me welcome you properly."

The men shook hands.

"How can I help you, James?"

"I want to buy all your stock to help trade for my daughter."

Marshall pursed his lips and whistled. "Okay. If you're gonna do that, you should also talk to Colwell and Wallace a half day down the road and purchase their stock, too. With all that to trade, we will surely get your daughter back."

"I'll do it," James said.

He settled up with Marshall and rode down to the other two traders to buy everything they had. In total, he'd purchased $1,000 of goods, more than enough to trade for three or four captives.

After concluding his business with the two traders, he stayed the night with them.

The next morning, a Shawnee Indian appeared outside. James and the two traders went out to see what he wanted.

The Indian spoke English and explained that a woman had just been purchased by Mr. Sprawling, one of Marshall's traders. James thanked the man and jumped on his horse, galloping back to Marshall's place.

It took four hours with James making good time. He sprinted from his horse and ran into the trading house.

"Where's Samuel?" he blurted out breathlessly.

The clerk reached for a paper. "He left a note for you this morning."

James snatched the paper from the young boy and read it.

My Friend, James W. Parker,

Sir: Having received good news, I start after the prisoner tomorrow morning. Mr. Sprawling has purchased a woman; I hope it is your daughter. Keep yourself here. The Comanches are now at Coffee's. You must stay here until I come back, and if God spares my life, I will have the prisoners. I have got three Indians engaged at two dollars per day. For God Almighty's sake stay here until I come back and see what can be done.

In haste, your friend,
SAMUEL B. MARSHALL

James rubbed his jaw and stroked his beard, deep in thought.

Seeing this, the clerk spoke up. "He said to stay here. Those Comanches will kill you before you ever see your daughter."

"Where is Sprawling's trading camp?" James asked, sliding a map over onto Marshall's desk.

"Farther up the Blue River," the clerk said, pointing to a spot. "But the letter said to stay here. Mr. Marshall was very precise. Let *him* fetch your daughter."

James hesitated momentarily before turning around and rushing out the door. He mounted his horse and galloped off. Rachel was waiting, and he wasn't going to waste one more minute.

The campfire popped and hissed at Sprawling's trading camp. Finding nothing else to do with his hands, James poked a stick at it for the tenth time.

He wanted to keep pounding the palm of his hand with his fist but knew that was useless. Once again, he'd failed to find his daughter.

The girl turned out to be another family's daughter and Marshall was hurrying her north to another trading post where she could be carried back home. He wouldn't return to his post for a week or more. This left James in a quandary.

"I'm considering following the Indians and see if I can find Rachel," he said over the campfire.

"How are you going to do that?" one of the traders asked. "Kill them all by yourself?"

"No," James replied. "I've heard they make captives fetch water from the creeks and rivers. I'll leave notes for the captives to find, saying I'm ready to help them escape. There's no chance a savage would understand it."

The trader leaned back and laughed. "That might actually work if you could get close enough without being spotted. Them Indians can smell a white man a mile away. And they send boys out in the morning to look for game. They'd see your tracks for sure."

"Would you two men join me?" James asked.

"I won't because I like my scalp. But Minnow here might."

A quiet, clean-shaven man whittling on a stick looked up from his work. His dark hair was trimmed close to the scalp. This style was much different than the long ponytails of the other traders.

"Would you pay me?" Minnow asked.

"Sure," James said. "Can you shoot?"

"I wouldn't be alive if I couldn't."

"Good. Then it's settled. Tomorrow morning, we'll head back toward the Red River. They seem to cross it with impunity. I plan to introduce a few of them to eternity."

The following day, James was up and ready to go. Thankfully, Minnow was also an early riser.

The pair got on their horses and took off in a westerly direction, willing to bend south when the land allowed it.

"So why do they call you Minnow?" James finally asked the trader.

"My name is actual François Minuet. I'm French but no one wants to pronounce my last name correctly. They just call me Minnow, and it's close enough."

"French, eh? From Louisiana?"

"*Oui*. My family is still there, running trading posts and trapping."

"Do you think this is a fool's errand?" James asked.

Minnow turned his head and looked directly at James. "I could only hope for someone like you if I fell into the wrong hands. Of course, I'd be scalped and killed before being rescued."

James nodded and fell silent. Minnow's words soothed him, but only barely.

The two men traveled for three days, stopping each night. On the third night, they hobbled their horses and ate supper. An hour later, they were fast asleep.

A noise awoke James. In the half-moon light, he waited until his eyes focused.

Seeing a slight movement, his right hand slid slowly to his rifle. Sure enough, he saw an Indian trying to cut the ropes holding the horses. Another Indian was not more than ten feet away.

James sprang to his feet and shouldered his rifle.

Blam!

He pulled his pistol out and fired again, certain he hadn't missed with his rifle but wanting to make sure. The two Indians sprinted from their camp.

Minnow was up next to him, grabbing the horses. He and James knew they were dead men if they lost the horses. It would only be a matter of time.

"Let's get out of here!" Minnow yelled.

"I concur!" James yelled back.

The two men grabbed their gear, saddled their horses, and rode in the opposite direction of their attackers. They pushed all night without stopping, constantly looking behind them. Even the horses seemed frightened.

When the sun rose, the pair stopped and looked all around them. For endless miles, they saw nothing but an occasional dip or rise in the terrain. The vast prairie gave neither them nor the Indians a place to hide.

Around 10 a.m., James and Minnow had their horses at an easy gait, finally relaxing. They had escaped with their lives intact.

As they pulled around some scrub brush, James noticed a movement.

Blam!

A ball whizzed past James's face, grazing his cheek and ear.

Before the smoke had cleared from the Indian's gun, James had his rifle up to his shoulder. He aimed it at the Indian still holding an empty rifle. James fired. The Indian crumbled forward and fell on his face.

"Ambush!" James yelled.

Minnow had a ball whiz past his shoulder. He dropped the Indian with one shot of his rifle.

James held his pistol steady and sighted a third Indian coming from the brush. Smoke streamed out the barrel as he saw the Indian jump up before leaning to the left and falling backward.

Suddenly, from behind a slight rise, the sounds of war cries reached the two men.

"Let's get out of here!" James yelled, kicking his horse.

Minnow was already ahead of him, racing his horse in the opposite direction from the war chants.

James took off after him, concerned with the stamina of his horse. But with God's providence, they made it five miles before slowing down.

They traveled another ten miles and stopped against a rocky outcropping. This allowed them to protect their backs while guarding their horses in front of them.

With a thick patch of sweet spring grass, the horses ate well. After all, they had earned it.

"That was close," James said when a campfire was going. "I thought we were goners."

"I did too," Minnow said. "Tomorrow, if you'll pay me off, I mean to leave and head east, back to the trading post. I'll not risk my life like that again."

James lowered his head. "I understand. And yes, I'll pay you off. You've earned it. If it had been just me, I'd be pinned to the prairie looking up at the Indians as they tortured me. God only knows what they would've done."

Minnow nodded. Both men were silent, considering how that would've played out.

Before he went to sleep, James added to his journal.

April 25, 1836- Minnow and I killed three Indians. I likely shot one more on April 24 but didn't wait around to see his carcass picked clean by the coyotes. One thing's for sure: I've found the Indians.

For weeks, James rode the prairie alone. He came upon another trading house and left his horse behind.

James wanted to swim across the Cash Forks of the Red River and preferred to be on foot. He figured he was less of a target and could better sneak up on any Indians. Besides, the Indians seemed drawn to any horse they could steal. Without one, they'd just be coming for a scalp and likely one or two bullets headed their way. The savages could weigh those risks.

Incredibly, James located the Comanche's camp—or at least one of their camps. He crept around the edges, looking for any white captives.

For days, he did this without being discovered. Then days turned into weeks and his food supply ran out.

He thought a lot about how to get some game. If he fired a rifle, the Indians would come running. He had to find another way.

After coming upon a prairie dog town, he had an idea. Using his hat, boots, and canteen, he filled each one to the brim with water from a nearby creek and dumped it into a hole. In seconds, two prairie dogs popped up. Using his bowie knife, he dispatched them without a sound.

He found a time right as dusk fell to start a fire. The sky grew dark, yet not so dark that the remaining light hid the glow from his fire. And the smoke, typically seen from miles away, would be hidden by the gray sky.

If he waited until the moon was full, some observant Indian could see the glow of the fire and sneak up on him in the dark. But right now, he could cook the dogs and put the fire out.

In the darkness, James ate his meal. Then he moved 500 yards to another camp he had set up just in case the Indians investigated his dead fire. It was a good plan and so far, it had worked.

By the third week, he'd still not seen any captives. He had moved with the band three times. Each time, they shifted west to another spot on a river, and each time, James followed and saw only Indians.

By the fourth week, there were no prairie dogs. But there were buffalo.

One evening, after the Indians had pulled up stakes and headed west, he waited until he could no longer see them. Then he went to a large herd of buffalo and shouldered his rifle. One shot and the buffalo dropped.

James left it where it lay and returned to a clear stream to set up a fire for broiling the meat. He was hungry and could barely wait to eat.

After the fire was blazing, he walked back to the buffalo and had a surprise. A white wolf, native to this area, had come upon the carcass and was already enjoying a tasty meal.

James threw some rocks at it but the wolf stood his ground. As more rocks flew, the wolf took a few steps toward James and growled, showing his white teeth in the fading light.

James rubbed his forehead. He didn't want to fire a second time to give any observant Indians a chance to fix his location. But if he wanted to eat, he had no choice.

Aiming his rifle, he crept closer and got into position. He couldn't miss at this range.

And he didn't. The wolf took the bullet and staggered away for a few feet before dropping to the prairie grass and bleeding out.

James moved to the buffalo and carved up large slabs of meat. With the meat slung over his shoulders, he returned to the fire that was still going strong. That night, he ate well.

The next morning, he would head back to the trading house and collect his horse. Then he'd ride home. But tonight, he'd stare up at the stars and wonder if Rachel could see them too.

He could only hope.

Chapter Eleven

Rachel worked at the never-ending chore of scraping flesh off buffalo hides. By now, she'd gotten better at working hides; she was faster than many Indian women. Her teenage youth helped, but so did her drive to explore the area around whatever camp they made.

Rachel was sure no white person had ever seen this country and was excited to be the first. She was also curious about how the Comanche fit into it.

However, deep inside her heart was the hope of reuniting with her husband and family. One day, it might happen. And if it did, she wanted to inform her fellow citizens on how to eradicate these savages. It was like she had been taken to hell and shown how it works. Her knowledge might help destroy her captors.

Rachel stopped and took a break.

No longer was she whipped. The women had seen her fight and didn't want a red-haired maniac coming for them. This allowed her more freedom of movement and slotted her into a higher level of the band's pecking order. She was not the lowest of the low. She had some status. Still, she was careful to use it.

Walking to a pot of water, she raised a dipper and took a long drink. Mary was with her.

"When do you think the men will return?" Rachel asked.

Mary studied the sky. "Let's see, they left two sundowns ago and it's almost noon today. They probably fought yesterday and are riding back right now. I'd be surprised if they didn't return by sundown."

The two captives knew what it meant if the men failed to return soon. The Comanche warriors would be dead or captured.

This tragedy would leave them open to a counterattack by the Osage. That was why the older men and injured warriors who remained in camp stood guard.

Kicking Knee had sharpened his lance and gathered up his bow and arrows. This morning, he mounted his favorite pony and rode to the outskirts of camp, sitting and staring to the east.

The younger warriors were farther away, also perched on their horses but on higher ground. They needed to see a great distance and warn the camp if trouble was coming.

Rachel felt the nervousness among the women. They tried to stay busy by making food and working hides.

Most males above fifteen had one wife, and the older ones had two or three. Kicking Knee had had a second wife.

According to Wild Rose, the second wife was bringing water from a stream in the dark when she slipped on some mud and hit her head on a rock. They didn't find her until the following day.

This wasn't strange as women worked all hours of the day and night. With the men up late singing and dancing, attention was rarely paid to who slept under the large buffalo blankets when they returned early in the morning.

The next day, Kicking Knee's second wife was found dead. The civil chief examined the scene and ruled it an accident.

One of the other Indian women told Rachel that Fist On Chest wasn't too surprised or broken up about it. She hadn't gotten along with the second wife, and it was a convenient fact she now had her husband all to herself.

Of course, this death turned other women away from Kicking Knee. No one wanted to become his wife, although most had no say in the matter. And Fist On Chest continued to satisfy her husband's lust, which kept his eyes from wandering.

All was well until Rachel came. But a fight had reordered Kicking Knee's household. Now, Rachel had to ensure she didn't slip and hit her head on a rock, especially one in the hand of an angry wife.

Rachel picked up a small pot of water and headed to Kicking Knee. She found him on his horse, holding his weapons of war.

Post Oak

Worry covered the old warrior's wrinkled, dark face; his pale eyes fixated on the horizon as he searched for friend or foe. If his men lost, today might be his last day on Earth. That made him sad.

Rachel stood next to Kicking Knee, saying nothing. She was unaware of the reason for this battle. She only knew there was some simmering conflict from the recent council.

Mary had told her the Osage considered the prairies their land, and the Comanche did too. The Comanche had beaten them back several times, but it was believed that one day, the Osage would gather up all their warriors and ride on the Comanche.

That fear was why Rachel's band combined with two other Comanche bands to take the fight to the Osage first. No one wanted to wait around each day waiting for an attack.

The good news about this tribal feud meant the end of any coordinated attack on Texas, Mexico, and the United States. These Indians couldn't stop fighting each other, much less come together and take on entire countries.

A noise came from a ways off. Kicking Knee stiffened and stared in its direction.

Suddenly, another warrior on a horse held his lance horizontal to the prairie and rode away from camp. Kicking Knee relaxed. This sign meant the men were returning. They would not be attacked by the Osage today.

Rachel walked back to camp.

Soon, the warriors could be seen riding slowly. It didn't look good.

"They have lost some men," Mary said. "They don't seem joyous."

As the warriors inched their way home, the Indian women tried to hold back but couldn't. They started walking toward the horses until their walk turned into a trot, then a full sprint. The women ran among the horses, looking for their man's fate.

Finally, the enormous horde made it to camp and a tally was made. Six warriors had been killed, their bodies draped over the horses. Fourteen wives and five daughters went to the bodies and wailed. They had lost their man.

Other women walked around dazed. Their men were not among the bodies, yet they weren't on horses either. Their frantic faces ran from warrior to warrior, trying to determine when their man would return.

One warrior dismounted. He carried a bundled blanket under his muscled arm and set the bundle down, opening it up. Three scalps stayed glued to the blanket, and several heads rolled out. This set off more wailing.

Every Comanche knew it was mandatory to risk their lives by bringing the entire body of their fallen comrades home. If time was short and the danger high, a head would suffice. If time was real short, they removed the scalp and brought that home. This denied the enemy the transferred power of their fallen comrade.

The battle had carved out a wedge of men from the band, making them weaker. But all was not lost. The Comanche had killed a good many Osage. That night, the camp's mood turned to elation and joy as the surviving men danced and sang. Each took his turn, recounting the battle and their brave exploits.

"These savages don't seem to understand this luck thing," Mary whispered.

"What are you talking about?" Rachel said.

"Luck. They keep their enemies' scalps as security for good luck. The more scalps, the more good luck. They believe this good luck is transferable from father to son."

"What about the dead Comanche warriors?" Rachel said. "I guess their luck didn't hold out."

"Exactly. Many of them took a large collection of scalps into battle, some of which were inherited from their fathers. Yet they were killed. So much for good luck."

Rachel shook her head. "They don't need luck. They need the Bible and salvation."

Mary smirked. "Once you're in the fiery abyss, don't be surprised when your fellow inhabitants are criminals and murderers."

"Yeah." Rachel nodded.

Three days later, they broke camp and headed west over the vast prairie. A heat wave swept through the land, causing the Comanches to forget the bitter cold of the past winter.

Rachel was initially grateful. She preferred the warmth to the cold, especially since they kept her wearing thin clothing.

Now, she wanted to stay warm and add weight to survive another winter. It would be here before she knew it.

Rachel also made plans to make herself a pair of moccasins. Mary agreed to help since she knew how. If the moccasins turned out well, she might even make a second pair and hide them in case something happened to the first pair.

In the scorching heat, the band trudged along. By midafternoon, the sun was at its hottest.

Rachel grew thirsty and smiled as she spotted a vast lake ahead. She thought of drinking its fresh, cool water with each step beside the mule carrying their lodge poles. Yet ten minutes later, they were no closer to the lake.

Rachel's thirst increased.

She found Mary and asked her about it. "See that lake ahead? We never get to it. What's happening?"

"We won't ever touch it because it's not a lake."

"What is it?"

Mary shrugged her shoulders. "An imagination? A dream? When the heat bakes the prairie, this happens. See those buffalo ahead?"

"Yes. They're right in it. I can see their wakes."

"But they aren't splashing around," Mary pointed out. "They're feeding on the grass, not standing in water."

Rachel couldn't understand it. When the band stopped for a break to take in water from their supply, Rachel sat down and noticed seashells and oyster halves embedded in the baked prairie.

"This was once an ocean," she said to Mary, showing her some shells.

"The lake we see but never get to is a ghost of the past. But where did all that water go?"

Rachel didn't know.

As they traveled west, they encountered some Mexicans living along a river. Early one morning, Rachel snuck away from camp and approached a Mexican milking a goat. He looked like a trader since almost everyone in remote locations traded for a living.

"Sir," Rachel said, speaking Spanish, "I'm a captive from Texas. My father and husband are dead, and I have enough land in Texas to pay you back."

"Pay me back for what?" the Mexican asked, looking up from his goat.

"I want you to buy me from my master, Kicking Knee," she pleaded, her hands together as if praying.

"I will do it," he said without ever stopping his work.

Rachel raced a hand to her mouth and thanked him profusely. Then she ran to find Mary.

"Guess what?!" she said, her voice cracking. "I found a Mexican who agreed to buy me. I'm going home!"

Mary put a hand on Rachel's shoulder. "Don't get your hopes up. Kicking Knee might not sell you since you are part of his wealth. The more wives he has making buffalo robes, the more he can trade for things he needs."

"But I'm not a wife," Rachel said.

"You wait on him. You feed him. At night, you bring him drink during his dancing and singing. And you lay with him. If he makes you pregnant, you will have his child. What else do you think you are?"

"His prisoner. His slave," Rachel insisted. "I'm not Fist On Chest."

"The only difference between you and Fist On Chest is that she occasionally seeks him out to couple. Otherwise, you and she are the same."

Rachel said nothing. Instead, she counted the minutes until she was free.

It never came. The band packed up and left the area. And nothing more was said about some Mexican purchasing her.

The band always kept moving. Plains. Hills. Mountains. More plains, always keeping the buffalo in sight. Where these animals went, so did the Comanche.

Their wanderings allowed Rachel to see many more wonders, which helped heal her from suicidal thoughts after the last disappointment.

During a day of blast-furnace heat, Rachel's band walked through a salt plain. She bent over and scooped up the grains. The salt resembled dirty snow on a freezing day.

Being light, the wind blew it for miles. She found places where the salt piled up to her knee while all around the ground was bare. It depended on where the wind blew it.

After weeks of travel, the band made it north of the Snow Mountains. The leaders chose a deep valley with the headwaters of some river directly in front of them. It wasn't their favorite camping spot. That was on the mountains' southside.

One afternoon, Rachel went in search of dry brush she needed to make a fire. She had to work at night to make her quota. As she scanned the ground, something sparkled.

Rachel picked up one of the particles and studied it. The rock was oblong, about three-fourths of an inch in circumference, and perfectly transparent. She turned it over and over. Then, she noticed a stream of concentrated sunlight coming from the object.

She got to her knees and held the stone steady. In less than a minute, the beam set some grass on fire. Rachel quickly put it out and realized she no longer needed dry brush to get a fire started. This object would do it for her as long as there was sunlight.

Rachel showed it to Mary. The pair decided it was a diamond.

In the valley, Rachel showed Mary the thousands of diamonds littering the ground. On sunny days, they could see pieces from a mile away as the sparkling light was strong and focused.

The two also found gold flecks. "There must be a gold mine around here," Rachel said.

She found larger gold pieces that Kicking Knee used for arrow tips. Yet she saw him exchange the gold for iron since iron was harder, lighter, and flew better.

Rachel and Mary laughed because the Indians had no concept of the value of gold.

One evening, Rachel worked hides south of camp when two Mexican traders appeared on horses, leading four mules packed with goods. Her heart skipped a beat.

She immediately rushed to them but the lead man spoke first. "Can we speak to your master?"

Rachel's eyes filled with tears. "Oh yes!" she said, trying not to cry.

She had been through this before, but it felt different because she had had a dream last night. The angel from the cave visited her.

This time, he had four wings and gave them to Rachel. She used them to fly away and back to her family. She was finally free.

Then she woke up and realized it was nothing but a dream. Now, another Mexican trader stood before her. He could be her way out of this cruel bondage.

Rachel led them to Kicking Knee. He had just eaten dinner and sat by the fire, satisfied and happy.

"*Senõr*," the trader said, "will you sell her to me?"

"*Si,* senõr," Kicking Knee replied.

Rachel almost fainted. Her unsteady legs caused her to sit down and listen to the transaction.

The trader made an offer, but Kicking Knee said no.

Rachel lowered her head in despair.

The trader offered more, but the Comanche still refused.

Rachel's heart slammed against her chest, knowing this might be her last chance out of this nightmare.

"I can give no more," the trader said, preparing to turn away.

Kicking Knee shook his head. But then, Fist On Chest appeared in his line of sight, her arms crossed and a scowl planted on her face.

Kicking Knee saw her and shifted to one side as the standoff between him and the trader continued. Rachel prayed to God to intercede.

The trader had seen Fist On Chest. He spoke with his companion, whose head shook several times.

The trader finally turned around and frowned. "Senõr, this is my final offer."

He laid it out for Kicking Knee as Fist On Chest stepped closer.

Kicking Knee looked away from everyone. He didn't like being pressured.

"Yes, I will sell her for that."

Rachel wanted to jump for joy but she had to be careful. The transaction was not over. She'd seen many deals over nothing more than a pot turn into fisticuffs.

She dared watch as the trader reached into a pouch on the first mule and removed several items. He handed them to Kicking Knee, who inspected each one. Satisfied, he waved at Rachel to join the traders. She was now theirs.

Rachel left everything behind, including her magic stone, and went to stand by the mules.

As they began to take off, she grabbed the trader and pleaded with him. "You must offer more for Mary, another white captive. My family has money. My uncle is in the Illinois Senate. Please!"

The trader scratched behind his ear. "I'll see what I can do."

He approached Kicking Knee and exchanged words. Kicking Knee leaned back and laughed.

The trader spoke to another warrior and he laughed too. Frustrated, the trader returned.

"He says there is no other white woman but you."

Rachel's face dropped. "That's not true! I've been living with her since I arrived."

"Where is she?" the trader asked, spreading his arms wide. "He said you could look through the camp."

Rachel hurried through the camp, calling Mary's name. For some reason, she was in hiding.

Then Rachel stopped. Mary would be there to say goodbye. It didn't make sense.

"Maybe she's off gathering firewood," Rachel mumbled to the trader.

The trader pulled Rachel to the last mule in line.

"These Comanche are tricky to deal with. We need to leave before they decide to kill us and take everything, including you. Besides, we offered a great price to get you. Don't you think they would be happy to sell another white woman if they had one?"

Rachel was frantic. "I can't leave without Mary."

The trader whispered, "Have you heard the name they gave you?"

"Yes. The Fighting Squaw."

The trader looked embarrassed. "He told me they also call you She Talks To Wind. They said you've been talking to yourself since you arrived. They think you're crazy. That's why they are willing to part with you. Kicking Knee said he worries you might kill him in his sleep. And with all that, you can't even tell me the name of her master, can you?"

Rachel gazed at the trader, unable to believe any of this. He was right. She didn't know who Mary belonged to.

How could that be? she thought. *Is it possible Mary is no different from the dream I had last night?*

Reluctantly, Rachel fell in with the traders, and they soon made it up the valley and along the rim, leaving Kicking Knee, Fist On Chest, and the rest of the Comanche band far behind.

The traders rode hard. Rachel was placed on a mule with the lightest load. The mule barely took notice of his rider as she weighed less than 90 pounds.

It was dark when they stopped to make camp.

As they relaxed around a campfire and ate some fresh meat from the Comanche, the lead trader told Rachel a man in Santa Fe had sent them to buy her and other whites from the Comanche. The man promised they would profit nicely.

"That's where we are headed," he said. "It will be a hard and dangerous trip through Indian territory, especially the Apache."

He explained that if they ran into other Comanche bands, they might not honor Kicking Knee's sale. The small group had a long way to go before she was safe.

"What day is it?" Rachel asked.

The trader took a piece of paper and made some calculations. "June 19, 1837."

Rachel leaned back from the campfire and gazed up at the stars. She had been captive for almost thirteen months. It seemed like a lifetime.

That night, she fell asleep out in the open and under the brilliant stars. For the first time, Rachel noticed their incredible beauty. Being free somehow changed that.

Rachel's mind raced. She couldn't sleep. The excitement and joy overwhelmed her.

Post Oak

The following day, Rachael was up first. She made a fire and found provisions to cook breakfast for the traders. The two men weren't used to having a cook, especially one as pretty as Rachel.

After breakfast, they loaded up and continued heading west.

At some point, they rounded the mountains and changed course to due south, pushing hard day and night. The weather was good, and they made it to Santa Fe in seventeen days.

Seeing the town, Rachel was overwhelmed with civilization. Everything moved so fast.

Within hours of her arrival, the local Americans crowded around the white woman as word spread of her ordeal. In hours, she was deluged with attention. Still wearing deerskin coverings, it was strange for her to see everyone else dressed like modern people.

Most wanted to hear about her captivity. This included several newspaper reporters.

As they jostled for her attention, a dashing man pushed them aside.

"Move back!" he shouted, a saber at his side. "She is under my protection."

Rachel studied the man. "Can you help me find a Mr. Donoho?" she asked.

"William Donoho, at your service, ma'am. Please come with me."

They made their way through the crowd to Mr. Donoho's residence. Once inside, a woman approached.

"Dear, what have they done to you?"

"This is my wife, Mary," Donoho said.

Mary. When Rachel heard that name, she was speechless.

Seeing her blank expression, William raced to fill the gap. "I sent traders out with instructions to pay for white captives. I heard of your disappearance and wanted to help your father."

"Is he alive?" Rachel pleaded.

"I don't know."

"Is my precious Pratt alive?"

William shrugged his shoulders.

"What about Cynthia Ann or Elizabeth Duty Kellogg, or John Richard Parker? They took us to separate bands—all Comanche, I think."

"I truly don't know," he said. "Wish I did but I don't because we're a bit behind the news this far from civilization."

Mary Donoho appeared with some clothes. "Try these on, dear. Perhaps they fit."

Rachel held the clothes to her face and cried. Before she collapsed, the Donohos moved her to a couch so she could get it all out of her system. It took an hour.

When she finally calmed down, Rachel learned that Colonel William Donoho was a Christian who felt it his duty to help her. He explained that they had reserved the best hotel room in town just for her.

After they fed her a meal, they took her to the hotel and checked her in. Rachel was asleep as soon as her head hit the pillow.

Twelve hours later, she awoke. It had been the first real bed in thirteen months. Even though the hotel room's floors were dirt, she was in heaven.

Before she knew it, a week had flown by. Rachel found herself adjusting nicely.

Mary Donoho came by to check on her and found Rachel worried. "What's the matter, dear? Do you need anything?"

"My monthly is late," she said in a whisper.

Mary closed her eyes and said a quick prayer. They both knew what this meant. She might have to give birth to a child who would remind her of all the unimaginable nightmares of the last thirteen months.

With an Indian baby, my family won't want me back, Rachel thought.

She, too, said a quick prayer. All she could do now was hope.

Chapter Twelve

It was Houston.

James dusted himself off and studied the town situated at the head of Buffalo Bayou. The spot wasn't much more than a collection of mud, tents, and cabins.

He tied off his horse in front of a newly built hotel that bragged of six rooms and hot baths and sauntered up to the front desk—six smooth planks held up by four stumps.

"I'm James Parker. Could I have a room, please?"

"Yes, of course, sir," the clerk said, getting up from his chair. He studied James. "Would you like a bath too?"

"I guess so," James grunted, "since you put it like that."

The clerk suppressed a grin and began filling out a piece of paper. "Have you been on the road long?"

"Only four months," he said sarcastically. "Mostly north of the Red River."

"Oh!" the clerk said. "You're *that* James Parker, The Searcher."

James furrowed his brow. "The Searcher?"

"It's been in the newspapers. The articles say you're crawling through Indian country to find your daughter, her husband, and their son. You're trying to avenge your father's death."

James wagged his finger at the clerk. "You got it wrong. The Indians killed her son, and her husband was never captured. Luther stayed behind and let me do all the searching. And two of my brothers were killed. There's also two more Parkers captive besides Rachel. I guess I need to correct the newspaper while I'm here."

"Okay," he said, putting up his hands. "We're still pulling for you. I hope you find all of them safe and bring them back home. We can't wait to read about your travels in the newspaper or maybe even a book."

"A book?" James stroked his beard. "The folks wouldn't believe what I've been through. Probably'd think it wasn't true."

"I don't know about that," the clerk said. "Here's your key, sir. Do you need help with your luggage?"

"No. I've got this pack and that's it. Thank you."

James was halfway up the stairs when the clerk called out to him.

"Sir, I just remembered I have a note for you."

"What does it say?" James asked, sure the clerk had already read it.

The clerk unfolded the note. "Please see President Houston when you arrive."

James stopped and turned around. "Where's his office?"

"It's the two-story plantation house at Texas Avenue and Main Street. They call it the Capitol building. Look for the columned porches and lots of people standing around trying to get in to see the President."

"Is he living there now?"

"Yes, but he just left yesterday for Nacogdoches. He has to pick up some items and wants to direct them himself."

James smirked. "Sounds like Sam, though it might be a girl or a bottle that needs picking up."

The clerk said nothing as James went back outside and mounted his horse. It took less than two minutes to find the Capitol—a large plantation-style house with several fireplaces and plenty of workers hammering and sawing on additions in the rear.

James tied up his horse and went inside. The place was a beehive of activity.

He found the receptionist. "I'm James W. Parker. President Houston wanted to see me?"

The receptionist left his desk and went to get somebody else.

"Are you James Parker?" a man asked.

"Sure am. What's going on here?"

The man produced an envelope with a wax seal on the back.

Post Oak

"These are orders for you. He told me to tell you that a treaty with the Indians is not possible. He's setting you loose on them. Good hunting, sir."

James's heart raced at hearing the words. He could feel it thumping in his chest as he tore open the seal and pulled out the letter.

Scanning it, he couldn't believe what he saw: he was being designated Commander-in-Chief of a military company to be called "The Independent Volunteers of Texas, without limit to numbers."

James's spirit soared when he read the last line: "It shall be your task to flog the Indians."

At the bottom was another wax seal designating it an official order of the Republic of Texas.

"Well, I'll be!" James said, slapping his thigh loudly. Several onlookers looked over at him. "Finally!"

As the man turned away, James stopped him. "Where's the post office? I need to send some dispatches right now."

"We don't have an official one yet. But you can send letters from Bert's Dry Goods store. It's down Main Street. Just head left out the door."

"Thank you kindly," James said, practically dancing out of the building.

Two weeks later, a man stepped off the stagecoach and James strode up to greet him.

"Nathaniel! It's great to see you. How was your trip?"

"Bumpy, brother. Does this hotel really have a bath?"

"Yes, and it's hot, too." James shook his hand. "Why don't you come in and have one."

"I think I will."

The two men went inside the hotel and arranged for Nathaniel's room and bath. When clean and freshly dressed, he joined James in the restaurant for supper.

"How far have you gotten?" Nathaniel asked.

"We've raised seventy-three men so far. Joseph should be here tomorrow from Austin. I hope he's bringing more men."

"How's our brother doing?"

"Good," James replied. "He's a tremendous help. How's the political temperature back home?"

Nathaniel was a senator in the Illinois state legislature. "Always arguing about money and who's going to pay."

James chuckled. "Some things never change."

The two men shared a laugh before turning serious. "Tell me about the attack and what you've been through," Nathaniel said. "I want to hear all of it."

James nodded. "Let's finish supper first. I'd rather tell it over a full stomach."

Joseph arrived in Houston the next day with eight more recruits. James had been hoping for at least fifteen, but he couldn't be picky.

Now that Nathaniel was here, James put him in charge of finding more men while he and Joseph arranged for weapons and ammunition. Several times a day, James drilled the men in formation and tactics. With each exercise, he could see each recruit's strengths and weaknesses.

Over the next ten days, Nathaniel delivered more men. James and Joseph worked them hard. At supper in the hotel, the three Parkers discussed a date to set off with them.

"I'm thinking July twenty-first," James said.

Joseph nodded. "That'll work so long as those rifles come in."

"They should," Nathaniel said. "I talked with the quartermaster or procurement something—whatever he's called now. He said those arms should be here in a few days."

"Any chance of more men?" James asked.

"We're trying," Nathaniel said. "I've put out more feelers and the newspapers across the state have run plenty of stories about it. There may be men riding here from Austin and other parts of Texas hoping to join. Other than that, these are the men we have. What is the total?"

"Ninety-six," James said. "We lost one to the fever and another when he shot himself in the foot."

Nathaniel thought for a moment. "That should be enough to handle any Indians we come across."

A clerk hustled to the Parkers' table and handed James a letter.

"What's this?" he said.

"It just came in from President Houston. He sent it from Dallas, but I think he's near Arkansas today."

"Okay," James said, growing concerned.

Like the first one, it had a wax seal on the envelope. He cut it and removed the letter.

> To James W. Parker:
>
> Some disturbing news has reached me about your actions which include murder and robbery. The Taylor family insists that you be held to account. I have also heard of attacks on friendly Indian tribes and other misdealings. Thus, you are hereby ordered to disband The Independent Volunteers of Texas immediately.
>
> President Samuel Houston

James dropped the letter and slapped the table.

"What is it?" Nathaniel asked.

"We've been disbanded!" James spat out. "And all over some vicious slander."

"What?" Nathaniel said, grabbing the letter and reading it. "What is this about?" He waved the letter around.

"After the attack on the fort, I heard rumors going around that I had cheated the Indians by giving them counterfeit money for some stolen horses. A big lie. Then I heard another rumor I killed Mrs. Taylor and her daughter so I could rob Major Hadley's house."

"That's preposterous," Nathaniel said.

"It's a lie because I was north of the Red River. I was out looking for Rachel when those murders happened. I have plenty of witnesses to testify to that."

Joseph turned pale. "What are we going to do with all these men? They're here because of us."

The three said nothing as they contemplated this extremely disappointing turn of events.

Nathaniel finally spoke. "I guess there's no reason for me to stay here. I'm going to pack and head back to Illinois. At least I got to spend some time with you, James. Now I need to head back to my family. Will you tell the men the bad news?"

James's face was sullen and dark but he still stood up and hugged his brother. "Of course. I thank you for coming down."

"Just wish I could've been there to kill a few of them Indians," Nathaniel said. "Maybe Dad or Benjamin or even Silas would've lived."

Nathaniel hugged his other brother, Joseph, and left the two men alone.

"What are we going to do?" Joseph asked again.

"How about you and I go into Indian country and see if we can find Rachel?"

Joseph thought about it for a moment. "Count me in."

"Let's get our things together. But first, we have to disband the men. Come and help me deliver the bad news."

The two brothers left the hotel with heavy hearts and angry minds.

It was October 31, 1837, when James and his horse sauntered into another Indian town just south of the Red River. It was his third in as many days.

Scattered along the big river were towns filled with Indians who were tired of fighting, running, and starving. Instead, they set up towns to trade with the whites. These Indians were friendly now and didn't plan on going back to the wilderness.

James glanced at his two companions, men who had joined to help find Rachel.

Brother Joseph returned to Illinois in late August after the two returned from riding 500 miles through Indian country. They had suffered from a lack of food and water and the almost deadly heat. James returned home to his family and saw Joseph off.

Once back home, James spent the next week recovering. Then, it was off again on another journey. He left on September 7 and returned on October 12, but like the earlier trips, he had learned nothing new.

After this last trip, James's health was in a precarious state. He remained at home for fifteen days to recover. And once again, he was gone.

James had ridden back to the Blue River and checked in with Samuel Marshall and the other traders, but no one had any news.

Now he was on a journey through these Indian towns, hoping someone had heard something about his dear Rachel.

"Let's stop here, men," James said, pulling up to what appeared to be the main structure. "I want to see if I can get some information."

James dismounted and tied off his horse. His two companions, the Stubbs brothers, did the same. One was called J.T. and the other one was simply Stubbs. They were looking for adventure and had tried to join the Independent Volunteers of Texas before it disbanded.

James found them when he returned from his last trip in October. Since they didn't need to be paid and were eager for some action, he took them along.

James walked through an open door and saw a female Indian suckling her baby. "Do you speak English?"

She shook her head and called out to a male Indian in another room. When he appeared, he asked James what he needed.

"Information. My daughter Rachel Plummer was kidnapped by some Indians over a year ago—May 16, 1836. Her son Pratt was taken too but I learned the Comanche killed him. They also took my niece, Cynthia Ann Parker, and my nephew, John Henry Parker. They may be with the Comanche. Have you heard or seen anything about them?"

The Indian scratched the side of his head. "No. We hear nothing."

"Have any whites been here?"

"Whites come through all the time, trading."

"I mean white *captives*." James felt his temper rising.

"No. No captives through here."

"If they do come or you hear about them, I'm willing to pay three hundred dollars for each captive returned to me. Do you understand?"

The Indian's eyes widened. "Yes. Money is three hundred dollars. I will listen for information. What is your name?"

"James Parker. I've been in all the newspapers for the last year and a half."

"Yes." The Indian nodded. "I've heard of you. 'The man who refuses to give up.' That's what they say."

"Yeah, well, there are others who say a whole lot of bad stuff. Don't believe it. Just think about those three hundred dollars."

"I will, James Parker," the Indian said sincerely.

James turned and left. As he walked out of the structure, he ran right into another Indian.

James was more startled than anything but watched the Indian's hands to see if he took offense. When the Indian held them up instead of reaching for the knife in his belt, James brushed past him.

"What did you learn?" J.T. asked.

"Nothing. But the Indian I just ran into wears a vest like the one I had at the fort. The buttons on my vest were made from the rind of a gourd."

He fished around his saddlebag for a knife.

"What are you going to do?" Stubbs asked, placing his hand on the butt of a pistol.

"I'm going to buy me a button. Mount up, boys. I won't be long."

James went back inside and tapped the Indian on the shoulder. "Excuse me, do you speak English?"

"A little," the Indian replied.

"May I buy one of those buttons from you? I need one for my shirt. Here's a quarter."

The Indian studied the coin and nodded.

James made fast work of it and cut a button off. Then he went back outside to his horse.

"What's the verdict?" Stubbs asked.

James held the button up to the sun as his face twisted in rage. "Start out of town ahead of me, boys. Get going—*now!*"

James organized his rifle on the horse's left side and his Huerta saber on the right. Then he checked two pistols to ensure they were ready to fire. They were.

Post Oak

James called the Indian back outside and questioned him about where he got that vest.

"I bought it off a trader," he replied, shifting from one foot to another.

James clenched his jaw. "Were you at Parker's Fort?"

"What's that?"

"A fort? Are you serious?"

The Indian swallowed hard and rubbed his hands together.

James narrowed his eyes. "I think that's my vest from the fort. Did you attack it?"

"No. Forts are dangerous. Many deaths."

A wicked grin spread across James's face. "Yeah, that's what I thought."

He mounted his horse and started trotting away as the Indian stood there watching him go. The sun was high and the sky was blue. It was a perfect day for a killing.

James stopped his horse fifty yards away and turned it around to face the Indian. In one smooth action, he drew the rifle from its scabbard and shouldered it.

"Thought you didn't know what a fort was," James muttered to himself.

His journal entry filled in the rest of the details.

> Taking a last fond look at my vest - with one eye through the sight of my trusty rifle - turned and left the spot with the assurance that my vest had got a new buttonhole.

James put his rifle up and wheeled the horse around.

His companions had started galloping fast at the sound of his rifle. James was 500 yards behind them and still had many Indians left to deal with.

One of them ran and grabbed the bridle of his horse. James withdrew his saber and slashed at the man. Cuts to his arm and shoulder caused the Indian to turn loose.

James spurred the beast on, and it responded.

Two other Indians ran to stop him, and James waved his sword at the closest man while steering away from the other. In seconds, he was free and racing to catch up with the Stubbs brothers.

The three rode hard for ten minutes before slowing to a trot.

James pulled alongside them and said, "Yep, it was my vest. Now they can bury him in it."

The brothers said nothing because they knew this might have stirred up a band of Indians to follow them and remove their scalps. If they hadn't fully understood the danger of being on the frontier, they understood now.

It was just after sunset when the three riders crossed the Sabine River and found yet another Indian town. Staggering across the main street were dozens of Indians, all drunk from whiskey.

The three riders stayed mounted and picked their way through the crowd. They had gone about halfway when an Indian grabbed the bridle of James's horse. In the dim light, James saw a knife in the Indian's right hand.

Perhaps he's already heard about what I did at the last town? James thought. *Or maybe he just feels like killing another white.*

James jerked free his rifle and slammed the butt into the man's forehead. A sickening crunch filled the street. To James's dismay, his rifle shattered into pieces, dropping to the mud all around his horse.

The other Indians rushed at the three riders. J.T. kicked one off as Stubbs ran over a man with his horse.

James pulled out his saber and yelled, "Let's ride, men. Fast!"

The Indians ran after the three riders, throwing rocks and whatever they could find.

In seconds, James and his band were free of the town and riding hard once again. They continued for another two hours before stopping at a riverbank. By then, their horses were exhausted and in danger of dying.

While the horses filled up on water and river bottom grass, the three men fanned out and prepared for an attack, using the riverbank as cover. It was going to be a long night.

By sunrise, it was clear the Indians weren't coming. Without sleep, the men mounted up and headed southeast, stumbling into a Texas settlement.

Once the horses were fed and put up in a stable, James and the two brothers procured a place to sleep for the night.

After several drinks, James said, "This tour is over, gentlemen. In the morning, I intend to head home."

"We are too," Stubbs said. "These are all the stories we need for a lifetime."

"I hope that's all you ever get," James added, "because the ones I have are terrible."

The three clinked glasses and turned in. This trip was another bust for James. He could only keep praying his Rachel would turn up alive.

October 28, 1837
Jesse Parker's Colony (near present-day Huntsville, Texas)

James arrived home to find his son-in-law Lorenzo Nixon and his wife Sarah visiting. Before he could talk to Lorenzo, Martha launched into James.

She was sick and tired of him being gone all the time. They were living in poverty and barely getting by, mainly from the kindness of neighbors.

"I don't want to hear about it," he said to Martha, grabbing Lorenzo and taking him outside.

"Did you find out anything?" Lorenzo asked.

"No," James said, spitting on the ground. "Absolutely nothing."

"You don't look well, James."

"I'm not. I've spent the past year and a half on the rugged frontier, eating very little and enduring harsh weather. I'm tired and sick and need to recover."

"What can I do?" Lorenzo asked.

James sighed. "You can head up north and see the traders I hired. Find out if they've heard anything."

"Where are they?"

James went back inside and drew a map. "I don't have much money," James said, handing him the map.

"Save it," Lorenzo told his father-in-law. "While you've been on the hunt, I've been making money. I'll start tomorrow morning and head up there before winter hits. Hopefully, I'll return with some news."

"God bless you, Lorenzo. I only wish Rachel had married a man like you."

For the next month, James rested up and recovered.

Late one night, a loud knock on his door woke him. He grabbed his gun and cautiously opened the door.

"G.S.! What are you doing here so late at night?"

It was G.S. Parks, an acquaintance.

"I have news for you, my friend. Good news!"

"Come in right now," James said.

He led Parks to the kitchen and lit a lamp. "Tell me. What is it?"

"It's Rachel. She's been found. And she's alive."

James collapsed into a chair and began sobbing. "Thank you, God," was all he could manage.

Chapter Thirteen

The citizens of Santa Fe were enthralled with Rachel Plummer's story. It was all anyone talked about as they could not believe she had survived.

During her first week in Santa Fe, the citizens raised $150, a substantial sum. They gave it to Reverend Calhoun, who promised to distribute it to Rachel. She went to see the preacher, but he didn't have the money on his person.

"I'll have to go by the bank and pick it up," he explained.

Day after day, Rachel asked for the money, yet the good reverend always had an excuse. She couldn't believe this man of God was a thief.

Colonel Donoho interceded, but no one could find the reverend. Or the money.

While Rachel waited for the funds to appear, she sat in Donoho's home and began writing about her captivity, which was still fresh in her mind.

On July 8, 1837, Rachel wrote:

> I found in Mrs. Donoho a mother to direct me in that strange land, a sister to console me in my misfortune and offer new scenes of amusement to revive my mind, and a friend – the best of friends – one who had been blessed with plenty and was anxious to make me comfortable. She continually poured the sweet oil of consolation into my wounded and trembling soul and was always comforting and admonishing me not to despond. Mrs. Donoho assured me that everything should be done to facilitate my return to my relatives.

At the start of her second week, Colonel Donoho came running to the house. "We need to pack now!" he cried out.

"What's wrong?" his wife Mary asked.

"There's been a rebellion. It's that Esquibel mess."

Juan Jose Esquibel was the mayor of Santa Cruz. He had received a bribe to release a criminal from jail. Governor Albino Perez suspended Mayor Esquibel and put him in jail for accepting the bribe. Yet Governor Pwerez was highly unpopular as a tax-raising outsider appointed by General Santa Anna. In July, local citizens rioted and freed Mayor Esquibel.

Now out of jail, Esquibel organized a rebellion against Governor Perez. The mob included unhappy Mexican citizens and thousands of Pueblo Indians.

"Why do we need to leave?" Mary asked.

"It's Governor Perez. He's lost his head."

"Oh, what's that fool doing now?"

"Nothing. He's lost his head—*literally*," Colonel Donoho said, grabbing a bag. "The rebels cut it off and put it on a stick. They're parading it through the streets. And they cut off Judge Hidalgo's hands and waved them in front of his face. It's only a matter of time before they start using us whites as target practice."

"Oh dear, William. This is terrible," she cried.

If Mary Donoho was scared, it was time to go because she was no pushover. She was likely the first woman to make the 1,100-mile journey on the Santa Fe Trail and the first U.S. female citizen to live in Santa Fe, a rough place at the time.

The colonel pointed at his wife. "Get our children together and pack only what you need. I'm going to find Carlos and get the wagon hitched up. When I come back, be ready to leave."

Four hours later, the Donoho family and Rachel were headed southeast along the first leg of the Santa Fe Trail. This direction was necessary as Elk Mountain blocked a direct route.

It was summer in the desert and very hot. Their first stop was in Las Vegas. As they approached the town, Rachel grabbed Mary's hand.

"What's the matter, dear?" Mary asked.

"I just got my monthly."

The two women smiled from ear to ear. Whatever Rachel might have to face on the Santa Fe Trail, she could handle it now.

January 3, 1838
Independence, Missouri

Lorenzo Nixon strolled up to the Donoho residence and knocked. Colonel Donoho answered the door.

"I'm Lorenzo Nixon. I'm looking for Rachel Plummer. I heard she was here."

"Yes, she's here. Come in. But let's step into my study first."

Colonel Donoho closed the study doors, and the two men took chairs opposite each other.

"Is something wrong?" Lorenzo asked.

Donoho cleared his throat. "We made it through Indian country and 1,100 miles of the Santa Fe Trail. It wasn't easy, and with all Rachel had been through, she didn't complain. Once we arrived here, she was inundated with gifts and well-wishers that first week. But then her past caught up to her. She's been wanting to leave on foot to travel back home to Texas, and we've had to hold her here. That's made her depressed. She stays in her room and prays all the time but it's tough for her. I just want to warn you that she may not be the same. I don't know how she'll react to seeing you."

Lorenzo exhaled loudly. "Okay, I understand. I'm ready for it."

Colonel Donoho stood. "Shall we?"

He showed Lorenzo to the second-floor bedroom and knocked on a door. It opened, and there stood a stunned Rachel. Facing her brother-in-law, she tried to move toward him but was frozen. Tears poured from her eyes and she started shaking.

"Are my father and husband alive?" her cracked voice managed.

"Yes," Lorenzo replied.

"Are Mother and the children alive?"

"Yes," he replied again.

Rachel ran to Lorenzo and hugged him. As her knees buckled, he and Colonel Donoho helped her to the bed.

Lorenzo pulled up a chair and sat with her, answering every question she had. Eventually, he was shown to a room and passed out due to exhaustion.

Rachel barely slept that night. Her life was about to come back to her. But would Luther accept her back?

The following day, Colonel Donoho begged the pair to wait until spring before attempting a 1,000-mile journey to their home in Texas. It was the dead of winter and too dangerous. But they would not be delayed.

The colonel furnished Rachel with a horse, and two days after Lorenzo's arrival, the survivors of the Parker's Fort massacre took off for home.

In the dead of winter.

In a raging snowstorm.

February 19, 1938
Jesse Parker's Colony (modern-day Huntsville, Texas)

A howling wind raged outside. James had spent several hours bringing in more firewood and now he was glad he had.

Through the window, he saw some movement outside. Grabbing a shotgun, he cracked the door open and peered out. It was Lorenzo with some gray-haired old woman.

James put down his shotgun and ran to help. Grabbing Lorenzo's bridle, he led the horse into the barn and the old lady's horse fell in behind.

When he closed the barn door, he went to help the woman off the horse, and she hugged his neck.

"Oh, Father!" she cried.

He held her back away from him. "Rachel?"

Post Oak

The woman in his arms was emaciated and covered with scars. Gone was her fiery red hair.

"Oh God, my precious Rachel. You've come back to us."

They hugged for a long time. She didn't want to let go but James forced her loose.

"We must get inside where it's warm," James said. "Come on. You'll catch your death of cold in here and we can't have that. Not after all you've been through."

Lorenzo held the barn door open, and James supported Rachel while going to the house. When Martha saw her daughter, she collapsed on the floor. Now, James had two women he needed to revive.

Three days later, Luther Plummer came riding up to the Parker house. Snow was blowing horizontally when he burst into the house.

Rachel saw him and started shaking. She didn't know how he'd react.

At first, he wasn't sure it was Rachel, but when he saw it was really her, he hugged and embraced his wife. Then he put her on his lap and said, "Tell me all you want to tell me."

The family relived some of the stories, while Luther heard the worst of it. Eventually, a room was given to the reunited couple and they entered once again as husband and wife.

Newspaper reporters soon descended on the house. Rachel Plummer and James Parker were big news back east. All the top newspapers wanted their stories.

Soon, a publisher came and procured the rights to Rachel's story. As she gained weight and recovered, she started writing her book, *Narrative of the Capture and Subsequent Sufferings of Mrs. Rachel Plummer*. Co-written with her father, James Parker, it became an instant bestseller.[2]

---

[2] And later a motion picture *The Searchers*, starring John Wayne and Natalie Wood. Released in 1956, it's considered one of the greatest and most influential films ever. Many consider it the best western ever.

March 21, 1839
Houston, Texas

Luther Plummer tightened his tie and buttoned his coat. As he walked through a side door of the church, he spotted James Parker just behind him.

Luther stopped and looked around. No one else was there.

Luther approached his father-in-law and tapped a finger on his chest. "This is all your fault. And I won't ever forget it. Understand?"

James swatted away his finger. "What's my fault? Hunting for your wife and child among the savages while you enjoyed the comforts of civilization?"

"No," Luther spat back. "For the Taylor business, the freezing rain, and what you put her through."

The Taylor business was the two murders James had been accused of committing. James received a note that some vigilantes were coming to kill him.

Late one night, he packed up his family and led a small train of horses through the wilderness, cutting trails by hand and staying in the backcountry for fear of being spotted on the main roads.

The Parker clan slept out in the bitter cold and rain, which was harmful to all of them, especially a still fragile and pregnant Rachel.

When they arrived in Houston, she gave birth to Wilson P. Plummer on January 4, 1839. Yet Rachel was very sick. She likely had pneumonia or something similar. Because of her weakened condition, she couldn't shake it.

"I didn't kill that Taylor woman and her child. It's all lies," James said. "And I had to stick to the backcountry to avoid the vigilante killers. They've been holding mock trials and hanging people. You should already know that."

Luther had blood in his eyes. "All I know is that we're here today because of you. And I will never forget it."

James poked his son-in-law right back in the chest. "You stay on that high horse, mister, and keep pretending to hold all the world's morals. Just think about that when you count all the money you made while I was crawling through prairie grass being chased by Indians."

Luther balled up his fist and was about to hit this man when the door opened. A woman called him over.

James stood there waiting for Luther to return so he could teach this city boy a thing or two about the hardened fists one gets from living in a rugged country. But then something happened. Luther dropped to his knees and began sobbing.

"What's the matter?" James said to the woman. "I've already paid for Rachel's coffin. There's no expense to him."

The woman walked over to James. "No, it has nothing to do with the funeral expenses. I just learned from the wet nurse caring for little Wilson that he died. He caught the same thing Rachel had."

James stepped back and pounded a fist into the palm of his hand. He'd lost Rachel two days earlier. Now her son—*his grandson*—was gone too.

"It's never going to end," he muttered to no one. "Never."

Before Rachel died, James learned that Pratt had not been killed; it was her newborn child. So, after the two funerals, he went back out looking for his grandson Pratt. He also searched for Silas's two children, Cynthia Ann and John Henry. He would never stop until he found them all.

Yet before he left Houston to continue his search, James self-published a pamphlet and distributed it throughout Texas. It was called *Defense of James W. Parker, Against Slanderous Accusations Referred Against Him*. Here is a brief excerpt:

> The public mind has been poisoned with charges, rumors, and reports of crimes committed by me of every character and degree, from the lowest in the catalog of petty villainy up to the most atrocious of which human depravity is capable; and yet so artful have I been, or so sluggish and blind has been public justice, that up to the present moment none have attempted to place me at the bar of a court and before a jury of my country, to answer a part or all of these charges.

No charges were ever brought against James, who eventually became a justice of the peace in Houston County.

As for Rachel, she'd survived the attack on the fort and the brutal Comanche and a journey from one end of the country to the other, only to die in the care of her family.

People around the Parkers always whispered that whatever business James had been involved in, it came back to roost.

Had his accusers endured the travails he went through, they would have hailed him as a hero who never gave up.

While she lived, Rachel was a sensation throughout Texas and the U.S. From her stories, the anger against the Comanche grew red hot. Everyone knew rivers of blood were coming, but no one knew who would do the bleeding.

The Comanche knew.

Show respect to all people but grovel to none.

Chief Tecumseh (1768–1813)
Shawnee tribe

Naduah

Chapter Fourteen

Cynthia Ann Parker awoke and stared up at three poles and a small hole.

Where am I? she thought.

Blinking several times, Cynthia Ann was desperate for answers. Then it all came rushing back in vivid images.

Her father, Silas, is killed and scalped in front of her. Her mother, Lucy, is trying to escape the savages, pressing baby Orlena against her breast and grabbing two-year-old Silas Jr. Cynthia Ann is holding hands with her young brother, five-year-old John Richard, when the Indians come for them.

She gripped the buffalo hide tighter, her fingers parting stiff brown hairs as she tried to stop the flood of memories. There was her mother again. Somehow, she escaped with the two youngest children and left Cynthia Ann and John Richard to fend for themselves.

Cynthia Ann was dragged to a spot where Aunts Rachel and Elizabeth were ravaged in plain sight of everyone.

Whenever Cynthia Ann cried, she was beaten. Eventually, she buried her head in her hands and stopped watching.

When the killers put her on a horse, she figured she was dead, so her mind went numb.

Whatever happens will happen, she remembered thinking.

During the long ride north, she saw the vast lands of Texas disappear behind her—the blue lakes, clear streams, dark-timbered forests, and endless green prairie. There was no food and little water.

After twelve hours of riding in front of a Comanche and tied to the horse, she was set down and allowed to relieve herself. Unfortunately, she had already let go on the horse. The Indian behind her didn't seem to mind.

Once the Indians made camp, Cynthia Ann was turned on her stomach and her hands and feet tied behind her back. It was a brutal position to be in and lasted for at least eight hours.

Occasionally, they slapped her for no reason, though she had long since stopped crying. There was no point. Nothing would change these murderers.

During the days of riding, they stopped to study a bent-over post oak tree. The Indians pointed in the direction of the tree and continued riding. This led to a freshwater spring. The water tasted wonderful, and for the first time she had her fill.

On the sixth day, she watched as Lucy, Rachel, and Pratt were given to other Indians, and they took off in three separate directions. Tears flowed from her eyes; she knew she'd never see them again. At least her five-year-old brother, John Richard, was still with her group.

On the seventh day, to her shock, she discovered that John Richard was gone.

Was he killed? Did another group of Indians take him to a different camp? She didn't know anything other than she was alone.

All alone.

At least the savages aren't abusing me like they did my aunts—yet.

It was almost sundown when she saw the village appear out of thin air. One moment there was nothing. Then it was there.

Her horse stopped, and the Indian behind her lowered Cynthia Ann to the dense, green prairie. Her heart raced as she inspected her inner thighs and butt, chafed from the seven days of hard riding. Her face and neck were deeply sunburned and she was hungry. But hanging over all that was the thought of being tortured and killed.

The Comanche untied Cynthia Ann's hands and let her walk around. Her legs ached.

Despite the exhaustion, her wide-open eyes and fast-beating heart searched for trouble. Whatever her future, it was about to arrive.

The Indian she had ridden with seemed important. He grabbed little Cynthia Ann's arm and roughly led her to a teepee, where he spoke in a strange language to a man and woman.

After a minute of this, the Indian looked down at her, said some words, and pointed to the couple. Then he pushed the nine-year-old to the woman, who threw her arms around Cynthia Ann. The man and woman were very happy and led her into their teepee.

After sitting on the ground, the woman dipped a dirty cloth into a clay pot of water and began washing Cynthia Ann's face and hands. When that was done, she cleaned the rest of her body. Cynthia Ann leaned back and let the woman rub salve on her chafed thighs.

The couple continued jabbering before letting Cynthia Ann have some water. She wanted to drink it all, but they slowed her down.

The man presented her with some dried berries and nuts, which she swallowed whole. He handed her some dried meat, and she devoured it, too.

Over the next two hours, they fed and watered their new child. It was clear to all three that she now belonged to them.

As the dark prairie night arrived, they moved Cynthia Ann to a pile of grass inside the teepee and ensured she was comfortable. The woman gently spread a blanket over her while she and the man crawled under a dressed buffalo robe. Before passing out from exhaustion, Cynthia Ann remembered staring up at the three poles and a small hole showing a tiny circle of the sky.

What felt like an eternity later, a hand gently shook her shoulder. Even though she'd been awake, Cynthia Ann slowly opened her eyes and saw the same smiling woman leaning over her face. The woman said something and helped her sit up.

A small pot of paste and a cup of water were presented. Cynthia Ann drank the water in one large gulp. Then she dipped a finger into the paste and took some to her mouth. It wasn't her mother's marmalade, but it was edible nonetheless.

Cynthia Ann sat there, adjusting to her new surroundings. She was in the enemy's camp, an outcome they had drilled on to prevent from happening. It was her worst-case nightmare, made ever more terrifying by her grandfather's campfire stories. Yet this woman was not so bad.

Could Grandfather be wrong?

After more water and paste, the woman fitted Cynthia Ann with a simple deerskin covering. What happened to her other clothes, she had no idea.

Outside, the woman called several children over. More words were spoken, and one of the young girls grabbed Cynthia Ann's arm, leading her to a field where the children collected flowers.

At times, one of the boys covered his eyes, counted to a number, and opened them as he proceeded to chase the other children. When he touched one, that child became "it" and repeated the process.

Cynthia Ann couldn't believe how fast these boys and girls ran. They were like deer, twice as fast as her since she had never run much. Each time, she was caught easily. Still, it was fun, and the morning passed quickly.

After the games, the young girls took her to collect more prairie flowers. They put the flowers into a clay pot and delivered them to an older woman who crushed the flowers into a fine powder.

One of the girls signaled to Cynthia Ann to follow her, and the pair found an Indian digging a hole with a knife. Unlike the other Indians, he looked sad.

So far, the sad Indian had scraped out a foot of soil from the ground. Cynthia Ann had no idea how far down he was digging, but three males stood around him, holding weapons. Apparently, they oversaw this dig.

Cynthia Ann and the other girl sat there for a while before walking to a field. Horses lingered around with a male holding each one by the reins.

Occasionally, two boys jumped on their horses and raced to another Indian some distance away. Items were exchanged at the end of each race, and Cynthia Ann assumed they were gambling on the outcomes. She had seen some of that when they traveled from Illinois down to Texas.

All around, the adults and children seemed to be content. Smiles were everywhere even though the women worked constantly. It was not what she imagined when they had pretended the fort was under attack.

After the races, the children went back to watch the man digging. By now, he was three feet down.

It was a wide hole, much like the well they had dug at the fort to store water inside the walls in case of attack. Of course, that assumed they had kept the gates shut and the Indians on the outside.

Maybe that's what he's doing, she thought. *Digging a well.*

As the dark night approached, Cynthia Ann's tummy rumbled.

The woman who appeared to be her new mother called and motioned her to the teepee. Outside, a gurgling pot of water hung over a fire. The woman handed her a sharpened stick and showed her how to spear the floating meat.

Cynthia Ann nabbed a piece and tasted it. The meat was so hot she had to wait for it to cool. Then she slowly chewed it. Again, it wasn't home cooking, but it was edible.

When Cynthia Ann speared another piece, she noticed a small pot filled with white crystals. Wetting her finger, she tasted the stuff and learned it was salt. She dropped a few sprinkles on the meat and ate it whole.

The woman was amazed. She had never seen anyone do that.

From that point forward, the woman would add salt to Cynthia Ann's food to make her happy. The woman even discovered that certain foods tasted better with a pinch of salt.

After dinner, several women came over and appeared to study the young girl's deep blue eyes. This fascinated the Indian women.

The older woman, who had ground up the flowers, presented Cynthia Ann with a fresh one. Her new mother placed it in her hair and uttered the word "Naduah." She pointed to Cynthia Ann and said "Naduah" several times.

Whatever Naduah meant, Cynthia Ann knew it was her name now.

Night fell over the camp as a few scattered fires flickered and popped. Cynthia Ann sat on a log and watched from afar as the men danced around a larger fire, singing loudly and occasionally yelling. Before she knew it, she was back in the teepee and fast asleep.

The next morning, Cynthia Ann awoke to the same water and paste. After breakfast, she came outside and saw the women breaking down the teepees and packing everything up on horses and mules. Cynthia Ann panicked.

Are they leaving? Will they take me with them?

Two men stood close by and drank so much water they vomited. After cleaning themselves up, they seemed happy. It was odd, like they had done it on purpose.

Several children ran around playing. Apparently, they didn't have to help with the packing.

The girl who had befriended Cynthia Ann the day earlier motioned for her to follow. The two came to the spot where the sad Indian had been digging. Now, the hole was deep.

As the digger climbed out, one of the males standing around grabbed the knife and tied his hands and feet. Then the digger was forced into the very hole he'd dug and made to stand up.

The digger did as he was told, speaking—no, *pleading*—with the other males. As he spoke, the three males tossed dirt in, packing it down with their feet now and then.

When they finished, the men scattered the leftover dirt across the prairie grass.

Cynthia Ann moved a bit to see the digger. His neck and face were above the prairie grass, but the rest of him was buried.

An old man pushed the men aside and removed a long, thin knife from a leather sheath. He dropped to his knees and inched close to the buried man's face.

With his wrinkled hands, he cut a tiny slit across the top of the digger's eyes. Then he gently removed the eyelids without injuring the eyes.

By now, the digger was crying and moaning, pleading for help in his strange language. Without eyelids, he couldn't close his eyes to what happened next: a male grabbed his scalp and, in seconds, cut it off cleanly. Blood streamed down his face. This set the poor man to screaming.

As the males walked to their horses, they laughed and pointed to the east. Cynthia Ann looked and saw the sun fully over the eastern prairie.

She glanced back at the buried man and realized he faced the sun with no way to shield his eyes. It was a brutal torture.

By now, the camp was broken down and packed up. Her mother came with a horse and put her on it.

As the horses moved east toward the rising sun, Cynthia Ann looked back to see the scalped, buried man crying, watching the entire band disappear as a small pool of blood formed around his neck.

A few minutes later, the male on a pony beside her pointed to his right. Two coyotes sauntered past the band, heading west toward the abandoned camp and the buried man.

When the buried man saw the coyotes approach, he screamed even louder. Several males chuckled but didn't stop. Instead, they kept moving to their next camp and whatever awaited the young white girl.

Chapter Fifteen

March 18, 1840
San Antonio, Texas

Two men stopped at the entrance to the saloon and dusted themselves off. The shorter of the two poked his companion in the arm.

"You let me do all the talking," Del Sands said. "Remember, you're here to observe and provide protection."

Del knew that was a joke. The man was a retired sea captain who couldn't steer a ship into a harbor, much less function on land.

"Whatever you say," Captain Hank Jordan said. "Can we drink now?"

Del shook his head. All Hank cared about was getting to his next drink.

"Yeah, just stay quiet."

Del pulled down his shirt, straightened his hat, and pushed through the saloon doors. It took a few seconds to adjust to the dim lighting. The place was sparsely attended as it was afternoon and there were only two people enjoying the bar. Del spotted his appointment.

"Mr. McDonald, I presume," Del said.

The two shook hands.

"I'm Del Sands. Pleased to make your acquaintance."

"Have a seat, gentlemen," McDonald said. "And you are?"

"I'm sorry, this is my colleague, Captain Hank Jordan."

McDonald shook his hand. "Please have a seat, especially since you're buying."

Del called over the bartender and ordered beers and whiskey for the table. He let everyone sort out their drink of choice, knowing Captain Hank would ensure nothing went to waste.

"So, how can I help you, Mr. Sands?" McDonald asked.

Tina Siemens

"Please call me Del. We've come looking for information on how to fight the Indians."

McDonald spit out some beer over the rough wood table and coughed before laughing heartily.

"Sorry for that," he said, regaining his composure, "but you two don't look like you're prepared for the mesquite and brush country."

McDonald stared at Hank. "What regiment do you command, Captain?"

"Uh, he's a sea captain, not an army captain," Del interjected.

McDonald leaned back and laughed again, shaking his head in disbelief.

"You misunderstand me," Del said. "We're not going to fight the Indians. We're putting together a book detailing the best tactics to *defeat* the Indians."

McDonald stopped laughing and took another sip of his beer, white foam clinging to his black mustache.

"Okay," he said, growing serious. "So tell me how you decided to take on this job."

Del cleared his throat. "A woman in Norfolk, Virginia, commissioned us to take it on. She read Rachel Plummer's book about being captured by the Comanches as well as other news stories listing dozens of women and children still in captivity here in Texas. The list even includes Rachel's son, Pratt. Her cousins, Cynthia Ann and John Richard Parker, are still hostages four years after their capture despite their uncle, James Parker, crawling all over Texas to find them."

McDonald nodded. "That's right. James Parker, The Searcher. He can't find hide nor hair of them because savages are smart and crafty—and deadly."

"That's where I come in," Del said. "I'm an efficiency master from New York. I observe and collect information, then assemble it into my reports. Once I learn the best way of doing something, I document it so others can benefit."

"If you say so," McDonald said. "But how did you and this sea captain get all the way from New York, Virginia, or wherever to the last safe outpost in the West?"

Del stopped and refreshed himself with an ample dose of ale before giving McDonald a partially true story, leaving out the bad parts that even his companion didn't know.

The real truth was that Del had run into some "financial issues," so he had to flee New York before he was arrested. He hopped on a cargo ship to the Caribbean and landed in Haiti. Fearful of being followed, he studied the docks each day for any incoming ship that might be looking for him.

After a week of this, he noticed a few things. A Spanish captain ordered his crew to rub a long leather strap laced with bent nails around the hull to remove barnacles. Crewmen on each side of the deck operated this strap, taking turns pulling it before letting the other side pull. By working the strap along the hull, the barnacles were removed, giving it a clean, smooth surface.

As all mariners knew, a smooth hull added speed to a ship at sea. With speed, a ship could outrun storms, pirates, and certain death.

The second clever device he observed was on a Dutch ship. It was a balanced and weighted crane with a cargo net made of thick ropes.

This crane allowed for swift loading and unloading of the hold as barrels were swung over the dock and ship. It not only saved a great deal of time but money, too, since the captain did not have to pay local stevedores to offload the cargo one barrel at a time.

As fate would have it, a ship from Norfolk docked one stormy afternoon and the captain came ashore. Del Sands noticed his men did not use a strap to remove the barnacles or a crane to offload the cargo. Instead, they slipped and slid down the gangway as they unloaded the barrels.

Later, when Del met the captain in the bar, he explained who he was, leaving out his financial issues while using a newly created name. Somehow, between Del's words and the alcohol, he convinced the captain he could save time and money.

The captain took him aboard and sailed back to Norfolk, where it turned out the captain owned a fleet of 28 vessels. In fact, he was quite wealthy.

Del set to work making the devices he had seen and employed them on all 28 ships. In the first year, the speed alone saved the fleet 118 sea days. This allowed for more trips and higher profits.

But the cargo net was the best of all. By rolling the barrels into the nets, the crane unloaded a ship in one-third the time it had previously taken. Again, this saved time and prevented the sailors from getting too drunk on land, thus delaying the next voyage.

Over the years, Del found other ways to save time and money while completely ingratiating himself into the man's business. Then tragedy struck. A hurricane took the captain-owner to the bottom of the Atlantic.

Without any legitimate heirs, his widow, Cora Covington, took over the business. Del quickly adjusted and worked on ingratiating himself into her life.

Later, he learned New York detectives were sniffing around Virginia for him, so he devised a scheme after finding the widow crying while holding Rachel Plummer's best-selling captivity book.

Del convinced Mrs. Covington to fund an expedition to the West and allow him to gather information on how to defeat the Indians. Getting paid to run away from trouble was a miracle. Now, all he had to do was tease his benefactor with occasional bits of information while dragging this commission out as long as possible. And not die at the hands of the Indians, of course.

As for Captain Hank, the Widow Covington became romantically attached to him. Her overly protective financial advisor, who'd been dead set against the funding of Del's crazy scheme, was not happy about all the handouts to Captain Hank.

Del saw an opportunity and suggested that perhaps the advisor would send the good captain along for protection. Suddenly, the financial advisor was on board with Del's *brilliant* idea since he could get rid of two rogues with one stone.

Del knew Mrs. Covington had more money than she could ever spend, so he figured there was no harm in this venture. Now, all he had to do was continue the charade for two to three years until the detectives left and he could safely return to Virginia.

Of course, he gave a shortened, safer version of this story to anyone who asked.

"So all I have to do is make notes about their tactics in this here book." Del held up a bright green hardback full of blank pages.

"I see," McDonald said. "It just might work. Lord knows we need more news and information on these savages and how they operate. I can tell you what I know, but the best man to talk to is John Coffee Hays. Jack, as we call him, is the best at figuring out the Indians and keeping his men alive."

"What does he do?" Del asked.

"He's a deputy sheriff here in town but used to do land surveys for headrights. I've been with him on several trips. While other surveyors and their men got killed, he didn't lose a man to the Indians. He also completed the surveys fast, so we all got paid."

Del set down his drink. "Where can we find him?"

"I saw him leaving town for some reason and expect him in tonight or tomorrow morning at the latest. We're having a meeting tomorrow with the Comanche. They've been attacking and killing whites on the frontier. They're supposed to bring in all their hostages so we can negotiate their new station."

McDonald gulped down the last of his beer and continued.

"Texas wants them to stay on the frontier west of San Antonio and Austin. President Lamar is insistent on it. I reckon you'll see plenty of them critters in town tomorrow. If you're looking for information, you came at the right time. In fact, you've hit the motherlode."

"Can we participate in the meeting?" Del asked, excitement rising in his voice.

"I don't think so because it's in the Council House with nothing but military men. You know, come to think of it, I might be able to sneak you in the side door for a few dollars. Afterward, you can track down Jack Hays and see if he has time for you."

"Sounds good," Del said, clapping his hands. "I'll see you at the side door with the cash. Until then, I'd like to hear everything you know about the fighting the Indians."

"That may take a while," McDonald said.

"We got all night so long as the bartender don't run out of liquor."

"Are you ready yet?" Del asked his companion as he checked his pocket watch. "I don't want to miss this chance to see real Indian chiefs up close."

"Yeah, I'm ready," Captain Hank said, shielding his eyes from the sun streaming through his window. "I hope it doesn't take too long."

"It won't. I talked to a Texas Ranger during breakfast and he said that as soon as the white captives are returned and counted, presents will be exchanged and negotiations for the treaty will be finalized. The deal was agreed to in January. He said two hours at the most."

"Good," Captain Hank said.

Both men knew where he would be after the meeting.

Fully dressed in their finest, the two men stepped out of the hotel and onto the dirty street, stunned at what they saw. Brightly painted Indian men, women, and children milled about with local citizens standing around gawking.

A few townspeople set up coins and paper money on a fence and watched the Indian children shoot at them with toy bows and arrows. Crowds clapped as the children consistently hit the targets.

It was the first time Del and the captain had seen Indians in person. With the children laughing, having a good time earning pennies for hitting targets, Del wondered if he had misjudged these people.

They weren't savages. How could they be? Their children were no different than any white man's, except for running faster and hitting coins with toy arrows.

Even though Del was completely amazed by the scene, he couldn't stop to take notes. Instead, he and Captain Hank hustled to a side door and opened it to find a soldier blocking their path.

Del mentioned McDonald's name, and the soldier asked for three dollars. After receiving it, he stepped aside to let Del in but blocked Captain Hank from entering.

"He'll need to pay three dollars too," the soldier said.

Del shook his head. "Just let him stay outside. One of us is enough."

Del turned to his companion. "I'll be out soon and tell you all about it."

Captain Hank nodded, rubbed his dry lips, and headed to a nearby tavern.

"Stand against the side wall and be quiet," the soldier told Del.

Post Oak

As he took his place, he pulled out his bright green book and started scribbling on a fresh page. This led to the first letter to his benefactor.

> To Mrs. Cora Covington
> 23 Brighton St.
> Norfolk, Virginia
>
> Dear Mrs. Covington,
>
> By the time this letter reaches you, reports will have been undoubtedly printed in your local newspapers. Regardless, let me provide a firsthand account of this unbelievable event.
>
> Using some personal connections, I gained entrance to the San Antonio Council House, a one-story building with a flat roof and dirt floor. Court is often held at the Council House since a jail is attached to it. A large courtyard sits in the rear, and this is where the Indian women, children, and some leftover warriors moved when the meeting began.
>
> I stood against the wall and watched the Texas soldiers negotiate to cease hostilities with the Comanche Indians in exchange for certain promises and goods. The Comanche have at least thirteen hostages.
>
> Months earlier, traders tried to negotiate for their return but were killed when the Indians thought smallpox had been placed on the goods. The Indians still kept the "infected" goods so it appeared the traders were killed out of greed alone.
>
> "Yet another reason not to trust these savages," said one of the officers there.
>
> The men in charge of this negotiation were two Texas colonels, a lieutenant colonel, and several other Texas officials. Each man sat in a chair on a platform facing the empty room.
>
> Before the Comanche were allowed in, one of the colonels explained the purpose of this meeting.
>
> Years earlier, a prominent Comanche chief, Spirit Talker, told a Texas Ranger the following:
>
>> "We have set up our lodges in these groves and swung our children from these boughs from time immemorial. When the game beats away from us, we pull down our lodges and move

away, leaving no trace to frighten it, and in a while it comes back. But the white man comes and cuts down the trees, building houses and fences and the buffaloes get frightened and leave and never come back, and the Indians are left to starve, or, if we follow the game, we trespass on the hunting ground of other tribes and war ensues. If the white men would draw a line defining their claims and keep on their side of it, the red men would not molest them."

Then the colonel gave the following speech about the many deaths the Comanche suffered from smallpox in January of this year.

"We've heard numbers like 500 and others like 4,000. Regardless, between the rangers harassing them and the smallpox killing them, they now want peace. We have told them that Texas will draw a north-south line west of San Antonio and Austin up past Fort Worth. Texas will agree the Comanche can occupy all the land on the west side of that line without being molested by Texas Rangers or whites so long as they stop attacking farms and killing whites east of that same line. This meeting is simply to recover the hostages and see how much money and goods it will take to get the deal done."

With this treaty, the Texans felt they could develop and settle their land in peace and hopefully trade with the Comanche, who have plenty of animal skins and excellent horseflesh. The colonel said President Lamar was adamant that Texas had to make this deal to stop the bloodshed, but the president also ordered the Indians taken into custody if they failed to bring in all the captives.

With that announcement, the colonel said he had assigned a captain to inspect and interview all the white captives returned by the Comanche. He summoned the captain for a report.

The captain entered the room and said he had just examined Matilda Lockhart, a fifteen-year-old. She had been captured with her little sister while picking pecans. Matilda had been held captive by the Comanche for two years, working as a herder and driving the large remuda of ponies the Comanche own.

Matilda told the captain directly that she had been at the main Comanche camp north of San Antonio just a few days earlier and saw fifteen other captives. Two of them had been adopted by the Indians and treated well. One of these was her sister.

"The Comanche plan to see how much we will pay for Matilda," the captain explained. "Then they plan to bring in the rest one at a time, raising the cost with each captive."

The colonel shook his head in disgust. "So they've failed to bring in *all* the hostages? Is that what you're saying?"

"Yes, sir," the captain replied.

"That figures!" the colonel barked. "At least we've recovered Matilda. Is she holding up well?"

The captain shifted his feet. "Sir, her head, face, and arms are full of bruises. She has sores all over her body and her nose is burnt off. All that's left is a large scab and two wide-open holes to breathe. Mrs. Maverick is taking care of her and heard the girl say that she had been 'utterly degraded' and would never again hold up her head in public, much less find a man willing to be her husband."

At that, several of the officers clenched their jaws and fists. They all knew the cold, hard truth. Most of the white girls and women returned with blank, empty stares, their wills and spirits broken. Death soon followed.

"Did she say anything else?" the colonel asked through gritted teeth.

"Yes, sir. She explained that the Indians constantly beat her. At night, they woke her and stuck glowing wads of fire to her flesh, especially her nose. Then they shouted and laughed as she cried in pain."

"And Matilda was someone who helped them drive their ponies?!" an angry officer blurted out. "Truly, I say they must be deranged."

"Or the devil!" another officer said.

"Simmer down," the colonel ordered. "It's an ugly business but we need to move on. So they're keeping possibly fifteen hostages. Who else did they bring in?"

"A small Mexican boy who's in good shape. But that's it, sir."

"More trickery," said the lieutenant colonel. "They'll never change."

"Bring the savages in!" the angry colonel's voice boomed. "Now!"

The door opened and in walked twelve Comanche chiefs, along with dozens of warriors and one woman dressed like the men. Each one was brightly painted and adorned with feathers, bear claws, beads, and other animal jewelry.

Mrs. Covington, I must say that it looked like actors in a play I'd once seen in New York. Yet these Indians carried real bows and arrows and knives.

As the Comanche delegation took their places sitting on the dirt floor, they seemed confident they had a better bargaining position. The colonel wasted no time.

"Where are the rest of the captives? You were told to bring all of them here for this negotiation."

The head chief, Spirit Talker, stood. He was bald and aged, but still cunning. Through a translator, the chief stated he wanted a high price for each one, including ammunition, vermillion, flannels, blankets, and other goods.

"The prisoners are held by various Comanche bands, each led by its own chief," Chief Spirit Talker said plainly. "I don't control them nor do they control me. However, I believe all the whites can be ransomed but the price will be high."

As I heard the chief's words, I could tell no one in the room believed him. After all, he appeared to be the head of the Comanche. Surely, he had the power to get the captives into town.

Then for some reason, the chief added these words: "How do you like that answer?"

The men on the platform were puzzled, each man trying to determine if the chief had just insulted them or was simply ineloquent with words.

The colonel signaled to a soldier at the main door. Suddenly, soldiers poured into the council room and lined the walls, pushing me closer to the platform.

When the commotion died down, the colonel said, "I'll tell you how I like that answer. We'll keep each of you hostage and set free the women and children in the courtyard. When they return with the white captives, the goods will be given to you and the treaty completed. You will be well treated and not harmed. But if your people start a fight, these soldiers will open fire and kill everyone."

The interpreter's eyes widened as he heard these words. He stood not five feet from me and I noticed his body start to shake. It was then that he told the colonel he would not translate that message to the chief.

"They will start fighting right now," he cried.

"I insist you translate it word for word," the colonel ordered, reaching for his sidearm.

The translator hesitated and glanced at the side door I had come through. Then he started translating the colonel's message to the chief. As soon as the last word left his lips, he turned and pushed open the side door, running outside and disappearing onto the streets of San Antonio.

In mere seconds, the world turned upside down. The Indians shouted their war whoops, drew their bows and arrows, and fired point-blank at the soldiers.

The colonel shouted to the soldiers, "Shoot these savages!" and they did.

Balls and bullets flew in every direction as soldiers fired at close range, many with arrows sticking out from their chests. Blood made the dirt floor slick, causing many combatants to slip, sometimes to a fateful ending.

Powder smoke quickly filled the room, making it hard to see who was winning.

Chief Spirit Talker pulled a knife and ran for the main door, getting there first before the other Indians. He stabbed a captain guarding the door before a soldier came up behind and placed his pistol on the chief's back, exploding the savage's body all over the injured captain.

A man named Lieutenant Dunning stood about twenty feet from me and reached for his pistol. Before he could clear the holster, the female Comanche pulled back an arrow and let it loose. I watched as the arrow went directly through the lieutenant's body and stuck into the wall behind him. He staggered backward and got off a shot, hitting her forehead and splattering her brains against the wall.

Lieutenant Dunning died twenty minutes later, telling a soldier with his last breath, "I killed him but I believe he has killed me too."

Poor Dunning went to his grave, never knowing that a woman had sent him there. What strength she had with the bow.

I'd love to tell you I was brave and didn't move from my place so I could witness the melee, but the truth is the side door was blocked by soldiers and Indians, either dead or fighting each other. I saw no chance to escape and instead stood still, hoping I might blend into the adobe wall and the Indians would fail to notice me.

The Indians flew in all directions, with soldiers shooting at them. Many of the savages were killed by these bullets, as were some Texans.

A few Indians escaped the Council House and joined the other men, women, and children outside. Individual fights took place in the streets with knives, guns, and whatever was available.

One child shot a judge with a "toy arrow" in the heart and killed him. Even the children are fierce warriors.

Some Comanche fled into nearby houses. Yet none escaped.

When the dust and powder smoke cleared, thirty-three Indians were dead, twelve of them chiefs. Thirty-two others were captured. And every one of their arrows that had found a target had been driven into the feathers, if not entirely through the body.

On the other side of the ledger were six dead whites. Among them were the local sheriff and two judges. One Mexican was also killed, while ten other whites were wounded. The captain whom Spirit Talker stabbed ended up living.

Upon interviewing the various participants and witnesses, I learned that the Indian women fought as well as the men and could not be told apart.

One story involved "Old Paint," a Texas soldier named Captain Mathew Caldwell who had fought many Indians. He was inside the Council House with me and injured by a musket shot to the leg. However, he grabbed a rifle from one of the Comanche and shot him to death with it. Then, he used the same rifle to beat another Comanche to death. But the gun broke into several pieces and was unusable.

That didn't stop Old Paint. He picked up rocks from the dirt floor and threw them at Indians. His wounds took a few days to heal, and he's walking around as good as new.

Another story involved two Indians who fled into a kitchen house in a local citizen's backyard. Troops surrounded the structure and found the door bolted.

The Indians refused to surrender, so soldiers crept onto the roof with balls of candlewick soaked in turpentine. Then they lowered the balls through small holes into the kitchen house and set the whole place on fire.

Post Oak

As the heat and smoke became too much to bear, the pair flung open the door and ran. The first Indian took two steps before meeting the business end of an ax, his head split clean open, like halving a cantaloupe.

The second one made it ten feet out the door before he was shot three or four times in his tracks. One of the soldiers put another bullet through his noggin for good measure so he could join his friend in the Great Beyond.

The colonel rounded up the Indian captives and installed them in the local jail for safekeeping. Then he told the widow of one of the chiefs that she could leave but needed to get the fifteen hostages her band held and bring them back to San Antonio. She asked for a pony and provisions and five days to accomplish this.

The colonel laughed and said, "I'll give you the pony and provisions, but you'll need at least twelve days to get there and back, wherever *there* is. If you're not back by April 1, all the hostages will be executed."

The woman said goodbye to the other captives and left. As she trotted out of town, I wondered what would happen to all the hostages—whites and Indians—if she was killed by an angry Texan two miles out of town.

A few days later, the Indian prisoners were moved to the San Jose Mission because soldiers manned it. The colonel worried a rescue attempt might be in the offing and the Mission would be harder to take than the local jail.

On March 28, nine days after the Council House Fight, as it's called now, at least 300 painted Comanche warriors circled the town and remained there as Chief Howling Wolf and a woman rode into the square and shouted insults, daring anyone to fight them.

They stopped in front of Black's Saloon, where an interpreter explained that Colonel Fisher had the captives at the San Jose Mission. If the Indians wanted a fight, he would surely give it to them.

The two Comanche went to the Mission and dared Colonel Fisher to fight them. They were told that Fisher was in bed sick and in no shape to fight anyone.

His next in command, Captain Redd, said there was a truce until April 1 and they must honor it. Redd had fought valiantly outside the Council House when the fight broke out, and he said if the Indians would wait until April 1, he and his troops would surely provide a fight worthy of their time and troubles.

Chief Howling Wolf insulted him and the other soldiers many times before riding away with the other Indians.

At this, Captain Redd found it difficult to hold back his soldiers since their comrades had been killed at the Council House Fight.

Captain Wells disagreed with this no-fight policy and called Redd a coward in front of the troops.

Embarrassed, Redd demanded satisfaction and a duel was arranged.

As both men stood facing each other, Redd said, "I aim for your heart."

Wells said, "I aim for your brains."

The two fired at each other and Redd jumped in the air, falling over dead on the spot. He had been shot in the head.

Wells fell over, too, as he had been shot near the heart. But he was alive and in agony, begging anyone to grab a pistol and kill him or let him shoot himself. He soon died a needless but painful death.

I can tell you from my humble opinion that these Comanche are the toughest enemy I have ever seen, for they can kill two battle-tested captains inside a heavily manned fort without firing one arrow.

Captain Hank and I will be here in San Antonio for perhaps a few more weeks while we hope to interview various Indian fighters, including the elusive Jack Coffee Hays. Everyone says he has the most information.

We are also hoping to meet up with James Parker, who frequents the nearby Austin area looking for financial support to find his grandson Pratt, niece Cynthia Ann, and nephew John Richard.

Thank you for your prayers and support. Having witnessed these savages up close, I can assure you your investment will be returned many times more in heaven when I pass this information on to the Texas and the U.S. governments and anyone else who wants to rid the Earth of these ungodly heathens.

Yours Respectfully,

Del Sands

Chapter Sixteen

Cynthia Ann waded into the muddy water and was immediately splashed by her brother, John Richard. She splashed back, laughing as she dodged the flying drops.

Her father, Silas, used a stick as a pretend gun and stood on the bank "shooting" at his children. Cynthia Ann knew he was a skilled Indian fighter since he told tales of his time defeating the Black Hawks in the area surrounding Chicago. He'd also been selected as an officer in the Texas Rangers back in 1835. This made him responsible for gathering neighboring settlers and farmers to "range" the frontier between the Trinity and Brazos Rivers.

Then there was her mother, Lucinda, or "Lucy" for short. She was chest-deep in the river, laughing at her kids having fun.

Even cousins Rachel and little Pratt were there. Everyone was having a good time.

Cynthia Ann turned to splash her brother again, but something below the water grabbed his legs and pulled him under. Her father, Silas, saw it and swam over to help, but he, too, was pulled under.

Then her mother disappeared below the water. So did Rachel and Pratt.

Before fully understanding what was happening, she felt a tug on her legs and was pulled into a muddy abyss.

Cynthia Ann sat up in bed, breathing hard, her face shining with sweat. Her mother, Singing Lark, rolled over and sat up too.

"Another bad dream?" she whispered, stroking the girl's face.

"Yes," Cynthia Ann replied softly. "I was with the whites again."

Singing Lark noticed her daughter no longer said, "*My* whites." She stroked the girl's hair.

"It's because we have joined camps with the other Comanche bands and you see their white captives. They remind you of the past. But don't worry, Naduah, the whites won't find you. You are ours. We found you."

Cynthia Ann thought back to a few months earlier when two traders came into camp and called her name. Her mother and father quickly smeared ash on her face and hands and hid her in the farthest teepee.

Even though her Comanche name meant "someone found," not one of the Indians wanted her found.

The men eventually left, and Cynthia Ann, now Naduah, was safe. She could never imagine going back to that life. These were her parents, and the tribe was her family.

It was still dark outside. Her foster father, Tabby-nocca or Lean Elk, snored comfortably under the best buffalo hide. The morning would be here soon, but for now, mother and daughter held onto each other.

As 13-year-old Naduah calmed down, Singing Lark continued brushing her brown hair from her sweaty face and began picking out lice. She cracked each one between her teeth, making a popping sound.

Naduah joined in and inspected Singing Lark's hair. It was easy because the white insects could be seen crawling through the black hair, eating skin, and sucking blood.

For a while, the pair crushed dozens of lice in their mouths before swallowing them for an early breakfast.

"Do you like your new jewelry?" Singing Lark whispered.

Naduah understood her mother. Singing Lark loved to please her precious daughter with gifts and constantly created new earrings for the girl. Singing Lark touched the piercing in one of Naduah's recently added holes. Her daughter had three holes in each ear, which conveniently required more earrings.

"Your father traded for that," Singing Lark said, pointing to Naduah's wrist.

"Yes," Naduah said, adjusting the silver bracelet.

This was at least the tenth time her mother had remarked on it and probably wouldn't be the last.

"I love him for it," the girl added.

Singing Lark smiled.

The faintest light of dawn crept in from under the teepee's canvas. Their time together would be the last until darkness returned and the men were out gambling, singing, bragging, and dancing. Then the pair would be free of the endless work and able to spend a little time together, gossiping and talking about possible husbands for Naduah.

Singing Lark helped her daughter up and they quietly slipped outside to begin the day's work.

One of Naduah's many chores was carrying water from the river. The men needed plenty of fresh water each morning so they could drink until vomiting it all back up. This helped them empty their stomachs, clear their heads, and prepare for the day.

Of course, all they did was hunt and fight. If food was aplenty and there was no one to fight, they lounged around camp, sharpening knives, practicing with spears and arrows, and mostly doing nothing except coupling.

The men coupled all the time whenever they felt like it. And the chosen woman stopped her chores and submitted to her man. When the act was over, the man slept while the woman went back to work.

One day, Naduah would couple with a man. Until then, she wondered what it would be like.

The camp was a combination of many Comanche bands. The chiefs had left days ago for San Antonio, where they intended to negotiate for the return of the white captives.

Right now, the remaining men awaited the chiefs' return so they could have a great feast and celebrate taking more riches from the whites. While the men waited, they mostly raced horses and gambled.

Naduah grabbed two clay pots and headed for the river. In a pouch hanging from her shoulder was a set of fishhooks and lines. Her mother loved the large trout in the river and was amazed at Naduah's skill in catching them with the fishhooks she had collected from a plant far west of here.

A rare desert cactus produced the perfect fishhooks and practically begged people to take them. Naduah had a collection of hooks in different sizes.

One of the older women showed her how to dry sinew and tendons from deer to make an almost transparent fishing line. By placing a bug or worm on the end of the hook, the fish was soon flopping on the bank, waiting to be whacked with her wooden mallet.

Except for the gurgling of the stream, it was quiet—so peaceful in this dense hill country. The sweet gum, ash, and oak trees stood guard, occasionally waving their boughs at Naduah. Sometimes, she waved back.

She studied the water and didn't see any trout. Instead of fishing, she filled the two pots with cold water and returned to camp.

It was still March, and the ground was cool to her bare feet. She easily avoided the thorns and bristles since the camp's females had tamped down a trail to the river. With so many teepees here, perhaps five hundred, the path was well-worn in no time.

Naduah made five trips for water. After that, she cut some deer meat for her mother to cook.

Last night, they enjoyed rabbit. Soon, they would head back north, and she would taste the succulent prairie dogs. But here in the hill country, it was deer, boars, and the trout she caught.

Fires were strategically placed throughout the camp. Several teepees shared a fire, making it easier for the women to stack and store the wood. The placement of each fire was vital since they had to be aware of the sun's rising and falling angles.

When meat was being cooked, no one could allow a human shadow to cross over the meat. It was a great sin.

If that happened, as it did once a month or so, the meat was spoiled and thrown out, and the offender was severely punished. That's why many times, the Comanche ate raw meat. This negated the shadow rule.

Another rule Naduah had learned the hard way was to not boil meat over the same fire as meat being broiled. Meat had to be cooked and eaten before the fire could be used to cook a different way.

No one knew why or from where these rules came; they just strictly followed them.

After sweating over the fire, Naduah served her father breakfast, saying little to him. He wiped his arm across his mouth and left to join the men.

Naduah served herself and her mother, sprinkling some white flakes over the fresh meat.

Singing Lark nudged her arm and whispered, "There he is again. He seems to find a reason to come by here."

Naduah glanced at the man and smiled. His name was Puhtocnocony, He Who Travels Alone and Returns. He was one of thousands of warriors in the Comanche nation.

Puhtocnocony, or later known as Peta Nonona, was twenty years old and belonged to a band in another division. He had been present when she was captured. Whatever his intentions, he had clearly been smitten with Naduah's brown hair and blue eyes, a rarity for sure.

With Puhtocnocony gone and breakfast over, Naduah joined her mother and took up their work on various hides. Her thick, strong wrists and hands had widened, growing muscular like her mother's.

All Indian women had large hands due to the daily scraping of animal hides. If a female had small hands, it was because she was still a child and exempt from work or lazy and would soon be sorted out of camp—one way or another.

Naduah stopped working on the hides to get more animal fat. Her friend had plenty and was happy to lend some.

Naduah grabbed a wooden gourd and headed to the center of camp where her friend stayed and Puhtocnocony was known to hang out. Naduah straightened the covering of her animal skin and pushed back her hair just in case she saw the handsome warrior.

As she navigated the fires and teepees, she came to the center and found Buffalo Hump and Yellow Wolf talking to a woman who had just dismounted her pony. Naduah noticed the woman was crying. As she spoke, several men gathered around her to hear better.

Naduah couldn't hear anything but saw the men begin cutting themselves in anger and disbelief. Many of the warriors cut off their sacred hair.

Afraid, she ran back to her mother, who grabbed Naduah and hid inside their teepee. Soon, they would hear from Lean Elk all about the horrific tragedy in San Antonio.

The day had been a complete nightmare. The Comanche at first denied that their loved ones were gone. The men questioned the woman over and over before anger took hold and they cut their bodies with knives. A man and woman cut themselves so deeply that they died by the evening meal.

Some men cut off their hair, a sign of great despair. Depression soon set in among all in the camp.

By the end of the first day, everyone had moved on to fury. It was time for revenge. But first, they had a lot of work to do.

The dead chiefs and warriors owned many horses. As was their custom, all the horses had to be killed and burned. That took two full days.

Then there were fifteen whites. Even though the delegation had returned Matilda, they still had her five-year-old sister.

Buffalo Hump gave orders, and soon, the women had constructed some small post oak trees into vertical supports. Skinny tree trunks seven feet long were lashed together, and Matilda's sister was tied to them with her back against the bark.

By now, she was crying, sure something terrible was about to happen. As the ropes cut into her hands and legs, she wailed louder.

Yellow Wolf stepped forward and examined the kindling beneath a pile of wood. He shifted some branches around and removed two pieces of wood.

"Too much," he muttered.

Yellow Wolf ripped out three pages from a book they had stolen on previous raids. The thin sheets were excellent for starting fires.

He touched one of the sheets to a pot of hot coals, blowing and coercing the fire to catch. When the sheet lit up, he shoved it into the kindling and repeated the process with the other sheets. Soon, a small fire was going.

"No, please!" the young girl cried as her hair caught fire.

A woman put the fire out and tied her hair up.

Yellow Wolf removed more wood. "The fire cannot grow too much."

It was clear he planned to make this last several days. This was the fate of several other captives.

Buffalo Hump asked for two fresh deerskins. Singing Lark and Naduah hustled the skins to the great chief and he sampled them around a captive white woman, satisfied they would fit. Then he ordered two of his women to stitch the hides together. When this was accomplished, they wrapped the combined hides around the distraught woman and sewed up the last seam with the woman inside. Due to small holes in the seam, she could breathe, though she had no access to food or water.

As the sun rose, the new skins dried and contracted ever-so-slowly, squeezing the woman's body into itself. The entire process would take two to three days, but eventually, the fresh animal skins literally squeezed the life out of the horrified woman.

As for other tortures, if they imagined it, they did it.

For some reason, two white children, Booker L. Webster and a Putnam girl, were spared. They had been adopted into the tribe and their Comanche parents didn't want to see them die. Eventually, they would provide eyewitness testimony to the world about this mass torture.

The mourning and torture went on for days. The men howled in agony while the women cried. Every Comanche had cuts on their bodies to signify their great distress.

On the fourth night, a big meeting was held. Chiefs Buffalo Hump, Yellow Wolf, and Santa Anna were the main deciders.[3]

"Spirit Talker was my nephew," Buffalo Hump said. "We can never trust the whites again!"

Hundreds of warriors around him nodded in agreement.

"We must take the fight to them!" Santa Anna urged.

"Yes," Buffalo Hump said. "And we will. Last night, I had a vision of what we must do. It was as clear and powerful as this scene before me now."

The men buzzed with excitement. A vision meant they would have good medicine on the trip as well as great success while being protected from the white man's bullets.

"Tell us about it?" Yellow Wolf asked.

Buffalo Hump stood up, adjusting the many brass rings on his arms. His naked torso glowed red in the firelight as a buffalo robe covered his loins.

From the chief's chest hung an impressive string of beads while a long mane of black hair fell from his broad shoulders. He had a serious countenance and was good-looking, even by the whites' standards.

---

[3] This Santa Anna is the Comanche, not the Mexican general

"I saw violence done to the lying white men of the Council House. I saw a great gathering of Comanche and together, we pushed every white man—Texans, soldiers, and others—back into the Great Waters, drowning them all."

Only the crackling of the fire could be heard as the warriors leaned in, listening intently to Buffalo Hump.

"We will break camp and head northwest back to our grounds. From there, we will send riders to all the other Comanche divisions and bands, urging them to join us for the largest raid ever. When we have assembled everyone, we will leave our camps and come through the land of the whites, killing, destroying, and burning everyone and everything. We will head straight for the Great Waters and destroy their cities. Then we will take the plunder and head back, killing and destroying anyone left."

"When will this great raid happen?" Yellow Wolf asked, amazed at the scope of this undertaking.

"As soon we can gather up all the Comanche. But soon. No more than four moons from now as the vision showed a great heat rising from the land."

"When do you want to break camp?" Santa Anna asked.

"When the whites are all dead. But first, we will send three hundred warriors into San Antonio to fight the soldiers and free our people, if we can."

The meeting ended, and Lean Elk returned to his wife and daughter to explain what had been said.

Naduah's mood, as well as that of the entire tribe, had shifted. Revenge and fury were tasks that had to be acted upon.

"What about the two whites left?" Naduah asked.

"They will be carried to San Antonio for trade," Lean Elk replied. "We need the white man's guns. They have killed too many of us, so we must start killing more of them."

Singing Lark wrapped an arm around Naduah. Everyone understood that death was in the future. All they could hope was that the whites died before they did.

Chapter Seventeen

July 18, 1840
Austin, Texas

Del Sands surveyed the dining area and saw one open seat at a table for two.

"Mind if I join you?" he said to the other patron.

"No, of course, please sit," the man said, rising from his seat. "Be my guest."

"Name's Del Sands," he said, offering his hand.

"Bruno de la Huerta," the man replied as he took it. "What brings you to Austin?"

Del pushed aside the knife and fork. "A fresh bed and better food. We've been looking for a man in the brush country and ran out of luck."

Bruno nodded. "Ah, a bounty hunter. Dangerous work."

"No, we're not bounty hunters. I've been looking for James Parker. He's The Searcher, the man trying to bring back his niece, Cynthia Ann, his grandson, Pratt, and his nephew, John Richard."

"I know James Parker," Bruno said, his face brightening. "I met him in Nacogdoches four years back, before his daughter Rachel Plummer had been returned."

Del clapped his hands. "This is divine providence. I'm working on a book about the Comanche and their tactics and wanted to speak to James about what he might know."

"The Comanche? I know something about them. Perhaps I can be a substitute."

"Of course," Del said excitedly, removing a bright green book from his pocket. "I'd love to buy you breakfast and hear all about it."

"A fair exchange, so I accept. Thank you."

After placing their orders, Bruno detailed the history of the Comanche and Apache, the same story he'd given to James Parker. Del took furious notes, lapping up all the information.

"When is your book due to be completed?" Bruno asked.

"I'm hoping to meet both James Parker and a Texas Ranger named Jack Coffee Hays by the end of this year. Then I'll write to my benefactor and see what she thinks. Hopefully, I'll have enough to rid us of the Comanche."

Bruno grinned. "Since my company sells blades for fighting, I am thankful the Comanche exists."

Del shot him a sideways glare.

"Where are you going to now?" Bruno asked, sensing a misstep.

"I'm headed back to San Antonio," Del replied, closing his bright green book. "Last time I was there, I saw the Council House Fight up close. Hopefully, things have calmed down a bit and there aren't any Comanche around to remove my scalp."

Bruno held up his forefinger. "If you do not see any, you can be assured that you will soon. The Comanche respect parleys and negotiations. They believe it is a great sin to violate that so they will declare war and attack Texans with a vengeance. Expect this sooner rather than later."

"They didn't respect the white flag they carried out front of Parker's Fort," Del said angrily, pushing back his chair and standing up. "They massacred that family."

Bruno stood up, too. "Mr. Sands, perhaps I do not have all the information. I am sorry. But if you want even more information about the Comanche and the rangers fighting them, find Philip Howard. His wife was captured by them and has a story to tell. They are staying at the hotel. I know this because I sold him a blade last night."

Del threw some money on the table. "I'll grab my companion and look for him right now."

"Good luck to you and with your book."

Before Del could get away, Bruno de la Huerta had one more piece of advice. "If you are ever in the market for a new blade, please remember the

Huerta brand. My blades will never break your heart, although they will likely break your enemy's."

"I'll keep that in mind," Del said as he left the restaurant. "Salesmen," he muttered to himself outside. "Always pitching something."

Del and his companion, Captain Hank, remained in Austin for four more days, interviewing James Parker and Philip Howard's wife. After discarding several drafts, Del finally completed the letter and sent it to his benefactor.

> To Mrs. Cora Covington
> 23 Brighton St.
> Norfolk, Virginia
>
> Dear Mrs. Covington,
>
> I pray you are well and prosperous. Captain Jordan and I are well, and this mission is proceeding with great success. I hope you are happy with my reports as I continue making a list of Comanche tactics. I will send that as soon as it is complete.
>
> By now, I'm confident you have read my last letter and the newspapers about the Council House Fight. Poor little Booker Webster returned with a five-year-old girl, her nose burnt off like Matilda Lockhart. After Booker detailed the torture and slow roasting of the remaining hostages, the citizens here are ready to kill any Indian on sight.
>
> Recently, we met with James Parker. He and his brother, Silas, had been Texas Ranger captains before the attack on their fort. During our meeting, I learned that the Parkers were a driving force behind creating the Texas Rangers. Ironically, we are trying to meet up with a famous ranger, Jack Coffee Hays, as he supposedly has a wealth of information we need for the completion of our mission.
>
> Mr. Parker detailed his searches to me, especially after his daughter, Rachel, died last year. Right now, he's recovering from his travels, as he roamed Comancheria this spring to see if anyone had news of his niece, nephew, and grandson. I have no idea how he's still alive.

While in Austin, we learned of another woman kidnapped by these nasty savages. After sitting down with her and interviewing numerous witnesses including some rangers, we heard a fantastic, scarcely believable tale-a bestselling book in the making. My quill struggles to capture the complete essence of it, but I will try my best.

Sarah Creath was a beautiful blonde girl with a graceful manner and a pure heart, a wonderful catch for any man. John McSherry saw this lovely creature and married her when she was but sixteen.

In 1828, the McSherrys traveled to Texas and settled along the Guadalupe River in a location known as Green DeWitt's Colony, southwest of Austin and southeast of San Antonio.

The McSherrys built a log cabin on Little Carlisle Creek, ten miles downstream from the nearest neighbor. A fresh, clear spring was just a few hundred yards from the cabin. The McSherrys were happy, and Sarah gave birth to a son.

It was a beautiful summer day when John McSherry went to the spring to fetch some water. He had been gone but a minute or two when his blood-curdling scream reached Sarah inside the cabin.

She picked up her baby and ran outside just in time to see several Indians killing her husband. Poor Sarah was horrified as a savage took a knife to John's head and removed his scalp.

For a brief moment, Sarah locked eyes with her husband and they exchanged an unsaid message: Save yourself for I am a dead man.

Realizing she could do nothing for her husband, she rushed back to the cabin and slammed the door shut, securing it with a strong board. With the baby on a blanket, Sarah grabbed up her husband's rifle and prepared to defend herself and her son.

The Indians roamed around and inspected the cabin. Like a porcupine with her shotgun occasionally sticking out, the savages soon left with poor John's scalp.

Sarah remained inside until a passerby appeared and discovered John's body. He took Sarah and the baby to another house in the colony, which was much safer.

The owner of the house was Andrew Lockhart, father of Matilda, whom the Comanches recently returned at the Council House Fight

Post Oak

in San Antonio. At this point, Matilda had not yet been captured, so Sarah was a mothering influence to the young girl.

From the Lockharts' home, the poor widow Sarah McSherry tried to put her life back together. She was only twenty-three.

Sarah had one thing going for her: she was still a beauty. It wasn't long before another man, John Hibbens, took an interest in her.

They married and produced a second child. Mr. Hibbens set up residence on the east bank of the Guadalupe River, the opposite side of where Mr. McSherry had built his log cabin and died. No sense tempting fate.

During the summer of 1835, Sarah expressed a desire to return to Illinois to visit her family for a few months, so Mr. Hibbens sent her and the two children up there.

In January 1836, Sarah returned to Texas with her only brother, George Creath.

Mr. Hibbens took an ox cart and traveled to Columbia, about thirty miles from the Gulf Coast and up the Brazos River to meet their arrival. After picking up the four of them, it was late afternoon when they began the 120-mile trip back to their home at Dewitt's Colony.

Sarah and the two children rode in the cart with John Hibbens driving and George Creath walking. Occasionally, they switched and George drove the oxen.

It was January 20, 1836, and they had almost reached home, lacking just fifteen miles, when thirteen Comanche warriors attacked. They killed Sarah's brother and second husband right in front of her. Again, they removed the scalps of the two men.

After plundering the wagon, they placed Sarah and her two children on ponies and rode northwest toward the High Plains, out of sight of all civilization. Yet on the second day of hard riding, the youngest baby from the loins of Mr. Hibbens continued crying.

The savages did not like the noise and Sarah tried desperately to quiet the child. It was not possible.

The Indians considered the eight-month-old baby too much trouble, so they stopped. One male ripped the baby from Sarah's arms, walked over to a post oak tree, and smashed its tiny head against the trunk, leaving the body in the crook of the tree.

By now, Sarah was so distraught she couldn't think straight. She was only twenty-six and had already lost two husbands, her only brother, and now her youngest baby.

They continued riding northwest and crossed the Colorado River while avoiding white settlements. As the cold wind picked up, the Indians stopped at the south side of a wall of cedar trees to wait out what appeared to be a freezing blue norther.

They awoke the next morning and decided to remain at their temporary camp, allowing the thick stand of cedars to block the frigid wind.

On the third night since her capture, Sarah awoke and took stock of her situation. In another day or so, she and her son would be so far into Comancheria that rescue would be impossible.

She looked down at her hands and legs and found them unbound. The savages believed that she was unable to escape due to the harsh weather and Sarah's distraught demeanor. The captors slept all around her, wrapped in thick buffalo hides, confident in this assessment.

Sarah's son was next to her, wrapped in a buffalo hide and asleep. She could wake him and try to escape but he couldn't travel too far since he was only three years old. And he would make noise. They would be caught before going far.

On the other hand, Sarah could leave her son and try to escape alone.

As she lay there thinking about this, she made the difficult decision to leave her son behind. Perhaps she could find help and rescue him.

She wrapped the buffalo hide tighter around her son and slipped away, barefoot and barely dressed.

Sarah had been overcome with grief, but the will to survive pushed her grief down and she formed a plan. She headed back to the Colorado River, hoping to follow it south and find some white settlements she knew were there.

But how far were they?

She didn't know.

Sarah found the river and walked in the icy water to cover her tracks. She quickly lost feeling in her feet. At some point, she heard her son crying for her.

She stopped in the river and waited for the savages to come, but they didn't. Perhaps it was the bitter wind, not her son's cries - she didn't know which. She kept on.

All manner of brush, thistle, and thorn ripped her clothes and flesh, yet she didn't stop. A faint glow of light soon appeared in the east. The sun was rising. Still, she kept on, frozen and bleeding.

By afternoon, she found some cows feeding near the river bottom. Believing these to be milk cows, she knew they would be called back home soon, so Sarah waited and watched to see what would happen.

Sure enough, the cows slowly began moving away from the river. She followed them and spotted a campfire.

Staggering into it, she found men preparing a meal. They grabbed Sarah's mostly nude body and covered her with blankets, warming her and offering water and coffee.

She couldn't say much until an hour later when she revived. Then she told them what had happened.

By God's providence, they were Texas Rangers headed to their designated patrol area. They knew the land well and figured she had walked ten miles in the harsh weather.

The sixty rangers loaded up their gear and raced away, leaving Sarah with a nearby family.

As the sun set, the rangers rode hard. They found the Indians' trail and had to stop for the night as they didn't want to lose it.

At sunrise, they sent some scouts ahead and found the Indians and their camp. Captain John Tumlinson sent half his men to the opposite side of the camp. Once in place, he yelled and commenced the attack. The Indians were caught by surprise.

The fighting was fierce with one savage shot dead. But he wasn't! He reloaded his musket and shot at Captain Tumlinson. The ball went through his coat and killed his horse. Another ranger sent the savage into eternity.

The rangers killed four Indians and the other nine escaped into the thick brush.

The rangers collected their horses and the stolen goods from Sarah's cart and prepared to return to camp. But a mule tore loose with an Indian on its back.

A ranger chased the mule and aimed his rifle at the rider. He pulled the trigger but the gun misfired. He pulled again and it misfired again. He tried a third time as another ranger rode up and knocked his rifle away from the fleeing rider. This time it fired, missing everything.

The two rangers slowed the mule and discovered the rider was Sarah's son. The ranger had almost killed him.

The rangers studied the dead Indians and realized they were the feared Comanche. The rangers scalped the dead, loaded the boy with the horses, and left for home.

Sarah was overcome when she held her son, Joseph Lewis McSherry, in her arms again. Her gamble had paid off.

Today, the skirmish is called the Battle of Walnut Creek since the action took place at that location. One of the rangers told me this was the biggest fight between their force and Comanche so far.

I am happy to report that within six months of her last husband's death, Sarah remarried a third time to Mr. Claiborne Stinnett, a former neighbor, and became known as Sarah Creath McSherry Hibbens Stinnett.

Unfortunately, Mr. Stinnett left on a business trip to Linnville, a city near Port Lavaca on the Gulf Coast, and has never been seen again—a likely victim of the ruthless Comanche.

Yet the good news keeps on coming, as a twenty-five-year-old man from Kentucky, Phillip Howard, married Sarah and they are currently happy and in love. She is now known as Sarah Creath McSherry Hibbens Stinnett Howard.

Such is life out here on the frontier. There's hardly any time for mourning as hardy, strong men are readily available for pretty young girls.

We are still in Austin and plan to head south for more information. I hope my reports continue to meet with your approval. And please send the next disbursement to the address enclosed so we can purchase two horses and tack.

Respectfully,

Del Sands

Chapter Eighteen

"There he is," Singing Lark said. "Hurry up and see where he's going." Naduah looked up from her work and saw a rider trotting into camp. It was Puhtocnocony.

"Here," Singing Lark said, handing a rag to her daughter. "Take this and clean up while you run to see the news he brings."

Naduah grabbed the rag and began wiping the grease off her arms and hands. She broke into a run as she hoped to catch up to the handsome warrior. She arrived just as he dismounted.

Buffalo Hump had been sitting on a log whittling down a stick and got to his feet after seeing Puhtocnocony arrive. The chief dropped the knife and prepared for the warrior's report.

"What do you bring?" he asked.

Puhtocnocony dusted off his leather leggings and took a swig from a skin of water.

Wiping his lips off, he said, "The tribes in the north refuse to send anyone. They are worried about the white man's disease. And they are fighting the Cheyenne and Arapahoe, who are being pushed south into the buffalo herds. They told me, 'Too much bad medicine in the south. We have our own troubles.' So they will not come."

Buffalo Hump shook his head in disgust. "How many warriors do we have from all the bands?"

"Four hundred, including Chief Howling Wolf. He is coming with his warriors."

Buffalo Hump touched his bear claw necklace as he walked in a circle, mumbling to himself.

Naduah moved closer to a teepee to hear more. Both men were focused on the news so they didn't notice her lingering around.

Finally, Buffalo Hump reached a decision. "We will travel with what we have. My vision demands it."

"What can we do to prepare for the march?" Puhtocnocony asked.

Buffalo Hump stared at the smoldering fire. Then he looked up at the cloudless sky and spotted a hawk circling the camp. It was a good sign.

"We will be gone one full moon, if not longer. We will need all the women and children but the old ones will remain behind. We will be traveling a great distance. Each one must be able to make the journey."

"I'll see to it," Puhtocnocony said.

By the end of the day, the warrior had completed the arrangements for the raid. Six hundred women would join the raid to feed and care for four hundred warriors. The women would also tend to the massive horse herd needed to support the journey by carrying the teepees, poles, meat, utensils, and everything else required to clean and sharpen weapons.

It would be the largest Comanche raid ever, permanently changing the whites' understanding of their most hated enemy.

August 4, 1840
Near Gonzalez, Texas

Texas Ranger Ben McCulloch reined his horse to a halt. Twelve rangers behind him stopped, too.

McCulloch said nothing as he jumped down and knelt on the prairie grass scorched brown by the Texas summer heat. He held his hand over the tracks, feeling for heat or moisture.

Sure enough, the tracks were fresh and everywhere. After crawling around for a few minutes, he sprang to his feet and checked his sidearm. The men behind him stiffened up.

"What is it?" the nearest rider asked.

"Comanche tracks. Maybe a thousand."

The other rangers swallowed hard. Two of them drew their rifles and prepared for an ambush.

Post Oak

McCulloch scanned the horizon. "They're about two hours gone. We need to follow them and see what they are up to. I've never heard of or seen a raid this large. No doubt payback from the Council House mess."

The rangers checked their weapons and tightened the strings on their hats. McCulloch knew his business and they'd follow him anywhere. Still, he wasn't dumb enough to take on a thousand Comanche. No one among the living was.

Four hours later, McCulloch and his rangers came upon a burning cabin. McCulloch surveyed the scene and found a dead settler with his feet cut off. He was about to leave when a teenage girl emerged from the root cellar.

"What happened here?" he asked the shaking survivor.

"I was helping Tucker Foley make some jam," the girl replied. "My family lives north of here."

McCulloch frowned, sure her family was already dead.

"These Indians came," she said. "Tucker was at the water hole when they roped him and dragged his body back here."

McCulloch studied the tracks to verify her story. "Where were you?"

"I was in the cabin and watched for a chance to escape. They cut a hunk of skin off the bottom of his feet and made him walk around and dance."

McCulloch winced. The summer prairie grass was scorching. It must have been painful.

"While they laughed and made fun of him, I snuck to the woodpile. They shot him dead and fought over his scalp so I was able to sneak into the root cellar. I thought for sure I was dead too. Even had a knife ready to kill myself. But they rode on."

McCulloch continued studying the tracks.

More than once a Texan had killed and scalped a fellow Texan, hoping to fool authorities. McCulloch believed that many local crimes had been wrongly pinned on the Comanche and his men had ridden after phantoms, chasing false stories while risking their lives. However, this girl's story checked out. It was the Comanche.

"I'm sending you with one of my rangers. He's gonna ride for the nearest town and raise some help."

The girl started bawling. "I'm scared," she managed through the tears.

McCulloch felt sorry for her but didn't have time to console young girls. He needed to stay behind this horde in case they turned and attacked a large city.

August 6, 1840
Victoria, Texas

Both mother and daughter were excited about the upcoming ball. Getting invited to the Johnson's Summer Gala was a big deal in Victoria. Everybody who was somebody would be there. Many a marriage had come from Johnson's grand balls.

Victoria was a proud town. Founded sixteen years earlier, it was called Guadalupe Victoria.

The name came from the first president of the United Mexican States. Incredibly, the Mexican-controlled city of Guadalupe Victoria had provided troops and supplies to the Texans to support their rebellion against Mexico.

When Santa Anna was defeated, the Mexican inhabitants of Guadalupe Victoria were driven out and replaced by Texans who dropped the "Guadalupe" for the simpler "Victoria."

Today, the mother-daughter pair carried sacks of fresh fabric they needed to make new dresses. After all, neither one would be caught dead wearing last year's dress.

"Let's hurry, dear," the mother said. "It's almost four and I need to get supper ready."

"Can I drive the rig?" the daughter asked.

"No. You always run this pair faster than they should go. I'll get us home safe."

The mother disengaged the brake and was about to slap the reins when her daughter grabbed her throat.

"What's the matter?" her mother asked.

The girl turned to her mother, clutching her neck as blood spurted through her fingers. For a brief second, the mother thought this was a sick prank.

"What's going—?" the mother managed before looking down to see a bloody arrowhead sticking out her own left side. A matching one appeared through her right side.

She spun around and saw the painted men on horses thundering down Main Street, a cloud of dust curling behind them. Her last thought was, *This can't be happening!*

It was undoubtedly the same thought other Victorians had as they ran from the Comanche, some with arrows sticking out of them.

Victoria was southeast of Austin and San Antonio, close to the Gulf of Mexico. Sure, they had an occasional Indian sneak into town to steal a few horses. But hundreds of warriors?

How did so many get here without anyone seeing them?
Where was the warning?

Screaming citizens scattered in every direction. Most dashed into buildings with some brave men taking up positions on the second floors and roofs, shooting rifles or any other guns they had at the invading horde.

Bullets zinged around the Comanche, bouncing off the tough buffalo hide shields and rarely finding flesh. The men were no match for the Comanche, as their assault was too powerful.

Buffalo Hump sauntered into town on a mighty steed and surveyed the situation. He planned to continue the slaughter, leaving an unbroken trail of blood from West Texas down through the Hill Country, between Austin and San Antonio, and all the way to the Great Waters. So far, no one had put up any resistance.

According to the plan, his men would soon dismount and go building to building and house to house, killing every citizen they could find. No one would be left alive. Before they moved on, they'd burn the town to the ground.

A warrior racing hard pulled up next to Buffalo Hump.

"What is it?" Buffalo Hump asked.

"Horses! Thousands of them."

The chief's eyes widened. "Where?"

"Around the edge of the city. It's like they were just waiting for us."

Buffalo Hump licked his dry lips and considered this unexpected development. In the Comanche Nation, wives and scalps were important to a man's wealth. But horses were the gold standard.

A man with horses could get all the wives he wanted. Such a man would never starve or go without anything. And that same man, the one with the most horses, was chief among chiefs.

The excited warrior danced his horse around Buffalo Hump. "Should we kill everyone here first or go for the horses? The whites are trying to get the horses to safety."

Buffalo Hump kicked his pony several times.

"Horses!" was all the warrior heard as dust enveloped him.

"Oh no!" McCulloch cried as he lowered his spyglass.

He was on a low bluff watching the carnage in Victoria. He slapped the ground in anger.

"What's the matter, Captain?" a ranger behind him asked.

"This horde was headed west of Victoria but peeled off several hundred warriors to attack the town. I didn't see that coming or I could've warned them. They will all be killed and the town burned to the ground."

"What can we do?" the ranger asked. "We have to do something, right?"

McCulloch crawled backward a few feet before turning around to face the man.

"We'll head west and try to find a small band we can attack. Maybe we'll draw the others away from Victoria and give the citizens a chance to survive."

"But, sir, can we risk dying before telling the others what's happening? Shouldn't we warn those ahead of the Comanche?"

"Who are those people, private? Do you know where the Comanche are going next? I can't afford to keep peeling off men to send messages. We're down to eight of us as it is."

"But, sir, if we create a diversion, how do we end up not dying? There are at least six of them for every one of us. We won't even be able to reload once before the sixth one kills us. And that's if every shot finds its mark."

McCulloch lowered his head. He knew the ranger was right. Of several bad options, the best was to keep following them and hope help arrived in time.

He stowed the spyglass in a saddlebag and mounted his horse. Fighting the Comanche was a nasty, dirty business.

The gentle waves lapped against the sides of the cargo ships. Each boat was tied up to the dock, waiting to be offloaded. A few more anchored a short distance away in Lavaca Bay, their crews no doubt in town living it up.

As the second largest seaport in Texas, much of the goods supplying the new country flowed through Linnville. The port city's warehouses overflowed with fabric, grain, clothes, and farm implements—the same goods Galveston received.

Inspecting all this was the job of a newly married major, Hugh Orem Watts. He stood in the hot summer sun and wiped the sweat from his forehead.

It was painstaking work, but customs had to be collected. The Texas Republic needed the money to pay the military, rangers, and crushing war debt.

A seagull floated effortlessly on the stiff breeze and came to rest on one of the tall posts. Fishermen had been known to toss out fish guts here. The gull hoped to fetch an easy meal.

Major Watts removed his pencil and studied the customs form. After making a few marks, he placed his signature at the bottom and handed it to a man standing next to him.

"Your shipment is approved," he told the vendor, who studied his watch.

"It's almost noon," the vendor remarked. "I think I'll take in some lunch. Care to join me?"

Major Watts grinned. "As a customs inspector, we can't take favors from vendors. You know that."

"Who said I was going to pay for your meal?"

"I know you. Instead, I think I'll go home and see what Juliet has cooked up."

"Major, if I had a wife as beautiful as yours, I'd find an excuse to be with her every chance I had."

"Yeah, just what I figured. I need to protect her from the likes of you."

The vendor didn't hear his response as he was too busy fixated on the approaching dust cloud.

"Ever see a storm rolling in like that?" the vendor asked.

Major Watts spun around and stared northwest at the brown horizon. He stepped up on a wooden block to get a better look.

Two miles away, he spotted a horse. It was followed by another horse.

"Is that the army?" the vendor mused.

The major blocked the sun from his eyes and continued staring at the ugly dust cloud.

"It must be. They're in a crescent formation. It's standard protocol when enveloping an enemy."

"But who's the enemy?" the vendor asked. "Us?"

The major's heart dropped when he saw half-naked men shift from the horses' sides to an upright position. Each rider was painted red and black. Some wore buffalo-horn headdresses, and all of them waved lances and muskets.

"Oh no, I've got to get home!" Major Watts yelled as he dropped his customs book and ran.

He willed his legs to move fast as he covered the distance, repeatedly imagining how his wife would be brutalized. But then a miracle happened.

She had seen the dust cloud and was running toward him, waving her hands. The couple collided in the street before turning away from the horde and taking off for the docks.

"We must get to a ship and out to sea!" Major Watts yelled. "Run for your life!"

Juliet Watts was unaccustomed to this, and her shoes were not made for running. She was holding back her husband.

"Leave me," she urged. "Here, I got your gold watch. Take it."

"I can't. You won't survive what they'll do to you."

The Watts stayed together and neared the docks as Comanche from the south arrived and commenced to kill anything that moved.

"Hurry!" Major Watts begged his wife. "To the water."

The couple leaped over a dune and sprinted for the beach. Dozens of citizens were already on the beach, wading into the waves as far out as they dared.

By this time, Juliet had lost her shoes and ran barefoot. Major Watts held his wife's hand as they crashed headlong into a wall of water. He tripped and fell face-first.

To Juliet's shock, an Indian came up from behind and grabbed her torso, carrying her back to the shore. As she screamed and tried to get free, she saw two arrows sticking out of her husband's back, a red stain growing around his floating body in the surf.

After being wed twenty-one days earlier, this Irish-born lass was now a widow.

Back at the docks, Buffalo Hump took charge.

"Open the doors!" he ordered.

The warriors flung open the warehouses and carried goods out, spreading them over the dock. Yet there was more killing to do.

The chief stared out at the Great Waters as whites desperately rowed small boats out of arrow range. Others swam for nearby cargo ships or drowned.

In less than thirty minutes, anyone living in town was either dead or safely floating at sea, thankful to be alive.

Or captured.

It took another hour until the first wave of women following the Comanche horde reached the docks. Naduah was among them and marveled at the plunder. She picked out a necklace and wrapped it around her neck as she began loading the horses.

All around her were fierce warriors wearing frock coats or trading their distinctive headdresses for top hats. Still others twirled umbrellas and tied red scarves to their horse's tails.

This celebration was in plain sight of the surviving citizens as they floated in Lavaca Bay, watching their lives and businesses turned upside down.

After loading the horses and mules with everything they could carry, Buffalo Hump ordered the town burned.

Like an Old Testament story, the city of Linnville, with its warehouses, hotels, stores, and homes, was utterly destroyed and wiped off the face of the earth. It was never raised again.

Chapter Nineteen

August 12, 1840
Lockhart, Texas

"What do we do?" Captain Hank Jordan blurted out, his panic rising.

Del Sands whispered, "Run for that tall grass over there and pray they don't see us."

The pair took off with Del, the fastest of the two.

Captain Hank made it two-thirds of the way before stepping into a prairie dog hole and wrenching his ankle. He limped and hobbled thirty more feet, collapsing in pain beside his companion.

"What happened?" Del asked.

"I think I broke my ankle," Captain Hank moaned in pain. "Ohhh, I'm done for."

"Quiet!" Del whispered, punching the injured man's arm. "Keep your voice down."

Del cautiously raised his head in the tall grass to see if the Comanche were nearby. Two warriors appeared on a rise, studying the landscape and tracks, hoping to find the missing white men.

Up to that point, Texas had been so much fun. Towns and cities. Hotels and saloons. Money by mail and letters in return. Except for the San Antonio Council House matter, the pair had faced little danger.

During the past two days, Del and Hank had been in a camp with Texas Rangers, soaking up their lifestyle while collecting some great Comanche advice. Then the alarm came that Comanche were coming through.

They had all heard about the thousand savages and their pillage of Victoria and Linnville, but no one knew where they would go next.

To tackle their formidable foes, the rangers spent several days gathering up every Texan who carried a weapon. So far, they had two hundred fighting men, each with repeating guns—either rifles or pistols.

The force had loosely formed north of Lockhart, hoping to run into the horde of Indians. The thinking was that the Comanche might return the way they came to the Gulf. With almost 2,000 stolen horses and mules plus their own thundering herd, the trail and dust clouds of 1,000 invaders would be hard to miss.

Del had been desperate to see some Texas Rangers in action and tagged along. He was all in when he heard Jack Coffee Hays was part of the posse.

But now, a Comanche scout team had ambushed Del and his companion, killing the ranger's cook while the pair just happened to be off in the woods relieving themselves. They had the good fortune to escape through a thick stand of trees and make it to some high grass.

Yet these two Comanche braves seemed determined to remove some white scalps. Del rubbed his hair, hoping he would enjoy that feeling for years to come.

"Do you have your pistol ready?" Del whispered.

"Yeah, but the pain is too much for me to bear. I know I can't walk anymore and I'm too heavy for you to carry me."

"Do you want to shoot yourself?"

Captain Hank stiffened. "No. I want to live if possible."

Del checked his own pistol.

"Oh, why did I ever leave the sea?" Captain Hank moaned.

"I have a plan," Del whispered. "Let me have the purse."

Captain Hank placed his hand over it protectively.

"Why do you want that? And right now? Especially when the Indians are creeping up on us."

He hadn't trusted Del from the moment he met the man, and this request just confirmed his suspicions.

"Because I'm going shake the coins and run to the left, drawing the Indians to me and away from you. I think I can lose them at the creek, wade through it for a mile or so, and make them give up. After all, they're just advance scouts and will probably return to their patrol before long."

Captain Hank thought this through. He had heard the rangers talk about how the Comanche often set the prairie grass on fire to smoke out prey—animals and humans alike. It might not be long before the world around them was in flames.

"What do I do while you're gone?"

Del placed a hand on the man's chest. "Lay still and wait until nightfall. I'll return with some horses and rangers and we'll put you on a pony. We'll get you to a doctor."

The captain stared straight up at the blazing sun, sorting everything out. Del's plan actually made sense.

One of the Indians called out to his companion. Del watched as the Indians studied the prairie.

"They're onto our tracks," Del said breathlessly. "It's now or never, Hank. *Make a decision.*"

Captain Hank handed over the purse and Del clutched it firmly, crawling backward out of the high grass and out of view of the approaching Comanche. He crept to his left, keeping the coins in the purse silent.

When Del had put two hundred feet between him and Captain Hank, he found some stones and threw them high in the air. The first one landed close to Captain Hank. So did the second one. The two Indians heard the noise and rushed to the spot.

Blam!

Del saw Hank's gun go off and a Comanche jump back, rubbing his thigh. The injured warrior screamed in pain. The second Comanche came from a sharp angle, raising a fourteen-foot lance.

Hank's scream joined the wounded warrior's as the lance descended into the grass and quivered briefly before becoming rigid.

The second Indian wasted no time bending over and slicing off Hank's scalp, holding it high in the air.

Del lowered his head and slid more to his left. He kept crawling on his belly until he heard more shots.

Hank's pistol had alerted the rangers and they were now on the trail of the two Comanche scouts. Del found some high grass and curled up in it. With any luck, the Indians would move on and he'd be spared.

"Can I get you another beer?" the cute waitress asked.

Del stopped writing and glanced up at the pretty face. "Sure, sweetheart. Why not."

He closed the bright green book and finished off his first beer. He cut a few pieces of steak and savored the taste, thinking about his list of Comanche tactics.

It was long but incomplete since he hadn't sat down with Jack Coffee Hays yet. It was like chasing a ghost. Hays was always "just over the hill" or "a mile or two ahead."

The task was frustrating but that just extended his mission. As long as his benefactor continued sending money, there was no need to wrap up anything. Interviewing Hays could wait.

The waitress set down his second beer and Del pulled out his money bag. Without the always-hungry, always-thirsty sea captain around, he had plenty to pay for this meal, his hotel, and several more weeks of good living. By then, the funds should be available at the bank and he could keep moving. All he had to do was finish this letter and get it off.

August 28, 1840

Austin, Texas
   To Mrs. Cora Covington
   23 Brighton St.
   Norfolk, Virginia

Dear Mrs. Covington,

  It is with deep regret that I inform you that Comanche warriors killed Captain Hank Jordan.

  We had been camping with some Texas Rangers when the savages ambushed our camp. Captain Jordan and I were gathering firewood and managed to escape the attack. However, four Indians tracked us down as we hid in the high grass.

Post Oak

Because I had twisted my ankle in the escape, Captain Jordan decided to attract the Indians' attention so I could remain hidden. It worked.

However, as he fled, the Indians closed in on him fast. Captain Jordan valiantly shot and killed two of them but was overwhelmed by the other two. His heroic actions saved my life. I am eternally indebted to him.

Speaking of debt, per your instructions, Captain Jordan carried the purse. Because the Indians stripped him clean, I was unable to pay the local undertaker, who collected the body, fashioned a comfortable coffin, and buried our hero in the hard, dry prairie cemetery.

It was difficult work, but I assured the digger that you would provide me with funds so I could cover his fees. It is only through credit and charity that I can stay in a hotel and have one meal daily. I beg you to send money to the address on the slip of paper in this envelope.

Now, onto the rest of the story. I do not doubt that you have read about the Comanche attack on Victoria and Linnville. While there have been some reports about what happened, let me complete the story.

When the Comanche entered southeast Texas, the rangers had time to form three companies of fighters. They knew this slow, bloated plunder train would eventually head back to Comancheria. All they had to do was determine where the raiders were headed and pick a spot to ambush them. It was a once-in-a-lifetime opportunity to kill some Comanche.

Captain John Tumlinson and his 125 recruits went first. This is the same Tumlinson as discussed in my last letter. He was involved in Sarah Hibben's escape.

By this point, every Texan realized the Comanche were retracing their path into Texas. It was an incredible blunder and one of arrogance on their part.

Captain Tumlinson intercepted the Comanche near Victoria, and he and his men dismounted to form up for an attack. The Indians each unleashed six arrows within a second while the Texans fired their weapons.

Unfortunately, Tumlinson's men were quickly surrounded. As he fought off superior numbers and probably prepared to die, the Comanche withdrew.

It was later determined that instead of scalping white men, they only wanted to block their plunder train from attack.

As the Indians disappeared, Tumlinson knew he was lucky to have survived.

On August 12, near Lockhart, the exact spot where Captain Jordan and I were stationed, the wagon train made its appearance. The whole scene was a sick dream, with Comanche warriors singing and grossly gyrating. Each one wore stovepipe hats and elaborate clothing with gold buttons down the back. I wouldn't have believed it if I hadn't seen it myself.

Major-General Felix Huston was in charge of another 200 fighters. His men call him "Old Long Shanks" or "Old Leather Breeches." He fought in the Texas War of Independence so he was very experienced.

Huston positioned his troops near Plum Creek, well aware the train would have to slow down to cross. He ordered his men to dismount and form a hollow square.

Because a recent lightning strike had burnt the prairie to a crisp, ashes flew through the air, blinding the eyes of anyone and adding to the searing heat of the day.

As the Comanche passed close by, Huston's actions quickly drew their attention. They encircled his troops, unleashing havoc. Arrows stuck in men, horses, and the prairie.

This time, the Texas troops looked to be crushed as the Indian women and children guided the plundered train into the Hill Country.

A Comanche chief with a massive headdress approached the troops, confident in his medicine and, thus, his safety. When he came close enough, several of the soldiers fired and hit the chief, who leaned forward in his saddle and was about to fall off. Yet several warriors came up alongside and steadied the chief, leading him to a stand of post oaks, from where a strange howling commenced.

Ranger Ben McCulloch and Matthew Caldwell knew that this was their chance. Whenever a chief is killed, the warriors lose their sense of purpose and direction.

The two frontier fighters urged Huston to mount up and attack the Indians.

You will recall Mr. Caldwell, or Old Paint, from the Council House Fight in San Antonio. Old Paint killed two Indian chiefs inside the Council House while suffering a leg wound. Be assured McCulloch and Caldwell are tough, smart Indian fighters.

Sure enough, Huston relented and ordered the men to mount up.

As the men charged, I watched the attack from the high grass, where I was still hiding. The Texans ran hard at the Indians and waited to fire until they were so close they couldn't miss. Their first shots dropped fifteen Comanche on the spot.

The troops then stampeded the Indians' horses and sent them smashing into the train. Horses, mules, and plunder spilled everywhere.

Stunned, the Comanche warriors were in disarray and chaos.

Not a hundred feet from me were several squaws guarding three female captives. When it appeared the squaws would be killed or captured, two warriors fired arrows at the white women, dropping all three.

I waited until the Indians disappeared and hobbled over on my bad ankle to the dead women, only to find two still alive. The first was Mrs. Nancy Crosby, the granddaughter of Daniel Boone. I found her gasping for air as two arrows had gone clean through her body.

She said she had been captured with her baby, but due to its noise, the Comanche killed it in front of her. A few minutes later, she died.

The second woman was Juliet Watts, captured from Linnville, Texas. She had an arrow sticking out of her but due to her whalebone corset, only the head pierced her skin.

There was some justice, though, when one of the squaws guarding the captives was injured. The soldiers arrived and found her lying flat on the ground. One of them used his boot several times to crush and stamp her face into the unforgiving prairie before sending another enemy to eternity.

After the skirmish, the rangers shot and harassed the Comanche for the next fifteen miles.

When the dust finally settled, most of the plunder had been left behind and two hundred stolen horses recovered. Upwards of 125 Comanche chiefs and warriors were dead, though others say only eighty. Still, they got away with an estimated 2,700 horses, a lot of mules, and most of the 1,000 beasts they came with.

The Texans lost just one man, although others claim no one died. Everyone agrees that seven Texans were wounded.

Later, the rangers heard a baby crying within a large stand of trees. They did not go in because it was a Comanche trick to lure men to their doom.

However, one brave (or foolish man) ventured in and discovered a baby Indian. The poor creature had been hidden by the retreating Comanche, who would likely come back to get him.

A man living nearby called Old Judge Bellinger adopted the baby, and it's doing well.

As for the plunder, it was reported to be at least $300,000 from Linville alone. Plus, the government had just delivered five hundred mules and a large stash of silver bullion.

When the plunder and bullion were recovered, it seems no one knew what to do with it. I suggested returning it to the rightful owners, but they quickly pushed me aside.

In a bit of frontier justice, lots were drawn and the loot divided up among the Indian fighters. Everything disappeared into the night, which happened to be a Comanche moon.

After the battle, I learned that the Texas Rangers value their Tonkawa Indian scouts. The Tonkawa are fierce enemies of the Comanche, and most of the Tonkawas roasted and ate some of the dead Comanche warriors after the battle.

Jack Coffee Hays was in this fight, which they now call the Battle of Plum Creek since it happened near Good's Crossing on Plum Creek. I failed to catch up with him but I will.

Thanks again for your prayers and financial support.

PS: I'm washing dishes and cleaning up at the hotel restaurant until your money arrives. They give me a little food for my labors. God bless.

Chapter Twenty

The endless prairie awoke from a night's slumber and life sprang forth. By midmorning, the spring day was refreshing. It was the perfect temperature after the harsh winter and right before the scalding days of summer.

Naduah looked over the two hides and made a straight cut so each side would fit snugly into the other. She grabbed some dried sinew and used a fingernail to peel off a piece. After holding it above her head to determine its length, she rolled up the string and stuck it into her mouth, moistening it thoroughly.

Once it was pliable, she removed it from her mouth and straightened out the sinew, inserting one end through the eye of a bone needle. Then she pierced the edge of the hide, taking her time to carefully sew it together with the other hide. It was tedious work.

Naduah was a stout nineteen-year-old. She had painted her cheeks with red-orange circles and her ears were covered in red dye. Even her eyes were lined in red. The red-colored look was common among Comanche women in this band.

Two women sat on the right side of Naduah with another woman on the left. Each woman worked over an animal skin until one of them stopped and said, "Look."

Up ahead were eleven white men on horses, slowly picking their way into the Comanche's camp, which stretched a half-mile. Several warriors ran alongside the riders, whooping loudly and yelling to each other that they should kill the white men.

Seeing this scene, Naduah panicked and dropped her needle, running fast to her teepee. Once inside, she hid under a buffalo hide.

Puhtocnocony saw the men, too. He immediately armed himself and ran to the center of camp, where the men were obviously headed.

To see white men riding into his camp so boldly was a stunning sight. *How could this happen?* he thought.

Pah-hah-yuco, or The Amorous Man, was head of this band. At more than two hundred pounds, he carried his girth in a stately manner while often enjoying the company of his many wives, hence his name.

Yet The Amorous Man was reasonable. Recently, he had kept his warriors from killing another delegation of white men and, thus, was well-respected by the whites as someone they could deal with. That was why, on this day, he was sought out by the white men on horses.

Puhtocnocony stopped just short of the chief's teepee and asked him, "What is your order?"

"Leave them be," the chief replied. "Let's see what they have to say."

Colonel Leonard G. Williams headed the delegation. He was an Indian agent from Texas with extensive experience with Indians.

Williams came to Texas at sixteen and, at twenty-seven, received a Mexican land grant for fighting in the Fredonian Rebellion. He had also fought for Texas's freedom so Sam Houston knew him well, giving him the rank of colonel. And his first wife, a niece of a Cherokee Indian chief, added more credibility.

When Sam Houston became president for a second time, he cast aside Governor Lamar's kill-all-the-Indians policy and appointed Colonel Williams as one of four commissioners to interact directly with the Indians. Since Williams spoke eight Indian dialects, he was ideally suited to the task.

Colonel Williams came to a halt in front of the big chief and dismounted his horse. So did the ten men with him.

"Chief, we have come to treat with you," Williams said in the Comanche's language. "Will you hear our offer?"

The Amorous Man nodded and pointed for the men to sit on half logs circling a small fire. Once the men were seated, the chief motioned for them to talk.

"I represent Texas, which, as of four months ago, is a state under the protection of the United States of America. This means I am also a representative of the United States."

Colonel Williams let that soak in before proceeding.

"We invite you to come to a meeting and enter treaty talks. Are you interested?"

The Amorous Man thought for a moment. "Where is this meeting?"

"On the Brazos River, northwest of Fort Worth."

"You are brave for coming here," the chief said. "I will speak to my people and give you an answer in five days."

"Thank you, Pah-hah-yuco. You are wise."

Once again, Colonel Williams hesitated. "I have also been instructed to look for any whites you may be holding captive. We are prepared to pay for them. Do you hold any whites?"

The chief glanced at Puhtocnocony, who heard the colonel's words.

"Bring her," the chief commanded.

Puhtocnocony shook his head.

"Bring her now!" the chief said again, standing up to enforce his order.

Puhtocnocony lowered his head and took off for his teepee. As he entered it, he found his wife shaking underneath the buffalo hide.

"Naduah, come with me."

"No!" she cried. "Don't sell me back to the whites."

"I will not. I promise. I will fight these men before I let them take you."

"Then why do I have to see them?" she said, lowering the hide to show her face.

"Because the white men are in the camp and the chief wants them to leave without bloodshed. All I must do is show you to them. Then they will go."

Naduah shook her head.

"Have I ever lied to you?" Puhtocnocony asked.

Naduah considered his words. "Do I have to speak?"

"No. I will stand by you."

The girl crawled from under the hide and desperately hugged her husband. Then, the pair walked to the chief's teepee.

As the girl approached, Colonel Williams moved into position to see her better. Once Naduah was within ten feet, he clapped his hands.

"I don't believe it! This here is Cynthia Ann Parker. She was taken ten years ago from Parker's Fort on the Navasota."

Several of the colonel's men moved closer to the woman, who wept loudly. None of them knew Cynthia Ann, only the colonel, as he'd spent time with her family before she was captured.

"Can I speak to her?" the colonel asked.

"Yes," The Amorous Man replied, "once you own her. Make your offer."

Williams rubbed his jaw. "Like you, I must confer with my people. I will set up camp nearby and return soon to make you a generous offer and hear your reply about attending the treaty conference."

Once again, The Amorous Man stood and held up his hand. "Let it be so."

The eleven men went back to their horses and rode out.

Once they found a spot to erect their camp, Colonel Williams summoned a young man.

"Jakes, I need you to ride fast to Austin and tell the governor that we have found Cynthia Ann Parker and she's alive. I'm going to try and ransom her back. Ask him how much I can pay because I intend to offer a lot to get her."

Jakes mounted his horse. "Will do, Colonel. I'll come back here with an answer or die trying."

The colonel watched the young man speed off and wondered if he would make it to Austin without losing his hair or his life.

Del Sands sat at the table, writing a letter to his benefactor. He signed his name at the bottom and chuckled, amazed he'd been able to keep this scam going for so long.

Six years earlier, he had come up with the idea to escape his New York creditors, never imagining that some widow in Virginia would still be paying him today to roam around Texas.

"Are you close to being finished?" the woman asked. "I need to start dinner."

Del glanced over to the comely brunette and smiled. "Darling, I just finished. Cook away."

The woman was Bridgette Moynihan. She was married to Thomas Moynihan, another rugged individual who believed he could take and hold land in Texas from the fearsome Comanche. But Thomas was gone, traveling to Dallas. That left Bridgette all alone in a remote cabin on the Guadalupe River, southeast of Austin.

A branch cracked outside the cabin, startling them. Del sprang to his feet and grabbed a shotgun, slamming a plank across the door to lock it against intruders.

Peeking through a window, he saw a horse ease into the yard barely twenty feet from the cabin. Several tree branches obscured its rider.

"It's just me!" boomed the voice from outside. "Don't shoot!"

Del squinted hard and could make out that the man was their neighbor, Barrett Gentry.

"Barrett!" Del yelled, opening the cabin door. "I nearly shot you. We thought you were a savage for sure."

"My wife calls me that sometimes. At least I have my hair on my head."

Del laughed and greeted the man warmly. "You got anything for us?"

"Sure do. A letter for Bridgette and one for you, too."

Del rubbed his hands together. He'd been expecting something from his benefactor telling him the money was at the bank, which was the case three times a year.

Barrett stayed in the saddle and handed the letters to Del, who was joined by Bridgette.

"Safe trip?" she asked.

"Yep. No problems. I think between the treaty talks and the Texas Rangers, we can forget about the Comanche coming through here. I'm sure they've moved west of San Antonio. Besides, there are plenty of settlers around here now. Shucks, there are five families within the same twelve miles. Why attack a crowded land like ours when they can ride west and take their pick without fear of a posse catching 'em?"

"Makes sense," Del said. "Still, I'll be glad when they're wiped off the face of the earth."

"Stay for dinner?" Bridgette asked her neighbor.

"Nah," Barrett replied. "Susie has something good cooking, I'm sure. But listen, I'll be back in a little while with that auger I borrowed. Much appreciated you letting me use it."

"What are neighbors for," Bridgette said. "We're all in this together."

"That we are," Barrett said, tipping his hat. He turned his horse around and took off north for his farm.

Back inside, Del held the envelopes behind his back. He knew Bridgette, like so many frontier women, was illiterate. He'd have to read the letters to her.

"Pick a hand and that's the one we'll open first."

In her excitement, she hopped a step and said, "It's like Christmas getting a letter out here, much less two. Okay, right arm."

Del produced the letter. "It's for me," he said as he tore open the envelope and started reading.

"Dear Mr. Sands. Mrs. Covington regrets to inform you that she will no longer finance your Texas adventures. Please return to Virginia with your writings and a complete accounting of the funds."

Del stopped reading out loud and read the rest silently.

> By the way, we have learned from some friends up north that you aren't so good at accounting for money. I'm sure they can't wait to talk to you when you arrive here.
>
> Regretfully, Strom Withers, Financial Advisor to Mrs. Cora Covington.

Del swallowed hard.

This means the detectives have tracked me down, he thought. *Withers knows that by telling me this, I won't come back. He's rid of me for good.*

"What else does it say?" Bridgette asked.

Del snapped to. "Oh, just directions to get there, which I already know."

He stood up and walked over to the fire Bridgette had just started in the hearth.

"Good riddance," he said, tossing the paper into the fire, watching the hurtful words disappear. He retook his seat and sat there brooding.

"What do you do now?" she asked.

Del thought for a minute. "I still have plenty of money since she's been paying for me to stay in a hotel and eat meals in a restaurant. Living here with you and eating your fine cooking has given me a surplus. And that's not counting my writings."

"Are they really worth anything?"

"Are you kidding me? I met with Jack Coffee Hays and emptied all the bullets from his brain. Plus, I interviewed Ben McCulloch and Old Paint, and a lot of other Indian fighters. I have a gold mine in tactics that defeat the Comanche. What's crazy is that the Texas and U.S. governments know none of this information."

Bridgette set a pot of stew over the fire and took a seat at the table, picking rocks out of beans.

"What kind of information?" she asked.

"Let me give you a taste of what I know," Del said as he opened his bright green book. "Hayes told me when you get into a tough fight with the Comanche and things look bad, find the chief and shoot him dead. The rest of them will stop fighting and do nothing as their medicine is broken."

"That sounds important to know," Bridgette said. "What else?"

"Hays would stop two hours before sundown and start a fire, cooking his meat and drinking coffee. Then they would mount up, ride until dark, and make camp without a fire. This made it hard for the Indians to know where he was. When he got close to the Indians, he made a cold camp instead of lighting a fire."

He turned the page.

"And never dismount your horse. That's sure death. Stay on your horse and charge at 'em. They like to be the bullies and expect you to run away. Take the fight to them and punch them in the face. He was adamant about never dismounting to fight."

Bridgette put down her beans and gazed at the man across from her. "Del, I never really understood what you were doing, but this is good information."

"It is," Del said proudly. "And Hays agreed with what I was doing."

He looked down at his book.

"Hays told me to ride the savages' ponies, not the heavy, slow ones the military uses to haul wagons. The Comanche horses go far without water and can find almost anything to eat on the trail. Those beasts are fast and light and quick, which allows them to ride rings around whites."

"That's so simple. I think even I could take those instructions and beat the Comanche," Bridgette said.

But Del didn't stop. He had a live audience. "And two more things. The Comanche are clever and love to trick you into an ambush. You will think they are fleeing and when you follow them, it's to your death. The second point is that the Comanche will come at night and try to steal your horses. If they can't, they'll make loud noises to stampede them. You must pound metal stakes into the ground and tie your horses off. And your horse guard must never fall asleep."

"I guess they'll risk their lives to get your pony," she said. "Right?"

"Not just that, but now you and your posse are stuck out on the frontier, days away from help and without a horse. They'll pick you off one at a time when you go to relieve yourself, sleep, or even gather firewood because they're patient. One by one, eventually, you and your men will leave a trail of bleached bones behind."

Bridgette clapped her hands. "Who will you sell this to?"

"The Texas government. I talked with a couple of officials and they showed great interest. Then I'll sell it at the same time to the United States. They'll both pay and never know the other has it."

"You're so clever," Bridgette said. "How much will you get?"

"Enough so you won't have to work for the next ten years. And the best part is that they could avoid paying me by collecting this information from the men who work for them right now. All they have to do is ask."

"That's wonderful, Del! Now read my letter."

Del picked up the envelope and tore it open. "This is from Dallas."

Bridgette leaned back and stared up at the ceiling. Del's statement was ominous since her husband had traveled there to pick up an inheritance from his dead uncle's estate. The trip should have taken two weeks, three tops—not six months. This letter might be bad news.

"Dear Mr. Moynihan, as stated in our last letter, we are holding a rig, four horses, and nine hundred dollars as your share of inheritance from your uncle's estate. We have been using the money to pay for the care of the horses and storage of the rig. In good faith, we can no longer do that. Thus, we are putting the rig and horse up for auction and will send you a draft with your share and a final accounting. We are sorry about this, but your failure to appear in Dallas and timely claim these items has necessitated our actions. Sincerely, Abe Barts, attorney-at-law."

Del set the letter down and studied Bridgette. She had been alone in the cabin for two months when they met in town. After explaining her situation, Del seized the opportunity to be her protector.

Once he moved in, the pair grew close as they assumed her husband was likely a permanent part of the Texas landscape. This letter all but confirmed his demise. No settler, no matter how incompetent, could take six months to reach Dallas. And Thomas Moynihan had not been incompetent.

Bridgette wiped away a tear. "I thought he was gone, but this pretty much irons the seam."

"Sorry, darling," Del said soothingly, "but you're mine now, and that's all you need to remember."

He went to her and held her close.

"Del Sands will take care of you. Once I sell this"—he pointed to the bright green book—"we'll move to Dallas and collect that inheritance. I can be Thomas Moynihan for a day. I mean, it's not like he's gonna show up and call me a liar. Right?"

Bridgette nodded and wiped off her face. "Let's have supper."

The two ate their bowls of stew in silence, each thinking about the future. In the space of an hour, two letters had changed everything.

Del got up and stoked the fire with a poker. Outside, the sun dipped to the horizon, sending rays off the Guadalupe River and into their tiny cabin. It was a lovely scene.

A noise in the yard caught their attention.

"Barrett's back," Del said, putting down the poker. "I'll get the auger. With any luck, his wife sent some of those sugar cookies. I can't wait to stuff my mouth with something sweet."

Del swung open the door and walked outside. "Barrett, you made it just before—"

A Comanche warrior grabbed Del and pulled him away from the door. Two more rushed inside the cabin. Del tried to pull the strong arm from around his neck but everything changed when a searing pain in his right foot set him screaming.

Tina Siemens

The warrior pushed Del to the ground onto his back as another sharp pain in his left foot caused his body to jerk. In seconds, two lances stuck out of the ground, keeping his feet from moving. The Comanche expertly pinned his hands to the hard prairie with two more spears.

By now, Del heard Bridgette screaming. He knew full well what was happening inside the cabin.

The warrior withdrew a knife from his hip and pressed the cold blade against his forehead. Del felt his skin being cut as he watched the Indian stand up, holding his bloody scalp. Being pinned down by lances meant Del could do nothing but scream.

After several minutes, Del was barely conscious, he could hardly watch as a warrior removed his bright green book and ripped a page out. Working on the side of the cabin, the Comanche used a flint stone and ignited the page, catching some dry brush on fire. The warrior moved to each side of the cabin, repeating the process.

When the warrior returned to Del, he skimmed through the book before tossing it at the cabin, which was engulfed in flames.

Del's eyes filled with blood from his missing scalp. After trying several times, he was finally able to close his eyelids and pray for death. He was coming to join Captain Hank Jordan. And the Indian woman whose head was crushed by a Texan's boot.

So much death in so little time. But none of that would ever matter to Del Sands, an efficiency master and professional con artist. His time on Earth was over.

A frustrated Colonel Leonard Williams sat across from The Amorous Man. The governor had made it clear in his message that Williams was to return with Cynthia Ann Parker or not to return at all. Yet the chief had already denied an offer of $500 in cash.

"Great Chief," Colonel Williams said, laying it on thick, "you have rejected cash so I offer you twelve excellent working mules. Two of them are loaded with goods. We have never offered so much for one captive. Please take all this and return the white woman to us."

The chief called over a man and whispered in his ear. The man vigorously shook his head.

"I cannot accept your offer," the chief said, looking back at the irritated Williams.

"Why not?" he asked.

"The man who owns this woman is very much attached to her. She is his chore wife and he has taken no other wives. He would rather fight you than sell her."

Williams cocked his head to the right and cursed. He took a second to gather his thoughts before staring at The Amorous Man.

"May I at least talk to her alone? I have been ordered to get this girl and can't leave without talking to her."

The chief considered the ramifications of this request. These eleven men were armed with guns that didn't stop firing. Each man might kill at least five Comanche before they were killed themselves. And maybe they killed more.

Puhtocnocony was a good warrior. Maybe he'd be a chief one day. Sure, he wouldn't like the whites talking to his wife, but he might be one of the first ones killed if the chief refused their offer.

After thinking about it, he ordered Puhtocnocony to take his wife to a nearby tree. "You may talk to the woman over there."

Colonel Williams thanked The Amorous Man and walked over to the spot. A few minutes later, a weeping Cynthia Ann Parker sat down, her back against the tree, and stared straight ahead.

The colonel kneeled and studied the girl. Her hands were broad and her wrists thick. She still had sky-blue eyes but everything else was pure Comanche.

"Cynthia Ann, do you remember me?" Williams asked softly as tears streamed down her face.

She ignored him.

"I met you and your father, Silas, at your fort on the Navasota River. Do you remember the fort?"

Again silence.

"Do you want to go home?"

Nothing.

The colonel was losing patience. "Do you want to see your uncle, James Parker? Do you want to sleep in a bed and go to a dance with other white girls?"

Nothing moved her. Instead, she sat there, tears dripping off her cheeks and saying nothing.

After twenty minutes of trying to communicate, Williams gave up and said goodbye to The Amorous Man.

Riding out of the Comanche camp, an aide kicked his horse and came up alongside.

"Colonel, Governor Henderson will be upset that we are leaving without her."

"Let him be upset," Williams replied. "I'm not allowing all of us to die for a girl who refuses to come home."

"What are you going to tell the governor?"

"That Cynthia Ann Parker is gone. She's one of them now and she's never coming back."

The colonel kicked his horse and took off. This conversation was over.

The aide shook his head in disgust. No one was going to believe this.

No one!

The federal marshal walked through the crime scene and examined the dead body.

"Is that her husband?" a deputy asked.

"No," the marshal replied. "He disappeared on his way to Dallas. That's some man staying with her. I guess he was supposed to protect her."

"Look here," another deputy said. "I see some bones among these burnt timbers."

The marshal gingerly walked over the charred wood and inspected the bones.

"That's probably the wife. The Indians had their way with her and burned the place down."

He took his hat off and slapped it against his thigh. "Man, these Comanche are tough."

"Do you think we'll ever defeat them?" the deputy asked.

"I don't know," the marshal said. "It's going to take someone with a deep understanding of them, someone who knows their tactics, the way they fight—strategies that work against them and ones that don't."

The deputy kicked a piece of wood. "Does such a man exist?"

The marshal walked over and stared down at Del's naked, mutilated body.

"If that man exists, he couldn't save this poor soul."

The deputies milled around waiting for orders until the marshal patted one of them on the back.

"Come on, let's get them buried and make our way to the neighbors' farm. I feel certain we'll be digging more holes today."

By 1856, twenty years had passed since Cynthia Ann Parker's capture at Parker's Fort and much had changed.

In 1842, six years after the Fort Parker raid, General Zachary Taylor[4] issued an order stating the government would pay good money for any white captive brought to Fort Gibson.

Located in Indian Territory near present-day Muskogee, Oklahoma, Fort Gibson experienced a "white rush" as many tribes, including the Comanche, cashed in.

The two young boys taken in the Parker's Fort raid—John Richard Parker and Pratt Plummer—were quickly brought in and redeemed.

Upon hearing the incredible news, searcher James W. Parker rushed north, arriving at Fort Gibson in January 1843. He discovered that neither boy spoke English nor was happy to be there.

They had been with the Comanche for over six years since they were very young. John Richard was now thirteen, and little Pratt was just eight. Pratt promptly ran away but was caught and brought back to James.

---

[4] And future 12th President of the United States

Instead of waiting for the weather to warm and the boys to acclimate to a new life, James left the protection of Fort Gibson with the boys in tow. He headed back south through the snow, harsh weather, and Comanche territory. Somehow, the three travelers made it home safely.

The older boy, John Richard, was returned to his mother, Lucy. She had survived the Parker Fort massacre and escaped with Silas, Jr. and baby Orleana. However, her successful escape meant leaving behind her daughter, Cynthia Ann, and son, John Richard. But now that John Richard was home, Lucy, grateful and tremendously blessed, worked hard to reintegrate him into the civilized Parker he was born to be.

Seven years after John Richard's return, Lucy sent him back out to the dangerous Comanchería to find and persuade his sister, Cynthia Ann, to return home. The odds were fantastically long of not only finding the girl but living to tell about it. Miraculously, he accomplished both.

Yet Cynthia Ann refused to budge. No matter what he said or offered, she was tied to the Comanche. Cynthia Ann Parker, now Naduah, would live and die with her tribe.

Little Pratt's life took a different path. His mother, Rachel Plummer, was dead, and his grandfather, James W. Parker ("the Searcher"), burned with anger at Luther. James refused to send Pratt back to Luther.

By now, Luther had remarried and produced two new children. Still, he demanded his son's return.

James claimed he'd paid $1,000 for both children and that Luther refused to reimburse him. This was a silly, stupid lie and easily debunked. James's church banished him for this conduct.

Seeking help, Luther went to Sam Houston, president of the Republic of Texas. Houston issued a written order to James to return the boy to Luther. James ignored the order and raised Pratt, keeping him away from his natural father.

Six years later, in 1849, gold rush fever spread through the country. Americans and Texans flocked to San Francisco to claim their share of the gold.

Many of these fortune-seekers raced across Texas and the Comanchería, bringing with them an unexpected assassin: cholera. When the disease hit the Comanche, it killed more of them than any fighting force could.

The cholera outbreak had cruelly come right on the heels of a smallpox epidemic. Due to this double hit, the population numbers of the Comanche and their ally, the Kiowas, were likely cut in half.

The ones who did survive were shocked and distraught. It was a devastating blow to a proud people.

One of the Americans making the journey to San Francisco was the legendary John Coffee Hays. Hays was probably the only man with the secret formula to beat the Comanche.

Sure, there were rangers like "Rip" Ford, who knew some of the tactics. But Hays knew everything, like picketing and guarding the horses at night. He knew how to live on the trail—in deep discomfort—while avoiding campfires near the enemy. His men stayed on their horses and charged at the Comanche, each holding two repeating revolvers that fired a total of ten shots. He and his rangers constantly practiced hitting their targets with deadly accuracy.

But Hays also knew not to follow the retreating Comanche too far, as it was likely an ambush. And when they were in danger, he focused on the chief and killed him, sending the attackers into chaos.

Short of germs, Hays and his band of Texas Rangers were clearly the most effective weapons against the Comanche. He even earned nicknames from them, like Bravo Too Much and Devil Yack.

Because of his trip to California, he removed almost all this vital tactical information from the battlefield. And the news was even worse for settlers on the frontier.

Now that Texas was part of the United States, the federal government was responsible for protecting them as well as fighting Indians. Unfortunately, no general or commander had a clue how to do it.

Instead, military leaders sent heavily armed men on strong, loaded-down horses to fight an enemy who rode circles around them while sending eight arrows arcing through the air before the first one hit.

To the Comanche's happy surprise, the federal troops often dismounted, allowing the warriors to shower them with more arrows as the soldiers tried to hit fast-moving targets. It was usually a tragedy for the poorly led soldiers.

For the Comanche, the inexperienced soldiers before them felt like a gift from the Great Spirit—a new future filled with hope. All these beaten-down warriors needed now was a leader, a great one to take the fight to these soldiers and finally rid the land of the white man and his cursed diseases.

Ironically, it would be a white woman who birthed their savior.

If we must die, we die defending our rights.

Sitting Bull (1831–1890)
Hunkpapa Lakota

Quanah

Chapter Twenty-One

The sky was a dense, inky blue. Quanah studied it for clouds or a storm and saw only tiny sparkles from the stars.

Somewhere across the prairie, coyotes howled, perhaps needing company or signaling a fresh kill. The coyote was a potent symbol for Quanah and all Comanche.

Hearing these howls and seeing clear weather ahead were good signs. This mission might have favor from the Great Spirit and thus result in success. He could only hope.

Quanah quietly gathered his shield and weapons and slipped from his tent. He was not yet twenty nor the great chief he would become, so he still felt a pang of uncertainty and nerves in his stomach.

He had been on many raids, killed several whites and Indians, and survived a hand-to-hand struggle, staring into his enemy's eyes before shoving the knife into his ribs. Quanah was strong and confident when it came to battle. But this was different. It was almost a betrayal. He was about to go against a powerful Comanche chief, and this was nothing to trifle with.

Crouching low, he slowly made his way through brush and tall grass, using the faint starlight to avoid snapping twigs and crushing vegetation. Being caught alone would not go well for him.

Several minutes disappeared until he found a game trail. Soon, it smoothed out.

Quanah was far away from camp and less concerned about the noise. Still, he couldn't be too careful.

The young warrior came to a dip and angled down. It was there that he saw his friends.

They had beaten him here, which was no surprise since they didn't need to take as much care. Their disappearance would not be missed, only his.

Quanah embraced each boy. Standing next to them were several girls, one for each boy. Only Quanah lacked a girl.

"Let's head to the creek bed," Quanah whispered. "She'll be there."

The group said nothing as they turned to face the ravine. Carefully and slowly, they descended a rough path until they reached the sand. Quanah's heart raced.

Will she be there? he worried.

Sure enough, a pretty young girl emerged from the shadows, carrying a large pouch stuffed with personal items. Her name was Weckeah, and she was the daughter of Chief Yellow Bear.

Even in the darkness, Weckeah's beauty made him tremble like nothing else. It was like he had known her all his life, mainly because he had.

They grew up together, running through fields, collecting flowers, and exploring the world around them. They learned how the tribe was connected to the land, the animals, and the Great Spirit.

As they grew older, their lives diverged. He learned to ride a horse, hunt, and fight. She learned to butcher a buffalo, tan a hide, and cook food. Despite having separate lives, they spent time with each other whenever possible, stealing moments here and there.

It was obvious to everyone they were meant for each other. Even Weckeah's father could see Quanah had chosen his daughter. But Chief Yellow Bear knew the hard truth. Quanah was half white and half Indian.

This half-breed could never be good enough for the chief's daughter. She had to marry and mate with a pure Comanche. There was no other way.

When Quanah asked the old chief, he refused to give his consent.

Weckeah was devastated when Quanah told her.

"I don't want anyone else," she cried. "I want you."

As Quanah held her, his fury took hold. He had to find a way to make Weckeah his wife.

Quanah set out to distinguish himself on raids. This he did well.

When he asked Yellow Bear again, he was rejected. Unfortunately, nothing short of killing every white man in Texas would impress the chief.

Quanah had no choice but to take matters into his own hands. He would "steal" a powerful chief's daughter and run away.

Quanah knew they could not survive on the plains alone. He could be out hunting and return to find an enemy had killed his wife.

And hunting was hard with one person. Having others drive game toward one hunter made it easier. That's why he secretly set out to convince other young men to join him.

A few had grudges against the chief. Some had lost a claim before the old man in council or were given positions and duties beneath them; others could see the budding leader Quanah was becoming. Still others came because their girls were attached to Weckeah, and the boys could not let the couple leave on their own.

Quanah formed a small group. He knew that when they established a camp somewhere, they could send word to other bands and possibly attract more dissatisfied Comanche. With blessings from the Great Spirit, they could make it.

Suddenly, in his mind, the face of Chief Yellow Bear appeared. Quanah couldn't shake it. This move would be disrespectful to him and something that could not go unpunished. A day of reckoning would come. Quanah knew it.

The group went to their horses, which had already been hidden behind some brush. When they mounted, Quanah studied his small band.

This might be enough to make it, he thought, *if the Great Spirit is with me.*

"Where are we going?" a boy asked as the horses walked over the dry creek bed.

Quanah had kept the place a secret until they were free of the camp. Too many plans had been spoiled by loose lips.

"The headwaters of the Concho River," he answered. "We'll settle there and hope for the best."

The men nodded.

With no more words, Quanah reached over and squeezed Weckeah's hand. They would soon be together as man and wife, share a teepee, and crawl under the same buffalo skin.

Their love would last forever, or at least until Chief Yellow Bear raised some warriors and came after him. Then Quanah would have to pay for this act in blood or horses. It could go either way.

October 12, 1856
Twelve years earlier, deep in the Comancheria

Naduah scraped another hide while her young son sat nearby, working on his shield. He ripped several pages from a book and added them to the first layer of dark brown hide.

Over the years, the Comanche had learned to incorporate the white man's books into their shields. They sandwiched pages between two buffalo hides and hardened the entire creation in a fire. This made it almost impossible for bullets to penetrate the second layer.

There was something about the paper that stopped the bullets. And the pages kept the shields light, a necessary quality when a horseman's speed was critical.

"Are you almost done with that?" she asked him.

"No," Quanah said. "I need two more days to get it just right."

"Good boy," Naduah said. "Your papa's shields have saved his life many times."

"A shield only works if you have good medicine," Quanah reminded her. "You must have medicine from the Great Spirit."

She smiled. This boy learned fast.

Near the center of the camp sat Puhtocnocony and another warrior, Tree Climber.

"What do you think of my son?" Puhtocnocony asked.

"Quanah makes good shields and arrows. He's smart and learns things before boys who are older than him."

"How is he at fighting?"

Tree Climber rubbed his chin. "Hand-to-hand, he's crafty and dangerous. The bigger and stronger kids had some trouble, but they all defeated him. He's too young to win those—*yet*."

Puhtocnocony nodded, pleased with those words.

"I've seen the small game he's hunted and killed. I think he will make a fine warrior," Tree Climber added.

A lone Comanche rode into camp and dismounted.

Puhtocnocony greeted the man. "What brings you here?"

"Buffalo Hump is heading to the white man's camp," the warrior said. "He will follow the white man's way."

Puhtocnocony hung his head. "How many more can we afford to lose?" he mumbled.

"Buffalo Hump's band was small," Tree Climber said. "They lost many during the last four years to the white man's sickness. He was unwilling to provide warriors for our raids. And he claimed there were so many whites around, the game had disappeared. His people are starving."

Silence enveloped the three.

The warrior pointed to Puhtocnocony. "Your son, Quanah, he is half white, half Comanche. Maybe he will be the one to lead us against the white man."

Puhtocnocony straightened his back and stuck out his chest. "I can do the job. I still have good medicine."

"Yes, you do," the warrior said, not wanting to cause a problem. "Will more white men come for your wife?"

"It's hard to say," Puhtocnocony replied. "We will only know with each moon and sun."

"Show him a place to stay," Puhtocnocony told Tree Climber. "We will have a feast tonight and dance, sing, tell stories. Maybe gamble. And then we will forget all about Buffalo Hump and how he accepted the white man's pity."

December 13, 1856
Fort Belknap, Texas

The young soldier made his way through the snow, carefully placing his crutches to avoid slipping. He spent half the time staring at the ground for sound footing and the other half seeing where he was going.

"Who's that?" a sergeant said, watching the boy hobble around.

"Billy Tyler," the captain replied. "He's our new clerk."

"A cripple?"

"His father's a general. Billy was born with a twisted leg that no sawbones can fix. He's been sent here to organize the place after that drunk Hammerly died."

"Fell on a pitchfork hidden in the snow," the sergeant recalled. "Crazy way to die."

"Yeah, well, that's what the report said. Hammerly owed the gamblers money. Sometimes bad things happen to good people who don't pay their debts."

"So now we have this cripple to get us organized?"

The captain straightened up and put on his cap. "Better make the most of it if'n you don't want the general breathing down your back."

"William Tyler, reporting for duty," the new soldier said, hopping on one leg as he held the right crutch with his left hand. He tried his best to salute without falling, but it was a pitiful sight.

The captain returned the salute. "Welcome to Fort Belknap. The sergeant here will show you to your office."

"Are there any instructions, sir?"

"Yes—organize everything."

Billy nodded, shifted back on both crutches, and followed the sergeant to a wooden structure.

As he walked into the first office, he found it a complete mess. Documents and files were scattered everywhere, and nothing was in its proper place.

"This here's your office," the sergeant said. "You'll deal with whoever comes through that door and let no one see the captain until you talk to him and get his permission. Understand?"

"Yes, sir," Billy replied. "Where's the general's office?"

"It's sergeant, not sir, and the general sits behind the captain's office. But he ain't hardly ever here. Captain Robinson runs everything and tells the lieutenant, who then tells me."

He eyed the boy skeptically.

"Keep your nose clean and on your own business and you'll do just fine. Otherwise, you'll experience Fort Belknap's reputation up close."

The sergeant was right about the fort's reputation. Situated one hundred miles northwest of Fort Worth, it was the northernmost fort in a line of twelve that protected the western edge of the Texas frontier.

Post Oak

Fort Belknap was primarily used as a supply depot rather than a defensive position. Troops slept in and around the fort, confident the Indians wouldn't attack. And they didn't.

Occasionally, the fort sent troops out to find the Indians—mainly Comanche and Kiowa—and kill them. Due to its general remoteness while still being close to the Comanchería, this gave these men a certain hardness. Billy knew he'd have to watch himself very carefully.

"I'll start cleaning up right now, sergeant."

"You do that, son."

The sergeant headed to the front door before stopping, turning back to Billy and grinning. "Say, son, do you play cards?"

It was another cold day at the Comanche reservation on the Clear Fork of the Brazos River. The sky was an insistent gray with no chance of sunshine.

A miserable bunch of warriors huddled around a small campfire, avoiding the gusts of cold wind from a winter that hadn't disappeared yet. Buffalo Hump was one of them.

"Have you seen the Indian agent?" the chief asked.

"No," a warrior replied sullenly.

Buffalo Hump spit into the orange-red fire. "We will starve to death. They don't care about us."

"The Comanche, Kiowas, and others raid nearby settlements, yet we are the ones who get blamed," the warrior said. "If horses are stolen, it's our fault. The only thing they make sure we get on a regular basis is firewater so our men are filled with the white man's evil spirits. We can't fight or hunt game. All we do is stagger around spouting nonsense. The more we drink, the more we are slaves to the white man. That's why other chiefs have taken their people off the reservation and back to our lands."

Buffalo Hump leaned over and placed his head in his hands. It had been 18 months since he surrendered to the white man. Life here was hopeless. They couldn't go on like this.

The warrior pointed to the west. "The old trails to our land are just over those hills," he said. "Let's leave this cursed place."

Buffalo Hump's dark eyes filled with light. "You are right. Tell our people to prepare to leave."

Another warrior touched his arm. "The white man will see us. They will come and kill us for leaving."

"No," Buffalo Hump said calmly. "Remind our people we are still the ones who made the Great Raid down to the Great Waters. Tell them to arrange everything inside their teepees tonight quietly. We will go to sleep early. There will be no late-night dancing or singing. I will assign a squaw to wake us before dawn. The white man never comes out here until the sun is well over the prairie and high in the sky. By then, we will be gone."

Several warriors stood up, and one of them said, "Yes, this is the right course."

Another said, "We will soon hunt game and feast like our forefathers."

Buffalo Hump got to his feet and pounded his chest. "We will be Comanche again. And we will be *feared!*"

Chapter Twenty~Two

May 19, 1858

Field Report of Action with the Enemy

Acting under the authority of Governor Hardin Runnels, Captain John Salmon "Rip" Ford assembled a company of Texas Rangers numbering one hundred.

On March 19, 1858: Captain Ford traveled to the Brazos Indian Reservation near Fort Worth and contacted Shapley Ross, the Indian agent. Ross ably stirred the anger of the reservation Indians against the Comanche and recruited 113 Indian scouts as follows:

> Chief Placido and his force of Tonkawas;
> Jim Pockmark and his force of Caddos and Andarkos;
> and some Shawnees.

April 7: Captain Ford left the Brazos Indian Reservation and carried troops and supplies north, establishing a supply camp near Fort Belknap.

April 15: Captain Ford's force crossed the Red River and proceeded deep into Indian Territory.

May 10: Captain Ford's force found arrowheads belonging to the Comanche.

May 11: Captain Ford's force came upon a small Comanche camp on the Canadian River.

May 12: Captain Ford organized his forces and sent the Tonkawas to take the camp. The Tonkawas attacked by surprise and killed several

Comanche. Two Comanche escaped and hot pursuit commenced, covering three miles of hard riding.

Captain Ford's troops were then led to a creek and discovered a large Comanche camp more than a mile long. The enemy numbered at least 400 against Captain Ford's troops, which numbered 213.

Captain Ford sent the reservation Indians ahead with bows and arrows, hoping to trick the enemy into believing they faced no guns or repeating revolvers. The Comanche fell for the trick and attacked with Chief Iron Jacket leading the charge, riding on his brightly colored horse. Chief Iron Jacket was known for wearing a Spanish mail shirt that stopped arrows from piercing his body.[5]

Once the Indian scouts and warriors had drawn in the Comanche, Captain Ford sent the rangers forward and they engaged the enemy. Iron Jacket's horse was shot and killed. Now on foot, Iron Jacket was shot several times and killed. When the enemy saw their chief dead and his medicine broken, they fled. The rangers engaged the enemy and killed many, unable to distinguish between warriors and squaws.

The battle raged on in the lowlands of the creek, the Canadian River, and the plains. Many Comanche were picked off by rifle and pistol fire.

After this enemy action, a count was commenced and informed them that 76 Comanche and two rangers were dead. Many Comanche were wounded, with only three rangers injured. Sixteen Comanche were taken prisoner.

After a lull in the fighting and tending to the wounded, a large Comanche force arrived, between 400 and 600 warriors. According to our Indian scouts, Puhtocnocony, also known as Peta Nocona, led the attack.

As the enemy force formed lines, single warriors came forward demanding our Indian scouts engage in individual combat. Our Indian scouts accepted the challenge, and each one rode toward the other with their

---

[5] Chief Iron Jacket was Quanah Parker's grandfather through Puhtocnocony aka Peta Nocona

lances, bows, and an occasional rifle. These single combats went on for 30 minutes with no one killed and not much damage done to either side due to the thick shields they carried.

With the men fully reloaded, Captain Ford reached the end of his patience and ordered a charge. This action scattered the Comanche, and the enemy fled as fighting continued for three miles while neither side lost a man. It gave the squaws and old men time to escape, although they abandoned their camp filled with cooking implements, teepees, and stores of dried meat.

Captain Ford determined the horses were exhausted and ordered a retreat. The enemy also retreated, and no further action followed.

Chief Iron Jacket's village was burned along with the meat, stores, teepees, and implements. The first small camp was also burned with everything in it. A great feast was held that night, and the Tonkawas remained awake all night celebrating.

Corporal John Bulsar
Clerk for Captain Rip Ford of the Texas Rangers

Billy Tyler sat facing Captain Robinson, watching him read Corporal Bulsar's report. Fort Belknap buzzed with the latest field reports. When the captain finished, he dropped it on his desk and cussed.
"The 'Battle of Antelope Hills,' they're calling it. Rip Ford and his Texas Rangers have completely embarrassed us!"
"Sir?" Billy managed.
"We are the U.S. Army. With Texas now a state and part of the Union, we're responsible for protecting the citizens and taking the fight to the Comanche. But because we aren't doing the job, the Texas legislature raised money and paid these men to raid the Comanche in a place where few dare to go. Even worse, the Red River is the official Texas border. They had no authority to cross the Big Red and enter the Indian Territory. Those dirty rangers aren't the federal government and don't care about boundaries or

rules. Now they're heroes because they killed some squaws and surprised the Comanche. I hear they even let those Tonkawa cannibals eat the dead Comanche at some big feast. Despicable!"

Billy shifted in his chair. "What are we going to do, sir?"

"I'll tell you what we're going to do." His jaw set. "We're going to recall the Second Cavalry from Utah."

"Will General Twiggs agree to that?" Billy asked.

"That's what this other report says. He's getting the authority to send our troops into the Comanchería and find some Indians to kill. Once enough of those critters die, we'll plant them on the reservation and be done with the whole affair. We just need to find a way to keep them there."

Billy stared down at his feet, and Captain Robinson knew what that meant.

"Do you disagree with this assessment, Corporal Tyler?"

"Sir, respectfully, yes," he replied.

Captain Robinson's face turned red. "Care to state your case?"

"There's too much corruption in the Indian agencies. Beeves meant for the Indians are diverted to others for under-the-table payments. We don't help them raise crops and the locals get stirred up and blame the Indians for anything bad that happens there. Even Indians in the wild come and steal from the reservation Indians and sometimes kill one or two of them. It's a miracle they stay as long as they do."

The captain turned his head away. "These Indians are liars. They promise to stay in exchange for blankets, food, and whiskey. As soon as they receive their payments, they're gone. It's not corruption on our part. It's a lack of honor on theirs. And Buffalo Hump is the most dishonorable of them all. He's promised twice to remain on the reservation and lied each time. Texas even set aside almost twenty-four thousand acres for those people. But it's all been a waste."

Billy remained silent.

"Son, have you ever been out in the field? Have you ever been attacked by these savages?" Captain Robinson was getting worked up.

"No, sir."

"Well, I have. During one battle, three men were separated from our company. They crawled through the dry summer grass and hid. The

Comanche lit the prairie on fire from the north, and the men crawled south. Then, the south was set on fire, so the men crawled east. But then the east went up in flames, forcing them west."

"Did they escape?" Billy asked.

"Two of them crawled to the west and were captured. The third braved the fire to the south and was horribly burned. He couldn't scream from the searing pain as he crawled to the woods, or he would've been captured. From there, he endured the pain and watched as the savages stripped the two men and staked them to fire ant beds. Soon, the fire ants crawled all over our boys. We heard their screams from miles away. The Indians stayed for a day and left. Once they were gone, we moved in and found the burnt man. He told us what happened."

"Did any of the men live?" Billy asked, fearful of the answer.

"The burnt man died in agony three days later, begging us to kill him. That's something I regret not doing. Of the other two, one died from ants crawling down his throat and choking him. The second man was alive only because he closed his mouth and breathed through his nose to force out the ants. He did that for a day and a half without sleeping, breathing out hard every few seconds, enduring stings on his lips, eyes, ears, chest, and other parts that only a man has. He was so ravaged by the ants that he begged us to shoot him. When I saw him, I almost threw up in front of the men. It was one of the easiest orders I ever gave. Yet no one would do it. So I stepped forward, yanked out my pistol and put a bullet through his forehead."

The captain looked out the window with a faraway stare.

"So when you go back to your desk, son, you think about that. Then don't tell me about any misdealing with Indians. They are nothing but liars and thieves. They all deserve to die."

"Yes, sir," Billy said before returning to his desk and slumping in his chair.

What did he know? He was just a clerk.

Chapter Twenty-Three

Billy Tyler glanced at the files on the desk. He had been at Camp Cooper for two days.

"How long will you be gone?" Billy asked.

Corporal Henson stroked a few hairs on his young chin. "I don't know, maybe two months. At least until we find some Comanche to kill. Captain Van Dorn said we have to show those rangers that we can do the job." He pointed to the files. "Can you handle all this?"

Billy gave a half-smile. "Don't worry, I'll hold things down while you're gone."

"What about your station over at Fort Belknap?"

"I trained an assistant. He's handling things while I'm here," Billy said confidently.

Corporal Henson stuffed some notebooks into a pouch. "That's smart, but it gets lonely. Nothing much to do."

Billy thumbed through some files. "Where are your past reports?"

The corporal waved at a stack along the wall. "In those six boxes. You're not gonna read all of them, are you?"

"Sure. I might find something useful that helps us defeat the Comanche."

Corporal Henson shook his head slowly. "If you do that, you should be made a general or something. Just don't let your wife hang around Van Dorn."

Billy stopped and looked up. "I don't have a wife, but if I did, why would that be a problem?"

Corporal Henson lowered his voice. "He has an eye for the ladies. They're attracted to him, especially when he tosses back those long blond locks and smiles. It's the twinkle in his eyes. And he wears fancy clothes.

When he turns on the manners and uses that educated vocabulary he learned, the women can't wait to be around him."

"Let's hope he's dangerous to the Comanche," Billy pitched in. "At least he won't find any women on the trail. That should be easier on you."

"Maybe," Corporal Henson said, strapping his pouch shut.

Billy reached over and picked up a muster report. Captain Van Dorn commanded four companies of the Second U.S. Dragoons and one company of the Fifth U.S. Infantry. Billy saw the name over a force of 135 reservation Indians and was stunned.

"Who's this white man, and how did he get command of all these Indians?"

"That's Sul Ross. His father, Shapley Ross, is the Indian agent on the Brazos Indian Reserve, but he was too sick to go."

Billy pinched his lower lip. He'd read about Shapley in other reports.

Shapley's grandfather, Lawrence Sullivan Ross, had been kidnapped as a child of six and lived with the Indians until he was rescued at 23. Shapley dealt with and fought Indians all his life. He knew how to speak their language.

"How did Shapley's son get to this command?" Billy asked. "He's barely twenty."

"The Indians must have a white commander, so Shapley recommended him. Said his son had grown up with Indians, including the Comanche. It seems that Little Sul, as they used to call him, just returned from the university, so he's all educated and smart. Van Dorn gave him the honorary title of captain specifically for this mission."

Billy set the report aside. "Sounds like you're going with a well-stocked army. My captain's hoping you find the Comanche and eradicate them. He says the Texas Rangers have made us look incompetent."

"Don't worry," Henson said, picking up his pouch and a box of supplies. "Our scouts will find every last Indian there is and turn their villages into ashes."

Henson headed out the door.

"Make sure this place is organized when I get back."

"I will," Billy said as he hobbled to the window to watch Henson leave.

He wondered what it was like to be on the trail and face danger. The idea was terrifying and exciting at the same time; it made his heart quicken. But then he refocused and emptied the papers from the top file.

Captain Van Dorn stretched his arms wide and gazed at the vast horizon. The turquoise sky meant there was no chance of rain, so his troops would have clear weather for the attack.

"The men are mustered, sir," the lieutenant reported.

Captain Van Dorn removed his hat, smoothed back his blond hair, and stared out at the troops. They had been riding north for one full week.

"Men, I have good news. Our scouts have located Buffalo Hump and the Comanche. They are camped on the west side of Rush Creek. Next to them is a Wichita village. According to the scouts, the Comanche often steal horses from the Wichita Indians. Why they are next to them right now? I have no idea."

At this, he shook his head. "Perhaps the Comanche attacked them and took over the village. Or maybe they are roasting the dead over fires. Who knows? The only thing for certain is a large mess of Comanche is just waiting to be slaughtered. And make no mistake about it, I intend that we are the troop to make it happen."

A loud "Huzzah!" rippled through the troops. The men were getting pumped up.

"Listen up," Van Dorn said, using his arms to quiet the troops. "We ride immediately. It's a day away, and I want to get close so we are rested and ready to hit them with everything we've got. Grab your gear and mount up. We'll show those Comanche the U.S. Cavalry can fight just as good or better than any Texas Ranger."

Another loud "Huzzah!" and the troops were dismissed. It was time to get the fight on.

Buffalo Hump sat in front of his teepee, hungrily digging into a tender chunk of buffalo. He was content since he'd just completed a peace treaty with Captain Prince of Fort Arbuckle. The white man promised not to attack Buffalo Hump so long as his people stopped raiding and killing white men, which he excelled at.

Prince gave him plenty of blankets and other essentials in exchange for this treaty. The best part was that the great chief could remain in the wild and on his people's land instead of rotting on a reservation waiting for the white man to feed him.

As if the day couldn't get any better, he also made peace with the Wichita by returning dozens of horses his people had stolen. It was the first part of this long-awaited peace conference.

Buffalo Hump was tired of all the fighting and dying, so he was settling scores and healing old wounds. It was time to live. Today was the first day of the rest of his *peaceful* life.

A warrior came running into his camp and skidded to a stop. Buffalo Hump leaned to the left to avoid the small dust cloud and sighed. It was always something.

"Yes, what is it?" he said, mostly disinterested.

"The bluecoats are nearby!" the warrior blurted out. "Maybe a hundred, and they ride with another hundred reservation Indians."

Buffalo Hump kept eating, refusing to look at the warrior. "Don't worry about it. I just signed a peace treaty with the bluecoats at Fort Arbuckle."

Another chief, Hair Bobbed On One Side, sat with Over The Buttes and spoke up. "It is nothing. They are probably riding to Fort Arbuckle."

"But the white man lies," Over The Buttes said.

Over The Buttes had disagreed with signing any of the white man's treaties and was now suspicious of all the bluecoats nearby.

He continued. "Remember, the white man said the food would arrive on the reservation and it did not. He said he would help make a crop and he did not. White men dress up like us and steal horses and kill other white men and we are blamed. I don't trust the white man with their blue coats and yellow stripes."

Buffalo Hump waved a massive rib bone at Over The Buttes and smiled blandly. "I do, and that's all that matters."

He turned to the warrior who had delivered the news. "The bluecoats will not bother us. I have Captain Prince's word in writing. Let's feast tonight and celebrate."

Captains Van Dorn and Sul Ross crawled up the crest of a small hill and pulled out their spyglasses, placing the eyepiece against their cheeks. Through the first hint of light, each man studied the scene before them.

Morning fog covered the ground, allowing only the tops of the Comanche teepees and domed grass huts of the Wichita to be seen. Between the Comanche camp and Wichita village was a large remuda of horses.

In the early light, the gray shades eliminated details. But from what was visible, it was almost too good to be true.

"I don't believe it," Captain Van Dorn said quietly as the two men crawled backward. "We've hit the motherlode. They should've set out pickets because they have no idea we're here. Prepare your men to be conquering heroes."

"Should I take the scouts and stampede their horses?" Sul Ross asked, trying hard to hide the excitement on his face.

"Yes, absolutely," Van Dorn replied, getting to his feet. "You may be young, but you surely understand this game of war."

"I'll get going," Ross said, dusting himself off.

"As soon as I see you waving a hat high over your head, I'll blow the bugles and charge. Get your men ready."

Before Ross could leave, Van Dorn grabbed his arm and pulled him back. "And do it very, very quietly, Captain."

"Sir, the first noise you'll hear is the horses running for their lives."

"Perfect."

Van Dorn walked back to his lieutenant and formed the men in two long columns, one hundred yards apart, with a guide on the right side. He ordered the left column to attack the south side of the Comanche camp while the right column swung around and raced ahead. He wanted those men to come back down from the north.

"Lieutenant," Van Dorn barked, "I'll command the south attack and you'll command the north attack. I'll give you four minutes before I sound the bugles. When you hear them, hold your line until we begin the attack. Captain Ross will soon be taking a position on the east side, and with the creek on the west, the Comanche will flee north, straight into your hands. I expect a lot of dead Indians from your men."

"Yes, sir," the lieutenant said before hustling off.

Captain Van Dorn led his troops to a position south of the two Indian camps. He sat high on his horse, watching Ross and his scouts disappear into the morning fog. Suddenly, a whoosh of vapor swirled up and horses dashed out, racing south through the Wichita village, damaging portions as they stormed through.

Van Dorn took in the smoke drifting lazily from the tops of the Comanche teepees. For a brief second, he chuckled, confident the enemy was fast asleep under thick buffalo hides.

Let's see how ready you are for me, Mr. Buffalo Hump.

Van Dorn spotted Ross waving his hat and gave the signal. The bugle blew and his men sprinted the five hundred yards, cutting through the fog.

The first thing they saw was a horde of panicked Comanche warriors running for their horses. At least a hundred went to get their mounts only to discover the horses were long gone. Now that they were afoot, the dragoons rode in and fired on anything that moved.

In seconds, Comanche men and women lay face down in puddles of blood, lapped up by the black dirt their heads were smashed into. But the firing of rifles and pistols didn't stop.

Sixty seconds after the first shot, every Comanche male had exited their teepee and armed themselves with whatever they could grab. It was their job to protect the women, children, and old men, to give them time to retreat to safety and stay alive, even if it meant giving up their own lives. And on this October morning, they surely would.

As planned, the retreating Comanche ran straight into well-armed dragoons riding down from the north. The northern cavalry showed the same amount of mercy as the riders from the south: none.

In a panic, the fleeing Comanche turned west and ran to the creek, helplessly splashing in the shallow water. As the floating bodies proved, they were easy pickings for the soldiers.

It didn't take long for the Comanche to figure out that due east was the only direction to go.

Through the fog, gun smoke, dust, and chaos of battle, Buffalo Hump led his warriors past the soldiers to several ravines, using bushes and thick brush to hide in. The soldiers saw this move and pursued the chief and his men. Leading the attack was Captain Sul Ross.

After stampeding the horses, Ross moved up from the southeast to form an eastern line. It didn't take long to become fully engaged in the hot action.

Comanche warriors ran straight into Ross's blazing guns. At one point, he worried about overheating the barrels or running out of ammunition. But that thought left him as he saw some squaws and old men brush past him.

Ross focused on the group and realized they carried a white child with them.

"Pursue!" Ross yelled to Lieutenant Cornelius Van Camp and two privates. "Grab that child!"

One of the privates snatched the small white girl and shot the squaw in the back. The rest of the fleeing group escaped through the fog.

The four soldiers gave up their pursuit and turned around to head back to the Comanche camp. As they took the first few steps, their stomachs dropped. Through the fog, twenty-five angry warriors appeared.

Before Ross could issue an order, Lieutenant Van Camp and a private were hit with a barrage of arrows, at least one piercing their hearts. The two collapsed and died on the spot.

Captain Ross felt an arrow slice into his shoulder, causing him to drop his carbine. He staggered back away from the advancing warriors and watched in horror as one of the warriors bent over and picked up Ross's weapon. It was all slow motion, even as the Comanche lifted the barrel and fired the rifle—*his* rifle—at *his* chest.

Ross fell onto his back, maroon liquid spurting from his chest.

The warrior who had just shot him dropped the carbine and reached around to pull out a long knife. As he approached Ross, the blade glinted in the first rays of the sun.

Ross knew he was about to lose his scalp, followed by his life, so he threw up his one good arm to grab the knife—anything to stop from being scalped. Suddenly, Ross had a revelation.

Post Oak

"Mohee? Is that you?"

The warrior stopped and stared hard at Ross.

"Mohee! It's me, Little Sul."

Incredibly, the two had played together as children. They even saw each other occasionally as they grew up.

"Please don't hurt me," Ross begged. "Mohee, please!"

Mohee hesitated, unsure what to do until an explosion ended the conversation. Ross felt guts all over his face and chest before passing out. He was not long for this world.

Captain Van Dorn, winding through the Comanche camp and still mounted on his trusty horse, blasted away, dropping warriors right and left.

Any idiot can do this, he thought.

As he swung his horse left, an arrow struck his stomach.

A belly wound, he thought, looking down at half the shaft sticking out. *I won't survive this. It's all over for me.*

He closed his eyes and slid out of the saddle.

Ten hours later, evening had settled over the blood-soaked prairie. The federal troops controlled the Comanche camp and Wichita village.

Sul Ross had been stretchered to the middle of the camp, where a surgeon operated on him. When he came to, another lieutenant gave him a report.

"Wh-What h-happened?" Ross stammered.

"You were about to be scalped, sir, and Lieutenant Majors used a shotgun to save your life. Two privates shot at the others and they ran for their lives."

"Mohee," Ross mumbled. "I'm s-so sorry."

"Sir?" the lieutenant said. He turned to a surgeon standing nearby. "Who's Mohee?"

"He's still groggy from the surgery," the doctor said. "Better let him rest."

"Wh-Where's Van Dorn?" Ross managed.

The lieutenant bent over and spoke close to Ross's ear. "He's still alive, sir, but barely. Took an arrow right in his belly button. The boys are saying he's a *naval* hero."

Ross failed to acknowledge the joke. "Did we rescue the little white girl?" he asked, his voice losing its power.

"Another warrior grabbed her, and we shot him. He was still alive, so we had to cut his throat, but we got the girl back."

The lieutenant noticed Ross's eyes closing. "Sir, the doctor says you will stay here for several more days until we can stretcher you back to the supply camp."

Ross closed his eyes and passed out, not hearing the last part.

Soon, his wounds became infected and so painful he begged and pleaded for someone to shoot him. No one would oblige.

While the two captains recovered, the troops burned everything to the ground. Nothing was left.

The nearby fields that grew tobacco, melons, and corn for Wichita were thoroughly destroyed. Their permanent grass huts were lit on fire, creating a nighttime glow in the sky that could be seen for fifty miles.

The troops even found the Wichita's winter food store and burned it all.

Known for their hospitality, the Wichita were peaceful Indians. They couldn't believe this had happened. But they had little time to think about it as they fled to Fort Arbuckle, hoping the bluecoats there would feed and protect them from *these* bluecoats. It was a terrible way to live.

The troops rounded up the dead Comanche and Wichita's—seventy warriors and squaws.

Over the next several days, many more died from infected wounds, with most leaving blood trails crisscrossing the prairie during their retreat. At night, the coyotes howled for their buddies to join them as they feasted on the dead.

Then it was time to review the butcher's bill. The dragoons and infantry had lost four men, with one missing and presumed dead or soon to be. Twelve men were wounded, including Van Dorn and Ross. Still, it was a one-sided victory.

In a daring feat of bravery and leadership, Buffalo Hump had organized his men and slipped into the brush near several ravines. The cavalry mounted and searched for them one bush at a time. This is where the soldiers were killed and wounded, as hand-to-hand combat was the order of the day.

After ninety minutes of close fighting, Buffalo Hump and his remaining warriors escaped through a hidden ravine. Every Comanche left with whatever they had on their backs. With winter coming, it would be tough to survive.

Ten miles away, Buffalo Hump stopped at a clear stream and took some water. He looked back at the fires burning his camp and pounded the ground, cursing loudly.

"The white man lied to me, and I will have my revenge!" he said to no one in particular.

He led his group farther north. They would have to die another day.

Van Dorn and Ross remained on the battlefield for five days until the pair were transported to the supply camp forty miles away. Ross was set on a litter between two mules. When the terrain turned rough, men stepped forward and carried his litter on their shoulders until they reached the supply camp, where the wounded would begin to heal.

Eventually, they made it back to Fort Belknap and better medical care. Sul Ross continued to feel pain over the next year. Miraculously, both men recovered enough to return to active duty.

As for the Wichita, an outraged Captain Prince at Fort Arbuckle took care of them—for a while. But it was the beginning of the end for the poor Wichita. Soon, they would be reservation Indians and never go back to their lands.

Once he was better, Van Dorn wrote a report detailing the attack and Ross's bravery. Newspapers across Texas and the country picked up the story, with exaggeration playing up the dead Comanche and Wichita's, along with the three hundred horses recovered.

Finally, the U.S. Army had subdued the feared Comanche. Both Van Dorn and Ross were celebrated.

The Wichita Village Fight, as it was soon called, was a tragedy of monumental proportions, a typical case of the right hand not knowing what the left hand was doing. Yet facts never stopped the spread of a good story.

Earl Van Dorn continued his womanizing and military career. When the Civil War arrived, he resigned his U.S. Army commission and rose to major general in the Confederate Army. He led troops and cavalry into many of the critical Civil War battles.

During one of the Confederate Army's military campaigns, Van Dorn made his headquarters in Spring Hill, Tennessee. On May 7, 1863, Earl Van Dorn was shot and killed by Dr. George B. Peters for committing adultery with Peters' wife.

Despite his success on the battlefield, some in the south chastised Van Dorn for his womanizing. Others honored him, at least until the Confederacy lost. Yet no one had a problem with his raid on Buffalo Hump and the Comanche days after the U.S. government signed a treaty with them.

During World War II, the U.S. Army set up Camp Van Dorn in his honor as a training camp in Mississippi. It's likely no Comanche attended.

Chapter Twenty-Four

Puhtocnocony sat on his horse, watching the white man reemerge from the fort. It was a beautiful day, and they had not ridden far. This raid would be over fast, and then they could head back to their camp north across the Red River.

These white men and their pathetic fort had horses and women to steal. Puhtocnocony planned to get one of the horses to build up his herd. He had big aspirations for himself.

The white man carried some food out in an attempt to appease the hundreds of mounted Comanche, Wichita, Kiowas, and Caddos. Each time these white insects built forts and houses, they scared away the game. Deer and antelope disappeared. Buffalo steered clear.

Homestead by homestead, these white invaders destroyed the Comanche's way of life. They all had to go.

Chief Tall Tree kicked his horse closer to one of these white men and, without warning, thrust his lance into the man's shoulder. The white man screamed and fell to his knees. This was good because screaming meant the man's medicine had broken.

The warrior beside Chief Tall Tree stuck his lance into the man's belly. Dipped with buffalo dung, a belly wound was always fatal. If the victim didn't bleed to death, a powerful sickness soon snuffed out their spirit. All Comanche knew that and usually aimed for the belly button with their lances and arrows.

Puhtocnocony avoided the crowd who wanted to stick their lances into the white man and count coup. Instead, he hurried his horse through the large gates and inside the fort, dismounting to catch a white girl.

She was young, too young, so he tossed her against a wall and went looking for more whites. He found one—a man pointing a rifle at him.

Blam!

Puhtocnocony fell backward and saw part of his right side blown off. Chaos erupted around him. It was difficult to see what was happening.

Chief Tall Tree soon established order and sent a squaw to attend to Puhtocnocony. It was late afternoon when he was able to sit up.

One of his friends had found some white paint and rubbed it all over his body. His friend urged Puhtocnocony to take some, but Puhtocnocony said no.

Soon, his friend was choking and gasping, his eyes bulging from their sockets. The sick warrior dropped to his knees, begging for help, yet Puhtocnocony could do nothing. He was hurt himself and didn't want to move for fear of ripping open the wound. All he could do was watch as some evil force killed his friend.

Puhtocnocony opened his eyes and tossed back the buffalo hide. Sitting upright, a light sheen of sweat coated his face. He wiped it off and blinked several times.

The dark dream again. Many times, it had visited Puhtocnocony, forcing him to watch his friend die from the white man's paint. Each time, Puhtocnocony could do nothing to save him.

He rubbed the old wound from Parker's Fort. On certain mornings, it still hurt.

A leg kicked his shin, and a woman rolled over in her sleep. It was Naduah, the white girl he'd tossed against the fence all those years earlier. She was under the buffalo hide with him, snoring.

Wide awake now, he crawled past Naduah and his two sons, Quanah and Pee-nah. They slept through anything.

Outside, he found a few embers from a dead fire and stoked it back to life. Darkness covered the camp, but the morning was almost here.

As Puhtocnocony rested against a log, warming himself, he noticed an old man sitting at another fire, some distance off. Puhtocnocony got up and went to him. It was Buffalo Hump.

"You are up early," Puhtocnocony said. "Can I get you something to eat?"

"That's a woman's work," the old chief said, staring into the fire and fingering a red-beaded necklace. "If I want something, I'll wake a woman."

Puhtocnocony was about to say more but decided to remain silent. He could see the chief was upset.

Ten minutes later, the crackling and popping of the fire was the only noise around, except for some loud snoring coming from a nearby teepee. Puhtocnocony drew his knees in to get up and return to his own fire, but the legendary chief spoke.

"The white man comes near our camp and soon our people die of sickness. The white man moves onto our land and destroys it. After the bluecoats attacked us at the Wichita village, I promised my men that we would seek revenge. But each day after our escape, I counted less and less. One moon later, many were dead from their wounds, and I was left with barely enough to hunt game for the surviving women and children. Though I want to with all my heart, I don't have enough warriors to raid and fight the white man. I want to give you a few men, but I can't spare them."

Puhtocnocony studied the chief's face. There used to be thin creeks and shallow ravines. All he saw now were deep canyons running up and down the old man's soul.

This was the same man who had led a nation to the Great Waters, ripping a gaping wound through the white man's world. It had been an impossible feat, yet Buffalo Hump had done it because he had good medicine.

The Great Spirit loved and protected this strong man. Now, seeing him defeated and his spirit dying like an ember on the outer edge of the fire, it was difficult and sobering.

"Join your people with ours," Puhtocnocony said. "Take our daughters as wives. Make more warriors. In the meantime, we can raid and steal the white man's young boys. Raise them as warriors to fight and kill the white man."

Buffalo Hump raised his head and stared directly into Puhtocnocony's eyes. "You have been good to us, He Who Travels Alone and Returns. You have been good to me. I am sorry I could not be there to fight with your father, Iron Jacket. He was a great loss."

Buffalo Hump hesitated. "How are your two boys from the white squaw?"

"Pee-nah is too young to fight. But I am soon taking Quanah on his first raid. Naduah is worried about him."

Buffalo Hump nodded, still staring at the fire. "The Eagle Dance turns boys into warriors. But at some point, all boys must become men in battle. They will either live or die. It is not up to us; only the Great Spirit decides when each of us dies."

This time, it was Puhtocnocony who nodded. "Women worry. Men fight. It will always be so."

"Maybe," the chief muttered. "Maybe not. But for now, *you* must seek the revenge I desire. Kill and destroy the white man. Destroy their way of life before they destroy ours."

Puhtocnocony reached out a hand and patted the old man's scarred thigh. Then he leaned back against the log and closed his eyes, soaking in the sounds of nature before it was all gone.

Soon, the rest of the camp would emerge from their slumber and teepees. Fires would be stoked and food cooked. But at this moment, all was quiet and perfect. There was still hope of what the day might bring.

Unlike his dark dream, Puhtocnocony could act and make a difference. He could save the Comanche's way of life.

Corporal Billy Tyler was back at Fort Belknap. Once again, he sat facing Captain Robinson, his superior.

Life on the western frontier had made Robinson gruff and surly. When he first arrived, he had a neatly trimmed beard. Now, it was unkempt and wild, holding crumbs from a hastily eaten breakfast or maybe last night's supper.

Robinson was also a jealous man, hating any officer who achieved some success. One thing he was not was a deep thinker. He cared very little about new ideas and instead clung to tactics that had worked in the past.

It was this kind of thinking that infected the military. "Don't think. Just do. Let Washington do the thinking." That kind of order was just what Robinson preferred: no thinking.

In his hand, Captain Robinson held the most recent field action report. But this time, it was written by federal soldiers about the Texas Rangers and their recent raids. And it was damning.

Post Oak

"Ha! Drunken rangers looking for Peta Nocona. Their horses stampeded at night. Had to return home on foot. This report says they remounted, went out, and crossed the Red River. Drank and fought among themselves until the Comanche burned the prairie around them, making sure their horses couldn't eat. Returned home to embarrassment and shame."

Robinson slapped the desk. "Reading reports like this puts me in such a good mood I almost want the troops to take a few days off and go into town. Almost."

He was no fan of the rangers and their disorderly ways.

"I've been so tired of listening to people say how great these Texas Rangers are, and now we all know the truth. They're nothing but a bunch of dirty, ragged drunks. It's a miracle they weren't all slaughtered."

Billy grinned insincerely and said nothing. He knew better than to ruin the captain's good mood.

Captain Robinson dropped the report and picked up a newspaper from Weatherford, *The White Man*. It was always filled with good stories about the Texas Rangers' incompetence.

"Look here," Robinson said, tapping the front page. "John Baylor says the rangers are worthless and their colonel is lovestruck. He declares that if anyone in Weatherford finds a ranger, they will hang that man. It won't be long before these Texans start looking to us to solve their problems. We're the only ones who can wipe out the Comanche."

Billy felt this was the best chance he'd ever have to bring glory and honor to himself, so he decided to act. Removing a lead bullet from his pocket, he set it on the desk.

"What's this?" the captain asked.

"It's a fifty-two-caliber bullet from a Sharps rifle. The hunting party that came through here a few days back gave it to me."

"And why would they do that?"

"This bullet can rid us of the buffalo," Billy said confidently.

"Oh really? So you have all the answers? Please tell me all about your secret weapon so we can win the war right now." The captain's good mood disappeared fast.

Billy swallowed and went forward even though this would be a tough sell. "Those men were killing buffalo. The hides fetch a good price back east. They're making a lot of money killing buffalo."

"So?"

"The main hunter told me the buffalo don't move or run when he shoots one dead. They just stand there, right next to their dead buddy or brother. He told me he shot fifty in one day and had to stop because he ran out of ammunition. If we stocked these bullets, he could've kept killing buffalo."

Listening to the young corporal, the captain leaned back. Since he said nothing, Billy continued.

"I have read all the reports from the very beginning of this fort and all the ones at Camp Cooper when I went down there to help out. I also saw copies of reports from the other forts and even the Texas Rangers. What I learned is that every time our men contact the Comanche, they find buffalo hides, blankets, and shields made of buffalo, and the bones are used as tools. They use every part of the buffalo to survive. If we stockpile boxes of these bullets, maybe give away Sharps rifles and ammunition to hunters, they can kill all the buffalo. We can starve the Indians to death. Then, a hungry Indian will come to the reservation and stay there if we feed them like we promised."

Captain Robinson leaned forward and stroked his beard, sending a few crumbs to the desk. "That's very interesting because I recently read a report that claimed there are maybe forty or fifty million buffalo roaming the frontier. During one mission, I saw a herd run past us for two days. There were buffalo as far as a man could see. And you say this hunter killed fifty in one day?"

"Yes," Billy replied cautiously, unsure which direction this was heading.

Robinson grabbed a pencil and started scratching on a piece of paper.

"Let's say we get a hundred men to kill fifty buffalo a day. Five, aught, aught, aught. That's five thousand a day. With the bad weather at times and not being able to find any buffalo, let's say the hunters can kill buffalo four months each year. Aught, aught, aught. That comes to six hundred thousand a year. Let's go ahead and say more men come, and they hunt longer each year. Somehow, the hunters kill one million buffalo each year. That means the buffalo will be completely dead in thirty-five to fifty years. Oh, and that assumes the buffalo never produces another calf. But you and I know fifteen million females will produce at least one calf each year. So cull that way down and say the buffalo herd adds only one million new calves each year. Since the hunters are killing one million a year, they will never get ahead. Right?"

Billy frowned. "Sir, the government could help transport the buffalo hides back east and provide security for the hunters. We don't have to kill every buffalo, just half of them. The Indians in the wild will have to fight each other for more land and hunting rights. Those Indians who lose will starve. If we start now, we can make a difference, maybe cut the herd down in half in five to seven years."

The captain's expression remained unchanged as Billy slid his detailed report to him. He had spent so much time and energy on those three pieces of paper that he couldn't fathom it was for naught.

"Sir, we can't beat the Comanche in a straight-up fight. They are too fast, too clever, and too accurate with their arrows. But we can starve them to death. Each settler we protect permanently rips up the prairie grass with their crude plows and mules. No prairie grass means no buffalo. The animals that live will be killed by our hunters. Between our human diseases and the death of the buffalo, we don't ever have to fight the Comanche," he said with conviction. "We just need to disease and starve them to death."

The captain tented his fingers. "Son, you stick to clerking and I'll stick to fighting. Until you ride out with us and see death up close, you have nothing to offer the army. Get back to work. I don't want to hear no more talk about giving away free bullets, or rifles, or killing fifty million buffalo." He chuckled after saying the words *fifty million*.

"We'll do the fighting, and you do the clerking."

"Knock knock," a man said at the entrance to Captain Robinson's office. "May I come in?"

"Bruno!" the captain said, rushing to greet the man. "Do you have my new sword?"

"Fresh from the forge," Bruno said.

He turned to Billy. "And you are?"

Billy thrust out his hand. "Corporal William Tyler, sir."

The blade salesman shook it. "Bruno de la Huerta at your service."

"Billy has been telling me his idea to get rid of the Comanche," Captain Robinson said. "How long did you tell me the Spanish have been fighting them?"

"The Comanche? Oh my, well, we have been fighting them for more than a hundred years. They pushed out the Apache and killed many Spanish and Mexican citizens. They are a scourge to our world."

"Billy wants to kill fifty million buffalo and starve them out," Robinson said condescendingly.

"I see," Bruno said. "That is a lot of killing."

"Unfortunately, the corporal here has never been in the field. So he doesn't know anything."

The captain glared at Billy.

"You can leave now. Bruno and I have some business to discuss."

Billy's face flushed red as he crutched back to his desk. Slumping in his chair, he sighed.

Through the thin wall, he heard the captain wad up his report and throw it in the trash. Billy rubbed his deformed leg and gritted his teeth.

If only I could prove I'm right.

November 26, 1860
Five miles northeast of present-day Jacksboro, Texas

Chief Puhtocnocony studied the creek in the morning light. A beaver picked its way through the water, searching for an early meal.

A slight movement to his left caught the chief's attention. It was his two scouts returning.

"What did you find?" Puhtocnocony asked.

"The man and his boy are cutting wood over that rise, too far to join his family when we attack. The house has no man there. A woman, a girl, and some children."

Puhtocnocony glanced around at the painted black faces. One of them was Quanah's.

They had done well to get this far in the white man's land. By camping without fire and enduring the cold, he had led them through the massive Cross Timbers section that ran north and south from the Red River down to Austin. By following the bent-over post oaks that pointed out the way, it had been relatively easy.

Staying in the trees hid their presence. But this tactic also allowed the rangers and bluecoats to sneak up on them. That's why Puhtocnocony had continually sent scouts in all directions. He didn't want to be exposed to the enemy on this revenge raid. All he wanted to do was kill, steal, and destroy whites.

Puhtocnocony nodded and tapped his horse with his foot. It was time to get moving.

Inside the house, Katherine Masterson, fifteen, and her sister, Jane, twelve, rolled dough in the kitchen. One was making bread, and the other was forming yeast rolls.

Their mother, Mrs. Landman, supervised everything. She married James Landman after her first husband, Mr. Masterson, died.

With Mr. Landman, she had two boys, Lewis, six, and John, her baby. It was the older Lewis who sounded the warning.

"Injuns coming!" he cried.

Mrs. Landman ran to the front door and cracked it open just in time to see an Indian put his fist up and push her back into the living room. As she fell onto her back, she was horrified to see his face and half-nude body painted black. A scarlet slash ran diagonally across his face and over his left eye.

Before she could take in a breath, the Indian was on top of her, stabbing the life out of this mother of six. When the two girls rushed to their mother's aid, they were wrapped up by other males and dragged outside. Their last vision of the house was seeing their little half-brother Lewis scalped alive, screaming in terror before they cut his throat.

But they didn't have time to cry. Katherine was set on a horse and Jane was tied to a rope and dragged behind another mounted Indian. It was too bad their father and older brother were away cutting wood for the winter. It wouldn't be needed now.

Once inside, Puhtocnocony directed his men to cut open the beds and spread the ticking and feathers everywhere. Then, his men went through all the belongings, taking anything that suited them.

"Fire?" a warrior asked his chief.

"No," Puhtocnocony replied. "The others will see the smoke and be ready for us. Leave it and the baby, too."

He turned to a scout. "Where is the next house?"

"That way," the scout said, pointing west through the trees. "Near the creek."

Puhtocnocony spotted Quanah guarding the horses. Quanah saw firsthand what he would be doing for the rest of his life, and Puhtocnocony wanted to make sure the boy wasn't shocked.

He wasn't.

"Let's go," the chief ordered.

Like the Landmans, the Gage family was busy. Mrs. Calvin Gage and her mother, Katy, supervised work in the kitchen.

Scattered about were five children: Matilda, fourteen; Mary Ann, ten; Hiram, eight; Jonathan, five; and Polly, eighteen months.

A mile away, looking for a second ox, was Joseph, sixteen. He had already penned one ox and needed to bring in the other one.

His father, Calvin, had been the county judge of Jack County when, a year earlier, he'd been thrown from a horse and died. Calvin Gage had been a respected man. Now, Joseph was the man of the house and doing his best to keep everything in order.

In the hot kitchen, the Gage women sweated. A woman's screams drew their attention to the front yard.

They opened the front door to see a warrior dragging their neighbor, Jane Masterson, behind a pony. The rider was painted black with a scarlet stripe running over his left eye and diagonally down his face.

Before they could fully comprehend this scene, the Indians were inside the house. They shot Mrs. Calvin Gage with several arrows and cracked her head with a club for good measure.

Her mother, Katy, was thrown on the dining room floor and stabbed at least four times.

The teenager, Matilda, was tied up and placed on a horse next to her neighbor, Katherine Masterson. So was young Hiram.

"Shut her up!" Puhtocnocony ordered, pointing at the screaming woman on the ground.

She'd been dragged a mile over rough terrain from the Landman house and was still alive. Several warriors stepped forward and brutally slayed Jane.

Her sister, Katherine, and teenage neighbor, Matilda Gage, screamed in horror as some of the blood hit their legs. Hiram refused to watch. Then Polly, the baby, began crying.

"Shut it up, too," Puhtocnocony barked.

A warrior grabbed the baby and tossed her high into the air. She landed with a thud on the cold, hard ground.

He did it several more times, leaving the baby for dead. With that done, the band of warriors took off for the next house.

Halfway there, Katherine and Matilda were nearly stripped bare, molested, and thrown on the ground.

The band continued on with little Hiram and whatever loot they had collected from the Gage and Landman households.

Once free of the Indians, the two half-dressed girls heard a bell ringing. It was Matilda's brother, Joseph. He must have found the missing ox and was leading it to the pen, as the animal wore a bell around its neck.

"We have to warn him!" Matilda cried, barely coherent. "He'll be killed if we don't."

The two girls ran toward the sound of the bell and stumbled face forward into Joseph. He was stunned at the sight before him.

"What happened to you?" he asked, lifting his distraught neighbor to her feet.

"Indians!" Katherine cried, trying to cover her body. "They came to our house and yours, too."

Joseph took off his jacket and covered her up. He didn't have anything for his sister, so the three carefully approached the Gage house and made sure the Indians had left.

Creeping inside, they found bed ticking and feathers everywhere. It was like it had snowed inside.

Among the chaos was his mother. She was alive but barely. So was Katy, his grandmother, and ten-year-old Mary Ann.

Outside, five-year-old Jonathan had been beaten but could still walk. And miraculously, so was baby Polly. Not one of the Gage family left behind died.

Unfortunately, one year later, little Hiram's bones were found a mile away. He had either been murdered or left in the cold to fend for himself and froze to death.

Another year after the boy's bones were discovered, Mrs. Gage died of the wounds from this attack. Folks whispered that she almost willed herself to go.

For settlers on the frontier, they understood. They either readied themselves each day for a fight to the death or suffered the consequences of an Indian attack. There was no middle ground.

Chapter Twenty-Five

November 27, 1860
Sixteen miles northwest of Weatherford, Texas

Holding a lantern, John Brown sang to his horses. They were corralled in a peach orchard near his house, waiting to be fed.

He loved spending time with horses; this time before sunrise was the best of the day. He had their full attention and enjoyed every minute.

Even though the Weatherford-Jacksboro road was a hundred yards away, in the quiet stillness of the early morning, John could hear the horse clops. The animal moved fast.

Instead of riding on, it turned onto his property and headed straight toward him. John couldn't imagine who would be out at this hour, as it was dangerous to ride in the dark.

A horse might trip in a rut and send the rider to his death. It happened constantly, especially with prairie dog towns everywhere. Only Indians were daring enough to try it.

Then it hit him. *Could this be a Comanche?*

Before he could run to the house and get his gun, the horse was on him. The rider leaped off and ran at him. In the light of his lantern, John saw it was a white man.

"Comanche!" he yelled out breathlessly. "They attacked us in Jack County. I'm headed to Weatherford to raise the alarm and ask for help in burying the dead."

John stepped back. "Comanche?" he said as he gazed up at the sky.

Even though the moon had disappeared, it had been the second night of a waxing moon, almost a Comanche moon, as they called it on the frontier. Whenever a Comanche moon appeared, the settlers prepared themselves for death.

"Oh no," John said. "What can I do?"

"I need a fresh horse," the rider said.

"You've got it. Let me fix you up with one."

John expertly removed the man's saddle and tack and put it on his fastest horse. Then he sent the man off.

John picked up his lantern and hurried to the house to warn Mary, his wife.

"What are you doing?" she asked as he packed some food and water. "Are you daft?"

"I'm heading off to warn the Thompsons," John replied.

"B-But shouldn't you stay here and protect us?"

"Yes, as soon as I warn the Thompsons. I couldn't live with myself if they got slaughtered and I could have told them what was happening. Grab the slaves and children and tell them to be on the lookout. Hide in the loft if you must but do it now. I'll be back shortly."

John ran to the corral and searched through his thirty-five horses for Barney, the slowest one. If the Indians came and he had to jump off and run for it, he didn't want to lose a good horse. Let them steal Barney.

Once Barney was saddled up, John Brown took off just as the sun peeked over the forest. A mile away from his house, he realized he had not brought a firearm.

Oh well, he thought. *Hopefully, I won't see any Indians. At least I have my trusty pocketknife if I do.*

Back at the Brown house, the two slaves lingered in the yard, staring down the road. One was an older woman, and the other was a young boy, Anthony, about fourteen.

"Do you think dey come?" Anthony asked.

"Maybe," the woman said.

Then she heard it. Horses. Lots of them.

She ran to a stump in the yard and climbed up, looking far down the road. Shielding her eyes from the eastern sun, she spotted fifty or sixty horses, each with a painted-black Indian on top.

"We gotta run for it!" she said to the boy.

"No," Anthony said. "I'll die with de missus and chilluns."

Before the woman could object, Anthony ran toward the house. She watched him go and took off for the high grass in the peach orchard. With any luck, they wouldn't spot her.

"Injuns coming!" Anthony cried to Mrs. Brown as he flung open the front door and sprinted inside.

Panicked, she gathered up her four children: Mary, ten; John, eight; Teranna, five; and Seaph, two months.

"Go upstairs, now!" she screamed.

The place was considered a log cabin mansion because it had an upstairs loft that was reached by a ladder. As soon as the children and Anthony were in the room, Mrs. Brown closed and locked the trapdoor.

No way you're getting in here, she thought.

She worked on calming herself, breathing slowly to get her brain working. Seeing her children around her and safe, she knew she was blessed.

In seconds, the Indians surrounded the house, whooping and hollering. It was tense, but Mrs. Brown felt very safe in this place. Suddenly, her heart skipped a beat.

"Wait!" she said as sheer panic raced from her stomach to her throat, constricting it. "Where's Annie?"

Annie was two and a half years old and not in the loft.

"Oh no!" she sobbed. "My Annie. My poor Annie. She'll be scalped alive."

"I'll get her," Anthony said, reaching for the trap door. "You keep de ax."

"But the Indians are here," she said, grabbing his arm. "John told me never to open the trap door. Never."

Before she could stop him, Anthony pulled up the door and quietly slipped down the ladder. Mary locked the door and sat on it in a pool of fear. Without the boy to help fight off the Indians, it was just her and the ten-year-old Mary. John, eight, couldn't even lift the ax.

"Where are you?" she cried out to her missing husband.

Minutes passed before Mrs. Brown heard a soft knock on the trap door. She had read all about the Indian's tricks and how they got people to open gates and doors, so she was sure the savages were an inch below her knees. Then she heard something.

"Missus, it's me."

Shaking with fear, Mrs. Brown moved over and opened the door only to see her boy slave carrying the baby. He had just saved the child's life—for a few more moments, at least.

"Where was she?" Mary bawled as she held her precious baby.

"In de kitchen house out back, missus. She was dipping ashes with a spoon."

"Oh, my love," Mary cried. "I thought I'd lost you."

The sounds of chains rattling soon reached her ears. John had chains next to the bits in the horse's mouth. Rattling chains meant he was home. He could protect them now.

Mary got up and peeked out the only window. The last thing she saw was feathers as an arrow struck her forehead, sending her backward and crashing to the wood floor.

Located two miles away on Rock Creek, the nearby Thompsons never received any warning. Instead, they heard the Indians coming and watched from a secured house as the savages stole their horse herd and merged it with the horses belonging to John Brown and others. For whatever reason, they turned southwest toward Palo Pinto County and disappeared.

The next morning, John Brown was found under a blanket of snow halfway between the two homesteads. He had been lanced several times, scalped, and his nose cut off.

A pocketknife was found close to the body. Apparently, he had wounded at least one Indian because a dead Comanche was discovered nearby. Other blood trails showed perhaps two more were wounded. It had been a valiant fight.

The female slave who didn't go into the house survived. She had hidden in some tall grass under a peach tree.

She told everyone she would have surely died if not for the tree because the Indians moved the horses all around. It was a miracle she wasn't trampled to death.

As for Mrs. Brown, she survived the arrow strike to her head, though she was left with a permanent scar at her widow's peak, a term that now applied to her.[6]

Puhtocnocony stopped his band for a rest. Finding Quanah, he pulled him aside.

"You've done well keeping our ponies together and looking out for any white men coming. I'm holding you back because I want you to learn. We attack the whites because they are destroying us. Did you notice that as we approached each house there was no game around? The whites chase everything away and it never comes back. They break up the prairie grass and set up fences so the buffalo don't come. They bring us great sickness. Many times, our enemy tribes have tried to live with the whites. But they can't. War always breaks out. Even some of the Comanche have tried to live with the white man, but they cheat us and freeze and starve our people to death. We can't live in his world because they are too selfish and consume everything. We either fight the white man or die. That is our way. Only the Great Spirit knows the future. But today, you can see we have had good medicine."

"Good medicine," Quanah repeated.

"Except for that last white man on a slow pony, no one has injured us. We will raid one or two more houses and return to camp to drop off our horses and plunder. Don't let down your guard because the white man can kill you when you least expect it. The metal from their guns travels great distances."

"I won't let that happen," Quanah told his father.

"Round up the ponies," Puhtocnocony said. "Our scouts have found some more whites, and we need to kill them all."

---

[6] Eighteen months later, the Widow Brown married Simpson Crawford after his first wife died. Crawford was a prominent rancher in Palo Pinto County. The couple remained married for 46 years until he died in 1908.

Everyone mounted up and checked their weapons. It was time to leave this place.

The Sherman family was a happy bunch because it was raining buckets outside, yet their roof held tight. That was always a blessing. And suppertime had arrived with plenty to eat—another blessing.

Ezra Sherman, an eternal optimist, had moved his family to the most dangerous part of the western frontier. His homestead, located in eastern Palo Pinto County, was very close to the western edge of Parker County. It was a new start for him and his young family, though the two oldest kids weren't his.

Martha and her first husband had produced three children, one of whom died. Billy, now seven, and Mary, six, were all she had left after her husband passed away.

Life on the frontier moved fast, so it wasn't long before she married Ezra Sherman and produced one-year-old Joseph. Now she was pregnant again, another blessing. The Shermans had lots to be thankful for.

"Children, suppertime," Martha called. "Come and sit down."

Ezra was already at the table. Little Mary took baby Joseph and set him in a crude highchair. Billy, a rambunctious child, was playing near the window when he saw some riders coming through the storm.

"Momma, come look," he said.

Martha hurried to the window and studied the riders. "Oh no!" she cried. "It looks like Indians are coming."

Ezra got up and peered through the thick rain. "No, it's only cowboys. Don't worry about it. We'll be safe."

Martha wasn't so sure, but she sat down and let Ezra say the blessing. Then they dug into the bacon and greens, fresh cornbread, and buttermilk.

Two minutes into the meal, the riders approached the cabin. Ezra got up, opened the door, and stepped out under the roof's overhang as water poured off the edges.

There before him were five riders, one the chief. Through the rain, Ezra saw that each Indian was painted black with a scarlet line running diagonally across their forehead, left eye, and cheek. It sent chills down his spine.

The chief raised up in his stirrups and whistled loudly. Dozens of mounted Indians hidden behind a hill came racing hard and surrounded the house, but not before young Billy escaped out the back door. He ran down the road toward the neighbor's house and hid in a brush pile.

Ezra watched the first six Comanche warriors enter his house, each with a tomahawk, knife, or lance. He thought of reaching for his gun but he didn't own one, not even for snakes and coyotes. That's how confident he was of his family's safety on this untamed frontier.

As for Puhtocnocony, he had been working hard for hours, raiding houses all over Parker County. Ironically, Parker County had been named after the uncle of Puhtocnocony's wife, Naduah. But he didn't know or care about names or county lines. This was just another white family destroying his way of life.

Puhtocnocony approached the man, rubbed his belly, and said, "Hambre."

"I'm sorry," Ezra said, "but we don't have any food or drink to spare. Maybe we could give you some molasses."

The Indians stared blankly, as they didn't understand English.

Martha bravely, or foolishly, picked up a broom and swung it at the intruders. "Git," she said.

When Puhtocnocony rubbed his belly again and pointed to the food, she said, "No you ain't," either meaning the Indians weren't going to take their food or their lives.

Though she wasn't clear, it wouldn't have mattered. These warriors were on a mission; nothing would stop them from accomplishing it.

Puhtocnocony and his warriors laughed at Martha.

"This one is crazy," he said, grabbing her long chestnut hair and feeling it. "Our squaws could teach her many lessons."

Martha pulled away from the chief and pushed the long hair behind her ears.

"Look, Mom," Mary said. "Red hair."

Martha studied one of the Indians. He was tall and, sure enough, had red hair.

"Perhaps he's white," she said to Mary. "It's hard to tell."

Puhtocnocony pointed to the door. "Vamoose!"

His warriors helped usher the family outside.

Just as they stepped onto the porch, to everyone's surprise, the rain turned into snow. It was colder, too, with temperatures dropping fast. Staying too long outside in this weather like this meant death, at least to white people.

"Let's go quietly," Ezra said to his family. "Don't disturb them."

Martha handed baby Joseph to Ezra while she grabbed Mary's hand. Without a second thought, the Shermans walked due east toward their nearest neighbor, the Potts.

When they had gone several hundred yards, Ezra looked back and saw the Indians still inside the house.

"God, please protect Billy wherever he is," Ezra prayed.

Puhtocnocony and his men ate the food and ransacked the house for valuables. After discovering a barrel of molasses in the outbuilding, the Indians took turns slurping up the brown goo.

Back inside, one of the men found a thick book. The Comanche knew well that the paper in these books saved lives when used in shields.

"This means life," the Indian said to his buddy as he held it up. The words *Holy Bible* were printed on the cover.

Regardless, he stole it.

The Shermans hurried as fast as they could. Their neighbor lived two miles away.

When they had gone a mile, they heard horses racing up behind them. Before they knew it, the Comanche had them surrounded.

Two Indians jumped down and took hold of Martha.

"No!" she screamed, letting go of Mary.

"Durn you, let her be!" Ezra demanded as he moved to rescue his lovely wife. But a lance pointed at his chest pushed him back.

Ezra watched helplessly as the warriors dragged his wife toward their cabin by her long chestnut hair. Unable to do anything for Martha, Ezra gathered up his daughter and baby and took off for the Potts. Maybe they could help.

When the warriors neared the cabin, they stopped before a large brush pile and stood Martha up. Several warriors inspected the woman.

At thirty-two, she could still turn a man's head. That was why it wasn't long after her first husband had died that Ezra put a ring on her finger.

He was a confident, honest, hardworking man who seemed like a good catch. Living on the frontier had not appeared that risky.

But it was too late for Martha to consider that decision now. The only things that mattered were surviving and giving birth to her child, which was due any day.

The Indians rubbed her chest, and one of them tore her blouse. The cold wind slapped at her bare skin.

She was startled but knew where this was headed. She'd heard the stories in town. No woman wanted to be a savage's pleasure.

Maybe they'll stop, she thought. But deep down, she knew what was about to happen to her body.

An Indian behind her ripped off all her clothing, and Martha started to cry. But she wasn't alone.

In the nearby brush pile, Billy lay flat on his stomach and watched the Indians. He thought about running out of the brush and distracting them. Maybe she could get away. He had to do something or his mother might be killed.

Unfortunately, Billy witnessed the unthinkable barbaric and inhumane acts of cruelty being done to his mother. He took a deep breath and prayed. If he was going to act, it had to be right now.

Billy rubbed his hands together and made a decision.

Chapter Twenty~Six

Ezra ran only as fast as little Mary could move her feet. With baby Joseph secure in his arms, he forced his legs to keep churning, tugging on Mary to hurry up.

He was close to panic, but he had to remain strong. Otherwise, what remained of his family would be covered under a layer of snow until the spring thaw or coyotes dug them up—whichever came first.

Exhausted, he reached the Potts' house and blurted out the tragedy. Begging for a gun to borrow, he left Mary and the baby behind and ran back to his place, wildly waving the six-shooter at anything that moved.

When he neared his homestead, he hid behind some brush and watched for any sign of the Indians. His milk cow wandered aimlessly around the yard, bawling at the three arrows sticking out of her milk sack and nudging something on the ground.

Finally, darkness arrived, with the moon not yet full. He ventured out to see what he could find.

Report of Depredation – Ezra Sherman and family, et al.

Not For Publication

An attack by 20 Comanche on the Sherman homestead commenced on November 27, 1860. The family was sitting down to supper when the Comanche approached. During the attack, the family was set free while Mrs. Ezra Sherman (Martha) was kept hostage.

Later that night after darkness, Ezra Sherman approached his cabin and found his wife, Martha, on the ground. She was barely alive and asked for water.

Ezra filled his hat from the creek and brought her water. After taking some water, Ezra lifted Martha and carried her to a bed that had not been ransacked. He worked at reviving his wife and listened to Martha's story.

According to Martha, the Comanche stripped her bare and laid her down on the ground. It was cold, wet, and snowing during this event. They took turns molesting her. Each one had molasses on his chest. Several had goose feathers stuck to the syrup. Inside the cabin, the other beds were found ripped open and the source of the feathers.

The Comanche stuck a lance in Martha. They removed pins from her hair and forced them completely into her skin.

One savage took a steel-pointed arrow and slowly pushed it into her shoulder blade. The arrow was removed and is now in the custody of the Palo Pinto Sheriff.

While still on the ground, they took a knife and sliced her scalp. Martha claims her long hair was stubborn and refused to come loose.

After finishing with the cabin, the Indians realized Martha was still alive. To kill her, they rode horses over her body. Yet by God's providence, not one hoof touched any part of her.

As the Comanche turned to leave, they shot three arrows into her body and left her for dead. The injured milk cow moved next to Martha for comfort but could do nothing to revive her owner.

Locals soon arrived at the Sherman house and tended to Martha. The following day, she gave birth to a stillborn child. She then complained about a "big old redheaded Indian." For the next two days, she talked only about this redheaded Indian, delirious and confused.

After surviving four full days, Martha Sherman died. She was buried next to a church near the Sherman homestead.

The cabin was inspected and found plundered. The Comanche even stole the family's Bible.

Before they left, the savages tried to set fire to the cabin but it was too wet and refused to light. Ezra Sherman's son, Billy, came forward at nightfall cold and afraid. He claims to have seen most of what happened to his mother from a brush pile. He wanted to help but was too scared and decided to do nothing.

Several agents and officers counseled Mr. Sherman and he now understands the importance of having and maintaining firearms on the frontier. He assures me that firearms will be part of his life as he cares for his son Joseph and Martha's two children, Mary and Billy.

A posse is being formed to chase down the Comanche attackers and degrade them.

End of report.

Word of the attack spread like freezing wind from a blue norther. It was soon learned that after the Sherman attack, the marauders hit the Eubanks's place but were fooled by two girls and a boy, who put on men's hats and jackets and took up stations on a fortified picket fence.

The Comanche charged but saw one of the "men" holding a shotgun and aiming at them. They broke off the attack just as the oldest girl fired, knocking herself off the fence. It was a close call.

An even closer call happened to their father, William Eubanks. That same night, the full moon was obscured by clouds as he tried to return home, leaving the sky nearly fully dark.

Somehow, Eubanks found himself among a herd of three hundred ponies. When he spotted the painted Indians in the dim light, he removed his hat and bent over flat on his horse's back, riding with the herd until he dropped behind and made a right turn at a thick stand of post oaks.

Once the horses and Indians were gone, he raced home to find his family alive and safe.

Post Oak

Another unbelievable event happened when some of John Brown's horses peeled off from the Comanche herd and returned home, including Barney, the slow pony John had been riding when he was killed. Because the misty rain and darkness obscured details and the raiders were in a hurry, they couldn't keep track of every horse.

All in all, Puhtocnocony's revenge raid through Jack, Parker, and Palo Pinto Counties was a great success. He had killed twenty-three whites, tortured and wounded five more, and captured and released two girls. He also made off with 150 to 250 horses. Only one Comanche died and two were injured, possibly by John Brown.

Puhtocnocony's men took plunder with them, including various clothing items and metal tools. They even stole a Bible, the pages of which they could not understand.

It didn't take long to see that the citizens on this part of the frontier would not take this raid lying down. Before the first sunrise following Martha Sherman's assault, a group was forming. These few men were about to change the lives of Puhtocnocony, Naduah, and Quanah forever.

Chapter Twenty-Seven

Charles Goodnight wiped the stinging rain from his face. It was cold, almost frozen.

At just twenty-four years old, he'd seen a lot. He knew how to hunt, drive cattle, and shoot. Growing up on the Brazos River bottoms, he'd even learned to track and scout from Caddo Jake, a young Indian boy.

Using all these skills, Goodnight had trekked across Texas and the Indian Territories, seeing all manner of death and destruction. But the complete scalping of his neighbor, Martha Sherman, shook him up terribly.

As soon as he saw the carnage and learned her story, he jumped on his horse and raced around the area, raising the alarm and recruiting men willing to travel deep into the Comanchería to find these ruthless scavengers. It would be their own revenge raid.

Goodnight designated Issac Lynn's house on the upper Keechi Creek as the meeting place. It was the right choice, being mostly west of the Shermans and a good starting point since they'd be headed west to cut off the Indians.

After warning the final homestead, he turned back and rode hard to Lynn's place, the rain unrelenting. When he arrived, he tended to his horse first because he would need the beast at its best. Where they were going, few men returned with their hearts beating and scalps intact.

Once his horse was taken care of, he hurried inside and closed the door, stamping his feet and trying to get dry. To his shock, Issac Lynn sat in front of a fireplace holding a long, forked stick over a crackling fire. At its end was a Comanche scalp, presumably from the dead Indian that John Brown killed.

Lynn turned the scalp this way and that to heat it evenly. This was the final stage of making the scalp permanent.

Post Oak

Having recently lost his daughter and son-in-law to the Comanche, Lynn didn't look well. It was not uncommon for prairie madness to take hold of these early settlers and never let go.

As more men arrived, Lynn turned to each one and said, "Don't forget about me, ya hear?"

Goodnight knew he wanted more scalps but truly, he was worried about the man.

Soon, there were seven men willing to ride after the savages.

Goodnight checked his long rifle to ensure it was ready to fire. Then he rubbed a finger over the engraving on the barrel: Matthew 6:33. Goodnight knew that verse by heart. "But seek first His kingdom and His righteousness, and all these things will be given to you as well."

"Let's get on the trail," Goodnight told his men. "They're driving hundreds of ponies and shouldn't be hard to track."

When Lynn turned his head, the flames in the fireplace behind him created a sinister optical illusion for the men who stood at the front door. Each flame appeared to come from his head, his face obscured in a dark shadow. The men carried this image with them as they left to ride the trail to an uncertain future.

Sul Ross rolled over, trying to get comfortable in his sleep. After being shot with arrows and his own gun two years earlier, the scars weren't ready to let him forget. He was half-asleep when a hand jostled him.

"Captain Ross, time to take 'em. I know these are the fellas we're after because o' what I found."

Twenty-three-year-old Ross snapped wide awake, something most men easily did on the frontier.

"What did you find?" he asked, grabbing his rifle.

"A pillow slip with a little girl's belt," Goodnight said. "And this."

In the lantern's light, Ross took the book from Goodnight. "A Bible?"

"Yes, sir. It's Mrs. Sherman's. It fell with the cover closed so the rain didn't ruin the pages."

Ross studied the Good Book and placed it in his saddlebag. "Have they moved?"

"No, sir," Goodnight replied. "They're still on the Pease River. Just where we left 'em yesterday. But we need to get going before they see our tracks."

Two weeks earlier, Charles Goodnight had led his posse 120 miles deep into Comanchería without bedding or other key supplies. As he neared the Pease River, he saw numerous Indian trails converging there.

With some careful scouting, he surmised it was a Comanche supply depot. This setup allowed the warriors to drive the stolen herds to this spot and drop off their loot.

From the tracks, it appeared several raiding parties used the location to load up on food and weapons before heading back out to kill more whites.

At the time, Goodnight determined that several raiding parties had returned to get refreshed. His eight-man posse had been heavily outnumbered. Instead of attacking, they returned to Parker County and found Sul Ross there.

Ross had just received a new commission from Governor Sam Houston to raise some men and fight the Indians. Houston had finally realized that negotiations and peace treaties would not work with the Comanche. The only viable solution was bullets fired from guns held by men with steely nerves and deadly aim. Sul Ross was chosen to lead such men and ride out into the Comanchería, where they would have to punish the Indians, if not kill them all.

In less than a minute, Ross was ready to ride. It had rained the night before and, in fact, had been cold since December 13, when they left Fort Belknap. The land was inhospitable when they'd set out, with its brown-colored prairies, muddy creeks, and barely a tree anywhere. The fog, rain, and cold wind had blistered his men.

Today, a blue norther appeared, blowing blinding clouds of sand and sending anyone alive—Comanche or otherwise—into shelter. But this was great news for Ross. His men would be hidden as they rode up from the south.

They would need every advantage because Goodnight estimated there were five hundred Comanche. They would also need the element of surprise if they were going to pull this off. Careers could be made from such a daring feat, and Ross intended to be known for this grand and courageous act.

Atop his horse, he studied his men. He had raised forty rangers, twenty-one U.S. regular troops from the Second Cavalry (the same bunch that had massacred Buffalo Hump's band two years earlier with Van Dorn and Ross), and eighty volunteer frontiersmen. Wisely, Ross made Goodnight his chief scout.

When they had ridden to within a few hundred yards of the camp, Ross stopped and turned to his troops.

"This is it, men. We know the Comanche are somewhere over this sand dune. Get your weapons out and wait for my signal."

The men pulled out their rifles and six-shooters and checked the loads.

When they were ready, Ross waved his hand and gave the order. "Let's ride, men!"

Former corporal Billy Tyler stared out the window of his small office. With Fort Belknap being shut down due to its unreliable water and the Civil War about to start, he'd been sent with all the files to a federal government office in Fort Worth.

The state of Texas would soon join the Confederacy, and the forts were Union property. No federal soldier wanted to be caught in Confederate territory, and most in Texas removed their uniforms and fought for the South.

Everything was changing, including the war against the Indians. Now, as he reread the field action report from the Battle of Pease River, he couldn't believe what it said.

Clearly, young Sul Ross was a hero. He fought hand-to-hand with Chief Puhtocnocony, known to the whites as Peta Nocona. Nocona's death gave a huge boost to the state's morale.

Under Ross, the rangers, federal troops, and volunteers all distinguished themselves by killing the warriors and other Comanches, leaving only two people alive—one of which was Cynthia Ann Parker, who was rescued while carrying a baby.

"We thrashed them out," Ross told the *Dallas Weekly Herald*. "All my men acquitted themselves with great honor—proving worthy representatives of true Texas valor. Not more than twenty of my men were able to get in the fight, owing to the starved and jaded condition of our horses having had no grass after leaving the vicinity of Belknap."

All through Texas, Sul Ross was celebrated, as was Governor Sam Houston. To the weary Texans, Governor Houston had finally made a dent in the Indian war machine that took so many lives. The frontiersmen soaked in the blood-stained victory that came with the news.

After the action, Ross led his troops to Camp Cooper, bringing Cynthia Ann and her baby, Prairie Flower. A summons was quickly dispatched to her uncle Isaac Parker, a former judge, legislator, and ranger.

Issac arrived in January and didn't recognize the blue-eyed girl. During questioning, she seemed to know some of the details of the 1836 Parker Fort raid. But when she was asked if she knew Cynthia Ann Parker, she stood, pounded her chest, and said, "Me Cyntha Ann."

That was good enough for Isaac. He agreed to take her and the baby home along with Ross's interpreter so he could communicate with her until she relearned the language. Then he started for his log cabin in Birdville, Texas, northeast of Fort Worth.[7]

Along the way, Isaac Parker stopped at Fort Belknap, where he received help from the Peveler family. They cleaned up the two Comanche and made them "presentable" to the white settlements.

Once this was accomplished, Parker headed to Fort Worth instead of his home in Birdville.

News of Cynthia Ann Parker's return spread fast. The frenzy was so great that the city of Fort Worth let out school so all the children could see her. Even Billy Tyler was going. But not before he questioned Private Hiram Rogers.

Rogers had been at the Battle of Pease River, and Billy wanted a firsthand account from workingmen like privates instead of the puffed-up version so often submitted by officers.

"How accurate is this report?" Billy asked the private.

---

[7] Birdville is now Haltom City.

"I'm embarrassed to say that I was present at the Pease River *Massacre*."

"What?" Billy said, astonished. "Why do you call it that?"

"I'll tell you why. The Indians were getting ready to leave when we came upon them. Their horses were loaded down and could hardly move. We fought and killed one, maybe two bucks. The rest were squaws, mostly shot in the back as they ran on foot or fled on horses. The toughest part of the action was a dozen or so dogs in the camp. They attacked us, and we had to kill them to avoid being bitten. That was the main defense—dogs."

Billy scribbled some notes. "What did Ross do?"

"He chased down some Indians on two horses. When he reached the first rider, she reined her horse over and shouted something like 'Americano.' Then she showed a two-year-old child hidden under her buffalo robe. Ross ordered Lieutenant Keliheir to stay with her while he rode down the other horse carrying two Indians."

"And then what happened?" Billy asked, writing furiously.

"Ross reached the second horse and fired at the closest rider. It was a Mexican girl who fell dead from the horse. The chief had a shield on his back, which stopped the bullet after it went through her heart. But she dragged the chief down, and they both fell off the horse.

"The chief hit the ground and was up firing arrows fast; one of them hit Ross's horse. As Ross tried to stay in the saddle while dodging more arrows, he got off a lucky shot that broke the chief's right arm. But Lieutenant Keliheir rode up and said he fired that shot. Whatever happened, Ross calmed his horse and shot the chief two more times. Everyone agrees with that part. Then the wounded chief crawled to a lone mesquite tree and wrapped his good arm around it to keep sitting upright."

"Did he die there?"

Private Rogers cleared his throat. "He started singing some Indian songs and talked to Ross through a Mexican interpreter. Ross urged him to surrender and promised he wouldn't be shot anymore."

"What did he say to that?" Billy asked.

"He said he'd surrender, but only after he died. Then he tried to throw a spear with his good arm but missed Ross. The chief fought to the very end. After throwing the spear, the chief talked to someone dead, saying he hoped he'd been a good chief for his people and a good leader. He wanted a safe place in the afterlife, but only if he was worthy.

"The Mexican interpreter translating all this was our cook and Ross's manservant. He begged Ross to kill the chief, and Ross refused. Instead, he let the Mexican interpreter do it with his Mississippi rifle. And that was the end of Peta Nocona." Private Rogers finished with a sad tone.

Billy looked up from his writings. "What made you think he was Chief Peta Nocona?"

"He wore a fancy headdress and a gold medallion hung from his neck. He also barked orders to the others when we first attacked. He had the two bucks stand behind their horses until the animals fell from our shots. Then the bucks dropped down behind the horses, using them as a breastwork to block more of our shots. It was a clever move. But the clincher was when I learned the Mexican interpreter had been captured by the Comanche as a child and was a slave to Peta Nocona. When he identified the man as Nocona, that was good enough for us. And before we left, Cynthia Ann Parker went to the body and cried over it like he'd been her husband or someone close. She also said one of the dead boys was her son but not her son."

"What did that mean?"

"We weren't sure, but the Mexican girl who was shot in the back had been captured as a child. She was just a teenager and supposedly one of Nocona's wives. Maybe the dead boy was from that wife."

"Then you headed back?" Billy asked.

"First, we rode our horses over the dead and dying, which was shameful. Then we looted and burned the place after Ross ordered every Indian scalped. He wanted to present Nocona's headdress and jewelry to Sam Houston along with the scalps."

Billy ventured out and asked the big question. "So you don't believe this was an epic battle?"

"Nah. It was only those two bucks who put up any resistance. And I guess you can add the chief at the very end, but really, we massacred mostly women and children."

Disgusted, Billy set his pencil down. "That figures. Since I've been at this post, we made a treaty with Buffalo Hump, then practically the next

Post Oak

day massacred his people by surprise at the Wichita Village Fight. Now we have the Battle of Pease River or really the Pease River Massacre. Except for Rip Ford's ranger expedition in 1858, everything we've done has been a failure or a joke or both."

Rogers shifted uneasily in his chair. "I know you're only a corporal, but should you be talking like this?"

"I used to be a corporal. Now I'm a civilian employee, so yeah, it's okay."

Billy changed the subject. "Are you going to Turner's and Daggett's General Store today to see Cynthia Ann? It's supposed to be crowded."

"Yes, sir," Rogers replied.

Billy reached over and grabbed a winter coat and his crutches. "If you'll fetch my horse, we can ride there together."

"Sure," the private said. "Let's see how she looks."

"Or what they've done to her," Billy muttered under his breath.

An hour later, the pair stood in a large semicircle with hundreds of local citizens, gawking at a grotesque sight. A stout blue-eyed female with short hair—a Comanche sign of mourning the loss of loved ones—and a deeply tanned face stood there terrified. A torn calico dress fell uncomfortably over her frame with a white scarf tied around her neck. Her hands were clasped together at her waist as tears streamed down her cheeks. Looking totally helpless and despondent, Cynthia Ann spoke some Comanche words over and over.

"What's she saying?" a young student asked the principal.

The principal turned to the translator, who said, "She's begging to be sent back to her people. That's all she keeps saying."

The crowds stood there and aahed and ogled. Some raised their hands to their mouths in horror. Others asked the captive questions she couldn't understand. A few made fun of her. It was nothing short of a trophy displayed to the masses.

Later that day, someone convinced Cynthia Ann to have her photo taken at A.F. Corning's studio, though no one was sure she understood what that meant. The picture showed her large, strong hands holding a baby as she nursed on her mother's right breast. There were also Cynthia Ann's sad eyes. She looked defeated.

Known as the White Squaw, this photo and her story were read and discussed from New York to London. No one could believe a white woman would choose to stay with the Comanche.

After being displayed, Cynthia Ann was taken to Birdville and Isaac Parker's massive log cabin. Most Texans would have been grateful to stay there, but Cynthia Ann was basically a prisoner.

Due to the twenty-four long years she had lived with the Comanche, this felt more like a capture than a rescue. Too much time had passed from the child taken to the woman she'd become. No one could put those twenty-four years in a box and bury it, though many tried.

One month after her return, Cynthia Ann was taken to Austin. Isaac convinced the legislature to grant a pension for her support and an education for her daughter, Prairie Flower. The amount was a generous $100 per year for five years plus a league of land. Still, she was despondent.

Those who saw her felt she would kill herself if she had the chance. She had already tried to run away several times. Clearly, she didn't want to be around whites.

At some point, Cynthia Ann understood her mother, Lucy, had died eight years earlier. With her father having died at Parker's Fort, she had no parents. Even her uncle, the Searcher James W. Parker, had died in North Houston.

Eventually, she was taken to live with her brother Silas Jr., who had barely escaped capture at Parker's Fort. Silas was twenty-eight and lived deep in the east Texas woods. It was not a pleasant time for Cynthia Ann or her brother's family.

Cynthia Ann never mixed with other whites and kept to herself, either sitting in the cabin or by a spring, staring at the land and the sky. She often took off down the road, walking back to her people, having no concept of the actual length of that journey. This led her to be moved to live with her married younger sister, Orleana, nearby.

Nothing much changed for Cynthia Ann until the Civil War came and the men left to fight. That meant the women had to do all the work.

Practically overnight, she was chopping wood and spinning wheels to make cloth. She also went back to tanning hides. They were so soft that folks from miles around brought her their hides.

Post Oak

When people were sick, she gathered herbs and roots and made healing medicines. She had found a purpose in living.

Once Cynthia Ann relearned to read and write English, her family promised to take her back to the Comanche as soon as the war was over. But Prairie Flower died in 1864 of pneumonia caused by the flu.

This changed her for the worse. She became despondent and depressed again. Most said her heart broke in two.

Though she lived six more years, the locals claimed her death seemed self-imposed, like she willed herself to die. She was just forty-three years old.

With the famous "white squaw" gone, it was her son Quanah Parker's turn to step up. Despite Sul Ross and others saying how the Comanche had been whipped and defeated, this young Comanche warrior would prove them wrong.

From 1861 to 1874, he let the world know his people were not dead. The U.S. Army discovered they had another dangerous Indian leader they'd have to ride out and kill before they could have any peace.

But they'd have to find him first. How hard could that be?

Chapter Twenty-Eight

Quanah Parker nursed his wound. Barely a few hours earlier, a bullet grazed his thigh. It had been a tough scrap.

Chief Bear's Ear had led him and other Comanche warriors through Texas on raids. They stole many horses and mules and drove the animals to far west Texas—Comanchería—where they hoped to cross the Red River safely and head north.

Unfortunately, soldiers from Fort Richardson spotted them and killed Chief Bear's Ear. The band became demoralized. Thanks to Quanah's quick actions in giving orders and taking charge, most of the men and stolen animals had been saved.

Once they crossed the Red River at an unexpected spot, the soldiers halted and let them go. But not before Quanah distinguished himself by hanging back and guarding the rear of the Comanche band. He even lowered himself to his horse's side to avoid being hit with bullets.

When a large bush appeared, he rode around it and raised up, charging an attacking soldier head-on. Quanah felt the bullets whiz by until one stung his thigh. Still, he fired several arrows and hit the soldier's shoulder, causing him to drop his pistol. The soldier wisely spun his pony around and retreated.

Quanah was about to give chase when other soldiers fired their guns and turned him away. That had given time for the last warriors to cross the river. Quanah then raced his horse across, thankful to find no quicksand.

Now, at a temporary camp, he smoothed a poultice of herbs and other plants over the wound, hoping to ease the pain and heal it. Quanah stared into the fire. He was truly alone; his family was gone.

After his mother's capture, his younger brother Pee-nah died of smallpox. Then his father, Puhtocnocony, died of an old war wound from the

Post Oak

Parker's Fort raid. Quanah was with him as he took his last breath and left for the Great Spirit.

He had heard that white men claimed Puhtocnocony was killed at the Pease River attack, yet there had been no reason for his father, a chief, to be there. Men didn't help pack up. Only the old men were left behind to protect the women, who did all the packing.

During the Battle of Pease River, Puhtocnocony had taken him and Pee-nah hunting. Later, the three heard that Puhtocnocony's Mexican wife was killed and his white wife captured.[8] More death and loss to deal with.

"We are ready," a warrior said.

Quanah got to his feet and walked over to a robust fire. He sat down, careful of his injured thigh, and faced the men.

"We have decided to make you our leader," the warrior said bluntly. "Where you go, we will follow. What you command, we will obey."

Under the bright stars and surrounded by the vast prairie, Quanah nodded. With the warrior's words, he was now a Comanche leader. His father would be proud but not surprised.

The box of files was ready to be sealed. The clerk stood by, waiting for Billy's approval.

Billy lingered over the contents list before finally nodding and letting the clerk take the box away. It would be stored in a large warehouse with other records. Maybe someday, someone would need them. But who that might be, Billy had no clue.

As he retook the seat in his Dallas office, his 10 o'clock appointment appeared. It was a reporter from the local newspaper.

"Have a seat," Billy said, pointing to one directly across from his. "What can I do for you?"

---

[8] Reports have long claimed Puhtocnocony had one wife: Cynthia Ann Parker. Yet Comanche were known to have multiple wives. This Mexican wife was likely added after Cynthia Ann and the reports were possibly romanticized by white writers who could not believe a white woman would have to share an Indian man with anyone else.

"I'm writing a story on the Indian raids through Texas. I hear you were with the Army and know a lot about Indians and raids, particularly the Comanche. What can you tell me about all this?"

Billy let loose a laugh. "That's a tall subject you're tackling. First, let's set some ground rules. You can use what I say but don't use my name or position. Understood?"

"Understood," the reporter said.

"Good. It's true, I've read a lot and know a lot. Even though the Texas Rangers and federal troops have resumed their patrols, the railroads are still having trouble laying down tracks because of the Comanche. It never ends. In fact, since the 1850s, the government has been certain the Comanche were defeated, but not so. They're clever and resilient even if the other tribes have been crushed."

"Like the Cheyenne?"

"Exactly," Billy replied. "Custer took plenty of men and weapons and beat them hard—twice, I believe. But the Comanche, well, we thought before the Civil War with Buffalo Hump back on the reservation and Peta Nocona dead, they had no one left to lead them. To our surprise, with the federal troops gone and the Texas Rangers fighting for the South, the Comanche ran amok. They had free rein over the plains. By war's end, they had built their tribe back up and found a leader."

The reporter looked up from his pad. "Who is that?"

"We don't know since the Comanche have dozens of bands, each led by a different chief. Some bands gave up and came in, especially after the Medicine Lodge treaty two years ago. But I heard several Comanche bands still refuse to give up. It's these bands that are riding all over Texas. Some even go into Mexico to steal, kill, and destroy."

"I've spoken with many citizens on the frontier," the reporter said. "They're demanding action, begging someone to stop the Comanche."

Billy cleared his throat. "The truth is we don't really know how to fight them. I've read all the reports, and the Comanche can outride and outshoot us. They lead our troops into ambushes and stampede our horses. They'll burn the prairie and leave our troops to die of thirst. Once our boys are afoot, they're just as good as dead."

"What about Kit Carson and the Comanche at that raiding post in West Texas? What's it called?"

"Adobe Walls," Billy said. "Yes, Carson took some federal troops out there along with some cannons and attacked the Kiowas, losing six men and returning with twenty-five wounded."

The reporter flipped through some pages. "From what I read, it said Carson killed maybe sixty Kiowa and Comanche and wounded a hundred more."

Billy held up a hand. "Four of the dead were Kiowas too old to flee their tents. And the Army can claim as many dead as they want because there are no bodies to show for it. But they did come back with scalps, which kinda suggests a death."

"How many did they have?" the reporter asked. "Was it close to sixty?"

"No, not that close." Billy liked drawing out the suspense.

The reporter leaned forward. "Well, are you gonna tell me how many scalps they had?"

"Sure," Billy said. "It was a single, solitary scalp."

Stunned, the reporter said nothing.

"Yeah, and Carson had to retreat in the face of three thousand Indians coming to attack him because he was running out of ammunition. Remember, it's us whites who write all these reports saying we're whipping the red man, yet the Indians keep coming. In fact, when Rip Ford, Van Dorn, and Sul Ross went on the offensive and took the fight to the Comanche, it was like stepping on a bed of fire ants. The Comanche sprang up and went on the offensive, utterly destroying huge swaths of Texas. There's no beating these people."

"Maybe there is. A Union war hero has a plan." The reporter consulted his pad again. "General William Tecumsah Sherman said, and I quote, 'The quickest way to compel the Indians to settle down to civilized life is to send ten regiments of soldiers to the plains with orders to shoot buffaloes until they become too scarce to support the redskins.' End quote."

Billy's face turned crimson.

"Something the matter?" the reporter asked.

Billy caught himself. "Sorry, it's just that years back I told my superior officer about that idea, and he convinced me I knew nothing about combat or fighting the Comanche. Now it looks like someone else who knows how to fight had the same idea."

The reporter explained that the government was stocking ammunition at the forts and encouraging buffalo hunters to come to the plains and make themselves rich on hides and tongues. "Do you think it'll work?"

Billy nodded. "Yes, it'll work. As more and more settlers destroy the prairie grass with farming and fence off the range, the buffalo won't come back. They'll congregate in spots, allowing hunters to kill hundreds a day. It won't take long."

The reporter closed his pad and stood up. "That's enough for today. Say, you're still single. When are you going to find some gal and get hitched?"

Billy pointed to his crutches. "What woman would want a man with a crippled leg? I can't do chores, and I can't protect them from harm. I'm useless to a woman. I'll be single for the rest of my life. But it's okay. I try not to think about it."

The reporter said nothing as he shook Billy's hand and left.

Weeks later, he published a series of reports about the struggles to rid the plains of the Indians, especially the Comanche. It would only stoke the government to encourage more prairie farming and the faster killing of buffalo.

Chapter Twenty-Nine

Weckeah kissed Quanah right before he mounted his horse. Whenever he rode off, she understood it might be the last time she saw him. And each time, Quanah smiled.

She had bravely gone with him and several others to start their own band. After sneaking out of camp, the small band attracted more than one hundred Comanche.

Over the next two years, the band grew. They went on many raids and were quite successful.

In time, Chief Yellow Bear realized he'd lost his daughter. If he weren't careful, he'd gain an enemy.

One day, the chief gathered up his people and rode to Quanah's camp. After holding a council to negotiate the price of Weckeah, Quanah offered twenty ponies. Yellow Bear accepted.

Quanah handed over the horses while telling the chief that he knew a ranch nearby where he could steal that many in one night. Whether that was an insult as the price was too low or a brag to impress his new father-in-law, no one was sure.

The next day, Chief Yellow Bear's people joined Quanah's, and a new, larger band rode northwest to the Staked Plain. Just like that, Quanah was fully recognized as a leader among his people.

September 30, 1871
Camp Cooper, Texas

Colonel Ranald Slidell Mackenzie studied his maps one more time. In an hour or so, he would lead a column of six hundred men into the deep reaches of Comanchería. It was a daunting task: find and kill Quanah, Bull Bear, Wild Horse, and Bull Elk—the Comanche leaders still terrorizing Texas.

Mackenzie was chosen for this mission because he had caught the eye of President Grant during the Civil War. Grant considered him the most promising young officer in the Union Army.

Although thin and shy, Ranald Mackenzie was determined to make a name for himself. He graduated first in his West Point class. He also had solid bloodlines since his great-grandfather was assistant secretary of the treasury under Alexander Hamilton. His grandfather was a prominent New York City bank president. His uncle was the top advisor to President Buchanan, a U.S. Senator, and a power broker in Louisiana. Another uncle was the chief justice of Louisiana. Even his aunt had pedigree, being married to Commodore Perry, who opened Japan to the U.S.

Mackenzie performed very well in the Civil War, proving himself a top-level leader. He led so much from the front that he was wounded six times: a .50 caliber bullet through both shoulders, an artillery shell wound in the leg, a shrapnel wound in the chest, and the first two fingers of his right hand blown off. As if that wasn't enough, a shell exploded and paralyzed him, leaving him on the battlefield for twenty-four hours before the surgeons could reach him.

After the war, he was given the Fourth Cavalry and expected to deliver the final blow to the dreaded Comanche. Mackenzie felt up to the challenge.

A captain carrying a lantern stuck his head into the tent.

"Sir, the men are itching for a fight. I feel like we're going to get some action this time."

"You think so?" Mackenzie asked halfheartedly.

"I do," Captain Carter said. "Not like Kicking Bird."

Mackenzie clenched his jaw at the mention of Chief Kicking Bird. The Kiowa chief was a sore subject.

Over the last year, the reservation Indians, including Kicking Bird's Kiowas, became jealous of the Comanche still free and running wild. The Comanche raided and stole whatever they liked, while reservation Indians like Kicking Bird were bound to their assigned plot of land. They couldn't leave it or would risk death. But they liked one aspect: being on the reservation meant they were safe and couldn't be touched by the military.

Post Oak

Somehow, the reservation Indians got smart. They left their plots and went raiding and killing before returning with the stolen booty, daring anyone to do anything about it.

These raids were neat tricks until Kicking Bird was spotted off the reservation. Mackenzie had been tasked with finding and punishing the high chief and started the chase on May 1, 1871, with his Fourth Cavalry.

Eventually, they lost the chief's trail. When they heard Kicking Bird was back on the reservation and thus safe, they were mad. They felt incompetent.

Mackenzie watched as the captain left. He gathered up his maps and stuffed them in a pouch. As he looked around his tent for any other papers, his clerk appeared at the entrance.

"Sir, a message from the general." The clerk handed a slip to Mackenzie, and he read it.

> Be on guard the moment you leave the fort. We must pay them back for Salt Creek!

That was another kick in the gut, as Salt Creek Prairie was the recent location of a horrendous disaster. One hundred fifty Comanche, Apache, and Kiowas had left the reservation and attacked a wagon train headed for Fort Griffin loaded with milled flour and cornmeal.

Five teamsters escaped to the woods, but seven were killed. Some of the teamsters endured having their fingers, toes, and private parts cut off. Heaping piles of hot coals were placed on their exposed abdomens. Some were beheaded.

The five survivors limped back to Fort Richardson, where they found General William Tecumseh Sherman. He had conducted an inspection of that exact same area the day before and realized he had just missed being killed.[9]

---

[9] Years later, Indians who were present at the massacre said they saw General Sherman, but the medicine man's dreams told them to attack the second group of white people they saw. Thus, Sherman lived.

For the settlers on the plains, the Salt Creek Massacre was the final straw.

General Sherman talked to "experts" about the Indians, especially the Comanche, and learned these were vengeance raids. All white men were to be killed. Any white man or woman alive would be slowly tortured. Babies would also be killed. Young children like Cynthia Ann Parker would be assimilated into the tribe and only killed if there was a good reason. Horses and loot were stolen because why not? The whites were looked at as insects—lice or red ants—tearing up the land and stealing the Indians' way of life. They all had to go.

General Sherman was forced to act.

It was quickly determined that reservation chiefs White Bear, Sitting Bear, and Big Tree had led the Salt Creek Massacre, as the settlers called the killings now. It was an easy investigation since the chiefs boasted about it when they returned to the reservation. Being there meant they were untouchable and gave them bragging rights.

Sherman strategized and devised a trick to have them report to Fort Sill. Once they arrived, they were off the reservation and taken into custody. Mackenzie was tasked with transporting the three chiefs to Jacksboro for a trial.

Along the way, Sitting Bear chewed away the flesh around his wrists and escaped his shackles. As he fled, he killed a guard but was shot and died.

In Jacksboro, the other two were convicted and sentenced to hang, but peace protests across the country and fear of an all-out Indian war prompted President Grant to order Texas Governor Edmund Davis to commute their sentences to life in prison.

Mackenzie now fully understood that he had to either kill the Comanche on the plains or bring them in to face a token punishment.[10]

---

[10] White Bear and Big Tree served only two years before being released on parole. Both were returned to the reservation where they immediately began raiding again. One year later, White Bear was caught violating his parole and sent back to prison, where he withered away, constantly staring out the window at his people's land. In 1878, rather than die in prison, he jumped headfirst from a high prison window and killed himself. Big Tree somehow avoided incarceration and converted to Christianity at the Immanuel Mission near Rainy Mountain in southwest Oklahoma, teaching Sunday school there. He was an important chief until his death in 1929.

Post Oak

Colonel Mackenzie went outside and took the reins of his horse. Because his last one was exhausted chasing Kicking Bird, he needed a new mount and procured the best he could find: a magnificent gray pacer.

Atop this fine beast, Mackenzie inspected his men: the Fourth Cavalry and Eleventh Infantry. Satisfied, he checked over the Tonkawa scouts. These Indians were vital because they could track better than any white man and knew well the Comanche and their tricks.

It was said that the Tonkawas and Comanche were bitter enemies. Mackenzie understood that an Indian would have to truly hate another Indian to team up with the white man. Regardless, he was glad to have all twenty-five of them.

When the men were ready, Mackenzie gave the order: "We march west until we find 'em." With that, the troops began searching for Quanah and his deadly Comanche band.

Under the early October skies, the Fourth Cavalry plodded along, mostly heading west but sometimes veering north. Ravines and draws were the only features that broke up the endless prairie—rolling green grass with tough mesquite and cedar trees.

On the fourth night, they reached the junction of Duck Creek and the Salt Fork of the Brazos, ten miles southeast of Blanco Canyon. Mackenzie ordered his infantry to set up base camp, and he would take the cavalry to find the Comanche. But before he did this, he sent out the Tonkawa scouts to see if they could find any trails.

While Mackenzie waited for the scouts to return, his men shot and killed several buffalo that gathered in the area. Each day, they feasted on fresh buffalo meat.

On the morning of October 9, the Tonkawa scouts raced in and said they had ridden down into Blanco Canyon and surprised a small Comanche scouting party. Obviously, the Comanche had been aware of the white soldiers coming so deep into their territory, something that had never happened in history.

The Comanche had been watching the bluecoats, yet they were surprised by the stealthy Tonkawas and fled. If not for the faster horses, the Comanche would've been killed. The Tonkawas gave up and returned to the base camp.

Mackenzie received the report and let everyone finish eating a hearty breakfast of buffalo. When they were done, he ordered the cavalry to mount up. He intended to pursue the Comanche scouts back to their village and attack them before the women could pack their mules and escape.

Blanco Canyon was vast, much like a funnel. At the wide end, Mackenzie set up his base camp, leaving infantrymen and supplies behind. To get farther into the canyon meant seeing the walls slowly close in.

Still, Mackenzie was unafraid and led his troops through the quicksand of the Freshwater Fork of the Brazos River. When they cleared that mess, his men spread out, the Tonkawa scouts guiding them along as they headed deeper into the canyon where no white man had ever gone.[11]

Mackenzie was at the head of his long detachment of cavalry when a gunshot rang out.

"The supply camp!" he yelled. "It's under attack. Quick, turn around and head back."

The riders turned their horses and raced back until a lieutenant trotted up to stop them.

"Sorry, sir. We had a nervous soldier fire a gun at an antelope in the brush. Nothing to report."

The colonel shook his head in disgust. "More wasted time. Let's turn around and continue on."

He reined over his gray pacer and headed back into the heart of Blanco Canyon, closer to his prey.

After riding most of the day, Mackenzie ordered his men to stop and set up camp. He chose a site hemmed in by bluffs to the east. He knew without a doubt that no one could climb down those bluffs and live to tell about it.

---

[11] Only the Spanish had ridden into Blanco Canyon in 1541 during their El Dorado expedition.

Post Oak

To the west was a stream with quicksand. To be safe, all he had to do was set out guards to the north and south. With that done, his men could sleep for the night.

"Fires, sir?" Captain Carter asked.

"Sure," Colonel Mackenzie replied. "And cook some food. I'm hungry."

Plentiful driftwood fueled the fires, and soon, the flames lit up the bluffs for miles around, helping his men keep an eye out for any intruders. After a full meal, Mackenzie turned in, confident he and his men were well protected.

Quanah sharpened his knife by the light of the stars. Buffalo Hump had given it to his father. When Puhtocnocony died, Quanah took it off him and kept it. The thought of Buffalo Hump brought him sadness.

After Van Dorn's raid, the great Comanche chief tried to rebuild his band, but the destruction of the winter stores made that impossible. Too many warriors had died, and not enough to feed the survivors.

Buffalo Hump moved his people to the reservation in Indian Territory and asked for a house and farmland. He wanted to be an example to his people for coexisting with the white man.

Recently, Quanah had received word that the feared chief had gone to the Great Spirit. The Comanche were running out of leaders.

A flickering light in the distance drew Quanah's attention. He found a rock outcropping and climbed up to investigate. When he returned, Quanah rubbed his hands together, his excitement building.

"The white man lights a great fire for us to find him," he said.

Bull Bear smiled, his white teeth visible in the dim light. "They are fools. It will blind them while we sneak in and steal their horses."

Quanah sheathed his knife. "Let's take some warriors and pay them a visit."

Bull Bear, Wild Horse, and Bull Elk chuckled as they gathered their men. This should be easy pickings.

Chapter Thirty

Midnight arrived, and the Fourth Cavalry was fast asleep. Fires died out. Only a few men guarded the north and south approaches, and some of those men napped.

Gathered in a large herd, the horses searched for late summer grass at the end of their ropes. Their tails twitched at the insects buzzing around, looking for flesh to bite.

A gunshot rang out.

More gunshots followed.

Bloodcurdling yells erupted everywhere as if the gates of hell had opened up.

The south guard fired pistols and carbines at the bluffs. Flames from their guns illuminated the horde of Comanche riders coming toward them. The riders rang bells, shook dried buffalo hides, and screamed their terrifying yells.

Several officers figured out what was happening.

"Get to your horses!" an officer ordered. He knew men who lost their horses in Comanchería soon lost their lives.

The horses were just as scared as the soldiers. The animals pulled on the ropes and became entangled with each other. Some were roped to iron pins driven into the ground. When the horses jerked the pins out, each piece of metal whizzed around in circles, hitting men and other horses. Men crouched low, trying to hold their mounts. But it was difficult.

The Comanche retreated and let out a victory yell. As quickly as it had come, the place was quiet and dark again. Very dark.

"That's Quanah's bunch," a disgusted Mackenzie said to one of the Tonkawas.

He nodded in agreement.

A sergeant came running. "Sir, we lost seventy horses and mules. And they got your gray pacer."

"Oh my!" Mackenzie said with clenched fists. "That was a fine animal. A lot of us will be on foot now."

The next morning, as the dull sky slowly turned yellow, Captain Carter rode down the lines to inspect the damage. A shot rang out and some soldiers rode up. Indians had come in again and stolen more horses.

"They took off that way," the lieutenant said, pointing to the south.

"Come on," Captain Carter said. "Let's get those horses back!"

The men rode fast and spotted the Comanche, but they had an insurmountable lead. By pushing their mounts hard, the soldiers gained on the thieves. As they drew closer, they could see the dozen stolen horses. The soldiers might finally win a skirmish with these clever bandits.

Seeing the troops closing in, the Comanche released the stolen horses and plunged into a timbered forest.

"Oh no," Carter said, "you're not getting away this time!" He ordered his men forward.

The soldiers followed the Indians through the woods and up an embankment over which the Comanche crested and disappeared. As he and his men reached the ridge, they had to ride over a low rise. When they did, their eyes widened and their hearts stopped. Fifty mounted Comanche were coming straight for them.

"Dismount, men!" Captain Carter ordered.

He counted and found he had five men, all veterans of Indian and Confederate battles, including Private Seander Gregg. It wouldn't be enough.

Behind him, to his surprise, Captain Heyl had followed him into the same ambush. Heyl had ten men but stopped well short of Carter's position.

In seconds, the Comanche circled, firing on Carter's and Heyl's men. Both groups returned fire and pushed the Comanche back a bit, giving Carter time to study the situation and his enemy.

Each Comanche was half-naked and brightly painted, ringing bells and making horrifying sounds. Another man carried a tall scalp pole with a woman's hair attached. Even their ponies were painted menacingly.

Carter watched as the Comanche flashed mirrors at each other to signal tactics and plans. He would be impressed with all this if he wasn't about to die.

The captain glanced up to a ridge and found women mounted on horses watching the battle. They were probably waiting to leave if their men lost.

Captain Carter studied the large rings the Comanche formed as they rode around their prey. Often, there were two or three rings, always riding in opposite directions from the adjacent rings. The outer rings reinforced the innermost ring and rescued fallen warriors. This tactic was efficient and effective as it confused soldiers trying to keep their gunsights focused on one rider.

Carter ordered his men to stop firing their weapons to save ammunition. He looked back at Captain Heyl and his men and realized they were all raw recruits. Each man had fear etched on his face. Even Heyl could tell his men might not hold up.

During a slight lull in the fighting, Heyl ordered his men to make a dash for Mackenzie's camp down the valley. Sure enough, they did and made it to safety.

With Heyl's force gone, Carter and his five men were all that was left. Surely, they were about to be slaughtered.

The Comanche circles tightened. Arrows flew from all directions. It was madness.

If the men focused on specific riders, others would come closer and sink an arrow into their flesh. Carter had only one chance to escape this.

"Start firing, men. You too, Private Gregg," Carter ordered. "We'll back up to the stream we crossed, try to mount up, and get out of here. It's our only chance. Make every bullet count!"

The five fighters followed orders, occasionally hitting a horse or a rider. Their good aim pushed the Comanche back.

Sure enough, Carter and his men returned to their horses and mounted up. It was time to make the run of their lives.

Private Gregg lagged behind, riding a horse still exhausted from chasing Kicking Bird over two hundred miles. His mount couldn't run fast and stumbled, sending Gregg to the ground.

The nearest warrior came closer. Incredibly, it was Quanah, the feared Comanche leader.

Quanah was painted a sinister black. Wide brass hoops hung from his ears, shining in the early light. He was half naked and wore a breechclout, leggings, and moccasins. Around his neck dangled a string of bear claws. His scalp was braided with otter fur and a bright red tie to set it off.

Quanah's white horse was decorated with silver metal and red flannel. Its flanks were painted with a double circle resembling a bullseye.

Quanah wore a full-length headdress of eagle feathers that hung in the wind behind him as he rode toward the stumbling soldier. Bells tied to his saddle rang terrifyingly, signaling his next victim that the killer was almost there.

Carter and his men turned back and fired at Quanah, hoping to save Private Gregg. But Quanah rode in zigzags, keeping Gregg between him and the bullets.

"Use your carbine!" Carter shouted to Gregg.

The private tried to, but seeing this nightmare coming toward him caused Gregg to panic. This was exactly what all the yelling, bell ringing, and paint were supposed to do.

Gregg pulled the lever back but not far enough, jamming his carbine when he tried to fire it. He tossed it to the ground.

"Use your six-shooter!" Carter yelled to the boy.

Gregg reached for his pistol, grabbing the butt and pulling it from the holster, but Quanah had closed the gap and fired his own pistol. Carter and his men watched in horror as Private Gregg's brains exploded all over the sand.

For Carter and his men, there was no time to mourn. They would soon be butchered by Quanah and the fifty riders racing fast behind him.

As Carter reloaded and ordered his men to do the same, Quanah spun about and headed back toward the canyon wall.

This is another trick, Carter thought. *Another ambush.*

Carter was wrong. Over the rise, he saw twenty Tonkawa riders screaming down the valley toward Quanah. Behind them rode Mackenzie and his troops. Somehow, Quanah had seen the dust from Mackenzie's men and saved himself.

Carter knew that the Comanche leader would have taken on the hated Tonkawas since the Comanche had the numbers in their favor. Yet it was the large cloud of dust that sent Quanah away.

Carter glanced up to the ridge and saw the Comanche women hand over fresh mounts to Quanah and his men. Using these horses, the Comanche rode even higher up the canyon walls, disappearing over the edge and onto the Staked Plain.

Mackenzie raced up to Captain Carter and ensured he and his men were okay.

"Yes, sir," Carter said, "but your arrival was not a minute too soon."

"Collect your dead soldier and let's ride," Mackenzie ordered. "We're going after them, one way or another."

Robert Carter gave himself an even chance of ever seeing his family again.[12]

As the Comanche band reached the level ground of the Staked Plain, Quanah barked his orders.

"Do what I say, and we might lead them into another ambush. These bluecoats don't know what they're doing. If the Great Spirit wills it, we should soon have more scalps for the pole."

"Hi yah!" the warriors and women yelled.

It was time for Quanah to show everyone why he was a leader to be feared.

---

[12] Captain Robert G. Carter would later receive the Congressional Medal of Honor for saving his men.

Chapter Thirty-One

As the attacks ended, Mackenzie found he had sixty-six cavalry members without a horse. The only choice was to send those men back to the supply camp and push forward.

Though he'd just taken a big hit in troop strength, the colonel was determined to find Quanah and the rest of the Comanche.

He pushed his men deeper into uncharted territory, discovering scenery that was both beautiful and rugged. Buffalo roamed in parts of the canyon and drank from crystal clear ponds. Wild ducks, swans, and curlews swarmed everywhere. No modern man had ever been into the Comanche's favorite campgrounds, so seeing these birds was a new experience for the soldiers. Sandhills and rugged ravines challenged their journey, but the Fourth Cavalry endured.

Occasionally, they spotted vacant wickiups where the herders—usually teenage boys and girls—had slept while watching the horses. But now Mackenzie was chasing them and had his prey in sight, or at least a trail in front of him. Like Quanah, he wasn't a man to give up.

Late in the day, the cavalry found the Comanche's empty village. All that was left were holes in the ground from the teepee lodge poles.

The Tonkawa scouts motioned for Mackenzie to come to a spot one hundred yards from the village.

"See here," they told the colonel, pointing to the ground. "These ruts are the lodgepoles the mules drag. Look at all the horse and mule tracks. They lead back up the canyon."

"We've got him!" Mackenzie exclaimed. "There's no way hundreds of Indians and thousands of animals carrying loads of tools and teepees can outrun us."

"Yes," the scout said, "but see here. These trails go back and forth, up and down the canyon walls."

"Which one do we follow?" he asked.

Another scout came running and spoke to the lead scout.

"What is it?" Mackenzie asked.

"They have double-backed on us. We must turn around and pursue."

Mackenzie removed his hat and slapped his thigh with it in disgust. They had been marching all day, and the men and horses were tired.

"We'll camp here for the night. If it was good enough for the Comanche, it'll be good enough for us. Hopefully, we'll guard our horses tonight. I'd hate to walk fifty miles back to the supply camp."

The night passed without incident, and early the next morning, the Fourth Cavalry was on the march. Soon, they picked up the trail before running into another problem. The trail led up the cliffs to the flat caprock plain above.

Mackenzie studied this feat and marveled, "How did they ever do that? It's almost vertical."

"We can do it, too," the scout promised.

"I sure hope so," the colonel muttered.

The troops went slow and carefully picked their way up narrow paths. It was hard and exhausting, but they made it to the top.

"Sir," Carter said, trotting back to his colonel. "You can see to the end of the world. There's not a tree or anything to break up the view."

Mackenzie joined him and stood up in his stirrups. "Why I'll be. It's like an ocean of short grass. But why can't we see Quanah and his people?"

A cold wind blew, hitting the troops like a slap in the face. They had just climbed up three thousand feet, which made it colder even if it wasn't mid-October.

Mackenzie wrapped his arms around his thin frame. "Let's get going. I don't want to see what else this wind brings."

The scouts led the troops along the solid, flat caprock. At times, some of the soldiers walked to the edge and peered over at the canyon below. It took a strong stomach to get so close to the edge.

After several hours, the scouts found the trail had gone over the edge and back down into the canyon.

Post Oak

"At least we'll be out of this cold wind," Carter said.

Mackenzie led the Fourth Cavalry down the steep trail where one stumble meant certain death. And there was plenty of slipping and sliding. It was extremely treacherous, more so than going up the canyon walls.

Eventually, they made it safely to the canyon floor and found dozens of trails crisscrossing each other. It took an hour for the scouts to determine that the Comanche horde had gone a mile or so before heading back up the cliffs, this time on the west side.

Disgusted, angry, embarrassed, and ashamed, Mackenzie led his weary troops back up the steep walls before once again reaching the caprock and the Staked Plain.

Captain Carter couldn't help but be amazed at this foe. Each time they had the Comanche in their sights, they were taught a lesson.

"We're in their land and they have the advantage, no matter how many men and rifles we have," Carter told another captain. "Right now, they're beating Three-Fingered Jack."[13]

The cavalry's working class had a slightly different opinion, which was evident when one of the privates whispered to his buddy.

"This Comanche chief is making fools of us. He's leading us around until our horses are gone. Then he's gonna turn around and pick us off."

His buddy nodded. "Yeah, just make sure your guns are always loaded. And save one bullet for yourself."

By late afternoon, the troops had all reached the caprock and formed up on the west side of Blanco Canyon. Again, they stared at a vast world of nothingness.

With only short grass, there was no branch or bush to tell them the wind was blowing. Then the men felt it: a cold norther coming to make their lives miserable.

---

[13] This was the name the men had for Colonel Ranald Mackenzie due to his two missing fingers. The Indians called him Bad Hand or No-Finger Chief.

Quanah stood atop his horse, a delicate balancing act, and squinted his eyes. The sun was behind him in the west, and he could see the bluecoats gathering on the edge of Blanco Canyon.

He and the other leaders were stunned. This had always been a safe place.

No white man has ever found our hideout, Quanah thought. *Who is this bluecoat that torments us?*

Quanah shook off his bad thoughts and rode to the back of the line, urging his people forward.

"The bluecoats are coming," he said. "Lighten your load of anything we don't need. And keep those lodgepoles digging in the ground. We must make sure they don't turn back. Soon, they will be ours, and that includes those Tonkawa scouts."

Truthfully, Quanah wasn't sure this would work. He was vastly outnumbered. His weapons were accurate up to sixty yards which put him at a disadvantage because the bluecoats could fire their rifles from one hundred yards and drop a warrior. Still, he had no choice. The white man was here, and he'd have to deal with them or die.

Mackenzie kicked his horse forward a few hundred yards and stopped. Rising in his saddle, he studied the vast ocean of prairie.

It was an awesome but fearful sight—a land of nothing, not a tree, twig, or stone. There were no mountains in the distance or ravines anywhere. It was hard to believe.

Mackenzie removed his hat and wiped the sweat from his forehead. The cold wind quickly evaporated it.

He and his men had been riding all summer long, wearing only summer uniforms. Now the weather was turning.

"We'd better find these Comanche before it gets colder," he said to no one in particular.

"Where will we get water, sir?" Captain Carter asked.

"From the Comanche," Mackenzie said.

"Sir?"

"They know where it is. They have to drink too. They'll lead us to it."

The captain nodded and kept quiet. He was pretty sure the only place the Comanche would lead them was hell.

Quanah rose in his saddle again and studied the weather.

Next to him was Chief Bull Bear, who frowned. "What do you think? A storm?"

Quanah watched some birds and followed their flight. "The Great Spirit is sending us help."

"I hope he sends some guns and bullets," Bull Bear said. "Those men can shoot."

"They won't shoot much when they're dead," Quanah said confidently.

"There are five hundred of them plus their Tonkawa scouts. If our women and children have to turn and fight, they'll be killed or eaten alive. It will be terrible."

"The Great Spirit sees us and won't let that happen. Just wait."

Quanah said it but he had no idea what the Great Spirit wanted. He could only hope.

As the sun fell and the sky turned orange, then red, Mackenzie stopped his horse and stood up high in the saddle. "Well, I'll be!" he said. "There they are."

Silhouetted against the western sky on the flat Llano Estacado were the Comanche people. Riders could be seen going sideways, protecting the massive caravan.

"We've got 'em, men," Mackenzie said. "Full speed ahead!"

His replacement horse was exhausted and could fail at any moment. But he wasn't crawling back to General Sherman to say he had given up the chase because he was worried about his horse. That would surely end his career.

As the Fourth Cavalry gained on the Comanche, Quanah employed a new tactic. He gathered his warriors and formed two columns riding toward Mackenzie on each side.

The Comanche came within gunshot range and tried to trick the soldiers into following them. But Mackenzie didn't fall for this ruse twice.

"Keep the men moving toward their women and children. That's the prize!" Mackenzie shouted. "Quanah will attack us on our own terms when we get close to his people. Be ready for anything."

The Comanche feints bobbed in and weaved out with no takers.

Eventually, Mackenzie formed a few squads of skirmishers and sent them out to harass and confuse the Comanche. They did just that, with no one on either side being wounded or killed.

The Tonkawas saw all this and stopped to paint themselves. They could see a battle coming and wanted to be ready.

Back on their horses, the Tonkawas rode on both sides of the soldiers, waving their carbines at the Comanche and firing off their own yells. Still, Mackenzie moved forward, his eye on the prize. He could see victory now. He was almost there.

All along the path, Comanche dropped more equipment to lighten the load on their mules and horses. The soldiers found iron and stone hammers, firewood, lodge poles, and cured teepee skins. Occasionally, a fire still burned. They were so close now, maybe a mile away.

The sun dipped below the horizon, darkening the land. Mackenzie studied the sky and saw it turn black.

"Should I sound the bugle for an attack, sir?" Carter asked. "They are right there."

A pellet hit Mackenzie's cheek. Then another.

"What is that?" he said as a freezing wind ripped through his shirt and stung his skin.

In seconds, frozen rain pelted his men and animals. He looked back from where he'd come. It was getting dark so fast that he couldn't see the canyon, much less the trail back.

Mackenzie rubbed his jaw. His supply camp was one hundred miles back there somewhere. If they charged through the darkness, his casualties would be high. And it was becoming bottomless-pit dark. He'd seen fights in the dark where men ended up shooting each other.

Could I actually lose this fight to Quanah? he thought. *Could he and his warriors ride around in the darkness and pick us off until there are only a few of us left? And what would happen to those men?*

More frozen rain hit his face. "We stop here!" he said loudly.

"Sir, can we light fires?"

"Yes. Burn whatever you can find. Make them big."

Just as the words left his mouth, the frozen rain turned to snow. Then the wind picked up so much that it blew horizontally to the ground.

Mackenzie watched Carter run away, barking orders. Once he was alone, he allowed his shoulders to sag.

He and his troops had summer attire. No one had coats or winterwear. They might freeze to death out here. If that happened, all Quanah would have to do was scalp his frozen corpse. It would be a Comanche victory for all time. He might even steal their uniforms and leverage this to take down a fort. Who knew what might happen?

"Here, sir, take this," Carter said, wrapping a discarded buffalo robe around his leader.

Mackenzie was so thin and had so many wounds from the Civil War that he would not have lasted the night. Both he and Carter knew it.

Ironically, he had the Comanche to thank for likely saving his life. And the buffalo.

As for his men, they drew close and huddled around fires, trying to look away from the blinding wind, snow, and rain—both frozen and liquid. If the Comanche had ridden in at that moment, all would've been lost.

It was a miserable and dangerous night.

The next morning, the ground was covered with a smooth layer of snow. The wind had let up, and the Comanche's trail was easy to follow.

Quite quickly, Mackenzie woke his troops and set off to bag his prey. But it soon became clear that the Comanche had a five- to six-mile lead.

He and his men would have to ride harder if they hoped to catch Quanah by late afternoon. And that was the deadline because the troops needed time to engage and defeat the Comanche before darkness returned.

Otherwise, they would be on the Comanche's land and vulnerable to small attacks or the stampeding of their horses. If Mackenzie's men lost more horses to Quanah, between the frigid temperatures and lack of food, Mackenzie's hair would surely be on that long scalp pole.

The colonel studied his maps. He was low on provisions, and the horses wouldn't last more than a few days' march. Each day out was another day back. If Quanah somehow eluded him one more day, he'd have to head to Fort Sumner in New Mexico. But that was a long way off. They might not make it.

Analyzing his options, he realized there was only one.

Mackenzie ordered a halt and called for Carter.

"Sir?" Carter said, easing his pony alongside his boss.

"Pass the word. We're turning around and heading back to Fort Richardson. I'll not die here on the enemy's land where he has the advantage."

Carter offered no opposition.

Soon, the Fourth Cavalry trekked back along the trail to Blanco Canyon and blessed warmth.

December 1, 1874
Dallas, Texas

Billy shifted several files around his desk. Every report from Colonel Mackenzie and his subordinates, like Captain Carter, was in these folders. This included the Blanco Canyon expedition and subsequent missions.

It all made for fascinating reading. He could easily see the words in a book one day. It would be a bestseller, for sure.

Billy couldn't believe how close Mackenzie had come to Quanah without getting him. The reports detailed how Mackenzie turned around on the frozen Llano Estacado and headed back down the same trail he'd been on.

After reaching the edge of Blanco Canyon, the colonel descended it once more.

Several hours later, the Tonkawa scouts found two Comanche following them. As the scouts raced out to fight them, the Comanche hurried their horses into a ravine with no exit. Mackenzie rode up and saw they had the two Indians trapped.

"Take fifteen Tonkawas and go on foot into the ravine," Mackenzie ordered. "Finish off those Comanche."

Time passed with no result. Mackenzie became impatient and grabbed a lieutenant. The pair walked to the ravine's entrance and peered down to see what was taking so long.

As Mackenzie shifted to get a better view, he heard a swish and a thud. Out of thin air, an arrow protruded from his thigh. He was rushed away to a surgeon and the metal point was cut out.

That arrow could've hit his chest, Billy thought. *Then where would he have been?*

Soon, Mackenzie heard shots fired, followed by silence. The Tonkawas informed him that the Comanche were dead.

An inspection found one Comanche had been firing a pistol when he was shot in the hand. The bowstring was full of blood. This meant he somehow managed to draw back the string with his bad hand and fire several arrows. It had been an incredible show of strength and willpower in never giving up.

Before the darkness covered the canyon, two cooks, along with Dr. Choat and Lieutenant Miller, headed back to the ravine and decapitated the two Comanche, stuffing their heads into gunny sacks.

When the dust settled, Mackenzie had lost the first round to Quanah. Almost a mirror image of his foe, Mackenzie refused to lose the second.

He sent all the sick and injured men to the supply camp along with word for reinforcements. Some of his horses died or had to be shot. He needed rations. The troops were hungry.

When the supplies returned, Mackenzie led a scouting expedition to Pease River, the site of Peta Nocona's supposed death and Cynthia Ann Parker's "rescue." Mackenzie guessed that Quanah would double back to this special spot while assuming the bluecoats would never suspect it.

After a snowstorm hit Mackenzie's scouting party, they returned, having found nothing. Quanah was still free and probably laughing at them when he took round two.

On November 18, 1871, Mackenzie and his troops arrived in Fort Richardson just as a blizzard hit the area. Every man and beast was cold and tired.

Since Mackenzie started chasing Kicking Bird and through the Quanah debacle, his men had been in the field for six and a half months. Sure, they had forced Kicking Bird back to the reservation, but all Mackenzie had to show for it was maybe a hundred stolen or dead Army horses and mules. Oh, and two Comanche heads in a gunny sack. This result wouldn't stop Quanah or appease the Texans on the frontier. Something more had to be done.

Mackenzie spent the next year resupplying and getting his men healthy.

In the fall of 1872, he set out again to find Quanah. Instead, he stumbled into another band of Comanche led by Chief Mow-way.

Mow-way had been on his way to talk peace with the Indian agents when he ran into Mackenzie, who attacked him. Mow-way saw 52 of his people killed and 124 women and children captured.

Mackenzie's men destroyed two hundred teepees, stores of meat for the winter, clothing, and equipment. He even took in three thousand horses and mules, entrusting those animals to the Tonkawa scouts.

The scouts drove the herd a mile away to a low area in the prairie and went to sleep. The next morning, the Tonkawas returned to Mackenzie's camp, leading a burro that carried their saddles.

During the night, the Comanche had slipped in and taken the entire herd—three thousand strong—without waking the Tonkawas. It was a miracle the Tonkawas lived to tell about it.

Billy imagined Mackenzie shaking his head. *It never ends with these Indians.*

He studied other reports from the frontier. Quanah had not been slowed. In fact, he had increased his attacks. Up and down the frontier, smoldering charred ruins collected around stone chimneys—monuments to all that remained of the settlers' homes. Gone were their horses, mules, cattle, and many of their lives. For sure, more white children were kidnapped while others were tortured to death.

Billy could feel Mackenzie's intense anger as the colonel sat in a fort somewhere and read the following words: "At almost all these attacks, witnesses report a tall, imposing figure, painted in black and wearing a long flowing headdress. This warrior, presumably Quanah, always rides a beautiful gray pacer, which was Colonel Mackenzie's former mount."

Billy closed the file and thought, *Mackenzie and the U.S. Army have certainly met their match. Will anyone kill this Quanah Parker?*

Billy was betting on Quanah, the Eagle of the Comanche, so long as the buffalo roamed the prairie. When that stopped, Quanah would be done.

Perhaps.

*It is better to have less thunder in the mouth
and more lightning in the hand.*

Apache Proverb

Herman

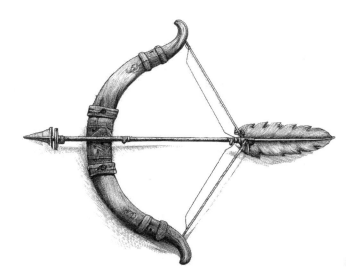

Chapter Thirty-Two

May 18, 1870
Squaw Creek, 25 miles northwest of Fredericksburg, Texas

"Come on, Willie, hurry up!" Herman Lehmann yelled. "We have to get to the fields."

It was a sunny morning in Hill Country. The persistent mosquitoes found a cool place to hide until later in the day when the sun went down and their unsuspecting victims provided a blood meal.

Willie, eight, ran after his big brother, trying to keep up. Behind Willie was Caroline, five, carrying two-year-old Gusta.

They all had a job to do: shoo the birds away from eating the tender stalks in the fields. Their mother had sent them to do this mainly to get the children out of her kitchen so she could clean up from breakfast and sit down at the table to enjoy a cup of coffee and breathe.

The two older boys ran through rows of future beans, sending birds flying. After ensuring the job was done, the pair sat in the fields with their two sisters and played in the dirt.

Why not?

It was a beautiful day with a perfect temperature. Anyway, there was nothing much else to do.

At almost eleven years old, Herman dug a tunnel in the dirt with his right hand. He studied a recent scar on his wrist that his sister had accidentally inflicted with a small hatchet. He'd been lucky. He could have lost a finger. Instead, he'd have this scar for life. *Oh well.*

The young boy focused on the work. His hole was supposed to connect with a hole being dug by Willie from the opposite direction. Herman stretched his arm through the tunnel until he felt Willie's fingers.

"Got it," Herman said, but Willie wasn't paying attention. Instead, his blank face stared at something behind Herman, who briskly spun around and found a half-naked man standing over him.

Bright paints and a hideous face shocked the boy. A buckskin around the man's waist kept him from being fully exposed.

Several other painted men surrounded Willie. In an instant, a warrior lifted up Herman as little Caroline ran for the house. A savage sent several arrows through the air, dropping the girl face-first.

The Indian slung Herman over his shoulder and carried him away. The last thing the boy saw was his baby sister, Gusta, crawling through the dirt, trying to survive.

By now, Herman had regained his wits. He struggled to get free, kicking and scratching. It worked, and he fell to the field, smushing some bean sprouts.

The Indian slapped his face hard and thrust it into the dirt, choking him. While he was down, the attacker stripped off Herman's clothes and threw away his hat.

The boy surprised the attacker by locking his fingers around the man's black hair and pulling hard. This distracted the Indian long enough for Herman to punch him in the gut. The German boy seized the advantage and dug his teeth into the savage's flesh, drawing blood.

The Indian yelped and faltered until another one came over and held Herman down. The leader joined them, grabbing the boy's legs and swinging him through the air, releasing him at the high point.

Herman hit a rock fence with a thud and saw stars. Before he fully came to, the Indians secured him with a rope and planted him on a horse.

With Willie on another horse, the Indians raced away, sending a naked Herman crashing through mesquite trees and thickets. He cried and screamed as thorns and branches scratched rivers of blood in his flesh. Yet the kidnappers didn't slow down.

They rode for some time, occasionally stopping to "collect" more horses. At nightfall, they separated Herman from his brother, and each abductor rode off in a separate direction.

Would Herman ever see Willie again?

The following day, an Indian spotted a young calf relaxing in the grass, soaking up the sun. The Indian untied Herman and signaled for him to catch the animal. Afraid, he did as commanded.

The Indian came over and cut the calf's throat. Then he opened the stomach, scooped up the ingested milk, and slurped it down. He gave some to Herman, who refused.

The man took Herman's face and thrust it into the calf's stomach, holding his nose until he had swallowed some milk. When the Indian let go, Herman promptly threw up.

The Indian cut out the liver and kidneys and forced pieces down Herman's mouth. He vomited it up.

The warrior collected the mess from the grass and forced it back down Herman's throat. He threw up again.

This back-and-forth went on several times until the man dipped the mess in the calf's warm blood and slid it down the boy's throat. The blood soothed Herman's stomach and he finally kept it down.

Whatever life this was, Herman didn't want it. He wanted to die and started looking for a way to make that happen.

Three days passed with the German boy still on a horse, naked and afraid. Herman's white skin had reddened, burned, and blistered in the sun.

His younger brother, Willie, had ridden north with six Indians, while Herman's six Indians took him west.

That evening, another band of Indians joined camp with Herman's group. A barbequed bull was cut up and served to everyone. Herman ate as much as he could keep down.

Still, they denied him water even though there were plenty of sources along the way. He knew from listening to his father that he would die the following day without it, but at that point, he didn't care.

The next morning, they rode northwest until Willie's band rejoined them. Herman was grateful to see his younger brother but noticed Willie was red and blistered, too. Both boys had trouble adjusting to the Indians' forked-stick saddles, with blisters forming on their bottoms.

Yet, the two boys were not given any water. With little ability to produce sweat due to lack of water, they would overheat in a few hours and die.

Somehow, the Indians knew this and led the boys to a muddy pond filled with bugs and smelling of frogs. Herman watched as the head Indian pulled some fresh grass at the pond's edge and spread it over the pond until the water was hidden. The Indian bent over and used his palm to cup some water through the grass. It was fresh, not muddy.

He motioned to Herman and Willie to do the same. The boys frantically cupped the fresh water into their parched mouths.

Finally satisfied, Herman was about to get up when the leader rushed over and pushed his head deep into the mud. The other Indians laughed and pointed as Herman wiped his eyes and mouth clean. Yet he dared not show his displeasure.

The band rested for several hours before riding north. It was late afternoon when they stopped on a hill and killed a steer resting in a cool spot.

Herman was summoned to help with the fire and watched how the Indian used only a certain kind of wood in a small quantity to keep the fire from generating too much smoke. Obviously, they didn't want the whites to see the smoke and come to investigate.

After a solid meal, the head Indian and Herman walked back down the trail to a slight rise. The Indian stepped up on a fallen tree and removed a shiny piece of metal from his pouch. By tilting the metal at different angles, he could use the sun's reflection to signal his scouts back down the line.

This went on for a minute or two until the Indian smiled. Herman guessed the signals meant they weren't being followed. There would be no rescue today.

With the West Texas sky turning shades of orange, the Indians mounted up and rode for a few more hours.

Just before evening dissolved into night, the band reached a small stream and found other Indians there. The women took Herman and Willie from the horses and washed and dressed their wounds, rubbing an herbal salve over their peeling skin. It felt good to be treated with kindness.

Soon, paints were produced and the two white boys were transformed into fearsome Indians.

On the fifth day, the band took off to the northwest, driving a herd of stolen ponies. One of the Indians had an injured leg from a shotgun blast. He'd been seen by a farmer as he crawled into the corral and was lucky to be alive. But now his leg hurt too much to ride. He was forced to walk, which was no problem since the band traveled at a leisurely pace.

As they neared a watering hole, another Indian rode up fast, his face filled with panic.

Herman watched the gestures and pointing and understood some Texas Rangers were camped at the watering hole. So far, the rangers hadn't spotted the Indians.

The head Indian barked orders and the stolen ponies were released. Then, at top speed, the band rode away from the rangers, constantly looking back over their shoulders.

The Indian with a sore leg tried to keep up but couldn't. Left with no choice, he jumped on the same horse as Willie and took off.

Unfortunately, the horse was tired. The injured warrior made its burden lighter by tossing little Willie into the brush. The horse seemed to gain a second wind but soon collapsed in exhaustion. Another Indian swooped by, picked up the man, and quickly caught up with the band.

Herman witnessed this all and cried from the depths of his soul. He knew Willie was likely dead and he'd never see his brother again. He was on the same horse as the head Indian and tied with rope to the forked-stick saddle, so there was nothing he could do.

Despondent, he thought about his mother. She and his father, Ernst Moritz Lehmann, had emigrated from Germany. When Ernst died in 1862, Herman was just five but remembered well how hard she'd cried. Losing her two sons would devastate her. It was unthinkably cruel.

Herman wiped his endless tears. Before his capture, he'd never seen an Indian, much less been harmed by one.

His mother's new husband, Philip Buchmeier, talked about Indians all the time. He was a local stonemason and was always on the lookout for savages.

But Philip had been working in town the day Herman and Willie were taken, so he couldn't protect them. The Indians took full advantage of his absence.

Herman glared at the sun. It beat on his blistered skin as the hard sticks cut into his groin. With nothing to do, he shook his head violently and let the tears fall.

"*Wo ist meine Mutter?*" he wailed in German. "I just want my mom."

Eight days from his capture placed Herman and the Indian band at the dividing line between the green hills of Central Texas and the desert of West Texas. For three days, they had not eaten or taken any water. The Indians feared the Texas Rangers so much that they didn't even stop to sleep.

It was evening when they finally dismounted at a clear creek north of Fort Concho. An Indian untied Herman and let him down. He was so pained that he crawled to the water, sliding in and washing his body as he drank his fill. It felt so good that he didn't want to get out, so he didn't.

An hour later, a thin moon appeared. It illuminated the frantic Indians looking for Herman. They called and kicked the bushes but couldn't find him anywhere.

From the safety of the dark water, the young boy watched all this and smiled. Eventually, they mounted up and rode off at a slow pace.

Herman was free, yet he was in the middle of nowhere. Coyotes howled all around, making him think, *I'll never find my way back home. Between the wolves, wildcats, and coyotes, I'll be eaten alive. Maybe I should run after the Indians. If they see that I returned on my own, surely they'll treat me better.*

Herman started running. Sure enough, the last Indian wheeled his horse around, picked up the boy by the hair, and set him down on the hard saddle. After several hours of riding, the band stopped for the night.

Herman saw an Indian pick up two sotol sticks and cut notches into each one. Then he pushed sand into the notches and rubbed the sticks hard, creating friction. Soon, a fire appeared. Several warriors lit cigarettes while another covered the fire enough to keep it alive but not to be seen from any distance.

Herman licked his lips, looking forward to some food. He hadn't eaten in almost four days and was famished.

One of the Indians called him over and tied a rope around his neck, fastening the other end to a bush. They strapped his arms behind his back and tied his feet together.

Herman watched in horror as they pounded forked sticks into the ground six feet apart. The leader slid a long pole on his back between the bindings. Then the Indians lifted the boy and secured the long stick into the crooks of the forked sticks. His chest barely touched the sand, and the slightest movement pulled the ropes deeper into his flesh.

Herman realized he would be suspended like that all night. It was a cruel torture, obviously a result of his escape attempt. These savages were sending a message: Your next escape attempt will be your last.

Herman tried to breathe but found it difficult. If he sucked in too much air, the ropes strained and choked him. It was searing agony.

Just before the Indians went to sleep, one of them placed a large rock on his back. This pressed Herman's face and nose into the sand.

It would be hard to breathe like this all night, much less make it to sunrise. He groaned and the Indian beat him severely.

During the night, each time he moaned or cried, an Indian got up and pulled his hair and ears hard, often beating him until he bled. Herman went in and out of consciousness, sure he'd wake up in heaven. He looked forward to it.

When the first rays of morning appeared, Herman was stunned to still be alive. One Indian pulled a gun on him while another drew back his bow and nocked an arrow. A third removed the rock and untied him.

He could barely stand. When he finally did, all the scabs on his body oozed with blood. That was fine because he wanted to die. He hoped for an arrow or bullet, but one never came.

The Indians waved off breakfast, so Herman had nothing. The water he'd taken the day before had given him a fever. It was the last thing he needed.

Soon, the twelve horses climbed the escarpment and reached the Llano Estacado. Herman gazed over an endless flat land, empty and featureless. It was not quite a desert but not a green prairie either.

The band rode for four hours before stopping suddenly. An Indian approached Herman's horse and pointed to two baby antelope in the grass. They ordered Herman to collect the animals and he did so without effort.

With a rope around the confused babies, Herman walked with them and followed the Indians a mile or two until they stopped to make a fire. To his horror, the Indians tied the legs of the two baby antelope and placed them in the fire, still alive.

The babies cried for their mother, squirming in the flames before burning to death. Despite this gruesome scene, Herman took the hunk of cooked meat they handed him and downed it fast. He hadn't eaten in four days and could hardly think straight.

These savages had no sympathy or respect for life. He made it his fervent wish that they would all die.

At nightfall, the two Indians stayed on foot and took Herman back down the trail where they had found the baby antelope. They were halfway there when the men shoved him into some tall grass, signaling him to stay quiet.

Soon, the momma and papa antelope came looking for their babies. With the antelope keeping their noses down to the trail, the Indians stood up and shot both with arrows.

That night, they savored more antelope meat. Herman didn't complain. He was still alive.

When it was time to sleep, the Indians tied him but didn't employ the hanging-stick-with-the-rock-on-back torture. Herman slept harder and deeper than he'd ever managed back home.

The next morning, the band was awake before daybreak and finished off the antelope for breakfast. They mounted up and traveled for two days without food.

Near the end of the second day, Herman saw a tremendous woolly beast with stubby horns. It ran hard with its short legs.

The Indians chased the beast and killed it. A warrior cut open the entrails and collected the stomach's contents, sharing it with his companions.

Then they cut out the liver and smeared gall all over it. One of them gave Herman a piece and he promptly threw it up. The Indian added more gall to the flesh and it stayed down.

From then on, Herman and his band found game everywhere. They ate well and Herman learned to eat whatever they gave him without vomiting.

After ten days of riding, they came to a knoll and stopped. The head Indian stood at the top of the knoll and waved a red blanket in a circle. He lowered the blanket and waited for a return signal.

Suddenly, he mounted up and the Indians kicked their horses into a full gallop, leading them to a village at the edge of a beautiful lake. Herman was now in New Mexico.

Indians from the village swarmed the riders, with everyone yelling and whooping. Herman guessed there were over 2,500 savages.

He was scared to death but fought hard not to show it. He had learned that tears and crying brought more beatings.

In seconds, dozens of Indians—women and children—surrounded Herman. A stout squaw grabbed his legs and pulled the boy from the horse. She proceeded to pinch his face and beat him senselessly. This was followed by rolling around on the ground and pressing her weight on him.

When she finally stopped, the rest of the village marched around him, dancing and yelling. The Indian train was led by the women, followed by the warriors. The children brought up the rear.

The women chanted while the men fired their guns and yelled. It was a celebration. Herman felt like those baby antelope tossed alive on the fire and feared his turn would soon come.

Out of the crowd, an old warrior pushed people aside and slowly removed a long blade from a sheath on his back. Herman's eyes widened as the edge neared his scalp.

The warrior grabbed his hair and set the knife to his forehead. Herman closed his eyes and prayed to God for help. He knew what was coming.

Sure enough, the blade cut into his scalp. When the old man was done, most of Herman's hair was gone. Yet his scalp was intact. The man had only dug the tip into his scalp and pulled out plugs of hair here and there.

Blood trickled over Herman's forehead and down his back. It wasn't long before his shoulders were red.

When the old warrior stepped away, another replaced him. This one carried a long, hot iron in his hand. Several strong men held Herman down so the warrior could burn a hole through his left ear.

The pain was so intense that Herman could barely scream. Just when he thought it was over, the man shifted to the right ear and burned a hole through it, too.

A woman approached and ran rawhide string through the holes. Herman closed his eyes and prayed it was over. It wasn't.

The same warrior took the red iron rod and burned holes in the boy's arms. There was no reason for it other than cruelty.

Herman fought and kicked and screamed and clawed, but to no avail. They did whatever they wanted.

Once again, Herman closed his eyes and pleaded with God to die. Despite the pain, it didn't take long for the boy to leave this place. In his mind, he was already gone.

Chapter Thirty~Three

February 10, 1875
Dallas, Texas

The worker raised the hammer and struck the nail, driving it into the soft wood with one swing. He repeated this three more times and set the hammer down.

"That's the last of them, sir."

"Okay," Billy Tyler said. "Load them up in the wagon and I'll be right there."

The worker opened the door and went back to the box, lifting and carrying it outside. When he had set the box in the wagon, he closed the door and remained outside.

It was cold outside and hard enough to heat these offices, especially facing north. Keeping that door closed was the only way to stay warm.

Billy straightened his desk and deftly shifted his crutches around so he could put on his coat. He heard the door open behind him and said, "I'll be right there. *Please!*"

"Okay," the voice said. It wasn't the worker.

Billy spun around and saw a clean-shaven man, perhaps forty, standing in the doorway.

"Can I help you?" Billy asked.

"I sure hope so. Name's Emmitt Hempstead. I'm with the War Department back in Washington."

"DC?" Billy said, stunned.

"The same one. Mind if I take a seat?"

"Uh, of course. Let me take my jacket off. I was heading to the archives with some boxes."

"I know," Emmitt said. "My man is riding with your man. They'll sort it out and you can fix it all later."

Billy took his seat and grinned. "Sounds like you know me somehow."

"I feel like I do," Emmitt said, lighting a cigarette. "I've read your reports. You have a keen eye for things others don't."

"Well, thank you, Mr. Hempstead."

"Emmitt. Call me Emmitt."

"Certainly, Emmitt. So what can I do for you?"

Emmitt exhaled a cloud of smoke. "We have a problem. We learned about it in the War."

The "War" meant the Civil War, which had ended ten years earlier.

The visitor continued. "You see, we treated the Reb prisoners well because we knew many of them would eventually be paroled back to the South. Some were traded and others escaped. Either way, we wanted them to tell their brethren how well they were treated. Do you know why?"

"I think so," Billy replied. "When a Rebel is fighting you but suffering losses or lacking food and equipment, he'll remember how well you treated his buddies and either back off or even surrender."

"Exactly," Emmitt said. "And that's where you come in."

Billy was confused. "You want me to run a prisoner-of-war camp?"

"No. We need you to check on one and see what's really happening."

"Where is it?"

Emmitt tapped off some ashes. "Fort Sill, Oklahoma."

"That's Indian country."

"Actually, it's an Indian reservation. There's a big difference. Many of the Indian tribes have come to the reservation, but they don't stay. We send them food, lots of it. Clothes, blankets, housing materials, farming equipment. I see the actual bills, and I know what we're spending. But the Indians aren't happy enough to stay. Something isn't right, and I need a man like you to sort it out; you know, get to the truth of what's going on."

Billy scratched his forehead. "But they won't tell me the truth. I'm a white man. They'll hide it."

"Right, and our soldiers and civilians will hide it from you, too. But if we send a clerk who's just there to archive some records—not a true investigator—he might have a chance. He can ask questions and gain information others can't. No one will suspect another bureaucrat shuffling papers from one tray to another."

Billy laughed. "I guess that's what folks think we do."

"It is. And we intend to use it to our advantage."

"When will this happen?" Billy asked.

"During a normal transfer of soldiers. We have a wagon train leaving Dallas in three weeks. The usual drovers, skinners, and supply wagons will come along. They need the soldiers for protection. The more, the better. I want you on a wagon headed up there. I arranged a nice one with a thick cover and bedding in the back to make your trip enjoyable."

Billy's mind raced. To be out on the prairie, crossing rivers and facing dangers. Campfires at night and hearty meals from the chuckwagon. It would be the adventure of his life.

Emmitt exhaled one final time and crushed out his cigarette.

"We'll outfit you with weapons and everything you need to uh… collect records for the archives. Are you in?"

Billy glanced at his crutches. He was thirty now, and this might be his last chance for adventure.

"How long will I be there?"

"Until you solve this riddle and tell me why the reservation system isn't working."

Emmitt Hempstead studied his man, trying to get a read before setting the hook. "But perhaps I've wasted your—"

"No!" Billy blurted out. "I'm in. I'll start getting ready today."

The government man nodded. "That's good because I already told Washington you'd accept. That's why they paid my way out here. Now I just need to brief you on everything you need to know and make sure you're outfitted properly."

"Then let's not waste a moment," Billy said, grabbing his crutches and rising from his chair.

Dozens of teepees covered the prairie, the tops glowing from the fires inside. One large teepee occupied the center of the camp. Inside, it was filled with smoke and Comanche warriors. At the head was Quanah Parker, holding a smoldering pipe.

"You have heard the others speak about White Eagle," he said. "They have told you what they saw and some of you know this is true."

The men looked at the medicine man. White Eagle was unlike any other medicine man. He was young, strong, and vigorous. His face was broad but smooth with piercing eyes. He wore no mask or buffalo skullcap and only a breechclout over his loins and a red sash around his waist to provide some color.

The moccasins on White Eagle's feet allowed him to move with a nimbleness others lacked. A red-tipped hawk's feather stuck out from his hair. A snake rattle hung from each ear.

White Eagle displayed two important things: confidence and stage presence—both in abundance.

Quanah exhaled some smoke and said, "You will see White Eagle conjure up the Great Spirit. Then you can decide for yourself if you will join me on a raid to seek revenge for the killing of my boyhood friend."

When he pointed the pipe at White Eagle, the medicine man moved to the front.

The Comanche warriors watched intently as this strange man picked up a handful of green cedar twigs and bent over a small fire, dropping them on the flames. A thick, pungent smoke arose.

It took a few minutes until White Eagle used a fan to push the smoke toward the men sitting in front. His helper sat behind him and tapped softly on a small drum.

The medicine man leaned over the fire and held his hands out, washing them in the smoke before bathing his chest and face. Then he started to chant, barely audible at first but growing in volume.

"Great Spirit, have pity on us. Great Spirit, make us strong. Through our brother, show us what to do."

The fire grew and cast a red light on White Eagle's face. He stood and stretched his arm up, staring at the small opening at the top of the teepee. Then he began a five-minute speech that ended with him receiving an important message from the Great Spirit.

Suddenly, he blurted out, "I can see a paint that stops the white man's bullets. I can make it."

White Eagle then detailed all the prophecies he'd previously made that came true. Quanah confirmed each one.

White Eagle leaned his head back and howled like a wolf.

The men had heard about White Eagle. Some even claimed they had seen the young medicine man raise a wagonload of cartridges from his stomach and bring the dead back to life.

Along with other promises, White Eagle said he would raise so much ammunition from his stomach that his brothers didn't have to worry about running out in a battle. But his biggest promise was that his medicine was so great that no warrior could be killed as long as he was present.

The warriors' heads were filled with smoke, their ears with his words. Then their eyes were treated to a miracle: White Eagle did the impossible, pulling an arrow from the smoke. And another. And another. The men were hooked.

When Quanah passed the pipe around, most of the men took it. A few believed White Eagle was lying and they'd surely be killed if they rode on a raid with that crazy fool, so they passed the pipe.

After the meeting, Quanah and White Eagle rode to the next camp. Quanah thought back to General Mackenzie. The bluecoat's raid had almost destroyed his Comanche band. Yet they had survived.

Once Quanah's people were safe, he would continue raiding all across Texas. It was to be a revenge raid. It hurt him deeply when his close friend was killed, and he now planned to kill and burn half of Texas. To do it he needed plenty of warriors to join him.

Quanah rode into a camp where several influential chiefs lived. He explained his idea for the raid, but the old men didn't like it.

This was a huge problem since these chiefs could turn most of the warriors against Quanah and his raid. He sat down with the men and listened to their concerns.

"While you burn Texas," a chief told him, "the buffalo hunters kill our animals. When you return victorious from your raids, you will find us all starved to death."

Quanah thought carefully about this truth. If the buffalo died, they would all die. It was a simple formula.

"But I must avenge my good friend's death at the hands of the Tonkawas," he pleaded. "They scout and lead the white man to our villages. I must kill the Tonkawas and the white men who hire them."

"Yes, you must," another chief said. "But first, plan a raid on the buffalo hunters' outpost."

"Adobe Walls?" Quanah asked. "Where we fought Kit Carson?"

"Yes. Kill all those buffalo hunters and tear down that outpost for good. The hunters will have nowhere to go and they'll stop killing our buffalo."

It made sense to Quanah. "If I do this, will you bless my revenge raid afterward?"

"Yes, we will," the chief said. "But you must kill them all at Adobe Walls. Leave nothing but ashes on the prairie."

"Then burn Texas to the ground," another chief added.

Quanah respected these old men. They were wise. With their blessing, he could raise a large force. And with White Eagle by his side, they couldn't lose. The Great Spirit would make sure of it.

Billy Tyler cleaned off his desk one last time. In a few minutes, he'd mount the wagon outside and begin a northward journey with the military leading the way. He'd been looking forward to this since Emmitt Hempstead had entered his office. Now, it was finally time to go.

Billy folded some papers and shoved them into his shirt pocket as the front door opened. A young girl holding a stuffed carpet bag walked inside and closed it.

Billy studied the girl. She had a large bandage on the left side of her face, most of it covered by thick, dark hair cascading over her shoulders.

The girl wore a light blue dress, drawn in tight at her waist, with shoes more appropriate for a party than walking the streets of Dallas. Judging from her appearance, she had to be under twenty years old.

"Can I help you?" he asked.

"I'm looking for William Tyler," she replied softly. "They said he'd be here."

"I'm William Tyler," Billy said, unused to hearing his formal name.

"Oh good. My name is Jennie Bunting. I need to get to Kansas and I understand you're leaving today. I was hoping to hitch a ride as I can't safely make it up there alone."

This stunned Billy. "Do you have a horse?"

"No, sir. I was hoping to ride in a wagon if there's room."

"Is that all of your belongings?"

"Yes, sir," she replied, patting the carpet bag.

Billy rubbed his lips as he contemplated this request.

Seeing his hesitation, she added, "I have money. I can pay my way. I just really need to get to Kansas."

"Do you have family up there?" Billy asked.

"I hope so," Jennie said, rubbing her large bandage. "My life is over in Dallas. I need to be with them."

Billy decided not to probe any further. If he was going to join the wagon train, he needed to get going.

"Okay, Jennie. You can ride in my wagon."

"Will your wife mind?" she innocently asked.

"No. I'm not married."

"Oh," she said, letting that hang in the air.

Billy grabbed his crutches and put on his jacket. "Come outside. I need to lock this place up."

"I can't thank you enough, sir!" Jennie said. "Truly."

"Thank me when we reach Fort Sill safely. In the meantime, call me Billy. All my friends do."

"Oh, I don't know," she said. "How about William?"

Billy thought for a moment. "That'll work."

He locked the door and helped Jennie with her bag. Then he smiled, noticing a slight spring in his step, as much as one could with a crippled leg.

Willie Lehmann was scared. The injured Indian had hopped onto his horse and now it was struggling to keep up.

Willie looked ahead at his older brother, Herman, and wished for help, yet none came. Herman was tied to the horse and couldn't do anything even if he wanted to.

Willie's horse stumbled and the Indian growled. A strong hand clamped under Willie's left arm and he was flying through the air. A thick bush cushioned his fall and he lay flat on his back for a few minutes, sorting everything out. By the time he stood up, Herman and the rest of the Indians were long gone.

He wanted to start crying, but he realized he was free of the savages. All he had to do now was get back to his mother, and quickly.

Willie walked southeast, the exact opposite direction the Indians had been traveling. The brush was fairly easy to navigate, and he found a road in less than an hour. It ran south toward civilization. His pace increased in his excitement.

Incredibly, an hour later, near Kickapoo, he met a man on horseback.

"What are you doing out here?" the man asked, his right hand on the butt of his revolver as his eyes scanned the bush for other Indians.

Naturally shy, eight-year-old Willie was used to saying little. "I fell off a horse."

The man looked around and gripped his pistol. "I don't see any horse. Are you alright?"

"Yeah," Willie said, unaware that his body was painted and that he wore Indian attire.

"Okay," the man said, kicking his horse and disappearing down the road.

Willie continued walking, thinking about that conversation. He looked down at his chest. It was covered with paint.

No wonder he didn't help me, he thought.

Willie found some mud and rubbed off most of the paint. Then he felt his head and removed the skull cap made from a calf's scalp. When he neared a ditch, he tossed the cap away.

Good riddance.

Willie took in a deep breath and said a prayer for another chance. Sure enough, a fully loaded freight wagon driven by oxen came down the road. This time, the boy was mentally ready.

"Hey, sir!" he yelled. "Can I have a ride?"

The freighter pulled back on the reins and grabbed the brake. "Sure, young fella. Hop up."

Willie climbed on board, and the driver took a closer look at him. "What are you doing out here?" he asked the boy.

Willie told him the whole story and the man was amazed. He told Willie he was headed to Fort McKavett and promised to take the boy home to his mother after he dropped off his load.

And he did.

Willie Lehmann had been gone for nine excruciating days. When she first laid eyes on her little boy, his frantic mother could hardly stop hugging him. Finally, he was safe at home.

The Lehmanns hoped with all their strength that their older boy Herman would soon join Willie. Each morning, afternoon, and evening, they stared out the windows of their small cabin, praying Herman would come trotting down the road on a horse.

He didn't.

But soon, they would have a different kind of visitor, someone who didn't bother to knock.

Chapter Thirty-Four

Confusion.

Nothing made sense. Herman felt someone dripping water over his chest but slipped back into unconsciousness.

Hours later, the boy awoke and found he'd been washed and cleaned, and his wounds dressed. Oil covered his body, which helped the scabs heal while keeping bugs away. Strangely, in all the chaos he'd endured, he felt refreshed.

Then a woman came for him.

She led Herman to a large blanket filled with various foods. Three Mexicans had just been in camp and traded the Indians sunbaked bread and cones of brown sugar.

The Indians set cooked buffalo next to pieces of raw meat. Herman was so hungry he could hardly decide which food to attack.

He hesitated and looked at the crowd surrounding him. All the men and women were quietly watching his every move.

Herman wondered what would happen if he grabbed the wrong food. Would he be declared hopelessly white and unable to assimilate into the tribe? If so, this would lead to death by torture.

He eyed several Indians holding ropes and other implements of torture. They stood ready to administer the days-long punishment. In fact, they seemed to be wishing for it.

When Herman reached for the raw meat and ate it, a gasp erupted. The Indian who had stolen him patted his shoulder. He would live another day.

All at once, the Indians laughed and made jokes, except for the ones who were clearly ready to dispense some untold torture. Disappointed, those men sulked away.

Herman ate for an hour before reclining back and patting his belly. Just when he was about to fall asleep, a warrior came over and fastened a jug around his neck. The warrior pointed to the lake and mumbled something. Herman understood the jug needed filling.

He walked to the lake while examining the jug. It was made of dogwood, woven together and cemented with pitch, a neat invention.

Several Indian boys showed Herman how to tip the jug on its side and allow it to fill. Once the jug was full, Herman couldn't stand up and carry it out.

The boys came over and helped him to his feet. Yet the heavy weight still hung around his neck. They released him, so he fell underwater.

The boys laughed and pointed at him. He was so weak that the jug was strangling him.

Quickly, a warrior splashed through the water and pulled the jug off, carrying it and Herman back to camp. Only then could he take a nap.

Three hours disappeared when a warrior woke Herman and forced him to wrestle other boys. He lost every round.

A woman came over and measured his body. Half a day later, she returned with a buckskin jacket and moccasins. They fit perfectly and felt good.

The chief then declared it was time to leave and move somewhere else. A sad little German boy looked to the east, certain he'd never see Texas again.

It had been two long weeks, a lifetime for Herman. The poor boy had been worked to the bone. He was placed in charge of watching over the herd of ponies.

Each day, they sat Herman on a small pony and he wandered around the remuda, calming the beasts and looking for wolves and coyotes. After being relieved by another boy, he went to camp and pounded up corn, skinned game, picked lice from other people's hair and cracked them between his teeth, started fires by rubbing sticks together, carried water, and dressed wounds. It was not the life he expected as an eleven-year-old.

By now, an Indian boy had been assigned to teach him the language. Herman was smart and picked it up fast.

He learned these people were Mescalero Apache. His stepdad had always told him the Comanche were the worst, followed closely by the Apache. He couldn't imagine how someone could survive anything worse than an Apache.

Herman was told the man who'd stolen him was named Carnoviste. He was a popular warrior and leader but not a chief. Herman could see Carnoviste held plenty of influence over the tribe.

At one location, the water was scarce, and so was the food. A squaw who constantly bossed Herman around sent him and the other boys to a mostly dried-up creek to catch fish. Herman waded out and pushed the fish to the other boys. They had about ten when Herman demanded one of the fish be given to him so he could eat it right there.

"No!" the boys said. "The Great Spirit will be offended. You can't eat fish here. We must take them back to camp."

The medicine man stood on the bank watching all this. He hated Herman and had been beating and injuring him since his arrival.

The medicine man loved fish since his diet was restricted, as it was an Apache belief that a medicine man couldn't be killed as long as he never ate swine. So when Herman wanted to eat a fish, he summoned the main chief.

As Herman argued with the boys to give him one, he heard some splashing behind him. Herman turned just in time to see the chief pick him up and toss him farther down the creek.

The German boy hit the mud face first. When he lifted his head and wiped his eyes clean, he saw a turtle and held it up.

The boys laughed at him but shrieked with joy when they saw the turtle. They ran toward him, and in a few minutes, the group had collected fifty turtles. Together, they carried the catch back to camp.

Seeing this, the squaws built a large fire and set the turtles over the coals. Many of the turtles tried to escape the searing pain, but the squaws picked them up and tossed them back onto the fire.

Once the turtles had all been roasted alive in their shells, the entire camp was summoned. A woman cracked each one open and pulled out pieces of meat. It wasn't buffalo, but it satisfied their hunger until the next meal, whenever that might be.

Life for Herman didn't improve. Each shift guarding the ponies made him feel desperately lonely.

Part of his job was to lead the horses to water. The pond was far from camp.

On one of these long trips, his body heaved with sobs from being so utterly homesick. Back at camp, he dared not let anyone see him cry. Otherwise, he'd be beaten or, worse, tortured as an escape risk. So it was no surprise he began hatching a plan to flee.

Each day, Herman snuck food under his buffalo robe and stored it away from camp. One morning, he took a water jug and slipped it over his saddle. He could almost taste freedom.

The big day was finally here. Herman led the remuda to water, but he filled his jug first. It was a clear day, and he let his pony drink its fill.

Herman stood on the vast land, gazing east at freedom and home. Then he mounted up and kicked the pony toward the rising sun. He would do whatever it took to escape these savages.

At first, the pony ran hard. Herman made five miles before his horse slowed. He urged it to hurry but the pony couldn't.

Herman hopped off and let the pony walk for a mile, hoping it would catch a second wind. Then he kicked himself for not stealing a younger, stronger horse from the herd. It would've been so easy.

He remounted the pony and kicked its side. The animal trotted a few hundred yards and slowed to a walk.

Herman wondered how far he could get before the band found he was missing. He twisted around to slap the pony's flank and felt his stomach drop.

A large dust cloud moved behind him. It wasn't the weather; it was the Apache, and they were coming for him.

He desperately kicked the pony, but it stumbled and tossed him to the ground. As he hit the dirt, he dropped the water jug and ran toward freedom.

Glancing back, he saw them gaining ground. Desperately, he sought out a place to hide, but there was nowhere to go.

Post Oak

Before he could turn around again, they were on him. A warrior dismounted and struck Herman all over with a rawhide whip.

After a thorough beating, he was tied tightly and carried back to camp. They gathered around him and held a large council. Once again, his life hung in the balance.

The final judgment was more whippings. Incredibly, Herman survived the escape attempt.

Why?

He had no idea.

The next day, they dispatched him to guard the ponies but sent another boy with him. Eventually, Herman made friends with the lad.

The boy taught Herman how to fix arrows and make a bow. And he learned more of the band's language and customs. At some point, Herman accepted his place and made no more attempts to escape.

Unfortunately, the whippings weren't his only punishment. His master, Carnoviste, added another chore to his long list. At random moments, the warrior took Herman into his teepee and made him perform unspeakable duties.

It was both shocking and sickening, but the boy had little choice as Carnoviste held a large, sharp knife. He had to submit and endure.

From his Bible training, he knew God would severely punish these heathens one day. He could only pray it would be soon, even if it meant he'd be taken. Anything was better than this degradation.

Two months raced by. Herman watched as his new father returned from a raid with eleven other warriors and a herd of stolen horses. They handed him hides, and he spent days scraping flesh off them.

Carnoviste and another warrior had suffered gunshot wounds. Herman was told his mother had fired the shots.

Not believing them, they showed him clothing and a small pistol he recognized as his own. Then they detailed how the warriors had killed his mother and sisters. His entire family was dead.

Before Herman could process this news, they commenced beating him severely for his mother's actions. When they finally let up, he was told that if either man died, he'd be tortured to death.

"And we'll make you suffer!" the medicine man added.

They forced Herman to pick shotgun pellets from Carnoviste's breast and the lower back of the other warrior. Whenever he caused pain, the Indian would grunt and howl, turning around to beat Herman.

It was a crazy way to live. With his family gone, this would be his life until the day he died.

Herman Lehmann thought long and hard about his predicament. Really, he had two choices: kill himself or become an Apache.

He couldn't decide which, so he put off making the decision until the next day. Maybe something would change.

Maybe not.

Chapter Thirty-Five

The horses pulled the lead wagon through the Red River and Billy Tyler slapped the reins. The sandy mud stuck to the wheels as they turned and churned to the far bank. One final pull from the strong team and they were free. It had been a successful crossing for him and his passenger.

"That was a good job, William," Jennie said, patting his shoulder.

Billy smiled. From a desk job to riding the Grand Prairie, he was proud of himself for making this transition.

It wasn't as hard as he thought. Having Jennie along to cook the meals while enjoying them next to her under a vast canvas of stars made Billy believe he could find someone willing to marry him. Maybe he already had.

The sergeant rode up and pointed to a flat area ahead. "Take your wagon to that spot and wait for everyone else. Then we'll form up and head out."

"Will do," Billy said.

The sergeant didn't turn to leave. Instead, he lingered and studied the young girl intensely until she looked away. It made Billy and Jennie uncomfortable.

"Is there something else?" Billy said, an edge to his voice.

"Uh, no. Not yet. But remember, we're in Oklahoma now—Indian country. Keep a look out because danger lurks everywhere." He spun his horse around and galloped back to the river.

"What was that all about?" Billy said. "It was like he was interested in you. Do you know him?"

"No!" she said emphatically as she touched her injured cheek. "He was probably staring at my bandages. I need to change them."

"Let me help you," Billy offered.

"Oh no, William, that won't be necessary."

"Please," Billy pleaded. "I can help. During emergencies, I assisted the fort's physician."

Jennie scrunched up her lips, contemplating his offer. "All right, then. That would be sweet of you."

Billy led the wagon to the designated spot and used a crutch to stand on the driver's box. He scanned the horizon and saw nothing but wagons and horses coming across the river to join them.

He set his crutch down and crawled to the wagon bed. The metal frame supported the sturdy fabric and gave the wagon the familiar Western frontier look.

A breeze flowed through the tunnel of canvas. Though it was almost too cold, it felt good.

Billy kneeled next to Jennie as she gently peeled off the bandage. She caught his eyes studying the wound.

"What happened to you?" he finally asked.

He had wanted to know her story from the moment they met.

"I was milking cows when a tool fell over and sliced my face."

Billy could see the cut from just below the hairline down to her jaw. It ran on a line between her left eye and ear.

"I'm so sorry," he said. "I'm sure it will heal up just fine."

He tried to sound positive even though he doubted his own words.

"You're sweet, William, but the doctor said I'd have this terrible scar for life."

"What about these stitches?"

"He gave me some tools to remove them. I have two more days and may need your help again."

Billy continued staring at the hideous wound. It was so serious that it could have killed her.

"William, press here," she said, grabbing his hand and placing it against the fresh bandage.

For a brief moment, she caressed his hand, causing a spark and tingle in Billy.

"There," Jennie said. "That should do it until we have to remove the stitches."

A horse raced up and skidded to a stop.

"Hey!" the private yelled, thrusting his head through the rear of the wagon. "Our scouts said Indians are coming. Form a circle like we practiced and get your weapons ready."

Billy sprung into action, pulling the wagon to a spot a few hundred yards away. When he had set the brake, a private unhitched the team and led the horses to the center of the circle. Billy moved his Winchester rifle and Sharp's long gun to his driver's box as Jennie brought him boxes of cartridges.

"Can you shoot those, William?" Her voice trembled.

"Yes. I won contests at the fort and even some money. Most soldiers assume a cripple can't do anything. But I can hit a polecat at two hundred yards. Can I hit an Indian on a fast-moving horse? We're about to see. But don't bet against it."

He spun the cylinder in a pistol and handed it to Jennie. "Take this. If an Indian tries to climb in the back, point it at 'im and pull the trigger."

"I-I don't know if I c-can," she managed.

"You can and you must. But Jennie, listen to me. If I get killed, leave one bullet for yourself. You don't want to be captured by these savages. I've read all the reports. Death is much better than what they'll do to you."

Jennie's eyes filled with tears, and Billy immediately felt bad. But he didn't have time to comfort her. Instead, he turned around, shouldered the Winchester, and prepared to end someone's life.

Augusta Johanna Adams Lehmann sat at her kitchen table, picking rocks from a bean pile. It had been six weeks since Willie miraculously returned from the savages and she hadn't stopped smiling.

The fact that Willie saw Herman alive gave her hope for her oldest son. If Willie could make it home, Herman could, too.

A noise in the yard caught Augusta's attention. It was Mina, her twelve-year-old daughter, screaming.

"Mom!" she yelled. "A big rock rolled down on us while Willie and I were watering the horses. It might be Indians."

"Did you see any?" she said, jumping up from her chair.

"No. But Dad said that's a trick they use. It almost knocked me down."

Augusta turned to her son. "Did you see anything?"

"No, Mom," Willie replied, nervously rubbing his hands. "But I don't want to be captured again."

Augusta walked into the yard and scanned the horizon. Max, the family dog, didn't seem worried. He lounged in the grass, occasionally snapping at bugs.

Her oldest son, Adolf, was irrigating a field a mile or so away with her husband. If trouble came, neither male would be around to help, at least not until late afternoon.

"Let's go inside," she told her children, hoping to redirect them. "I have some sewing for you to do."

Mina and Willie followed her in. Augusta quietly moved a shotgun closer, checking that it was fully loaded and ready to fire. Soon, everyone had calmed down.

Little Caroline played with some paper near the fireplace. Incredibly, she had survived the attack by fainting as she ran toward the house. The arrows had flown over her head, just missing her.

The Indians must have thought they had killed the girl because they broke off the attack when the boys started struggling and making noise. Even the baby was left wiggling in the dirt, alive and unhurt. It had been a true miracle that so many of them survived.

The cabin was quiet when Max started barking. Mina went outside and saw nothing.

"Did you see anything?" Augusta asked her daughter.

"No," she replied. "Dad and Adolf must be returning."

Augusta sighed. She'd feel better when her husband was back to protect the family.

Max barked loudly again. Mina looked back and saw twelve massive Indians riding toward the cabin at full gallop. They held their shields before them, moving them around as they rode.

Mina's legs froze. Seeing these hideous creatures painted for war with their braids flying through the air like black snakes springing from their heads caused her to shake.

Somehow, her legs started moving and she ran to the front door.

"Apache!" she yelled. "They're coming for us!"

She hit the door and slammed it behind her, sliding the wooden block into place. Her mother was already grabbing the younger children and moving them to the safest place in the cabin.

Locked inside with no way out, Augusta prayed while Mina watched the Indians. They circled the house fifty yards away and slowly drew the circle tighter.

Mina grabbed an ax and prepared for her final day alive.

Rocks crashed through one of the windows. Sticks followed.

Mina forced the children under the bed and kept pushing them back as they tried to crawl out. The children just wanted to be with their mother.

Mina peered through a crack in the wall and saw four Indians stealing their horses, leading them away from the farm. Two Indians fired at least twenty gunshots at the cabin, splintering wood and making the children cry harder.

When the shooting stopped, Augusta peeked out the window just in time for a lance to whiz past her temple. The spear slammed into a table, and its shaft vibrated.

"I'm gonna shoot out the window," Augusta said.

She held the wooden stock while Mina grabbed a rag and lifted the heavy barrel to the opening.

Seemingly out of thin air, the leader appeared in the window, holding his shield near his face. Augusta pulled the trigger, and the blast sent her backward.

Outside, the leader dropped to the ground and screamed. Three Indians ran to get their man, the closest one holding up his shield.

The brave German mother racked another round into the shotgun as Mina lifted the hot barrel with the same rag. Augusta took careful aim and blasted the man's shield, sending pellets everywhere. Another Indian shrieked and hopped around in pain.

When a second window crashed open, Augusta moved everyone into the main bedroom.

"Close the door!" Augusta ordered, and Mina slammed the bolt home.

Now, they were even more trapped.

Augusta picked up Mina's ax and stood by a window. Mina held a long cane knife and crouched by the only other window in the room.

A few seconds later, they heard the Indians inside the cabin ripping up their beds and taking whatever they wanted. It was a terrifying two minutes, but finally, the savages left.

Once Augusta was sure they were gone, she and Mina ran outside and found Max. The yard was torn up from hoofprints, with most of the grass covered in his blood. He had fought the Indians but taken several lance wounds.

Poor Max crept over to Augusta and collapsed at her knees. She stroked the dog's bloodstained fur until he took his last breath. Then she and the children cried. Not only were they distraught at losing their family pet, but they needed to release the fear and sheer terror that had built up during the attack.

When her husband Philip and her son returned that evening, they discovered a box of Herman's clothes had been stolen. Philip wanted to take off after them, but Augusta begged him not to.

Eventually, Philip cooled down and realized his job was to stay with his family and protect them. Besides, he'd already lost his horses and family pet. He didn't need to lose his life, too.

Quanah and White Eagle looked out over the long train warriors. Four hundred strong, consisting of Comanche, Cheyenne, Kiowas, and Arapahos. They had left Elk Creek in the northern panhandle of Texas and were heading west.

White Eagle was quite a sight. He had painted himself and his horse yellow. Due to his strong medicine, this special paint would repel the white man's bullets. He had promised that nothing would harm them as long as the warriors used his yellow paint.

White Eagle had also tied scalps from his bridle, letting them swing back and forth as his horse moved along. His appearance gave the warriors confidence that the white man could not hurt them one bit, especially since most of them had seen the medicine man perform miracles.

White Eagle even predicted the warriors would first kill a few white men before they arrived at Adobe Walls. And that had happened. Soon, they would destroy the hated Adobe Walls and the men inside.

Post Oak

Adobe Walls was a trading post for buffalo hunters and the white man's oasis in the Comanchería. The outpost was situated on a flat piece of prairie that gently sloped to a little creek. The Canadian River ran just southwest of the post. It was a perfect spot for the buffalo hunters to drop off their hides, drink some whiskey, and fill up on ammunition before heading back out to the prairie and killing 2,000 more buffalo.

For the Indians, Adobe Walls was destroying their way of life. That's why it had to be wiped out completely like Buffalo Hump had wiped out the port town of Linnville, Texas.

Quanah reached a distant bluff overlooking the trading post. His people had been there before when Colonel Kit Carson led some federal troops from Fort Bascom and took on the Comanche and Kiowa.

After that battle, some of the buildings had been burned while others had fallen into disrepair. The Plains Indians were sure Adobe Walls would be abandoned. And it was for many years. Somehow, it had been rebuilt. This allowed the white hunters to slaughter the buffalo for their hides and tongues only—a tragic waste of a vital resource.

White Eagle pulled up alongside Quanah. "Where will we stop?" he asked the leader.

"That place down there, in the trees," Quanah said, pointing to the south. "We'll gather everyone together and rest up. Then we attack in the early morning."

"It will be a great victory," White Eagle said. "I promise."

Quanah nodded his head. "I know."

White Eagle grinned. His fame was about to explode. And with fame came wealth, enough to provide for many wives. He had several already picked out. The only way this wouldn't happen was if any of the 400 warriors ate a skunk along the way.

Skunks were a favorite of the Indians. They were sweet and easy to catch because they waddled along, unworried about any harm since their stink was so horrific.

Yet Indians grew hungry when they went on raids. They didn't carry enough food so they had to hunt along the way.

Skunks were such easy food that this commandment to forgo them upset the warriors. But they would do it for a good cause and certain victory.

White Eagle was sure the Comanche would regain control of their lands. The buffalo would return and become plentiful, and the white man would be eliminated.

"You just have to avoid killing a skunk," the medicine man said, sounding a lot like the Parkers in 1836 when they preached over and over about keeping the fort's main gate closed. "That's all you have to do," White Eagle continually told the warriors. "How hard can that be?"

Indeed…

Chapter Thirty-Six

Herman heard the rope creak as the Indians lowered him down the 200-foot-high bluff. It was dangerous, but the reward would be worth it.

When he was even with the cave entrance, he hooted for the rope to stop. Herman hopped off and stood inside the cave, untying the empty water bladders around his waist.

For a moment, he studied the treasure. Honeycombs were everywhere, extending as far back as he could see. Though some were black and ruined, there was plenty of fresh honey.

He hurried and filled the pouches as the bees buzzed around him. After tying them back to his waist, he grabbed the rope and hooted again. Soon, he was up on the bluff.

This routine was repeated three times before they had more honey than they could ever consume.

"Can you pull these out?" Herman asked his buddy.

The Indian found the bee stingers embedded in his skin and removed them.

"Come on, let's get back to camp," he said.

The five boys mounted their ponies and took off. As they rode, Herman thought about his life.

It had been at least a year since his capture, and he had fully assimilated into the tribe. By now, Carnoviste treated Herman like a son, except for the one act that would cause a lynching among white people.

Carnoviste taught the boy to jump from the ground and mount a wild horse while running. Herman also learned how to shoot arrows while mounted and sling his body around the horse's neck to avoid being hit by the enemy.

Recently, he'd made a shield for himself. The entire process took several days.

When it was done, the shield was set up as a target and arrows and bullets were fired into it. If one pierced the shield, it would've been tossed into the trash. Fortunately, Herman's shield turned back all projectiles and he got to keep it.

Carnoviste showed him how to string up the shield so he could carry it on his back or arm, furry side inward for comfort.

The warrior borrowed some paints and decorated the smooth side with a moon and stars. This allowed Herman to use it as a compass and guide during raids.

Carnoviste also painted turtles, serpents, and other symbols, which were clever maps guiding him around Texas and New Mexico. If the whites got ahold of the shield, they wouldn't know how to use it.

With this piece of equipment, Herman could always find his home.

Racing horses was a huge pastime. So was gambling on the outcomes. At night, the Apache gambled with a stick game.

Herman was amazed that warriors would lose all their possessions, along with their wives and children. It was crazy to watch the women and children being told they had a new husband and father, who quickly consummated the new relationships.

Laughing Eyes was Carnoviste's wife. She had no children and absolutely adored Herman, showering affection upon him every day. It was clear why he'd been kidnapped: Laughing Eyes.

From the first day, she called him En Da, which meant White Boy. Whenever Herman needed protection or consoling, he ran to Laughing Eyes. She always babied and took care of him.

Something Herman hated watching was the cruel treatment the Apache men dished out to their wives. At times, it was downright brutal. Herman couldn't understand why the women never killed their men. The men certainly asked for it.

One day, a Mexican trader arrived and made some deals with the warriors. The Mexican treated the women kindly and one of them succumbed to his charms. This woman was married to Whitewood, a friend of Herman's.

Once Whitewood discovered the adultery, he located the trader and used his long knife to slice open his midsection. After pulling out some intestines and showing the bloody mess to the still-alive Mexican, Whitewood grabbed several buddies and held his wife down. Using the same bloody knife, he cut off the end of her nose.

The woman screamed and howled, but no one helped her. Bleeding profusely, she gathered up some belongings and left the camp on foot. Herman assumed she'd be eaten by the wild beasts of the night.

Despite his actions, Whitewood was distraught. He announced, "I will never come back from this raid. I am going to die."

Herman brushed it off and assumed his friend would find another girl.

The raiding party traveled to Kickapoo Spring, about 150 miles northwest of Fredericksburg. Approaching it, they spotted a well-dressed white man on a large gray horse.

Before they could discuss a plan, Whitewood said, "I will get that man."

He adjusted the long string on his shield so the furry side faced the enemy.

The chief grabbed the reins of his horse and said, "The Great Spirit will not assist a warrior who is so unreverential. Turn your shield around or the bullets will pierce your body."

"The white man and I must both die!" Whitewood said, jerking the reins free from the chief and racing off toward the white man.

The white man pulled a .44 caliber Colt revolver and fired several times. At the same time, Whitewood sent the lead from his Winchester rifle forward and continued racing toward the man.

Herman and the other warriors sat on their horses, stunned at this turn of events.

The white man wheeled his horse around and retreated as Whitewood's horse slowed. Herman watched his friend slide from the saddle and fall to the black dirt. The white man slowed, too.

As Herman and his raiders neared the white man, he fell from his horse. Herman jumped off first and found the man on his side with four bullet holes in his chest.

Breathing hard, the white man raised his heavy Colt at Herman and tried to pull the trigger but didn't have the strength. The man struggled with the gun several times before giving up. Then he rolled over on his face, took one last breath, and stopped moving.

Herman ran back to Whitewood and rolled him over. His shield had three holes to match the ones in his chest. His back showed three exit wounds. Poor Whitewood was dead.

Herman immediately claimed the white man's fine Mexican saddle. It was embossed with silver.

His chief went through the saddlebags and found a nice red blanket, a stout, heavy bridle, and a large quantity of silver. Then he held up a roll of green paper.

"What is this?" he asked, handing the roll to Herman. "We find this stuff on all the whites."

Herman unrolled each sheet and found a picture on it with a number in each corner.

"I don't know what it is," he said, handing it back.

The chief tore up the sheets and let them fall to the ground.

"Put Whitewood on his horse and let's get out of here. The whites will have heard the gunshots and come to investigate. I don't want to be here when they arrive."

"What about the white man?" a warrior asked. "Can we scalp him?"

"No!" the chief replied. "Don't touch him. He was brave and fearless."

The group did as commanded and rode to a nearby ravine. There, they found a cave and set Whitewood inside, covering him with buffalo robes. At his sides, they laid his weapons.

The chief took Whitewood's horse to the cave's entrance and cut its throat, leaving the body where it fell. Then he collected the reins of the white man's gray horse and the raiders moved on.

Two days later, the Indians awoke from a long night's sleep and had breakfast. Herman was given the responsibility of handling the gray horse, so he hung back from the main force.

By noon, they found an established road and spotted an oxen team pulling a wagon away from them. Its occupants were unaware of the terror riding up on their rear.

When the people in the wagon finally noticed the Indians, it was too late. Two warriors killed the white man and woman. The woman held a baby girl in her arms, and she, too, was killed. All three were scalped.

A girl, about eight, and a boy, six, were found hiding in the wagon's bed. The siblings were taken as hostages.

The chief ordered the oxen killed and the wagon burned. The raiders continued on, pushing their stolen herd of horses in front of them.

Once they had enough horses, the chief turned the party back to the north.

A few hours later, they entered a ravine and four white men on fast horses appeared out of thin air. They rode between the stolen remuda and the Indians.

It was a daring maneuver, which shocked the Apache. But they quickly rallied and fired several times at the whites.

Unfortunately, the whites were too fast and made off with the Indians' stolen herd. In a matter of seconds, the raiders had nothing to show for their trip.

"Did they get the children?" the chief asked.

"No," Herman answered. He had been caring for them.

"At least we have them," the chief said, sighing.

The group turned back to the south and rode for four days, looking for more farms to rob.

The children cried constantly and refused to eat. By the fourth night, the Indians were frustrated with their hostages.

"They make so much noise we can't steal anything or we'll be caught," a warrior complained.

"I'm trying to keep them quiet, but they're upset," Herman said. "Just give me more time."

Carnoviste rode up alongside the children. "Take care of them," he said, looking directly into the eyes of several warriors.

Two warriors, one on each side, approached the horse carrying the crying girl. They grabbed an arm and a foot and lifted her off the horse. Another warrior took the horse, suspending the girl in midair.

The warriors swung her back and forth three times before releasing her high in the air. She somersaulted twice before hitting the ground with a thud, and the crying stopped.

The boy had to watch his sister killed before he endured the same death.

"Ride over them," the chief ordered.

The Indians trampled the bodies before hanging them in trees for the vultures to pick clean.

Herman looked away and tried to be strong. Still, it was hard. They were just children.

A short time later, the Indians rested at Beaver Lake in West Texas. A buffalo was killed and the raiders sucked on its ribs.

A few warriors jumped in the water to bathe, enjoying the cool temperatures. Herman watched another warrior remove his breechclout and carefully fold it, placing the garment next to the fire to stay warm. The warrior was about to go for a swim when his stomach exploded into the campfire. Another warrior's brains cascaded over the roasted buffalo meat.

The Indians lounging flat around the campfire couldn't understand what was happening. Then they heard the distant explosions just as the Texas Rangers raced into camp. The white men shot anything that moved.

Herman grabbed his rifle and ran to some nearby brush. When Carnoviste and the chief joined him, they looked for their horses and found they were gone.

Carnoviste pounded the dirt. "It's those rangers again!"

Herman and three others survived, but they were on foot. It took four days to make it back to the main camp.

Over the next week, warriors arrived at different times, all bringing news of others who had died. The final count was five dead and one severely wounded. That man died a few days later.

The squaws howled and cried, using knives to cut themselves to pieces. The wounded warrior's squaw burned herself with a red-hot iron rod when he died.

To make matters worse, another raiding party returned defeated, with one wounded and another killed. Incredibly, a third party arrived, announcing four dead and one taken captive.

More howling and self-mutilation followed.

"We have somehow offended the Great Spirit," the chief announced.

Post Oak

Herman thought back to the girl and boy they had killed. He was about to say something when he decided against it.

The medicine man approached and said it was up to him to deal with this problem. He started yelling incantations and raising his arms to the sky.

Later, he made his way up a hill and waved cows' tails. When he came back, he ordered everyone to fast.

The next morning, a fourth raiding party returned with stolen horses and fresh scalps, which changed the camp's mood. Celebrations erupted and all the dead were forgotten.

Well, not all of them.

Chapter Thirty-Seven

Billy Tyler stared down the sights of his Winchester rifle, waiting for the Indians to appear. But they never did.

"False alarm!" a private yelled. "The Indians turned west and are leaving us alone."

Soon, the sergeant rode over. "We're gonna ride for three more hours and camp. Get this rig headed north and keep your eyes peeled for Indians or they might get peeled for you."

Billy nodded but noticed the sergeant gawking again at Jennie, who was climbing back to the driver's box. Billy released the brake and slapped the reins, letting the horses and the wagon put the creep behind them.

"You sure you don't know that fella?" Billy asked Jennie.

"I'm sure, William. I'd tell you if I did."

They rode for three hours and stopped with the rest of the wagon train. Jennie joined the women as they started fires and kettles boiling. Billy was checking the rear axle when the sergeant reappeared.

"Hey, fella, is that your woman?" the sergeant asked, pointing to Jennie.

"What do you mean?" Billy replied.

"She your fiancée or wife?"

"No, but she's a passenger in my wagon, and therefore, it is my responsibility to see to her safety. Why are you so interested?"

"I want to have some sport with that one," the sergeant said lewdly.

"No, you won't," Billy said, bowing up to the sergeant.

"Whoa, fella. You're cripple and all so you shouldn't be tempting a man to beat you to within an inch of your life."

Billy leaned against the wagon and reached his left hand inside to grip the butt of his six-shooter. The bottom of the sun touched the western horizon behind him, giving Billy an advantage.

The sergeant squinted. He was taller than Billy and the sun was directly in his eyes.

Billy pulled the butt of the gun free from the holster and whipped it out of the wagon as the sergeant hit him in the face before he could pull the trigger. The gun tumbled harmlessly to the prairie and the sergeant picked it up. Then he commenced to beat Billy senselessly.

James Hanrahan stepped into the doorway of his saloon. The night was warm and humid. Lightning bugs floated through the air as the nearby stock made muffled sounds. A horse shook the flies off while others searched for fresh grass.

To the east, a stand of cottonwoods hid the owls, hooting for each other. And just over the forest sat a full moon, making it a perfect night for a Comanche raid.

Actually, Hanrahan knew one was coming. Camp Supply in Oklahoma had learned that Quanah was coming for Adobe Walls. The traders there sent a government scout with six soldiers south to warn the outpost.

Several hours earlier, the government scout told the two merchants, who then told Hanrahan. All three men decided *not* to tell the buffalo hunters and other proprietors. They feared they'd abandon the outpost and either stop spending money or not be there to defend it.

The three men had all their money sunk into Adobe Walls. If it fell, they'd be busted.

The two merchants wisely decided to leave. They had a man to run their large shop and left him in charge, though they neglected to tell him about the coming attack.

That left Hanrahan standing in his doorway, staring at the other buildings, their wide-open doors and windows hoping to coax a June breeze inside and cool the inhabitants. With a scene like this, a silent Comanche attack would wipe them all out before they could fire a shot.

Hanrahan pulled out his pocket watch and learned the time: 2 a.m. Behind him were a dozen men scattered over the saloon floor, hidden inside their bedrolls. Several snored loudly and all were fast asleep.

Hanrahan needed the men to be awake, alert, and ready for the attack. But if he told them about it now, they'd mount their ponies and fly away. If he didn't tell them, they'd all be slaughtered.

There was a third scenario: he could tell the men, they could prepare a defense, and the attack might not come. If the attack came the following day, the hunters might be gone or asleep. Drinking, gambling, and sleeping were all they did since the main herd of buffalo had not yet appeared.

Then he had an idea.

A loud crack happened just outside the saloon. The men inside sat up and reached for their guns. Most were hazy from too much to drink and too little sleep.

"What's going on?!" a hunter asked.

"The ridgepole is cracked!" Hanrahan yelled, rubbing his hands over the wooden support. "It's about to go. We need to shore it up and fast!"

When the men heard this, they fully understood the ramifications. The ridgepole supported the beams which held up the roof. If the roof collapsed, they'd be buried under wood and dried mud. Maybe they'd survive; maybe not. Either way, they would lose the only saloon for miles around.

Two men ran outside, climbed onto the roof, and began pulling mud off, hoping to lighten the load. Another ran to the creek to find long pieces of wood to shore up the ridgepole. Everyone worked hard for three hours until the roof was sufficiently shored up.

Hanrahan's watch now read 5 a.m. He turned to the men and found many of them rolling back into bed.

"Free drinks to thank you men for saving my saloon."

"Yay!" a man yelled.

The others made their way to the bar for a drink on the house.

"What about you, Dixon?" Hanrahan asked.

"I'll pass," Dixon replied. "I'm gonna get an early start on finding the buffalo. The faster I find 'em, the faster I can get back here and drink."

"What about your horses?"

"I sent Ogg down to the creek to get 'em."

"Why don't you stay and have some grub?" Hanrahan pleaded.

Post Oak

He needed every gun and Dixon was an excellent shot. Plus, seven skinners would go with him. This would leave the outpost with twenty people to fight the Comanche, two of whom were women.

"Nah. Got to get out there," he said as he rolled up his bed.

After tying up the bedroll, he grabbed his long gun and walked out to his wagon. The bedroll was too big to put into the wagon with one hand, so he set the gun on the ground and tossed it in the back. Then he turned around, picked up his gun, and stared to the east in the direction of the horses. Behind the corral, hardly visible in the reddening sky, was a black mass emerging from the trees.

Dixon squinted and stared hard, trying to comprehend what he was seeing. When the mass fanned out and the horses' hooves pounded on the prairie, Dixon heard the war-whoop and realized they were in trouble. There'd be no buffalo killed today.

"Indians!" he yelled even though the war whoops had already signaled the outpost inhabitants. "Get your guns ready. Hurry!"

Hanrahan ran outside, straight into Dixon.

"Help me barricade this place shut!" Hanrahan yelled.

But Dixon had set his gun down and tied his horse to the wagon. By the time he fetched his gun and turned around to the saloon, the door was closed.

"Let me in!" Dixon yelled as he turned and fired a shot at the horde.

His helper, Ogg, joined him and collapsed at the blocked entrance. He had raced from the creek barely ahead of the riders and was exhausted.

Hanrahan opened up just in time and pulled the two inside, closing the door behind them as arrows smacked into the adobe walls and door. Inside, fifteen men shoved sacks of grain and furniture against the windows and doors, anything to keep the attackers at bay.

Off to the side, Dixon had his back to the cool Adobe Wall. He checked his boxes of cartridges and loaded his long gun. Death was coming for a whole lot of people, and he was determined it wouldn't take him—at least not without a fight and a whole lot of gunsmoke.

Billy awoke to find himself in the back of a wagon, his shirt undone and a girl dabbing his face with a wet cloth. He allowed his eyes to open wider and take in the entire scene.

Jennie leaned over him, the moon's rays streaming through the opening and lighting up her green eyes. He had never noticed them before, but now they comforted him.

"The brute loosened one of your teeth and bruised your face. I put some salve on the cuts to help heal them faster."

"Thank you," Billy whispered.

"It's the least I could do, William."

"Did he d-do anything to you?" Billy whispered.

"What do you mean?" Jennie replied, genuinely puzzled.

"Oh, nothing," he said and drifted back to sleep.

The following day, the wagon train came to a river. The best crossing was down through a ravine, but it was too narrow and only one wagon at a time could make the trip. For this crossing, Billy's wagon was last in line.

He and Jennie watched the wagon in front dip down and disappear toward the river crossing while they stayed up on the bank. The sergeant and a private circled around Billy's wagon to ensure they made it, too.

Suddenly, a bullet ripped through the wagon's fabric.

"Indians!" the sergeant yelled. "Get your guns ready!"

Billy jammed the brake home and crawled to the rear of the wagon. In seconds, he saw dozens of riders racing toward them, a flock of arrows filling the air over their heads.

Billy sighted his Winchester and dropped the closest rider's horse. The Indian fell but was on his feet, running toward the wagon with a tomahawk in one hand and a shield in the other.

Billy fired at the attacker's exposed legs, sending the Indian down. He hit the prairie and writhed in pain.

Billy glanced to the left as he cocked his gun. The private fired his gun at a group of Indians. The sergeant's horse had been shot and the Indians quickly surrounded the dazed soldier, dragging him away by his shirt collar.

Billy looked away and saw a rider coming to help the one he'd just shot. Billy fired the Winchester and dropped the second horse. This time, the beast trapped the Indian underneath.

Billy took careful aim and splattered the Indian's chest against the horse. To Billy's surprise, a third Indian rode over and Billy dropped him straight from the saddle.

Billy reloaded and looked to his left again. The sergeant was trying to get free, but the Indians were intent on getting their hostage back to camp.

"Hand me the long gun!" he ordered Jennie.

She grabbed it with two hands and gave it to Billy. He shoved a cartridge into the breech and armed the gun, aiming it carefully at the Indians who were carrying the sergeant away.

Billy could see the sergeant's face. His eyes were fully panicked as the last wagon drew farther away. The sergeant knew what was coming.

Billy breathed deeply and exhaled slowly. Then he pulled the trigger and the gun exploded in smoke.

Jennie stared out the back in time to see the round hit the sergeant in the chest, killing him instantly.

"Oh no!" she cried. "You hit the sergeant."

Billy ignored her and fired again. An Indian fell to his knees until two buddies helped carry him away.

Another one quickly scalped the sergeant and left his body for the prairie scavengers. Now they ran hard, just wanting to be clear of this deadly white shooter.

Billy set the long gun down and picked up his Winchester. There were no other riders or Indians anywhere except the first one he had shot. That Indian was trying to crawl to a nearby depression in the prairie and hide.

Billy aimed carefully and fired. The Indian jerked. Billy shot the man three more times before being satisfied he was dead.

The private came riding over and looked in. "You've been shot!" he said.

Billy glanced back at Jennie and saw two arrows sticking up through her skirt. The points were embedded in the wooden planks.

"No," she said, ripping the fabric free of the arrows. "They missed me!"

"I meant him," the private said.

Billy turned his head fully around and saw an arrow sticking out from the back of his bad leg.

"I'm gonna fetch the others," the private said before galloping off, leaving the two on their own.

Jennie tied some cloth just above the arrow and wiped away some blood. "How do you feel?" she asked.

"I don't feel anything."

Jennie caressed his still-swollen cheek. "We'll get you better. Don't you worry."

Billy turned back and loaded both guns. "They might return since it's just us. Let's keep a lookout."

Jennie lowered herself next to Billy as they stared out the back of the wagon. "Listen, William, I need to tell you the truth." She hesitated. "A farm tool didn't cut me; a man did. I need to tell you something."

"No, you don't, Jennie. No. You. Don't."

She closed her mouth.

"Not now, at least. Please," an irritated Billy said. "Let's just get through this first."

She nodded and shielded her eyes from the sun. The endless prairie was still brown from the winter but a few flowers had popped up, each a brilliant hue. Except for the dead horses and men, it was a beautiful day.

Quanah sat up and studied the sky through the thick trees. He had barely slept, and morning was close. If they were going to attack, now was the time.

The warriors had already hobbled their extra horses in the woods, and the saddles and blankets were hidden in the trees. Each warrior covered his face and some of his body with White Eagle's bulletproof paint. In the faint light, they looked like yellow ghosts.

Four hours earlier, White Eagle sent scouts to Adobe Walls and confirmed the hunters were asleep and the buildings wide open. It would surely be a slaughter, just as White Eagle guaranteed.

Quanah and another leader roused the men. The two men organized the warriors into four long columns. Then they mounted their ponies and began the march through the woods.

The attack force was an hour away from Adobe Walls, so they needed to hurry if they wanted to hit the place before anyone was awake or the sky was too bright. Before it was too late.

Post Oak

Quanah rode at the head of a middle column but had trouble keeping the young men back. The warriors were excited and wanted to be the first to kill a white man or seize their horses and fine saddles.

Eventually, the four columns reached the creek and the edge of the cottonwoods. They stopped and waited for everyone to catch up.

Quanah was at the edge of the cottonwoods. One more step and his men would be on open ground, available to be seen by any white man who was not asleep.

When the signals from the back came forward, Quanah nodded at the other columns and led his horse from the dark forest. He motioned the men to stay quiet so they could creep forward undetected as long as possible.

As they came within 200 yards of the first structure, they were seen by a man fetching horses, so the warriors sent their horses racing forward. Several found prairie dog holes and stumbled, sending their riders to the turf. The rest flew like the wind.

Quanah spotted a white man rising from a bedroll in the back of an open wagon. He drove his lance through the man's chest and he died right there.

The white man's brother was killed by another warrior along with their large Newfoundland dog.

Quanah steered his horse to the saloon and found the main door closed. He backed the animal to the opening and signaled his horse to kick the door in. The horse gave several mighty kicks, but the door held.

Quanah knew the sod walls were two feet thick and wouldn't burn. Like prying the shell off a turtle, he stood up in the saddle and climbed onto the roof, determined to make a hole in it. He desperately wanted to shoot down on the hunters.

The rugged outpost had only one street and it was chaos. Most of the hunters' horses had been run off by the Indians or the shooting. The Indians on horses now controlled the street, firing into buildings while guns fired back at them.

The inhabitants of each building had barricaded themselves inside, shoving anything they could find against the doors and windows. A few buildings held women, each knowing exactly what fate awaited them if the doors were kicked in.

From small holes in the walls, the white man's guns fired out. Indians were shot. Yellow Bear, Quanah's father-in-law, suffered a broken leg.

Quanah saw one of his friends lying shot in the street and jumped back on his horse, racing to the man. Quanah leaned over and picked him up before speeding him to safety. Sadly, though, the man died.

The buffalo hunters who saw the act talked about Quanah for years, marveling at the sheer strength and agility it took to lift a man from the street at full gallop while the rider's hand and foot clung to the saddle.

Quanah and his men continued poking at the roofs, firing through the wood in the windows and trying to break down the door. Yet the Comanche casualties rose.

Quanah's horse was shot out from underneath him, throwing the warrior clear. Crawling to an animal carcass, he hid behind it and waited for help.

Instead of help, he received a bullet in the shoulder after it deflected off the buffalo powder horn hanging around his neck. The horn saved his life.

He immediately crawled to a thick row of plum bushes and waited for a rescue.

Nearby and away from the action, the older chiefs and White Eagle met to decide what to do. Without Quanah leading them, the men were losing courage.

Instead of attacking the buildings, the warriors rode in circles around them, occasionally firing guns and arrows. Nothing worked. The white men of Adobe Walls simply wouldn't die.

Inside the saloon, one of the occupants, Bat Masterson, reloaded his gun. "Anyone have some water?" he asked through a thick haze of acrid gun smoke.

"It's all gone," Hanrahan replied. "We'll have to make do."

"If they keep riding around long enough, we'll kill them all," Masterson said.

Dixon nodded. "Yeah, I've killed five and wounded more than that. Surely, they're about to give up."

He was wrong. The chiefs sent the warriors back for more direct attacks on the buildings. They were frantic to find a way through.

White Eagle, the brilliant young medicine man, rubbed his hands nervously. "Do the white men have new weapons? How can this be happening?"

The chiefs ignored him and his previous guarantee.

Four hours after the first attack, the sun was at its height and noon had arrived. All over Adobe Walls lay dead or dying Indians while the hunters kept firing.

Quanah studied the town from his hiding spot and saw rifles sticking out of holes like an alarmed porcupine. Up on the hill was White Eagle, refusing to believe what he saw.

"How can this be happening?" the medicine man muttered to himself.

Throughout the attacks, a bugle blew, signaling the Indians when to attack or retreat. As an army veteran, Masterson understood the calls. He told the men when to prepare to fight and when to relax. Deciphering the bugle calls helped the men in the saloon immensely.

Late in the fighting, the bugler was seen crossing near the wagon where the two white men and their dog had been killed. He was a black man, a Buffalo soldier, thought to have deserted from the 10th Cavalry.

One of the hunters leveled his .50 caliber Sharp's rifle at the man and shot him through the back. The bullet ripped the man's chest in half, and he fell dead on the spot. There would be no more bugle calls.

Quanah was finally rescued, and the chiefs discovered the young leader had been shot. Yet Quanah continued to fight as he organized a retreat. The warriors had no problem following him away from Adobe Walls to the safety of a bluff a half mile away.

On the bluff, the leadership sat on their horses and talked about this terrible battle. Quanah curiously watched some smoke coming from a rifle at the outpost. The hunter had set himself up on a wagon outside one of the stores and fired his long gun. Quanah shook his head, knowing they were too far away to be hit. Yet a few feet away, the head of White Eagle's horse twitched and the animal collapsed.

A warrior walked over and saw a smoking hole in its skull oozing blood. The chiefs noticed the famous yellow paint had failed to stop the medicine man's horse from being killed. Several men glared at White Eagle, who had been off the horse then.

"Let's move farther away," a chief ordered.

The leaders rode an additional three-quarters of a mile and found another bluff to watch the scene back at Adobe Walls.

Quanah was ten feet away when an old man groaned and slid from his horse. Quanah looked back at the same hunter and again saw smoke rising from his gun. He could not believe it.

"How is this possible?" Quanah muttered.

The old Indian had been hit by a bullet but was just stunned. Still, the leaders moved everyone out of sight of the outpost and gathered to discuss their next move.

When White Eagle arrived on foot, a Cheyanne warrior climbed off his horse and beat the medicine man silly. He was saved from death when the chiefs intervened and pushed the warrior away. But not before the warrior leaned over and yelled, "You promised their bullets couldn't touch us through this paint. You promised!"

"Someone ate a skunk," White Eagle moaned through bloody lips. "I told you about that."

"A skunk?" the warrior spat. "You're a liar! You have polecat medicine."

To Indians, this was a serious insult.

"From this day forward, you are no longer White Eagle," the Cheyenne said. "You shall be called Isatai." This was Comanche for *Coyote Droppings*.

"Isatai!" the others yelled. "That's his new name."

Others farther down the line yelled out, "Isatai! Liar among liars! Polecat medicine man!"

Quanah watched all this from a fresh mount and rubbed the wound with his fingers. Soon, his hand was orange, a combination of his red blood and the supposedly "bulletproof" yellow paint.

He thought of his wives and kicked his horse to the east. He needed to get back to camp and tend to this wound. Then he would round up the warriors and burn Texas to the ground.

"I will have my revenge!" Quanah said through a clenched jaw.

Chapter Thirty-Eight

Herman stoked the fire to keep it alive. Another warrior, Bucking Horse, was up early and near the fire.

"What are you doing?" Herman asked.

"I'm going to kill antelope," Bucking Horse replied. "I'll get so close that I can reach out and touch one."

Herman looked around the silent camp, confused. "How will you do this?"

Bucking Horse showed him an animal skin.

"I cut the last antelope as one full piece. Now I'm stitching up the hide so it will fit me. I'm going out in the morning and crawl on all fours. The antelope sleep under the trees and move at daybreak. I'll kill three of them before they can get up. My cleverness will feed the entire camp."

Herman could see Bucking Horse was impressed with himself, although it was unusual to see a man sewing or doing any work since women did everything. But he had beaten his only wife's face so hard, she couldn't see through her swollen cheeks. If he wanted this done, he had to do it himself.

The next morning, Herman watched as Bucking Horse eased into the antelope hide and crawled away. Herman had to admit it looked real.

A few minutes later, another warrior came by to check on Bucking Horse's wife. He had wanted to marry her, but her father refused. Instead, Bucking Horse paid the hefty price and could now beat her whenever he wanted.

An hour later, two warriors carried a large antelope hanging from a stick. They dropped it in front of Bucking Horse's tent and his wife emerged.

Through a half-opened black eye, she touched the antelope and began removing the hide. Herman watched in horror as Bucking Horse emerged from inside the antelope.

"Was he eaten alive?" Herman said as he pulled his knife free.

Spinning around, Herman scanned the area for a monster antelope that ate Indians.

"No," she said. "He was killed by another warrior who thought he was an antelope. Now he rests with the Great Spirit."

Herman put his knife back and pondered how she could know this since she'd been in the tent, and the men carrying Bucking Horse said nothing.

That afternoon, Carnoviste arranged for Bucking Horse's burial in a tree, the usual spot for a warrior. Soon after, the band moved to another location.

Once there, Herman noticed the widow had a new suitor. He caressed her face as the bruises slowly disappeared and her eyes opened. The lucky warrior finally got his girl.

Herman chuckled.

Where there's a woman, there's a way.

The Apache raiding party leaned back and enjoyed their feast. They had killed a buffalo and were enjoying the meat. Herman was one of twelve warriors relaxing and resting when another Apache ran into camp.

"Four buffalo hunters heading toward us!" he yelled. "Follow me."

The warriors grabbed their weapons and crept to the top of a hill. Sure enough, four men approached their camp, perhaps having seen the smoke or hoping to climb the hill and see more buffalo.

When the hunters were close enough, the Apache raced over the hill and chased the four men. Three of them ran to a nearby embankment and lodged themselves behind rocks, their guns pointed outward. The fourth man ran back to camp, but he was too slow. Herman and his group caught up to the man and discovered he was Mexican.

"Where are you going?" one of the Apache asked in Spanish.

"To camp," he replied.

"How many others are there?"

"Only me. I was supposed to guard it."

Post Oak

The leader ordered Herman to guard the Mexican. "And don't let him escape," he commanded. "We will check out the camp."

In less than five minutes, Herman heard shooting. As he looked in the direction of the camp, the Mexican picked up rocks and threw them at him.

Herman fired an arrow that grazed the man and he threw up his hands. Herman kept another arrow trained on the man to avoid any more problems.

Soon, his party returned. Carnoviste said the camp was full of hunters and they were lucky to have escaped without injury.

"The Mexican lied to us," he proclaimed.

"He tried to kill me by throwing rocks at my face," Herman said.

"Kill him," Carnoviste ordered.

Herman drew back the bow and sent an arrow through the Mexican's heart. The man fell over on his face, dead.

"Now scalp him," Carnoviste said.

Herman resisted as he'd never scalped anyone. Yet the chief threatened the boy with all kinds of harm if he refused.

Herman pulled out his knife and cut around the top of the scalp. Then he yanked on the hair and off it came, making a sound like a popgun. He had his first scalp.

Since the Apache never used an arrow after it had killed a man, they made Herman find it and cut a cross on the shaft.

"Lay the arrow on his back," the chief told Herman. He complied.

Soon, the men stood around, blowing smoke from a pipe over their breasts. They held their palms up to the sky to celebrate the victory the Great Spirit had bestowed on them.

As Herman cleaned off his knife, the Indians told him to mount up so they could head to the next settlement and kill more people.

Over three years had passed since Herman's capture. He was fifteen, and his past life a distant memory. The German boy now lived and fought hard for his adopted tribe.

It was early one morning when Herman and his young Indian friend, Bobo, went hunting. Herman was stuck on a balky dun mule that had been hit in the head too many times for its stubbornness.

Herman kicked the mule to run but the animal stopped and whirled around, disobeying his command. It was entirely frustrating. Plus, they had not yet killed anything, so the trip was a bust.

Up ahead was a hill. The boys headed toward it to see if there were any animals worth killing. When they looked up the slope, a horde of painted Comanche warriors crested the hill and spotted the two Apache boys.

The Comanche hated the Apache and vice versa. Instantly, Herman reined the mule around and kicked its side, but the mule stopped.

"Wait, Bobo!" Herman yelled as his friend took off on the horse. "Wait for me!" he cried again.

Bobo didn't heed Herman's plea and instead raced for camp. In seconds, a hail of arrows filled the air.

Herman heard a thwack and saw an arrow sticking out of the mule's rump. Before he could turn back, the mule had taken off. This time, it needed no coaxing.

Herman hugged the mule close so as not to catch any air and slow the mule down. In less than a minute, the mule had caught up to Bobo.

"Wait for me!" Bobo yelled as Herman raced by.

Herman kept on going.

When he reached camp, the mule refused to stop. Instead, it raced between the teepees, knocking women and children over and didn't stop until it had reached the horse herd, which was grazing peacefully in a meadow. There, the mule skidded to a halt and kicked his back legs, trying to rid itself of the arrow.

Herman hopped off and grabbed another pony, hurrying back to the camp to fight the dreaded Comanche. The fight was a full-on brawl. Much of it was hand-to-hand combat.

The fighting lasted from ten in the morning to sundown. Only then did the Comanche withdraw and leave their dead behind.

Herman searched through the dead and found Bobo just before the camp. He'd been caught, killed, and scalped.

Twenty Apache warriors were also dead and eight more were seriously wounded. The medicine man said prayers and incantations, but four of the wounded died that night. One more passed the following morning.

Dozens of Comanche were dead, too. And many had left the battle wounded, some of them surely dying over the next few days.

Herman and the other warriors collected the dead Comanche's guns, bows, arrows, shields, and horses and divided the spoils. The dead Apache were given proper funerals, while the dead horses and Comanche warriors were thrown in a hastily dug pit and left uncovered for the vultures, wolves, and coyotes to enjoy.

The next day, they moved camp farther north but happened to intercept some Comanche spies. One was killed and the other surrendered.

Carnoviste drilled a hole between the two bones of the spy's lower arms and threaded rawhide strings through the holes. Then he hung the man to a mesquite tree and left him for the birds.

Later, an unfaithful squaw with her nose cut off snuck back to the tree and cut him down. The warrior escaped and returned to his people.

Two months later, it happened again. Herman's band was surrounded by Comanche and another fight raged.

Many Comanche warriors were killed, but they managed to capture the Apache women and children. They also killed forty Apache warriors.

Herman, one hundred warriors, and six women escaped on foot, their horses and equipment all seized by the enemy. The Apache band was destitute and desperate until they linked up with 150 well-stocked Apache. The two bands merged and sent out riders to all the other Apache bands.

A meeting took place at a lake in Arizona. While the tribe waited for everyone to arrive, the warriors collected weapons and ammunition and fashioned arrows, bows, and lances. Every teepee had men and women making instruments of war.

When the men weren't making weapons, they were training ponies. A massive war was coming and they wanted to win it.

Victorio was an important Apache chief. He took several scouts and left to find the Comanche. He wanted to be ready to ride when every Apache warrior made it to the meeting.

Three days later, he returned alone. His scouts had been killed and he had barely survived.

A large council was held where two separate opinions emerged. The first was to fight and kill the Comanche. The second was to unite all the Indians and kill the white man.

With the Comanche's increasing firepower and their skills on the horse dominant, plus the devastating recent losses of numerous Apache warriors, the second opinion prevailed. They would seek out the various enemy tribes under a flag of truce and work to destroy the white man.

After several months, treaties with the enemy tribes were made. The Apache's women and children were returned.

The Comanche demanded the men who had strung up their warrior with rawhide strips, but the Apache swore those men had been killed in battle. Carnoviste, one of the men who had done it, stood by while the chiefs promised the Comanche they were telling the truth.

The woman who had cut down the Comanche warrior from the mesquite tree was kicked out of the Apache tribe and sent to the Comanche to live, no doubt telling the Comanche that the Apache had lied. Nothing came of it.

Over the next twelve months, after more attacks from white men and bluecoats, the chiefs of Herman's Apache band gave up and made a treaty. They were placed on some land in New Mexico, nothing more than a crude reservation.

The inspector came to Herman's camp looking for white captives. Herman and another boy were forced to hide out in the forest.

The other boy kept slipping back to camp, hoping to be spotted by the inspector. Snapping Turtle carried the boy away and tied him to a tree without food or water.

The inspector stayed for three long days. When he left, Herman was allowed to return to camp while the other boy was left tied to the tree.

Days later, they found him dead of dehydration, still tied to the tree. They let the beasts of the forest deal with him.

While on the reservation, some of Herman's friends stole a few horses from nearby settlements and had to flee. Soon, the rest of the band fled, too.

Post Oak

They roamed back over their favorite lands before crossing the Pecos River. The chiefs prepared everyone for a raid into Mexico, but cholera broke out among the Apache. Many died, including Laughing Eyes, Carnoviste's wife.

Herman was crushed and cried hard. He had grown thoroughly attached to his new Apache mother.

During her funeral, Carnoviste killed her two favorite dogs and set them next to her in the burial ground. A woman placed Laughing Eye's trinkets and property there.

Carnoviste pointed to Herman since he was her property. A warrior led the grieving boy to the grave and readied his knife to cut his throat.

Dramatically, out of the crowd dashed a young maiden. She cried, "No! Please spare him!" as she flung her arms around the boy.

Surprised at this, Carnoviste relented and allowed Herman to live. But how long could this go on?

Between the white men and bluecoats, the diseases, and the cruel Apache customs that might kill him at any moment, he wondered how much longer he could stay alive. Sooner or later, there would be a bullet or arrow with his name on it. It was just a matter of time.

I was born upon the prairie, where the wind blew free and there was nothing to break the light of the sun. I was born where there are no enclosures and where everything drew a free breath. I want to die there and not within walls… The white man has the country which we loved, and we only wish to wander on the prairie until we die.

~ Comanche Chief Ten Bears

Henry

Chapter Thirty-Nine

June 6, 1871
Rudnerweide, South Russia (present-day Ukraine)

Henry Kohfeld's father, August, leaned on a shovel just outside the barn. He had been working hard and needed a break.

His wife joined him, carrying a glass of water. He took a long drink and handed it back.

"What did Johann tell you?" Katharina asked.

"It's happening again," he said, wiping his brow with a handkerchief. "I knew it would. We all did."

It was an old story that started in 1536. An influential Anabaptist church leader, Menno Simons, led a small group that became known as *Menno*-nites. These Mennonites were first based in the Netherlands but have been forced to migrate from one place to another when their religious freedoms were taken away. From the Netherlands to Prussia (present-day Poland) to South Russia, they could never be secure.[14]

Katharina nodded. She knew all this and remained silent to let her husband vent.

"And now they're forcing us to move from here after we turned this barren land into a fertile paradise!" he said indignantly. "Remember when there was nothing but overgrown bush on this land?"

Again, Katharina said nothing.

---

[14]This "persecution" continued for the Mennonites 100 years later when another group of Mennonites decided to leave Mexico due to difficulties feeding their families and enter the United States. They were forced to look for a place to call home and make a better living. Their journey and struggles became international front-page news and was told in the book *Seminole: Some People Never Give Up* by Tina Siemens.

Post Oak

"But of course, we suffer in that we don't have a permanent dwelling here on Earth."

August caught his breath before continuing. "It's God's way. He is sending us somewhere else for some other reason. Our duty is not to ask why, but simply obey."

"Let's not tell the children yet," Katharina suggested. "They will be crushed."

"I agree. I have a meeting this afternoon to discuss our options. I'll learn more then."

The couple hugged each other and walked back inside, unaware that eight-year-old Henry had been listening through cracks in the barn wall. He turned away fast and exited through the back door, running to his favorite tree.

Hugging it, he stared at his family's land and the neighbors' tracts on both sides. Each 175-acre lot was narrow but long. Any piece of land that didn't have a house and a barn had orchards of mulberry and apricot trees as well as acres of turkey red wheat.

As he contemplated the words he'd just heard, he found the mark he'd made a year earlier on his favorite tree. Henry had been afraid of getting lost. He always wanted to find his way home. In his young mind, somehow, the trees would tell him how to get back.

Now his parents were talking about leaving. He was scared, but maybe there was a way they could stay.

At this moment, Henry Kohfeld had no idea what God's plans were for him or who he'd meet. If he had known, he would've never stopped hugging that oak tree.

Two Weeks Earlier
Moscow, Russia

"Do you have it ready?" the boss asked.

The Russian bureaucrat looked up at the impatient man standing before him, hands on hips.

"Yes. Here it is." The bureaucrat slid the document across the desk and his employer picked it up.

"I must make the presentation to the minister in one hour and you are handing it to me just now? Therefore, I must insist *you* give the presentation."

The bureaucrat had been ready for this. His boss was utterly incompetent, and it was doubtful he could even read. That's why the bureaucrat had worn his best suit to work. He assumed it would go down like this.

"Of course," he said. "Let us go now."

An hour later, both men stood before the minister and two other officials. The minister signaled for the bureaucrat to start.

The man cleared his throat. "To provide some background on this problem, I must detail a few facts. In the 1530s, the Mennonites were persecuted in the Netherlands because they refused to join the state churches. Many of them fled to Northern Germany and Prussia. As you might know, Prussia made a special agreement with the Mennonites because it needed help replacing its citizens who had died from the Great Plague."

"Was Prussia's 'special agreement' the same as we made with them?" the minister asked.

"Yes, sir. It granted them certain privileges and, most importantly, exemption from military service. The Mennonites are peace-loving people who refuse to fight or engage in violence."

"I guess someone else has to fight in their place so they can be free," the minister said, visibly disgusted. "Continue, please."

"The Prussians also needed help with draining the swampland and knew the Mennonites were expert dike builders. These people can convert swamps into rich farmland. Sure enough, they added land to the country and turned it into a bountiful producer of food.

"But the Mennonites have large families, sometimes fourteen children or more. By the 1780s, their population growth worried Prussia and King William III. The Prussian government was highly militaristic which clashed with the Mennonites' pacifist religious beliefs. Eventually, the Prussian government tied land acquisition to military service. Since the Mennonites could no longer acquire new property without giving up their pacifism, many chose to leave the Prussian territory."

"Exactly!" one of the officials blurted out. "It also freed up all their land."

The bureaucrat nodded. "Yes. Then, our Empress Catherine II sent emissaries to the Mennonites and urged them to consider settling in South Russia. She offered a special agreement consisting of economic privileges, religious freedom, and, of course, the all-important exemption from military service. The Mennonites accepted."

He paused to look over the room. Some of the men in the audience leaned forward and listened attentively.

"Practically overnight," he continued, "they took the land and worked from sunrise to sunset six days a week. Now, ninety years later, the Mennonites have planted seven-and-a-half-million trees while erecting mills and factories that produce wood, brick, and silk. They have metal forging operations as well as oil presses, and the men are very inventive." [15]

The bureaucrat took a sip of water. "Their pastures overflow with plump animals, and their villages have no poor people. It's truly a miracle that they were able to turn the dry and barren steppes into what we have today. South Russia now feeds all of Russia and other parts of the world."

"But their population has overtaken the country," the minister said.

"Yes," the bureaucrat replied. "It has doubled every twenty-five years."

"That's why we must act now!" The minister pounded the table. "Prussia clamped down on them and kept the fertile land when they left. It's worked before. It'll work again."

The bureaucrat raised his hand. "But sir, if I may. If you chase the Mennonites away, many of the fields will not be planted. And the factories will go with them."

"Ah, but we are not the Prussians. They acted harshly. Instead, we will be more subtle. We will give the Mennonites, say, ten years. By then, most of them will have gotten used to the new rules and not leave. Perhaps we will lose almost no one."

"Perhaps," the bureaucrat said. *And perhaps we will all starve,* he thought grimly to himself.

---

[15] In 1907, the first airplane to fly over Russia was invented by three Mennonites. The HUP airplane was named after Kornelius Hildebrand, Peter Unrau, and Henry Plenert. This incredible feat came just four years after the Wright brothers' success at Kitty Hawk in the U.S. and is barely known throughout the world.

The minister grabbed a quill pen. "Before the ten years expire, we will stop them from buying more land. As their families explode, they will have to crowd onto the land they already have and perhaps seek to negotiate an accommodation."

"Do you really think this will work?" the bureaucrat asked, trying one last time to restore sanity.

"You'll see," the minister said, smiling. "We are smarter than the Dutch and the Prussians. Besides, we need a scapegoat after our losses in the Crimean War. We have all that debt. With the serfs freed, so many of our fellow Russians are bankrupt after losing all that free labor. It's a complete tragedy. So it's perfect timing for these wealthy Mennonites to pay off all this debt."

"Bravo," the official in charge of bootlicking said.

The minister held up a glass of sweet wine. "It will work. After all, what are they going to do, fight us?"

Laughter filled the room. Everyone enjoyed themselves except the bureaucrat. He was the only one who could see what was coming.

October 1873 – Two Years Later
Chortitza Colony, South Russia

A large group of Mennonite men gathered under a massive oak tree, its umbrella stretching far and wide, providing a protective cover for most of them. The oak tree had been here for centuries and was an important symbol to the village. So many important meetings had been conducted under its fatherly limbs.[16]

Henry, now ten, had ridden with his father but was ordered to stay clear of the men. Yet he was a curious boy. He found a nearby cart and hid in it, hoping to listen to whatever was said.

The leader stepped up onto a wooden crate and clapped his hands. "Men, as you all know, we now have eight years to leave this place. If we stay, we must fight in their wars."

---

[16] To see this tree, search online for the "700-year-old Zaporizhzhia Oak."

Post Oak

An angry murmur rippled through the crowd.

"I understand your feelings. That is why we voted to send delegations to Canada and the United States. Both countries have lands that need settling. Now the men have returned and reported that Canada will grant the same privileges we received from Catherine the Great in South Russia. And there is land available to us, but it will be at market price and not given away. Our delegation reports that winters are frigid and the snow is deep. Still, it is a beautiful country, I'm told."

"What about the United States?" someone called out.

"I'm getting to that," the leader said, waving his hands to quiet the crowd. "Our men traveled from Canada through Minnesota, south to Nebraska and Kansas, then farther south through Oklahoma and Texas and into Houston. Even though Texas and Oklahoma have problems with Indians, they are being defeated and moved to reservations. Our people found vast lands available, most of which can be claimed for a small filing fee. The usual allotment is 160 acres. There is also water, but it needs to be diverted and controlled. To our men, the land appeared fertile, ready to submit to the plow, unlike what we encountered in Prussia and here."

"Will the United States grant us special privileges?" someone else asked.

"Our men met with President Grant and he would not provide us special privileges. But rest assured, the United States has many boys and men to fight their wars. The location of this available land is away from the big cities in the east. It is likely they will leave us alone for some time. We also learned that the cost of their land is so cheap it's hard to pass up. As we have learned in the past, paying top dollar for land might be a bad investment since no government can be trusted to keep their word for too long."

Another murmur rippled through the crowd.

A third man shouted out his concern. "If we go to the United States, will the Indians attack and kill us?"

The leader nodded. "It is possible. But we shall settle in areas where they have been subdued."

"Still, you are saying it's possible."

"Well, yes. There are a few especially violent tribes roaming the territory south of Nebraska and Kansas, mainly in Texas and the Oklahoma Territory."

"Perhaps we can negotiate with their leaders," a man suggested.

"Perhaps," the leader replied, removing a handkerchief and dabbing at the sweat on his cheeks. "One tribe is led by a half-white, half-Comanche man. He is greatly feared. Attacks are frequent on the settlements in Texas, but are not our religious freedoms being attacked here?"

Several men looked down at their shoes while others rubbed their hands together. The thought of being attacked by Indians terrified them. Even young Henry shuddered.

"What is this man's name, the half-white, half-Comanche?"

"His name is Parker. *Quanah* Parker."

Chapter Forty

A massive outcropping rose two hundred feet above the Comanche camp. Its crescent moon shape provided shelter like a harbor for boats, making it one of their favorite places to camp.[17]

Quanah had scaled the butte and now stood tall, staring north to Blanco Canyon, the location of his famous battle with Colonel Ranald Mackenzie four years earlier. Now a general, Mackenzie, still chased the Comanche leader.

Just nine months earlier, the general caught up with Quanah, forcing him to lead his people through another escape. Some might consider it a victory over the white man's army, but Quanah knew better.

After Quanah's failed attack on the buffalo hunters at Adobe Walls one year earlier, the bluecoats sent three generals to find, pursue, and kill him and his people. The armies came from different directions, often pushing Quanah toward another general.

This strategy triggered a series of running battles barely two months after Adobe Walls: one in August, four in September, and two in November. Each time the Comanche contacted the bluecoats, they lost some warriors.

The big loss, however, was always stores of dried buffalo meat. It was becoming harder to find the beasts, and it took longer to replenish their food supplies. The warriors were constantly hunting game and not always guarding the camps.

When the bluecoats attacked, hurried escapes meant leaving clothing, teepees, lodgepoles, and utensils behind. These abandoned items also took much time and labor to replace—if they even could—not to mention the

---

[17] This formation is located at present-day Gail, Texas.

loss of morale. Mackenzie's war of attrition was eating away at the last of the free Comanche.[18]

Then there were the ponies. Having huge horse herds served multiple purposes for the Comanche. First, they used fresh mounts to harass and attack the whites, a considerable advantage the Comanche exploited over any attacker. Next, it was a sign of wealth. Losing horses meant a loss of status. Finally, in times of stress, horseflesh sustained the Comanche. It was a backup food supply when needed.

Yet the huge herds were easily spotted and took great effort to keep from being taken by the bluecoats. And the horses ate grass, which sometimes dictated where the Comanche had to go. During each bluecoat encounter, horses were lost. This not only reduced their fighting readiness but sank the band's morale.

Quanah tossed a rock off the outcropping as he thought about his last contact with Mackenzie. It was at the Comanches' favorite hideout in Palo Duro Canyon, north of the Blanco Canyon and the deepest, most secret part of Comanchería.

After getting over the shock of seeing the bluecoats in these distant and secluded campsites, Quanah led yet another escape, losing some warriors and stores of food. But the most significant loss was over 2,000 horses. Before Quanah could organize a rescue of the animals, Mackenzie shot them all, save a few he doled out to the scouts. It was a brutal but effective tactic.

Quanah sighed. Through skill and the Great Spirit, they had survived the winter. Between finding game and eating horses, they emerged in the spring still intact as a band but barely.

Quanah assumed Mackenzie would continue to use the same three-general approach until his people were slaughtered by the soldiers or starved to death. But there was another option.

A few days earlier, a white man, Dr. Jacob J. Sturm, had found Quanah's camp with the help of three Comanche reservation Indians. Dr. Sturm was a physician and interpreter at Fort Sill. He'd married a Caddo woman

---

[18] These battles in the Texas panhandle from August to November 1874 later became known as the Red River War.

and lived with her people to immerse himself in Indian culture. Thus, he was the perfect person for this vital mission.

Dr. Sturm delivered Mackenzie's message: surrender to the reservation or I will hunt you down to the last man. Of course, Dr. Sturm put it in words that were friendly and palatable to Quanah's people.

Then there was Isatai. The young medicine man had lost a great deal of respect after Adobe Walls. Undeterred, he kept trotting out the skunk excuse.

Many of the Comanche continued to believe in Isatai's medicine because he kept making predictions that came true. Quanah was one of them who still believed.

Isatai had been his partner, and together, the two young men hoped to restore the Comanche to their former glory. But Quanah was still haunted by the incredible range of the hunters' long guns. A warrior would be dead before he heard the sound of the gun that killed him. How could anyone defeat weapons like that?

But the misery didn't end there as hardly a day went by that he didn't hear the thunder of the Sharps rifles destroying 1,000 buffalo somewhere on the prairie around them. The carcasses that could feed his people for months, if not years, were left rotting in the sun for the fat coyotes and wolves.

The population of these predators quickly exploded, allowing them to work in packs to take down other game the Comanche needed. It was a vicious cycle. To find buffalo or any game now required longer rides and more effort to return the meat to camp if they could even find anything to kill. It was all so depressing.

After Sturm's arrival and the receipt of Mackenzie's message, the chiefs convened. Quanah was not yet a chief but still had great influence, especially in war matters.

Isatai also influenced civil matters. He believed they needed to surrender or plan on dying here on the prairie. So many other Comanche bands had gone in, and theirs was one of the last ones left in the shrinking Comanchería. They simply lacked allies to fight with.

Then there was the weather. So far, the spring and early summer had been dry. It was hard to find game, which meant more effort and more hunger.

Quanah bent over and rubbed his hands with dirt, letting the wind carry it away. For hundreds, if not thousands of years, all his forefathers were buried here in Comanchería. They would be left behind, as would the exciting buffalo hunts and the nighttime rides to attack white settlements and steal horses.

If they surrendered, would they even be allowed to keep horses? The young Comanche leader had no idea.

There was really no choice. The white men knew all their campsites in Comanchería. Sooner or later, those long guns would be set up on the edge of some bluff and pick them off one by one. It was time to go in and face whatever fate awaited them.

But one thing was certain in Quanah's mind: he would survive. And if he could survive, maybe he could thrive. Perhaps he could beat the white men at their own game. Who knew what the Great Spirit might have in store for this brave warrior, the last of his kind?

Herman sat around the campfire, his head in his hands. Losing his Apache mother was soul-crushing. Making matters worse, others around him were sick and dying from the white man's diseases.

The medicine man who hated Herman told the camp he would get rid of the pestilence. Even though it was deep into winter, he climbed to the top of a mountain and spent time there, offering up prayers for The Great Spirit to come to their aid and rid them of their sicknesses. Below, his people were huddled in their teepees, trying to stay alive.

The next morning, the medicine man returned to camp and ordered a hole dug near the river. He placed large stones in and around the holes and made a big fire.

The heated stones were placed in airtight teepees, and the sick Indians were stripped and placed inside. Each one was forced to stay as long as they could, sweating and sweating until each one staggered outside and then into a cold plunge in the river.

They remained in the icy water for several minutes, with icicles forming in their hair. Then they were helped out, and women rubbed their skin with wet grass and a rough blanket before covering them in a warm buffalo robe. Finally, each one was given hot, bitter tea made from a plant root known in the area.

When all the ill had endured this regimen, each healthy Indian, including Herman, underwent the same treatment. Then they moved camp with the healthy carrying the sick. Miraculously, the plague went away with no more deaths.

Once they were all well, Herman's Apache band moved around the plains until they contacted the bluecoats. At first, they led the soldiers onto the Llano Estacado, but the soldiers found a spring.[19]

After dodging them for weeks, the chiefs decided to head back to the reservation in New Mexico. Everyone promised not to run away.

The Apache settled on reservation camps about fifteen miles apart. A few weeks after they arrived, an old Apache made the trip from one camp to see Herman, bringing a sizable quantity of beer. Soon, he and Herman were completely drunk.

The intoxicated man made fun of Herman and teased him, reminding Herman how he had made fun of the boy and treated him when he was first captured. Herman remembered this and took offense, pulling his pistol and shooting at the old man.

The Indian dodged the bullets and escaped as Herman staggered after him, firing the gun until it was empty. Herman tumbled into a ditch and lay there until the next morning.

Herman could see that drinking beer, whisky, and mescal on the reservation was constant with the Apache men. Drunk Indians fought each other and sometimes died. They were rudderless and had nothing to do but wait for their government handout.

Herman's friends fell into a feud with another Apache group, and a brawl soon erupted. He and his buddies killed each member of the opposing group.

Not wanting to stand trial with the Apache or the white man, a sizable group of Apache left the reservation and headed south to Mexico. It was time to be free again, as staying on the white man's land was no way to live.

Maybe the soldiers would give up and never find them.

---

[19] The spring is located in what would later become Seminole, Texas.

Dr. Sturm's reports finally reached General Mackenzie. He sat at his desk, reviewing them, when the appearance of Tatum, the Indian agent, followed a knock on his door.

"Sir, we have Chief Bull Bear here," Tatum announced. "He wants to speak to you about his son."

"What's this about?" Mackenzie asked.

"One of the conditions for his Comanche band's surrendering was the return of the white and Mexican captives. Chief Bull Bear has complied, giving us four whites and twelve Mexicans. In return, we reunited his band with a hundred women and children you captured."

"Okay. So far, this all sounds fine," Mackenzie said impatiently. "What do you need from me?"

"Chief Bull Bear returned a Mexican named Presleano. This young boy was raised by the chief from maybe four or five years old. He loves this boy like a son. It's also very clear the boy loves the chief. However, I think the boy's family wants him back, although no one knows if they are alive. I believe Presleano would be willing to go back home if he is questioned properly. That's why the Chief Bull Bear wants to see you."

"But we don't even know if the boy has any family left to go back to. Right?"

Tatum nodded.

Mackenzie set down the reports and sighed. "Show him in."

A great big bear of a man with curly hair walked into Mackenzie's office. It was easy to see the fierce warrior in Chief Bull Bear, as he had fought many great battles and was still alive to celebrate each victory.

Mackenzie could only imagine what hand-to-hand combat with such a man would entail. He had no doubts that the chief would always come out on top and his opponent would be left bleeding out on the vast prairie, minus a scalp.

Now, thoroughly defeated, Chief Bull Bear stood there, tightly holding the hand of the young Mexican boy. It was a contradiction from the unbeatable warrior to a loving father.

Mackenzie studied the chief's countenance. It was not one of confidence. Instead, his face was filled with worry.

For the first time in his life, the great chief was not in control. He needed the white man's help.

"What can I do for you?" Mackenzie asked.

Through a translator, Chief Bull Bear said, "The other prisoners we have brought in belong to your nation. Yet this boy was captured in Mexico and does not belong to your government. You have no special right to him. I love him as my own son, and he loves me. I cannot part from him, and I know he wants to remain with me. If you will not force him away but leave it to his own choice, I shall be satisfied."

Mackenzie nodded. "Let it be as you say."

Chief Bull Bear suppressed a grin. He was almost there.

The interpreter started asking Presleano about his parents. The boy said he had no memory of them other than Bull Bear and his wife.

"They are my parents," Presleano proclaimed, still tightly holding his father's hand.

Agent Tatum cleared his throat. "Do you wish to remain with Bull Bear or go home to your own people?"

Presleano smiled. "I want to stay with him," he said confidently, pointing to his father.

Chief Bull Bear's face lit up with joy. But as he reached to take the boy from the office, the agent pulled him away from the chief and sat Presleano on a couch between himself and the general.

"Don't you want to see your brothers and sisters?" Tatum asked in a gentle voice. "Don't you want to go with them?"

Complete silence filled the office as the boy seemed confused. This matter should have been closed, but for some reason, it wasn't.

The boy glanced at his father, then back to the general and Tatum. Was it possible he said something wrong? Might he get in trouble?

Suddenly, Bull Bear's victory was not so assured. Everyone in the room could feel the tension.

Presleano lowered his eyelids, scared and unsure what to say.

Tatum tried once more. "Surely you want to see your family, right? They love and miss you."

Presleano's chin shook as he stared at the floor. Finally, he released a few meek words. "I want to go home."

Bull Bear's back stiffened, and his face went blank.

"Then I will send you home," Tatum said, closing the matter.

Mackenzie and Tatum glanced at Bull Bear and noticed his lower lip quivering. Before the massive Comanche warrior could turn to leave, tears streamed down his proud cheeks. He had just lost his son—his only son—his *precious* son.

Realizing the men were staring at him, the great chief turned, opened the door, and walked through it.

Outside, Billy Tyler rested on his crutches, waiting to see the general. He was confused at seeing Chief Bull Bear, his eyes cloudy, cheeks wet, and his right hand shaking. The chief grabbed his hand to steady it, and Billy could tell something terrible had just happened.

Soon, a Mexican boy was led out in another direction and the clerk called Billy in.

"Sit down," Mackenzie ordered.

"Is everything okay, sir?" Billy asked.

"Just had some unpleasant business, but we are past that." He handed Billy a document. "This is from Washington. It orders you to make your reports to me. I will make changes as I see fit."

Billy read the document. "So you know why I am here?"

"Yes, but only me. As far as anyone else knows, you're just here to archive records."

He looked at Billy's leg. "How are you healing?"

"Good. I had excellent care along the way. And your surgeon cleaned it all up."

"At least you can tell your grandchildren about the time you were shot with an arrow."

Billy thought about that. Before grandchildren came children. And children meant marrying a woman. But who would want him?

The only possibility was Jennie. He had spent the first few weeks setting up his tent and organizing his work and hadn't spoken to her yet.

"So, what can you tell me since you have been here?" Mackenzie asked.

"I haven't identified every scheme, but it's clear that all the government rations and money are not reaching the Indians. Between the suppliers and our people here at Fort Sill, fraud is rampant. Then there's the Ice House."

Mackenzie shifted uncomfortably in his chair. "Yes, I know about that."

"Sir, I must implore you, it's barbaric. Even the roof is missing. We lock the warriors inside and once a day an army wagon comes along and tosses fresh meat high over the wall to the other side. The meat hits the floor and the men race to tear it apart. During cold spells, some wood is provided to heat them. Even though they can eat raw meat, it's safer to cook it, which they can't do."

Mackenzie rubbed his jaw. "Hmm, I see your point. But the Ice House serves as a shock to let these Indians know who's in charge. We don't keep them there longer than a few months. But they leave knowing the Ice House is always there if they break the rules."

Billy shook his head. "But then we starve the rest by shorting their rations through fraud. And our leaders are surprised when they leave the reservation to find game to eat."

"You are right," Mackenzie said. "I'm going to investigate this fraud right now."

"No, sir," Billy said. "I beg you to let me do it. The second you start poking around, the fraudsters will stop their capers. Let me get close and learn about their schemes because they don't fear me. After all, I'm a simple clerk on crutches handling paperwork. I'm no threat."

The general hesitated. "Okay, son, we'll play it your way. But I have just learned that Quanah Parker is coming in with his people. I need his help to bring in the stragglers, and I don't need this fraud sending him and his people off the reservation. I want regular reports. Just do it discreetly, preferably when my clerk is gone."

"Yes, sir," Billy replied.

He left the general and hobbled to the center of the fort, which was bustling with activity. Jennie stayed with another woman in a room near the officers' quarters inside the fort while his tent was outside the walls. Since they had arrived at Fort Sill, he'd seen various soldiers talking with Jennie. What they were saying, he had no idea. But perhaps it was time for that talk. He wanted to see where they stood with each other before she fell into the arms of some lieutenant.

Quanah and his Comanche band made their way east and north toward Fort Sill and permanent reservation life. Each day, he could feel their way of life slipping away. The prairie felt less free.

Before they left camp, the band held one last medicine dance. No one knew if they would be allowed to continue having them on the reservation. Even if they could, this would be their last free dance. Quanah had savored every moment.

As they made their long journey of surrender, they took their time, stopping at every favorite spot along the way. Like Quanah, each Comanche felt, smelled, and tasted the last vestiges of Comanchería and freedom, hoping to store up a lifetime of memories in barely a few weeks.

Quanah and his fellow warriors had heard about the Ice House. They were resigned to their fate and would endure the white man's punishment.

On June 1, 1875, the Comanche arrived at Fort Sill. Their arms were seized and the men were taken to the Ice House to await chunks of raw meat tossed over the walls.

The downcast women, children, and old men shuffled sorrowfully to their assigned camping grounds and began setting up their teepees. It was all so quiet.

General Mackenzie had Quanah brought to an open part of the fort. In front of many spectators, the two warriors met and shook hands, each man studying the other.

Billy Tyler positioned himself to see this meeting and was stunned. Quanah was tall and erect, his dark skin set off by penetrating blue-gray eyes. His body was well-proportioned and his features powerful. To Billy, he was the best-looking Indian he had ever seen.

The meeting was less than a minute. Mackenzie told Quanah to make sure his people were settled properly and to come to him if he needed something.

Mackenzie also told Quanah he was counting on him to head back out and bring in the rest of the Comanche holdouts. Quanah listened intently and nodded. And that was that.

It appeared to Billy that Quanah was not going to the Ice House but to the campgrounds of his people. This was quite the treatment for such a dangerous and deadly foe.

"Sir, can I speak to you for a moment?" Billy asked.

General Mackenzie waved him back to the office and closed the door. "What do you have for me?"

"Sir, the reservation is turning into a refuge for criminals, especially murderers, rustlers, and thieves. I just heard that two herds were stolen from the Comanche and Apache. The chiefs are very upset. They are coming to see you about it."

"Oh no," Mackenzie moaned. "Not another problem. Why are the criminals so attracted to this reservation?"

"The law, sir. The local and state laws don't apply since this is federal land. They can't be arrested on it. Even if the sheriffs come onto the reservation, there are so many creeks and cracks in the land to hide in it's hard to track them down. Also, some law enforcement officials are still scared of the Indians. They know too many kinfolk who were killed, raped, and scalped. The criminals know this too and use the reservation as a home base."

"All right, son. Thanks for telling me. I'm going to put three squads of men to patrol the reservation. See if I can put a dent into these thefts."

"But that's a lot of territory," Billy said.

"Not really. I only have to put them near the herds of ponies, and that's a much smaller area."

Billy nodded. The general was indeed smart.

After the meeting concluded, Billy went to find Jennie. He spotted her outside the fort, walking back from a Comanche camp. It was time for the talk.

"Jennie, how are you doing?" Billy asked eagerly.

"Fine, William. How's your leg?" the young girl said.

"Almost healed," he replied as the pair stopped to talk.

The light was fully on Jennie's face, and Billy stared at the scar. He could barely see it.

"I know," she said, watching his eyes. "The scar is hard to see."

Billy's mouth hung open. "How did that happen?"

"Some Comanche woman made a poultice of herbs and who knows what. She put it on my scar for half an hour and made me hold my face over a kettle of steaming water. I've done it three times, and the results have been amazing. It seems to tighten my skin and hide this scar."

Billy was at a loss for words. The girl before him was beautiful. It was almost too good to be true.

"Listen, Jennie, I wanted to have that talk, the one you mentioned in the wagon. I was wondering if you may be interested in me, you know, as a boyfriend and, maybe one day, a husband." Billy held his breath.

"Of course I am, William," she said, touching his arm. "But I didn't think you were interested. When we arrived here, you didn't speak to me. I thought I had offended you somehow."

Billy exhaled, relieved. "I'm sorry for that. I had to get settled and understand the work. But that's all past me. I have plenty of time to talk now. Let's go for a walk, maybe toward Medicine Creek." Billy shifted his crutches to start walking.

"I'm sorry too," Jennie said, stopping him. "But Lieutenant Haverson has shown some interest, and I'm with him now."

Billy's eyes widened and his heart constricted. He had waited too long. His one chance had just evaporated in the haze of eligible men at Fort Sill.

Impulsively, he slapped his good leg. Then again.

"I understand," Billy said calmly, trying hard to regain his composure. "I'm happy for you but sad for me."

"Thank you, William," Jennie said, touching his arm again. "We'll always have that trip up from Dallas. I cherish the memories of your bravery."

Billy nodded, spun around, and started hobbling away. He didn't want Jennie to see his eyes filling up. At least his hand wasn't shaking like Chief Bull Bear's. But he was pretty sure his heart had just been ripped in two.

For the love of God, this life was a cold, cruel one.

Chapter Forty-One

General Mackenzie and the Indian agents quickly figured out the structure of the various tribes. With the Comanche, there were dozens of bands, each one controlled by several chiefs of war. Other chiefs handled the civil manners.

Instead of following orders from one chief, a single warrior could organize a raiding party and take off. This presented problems when trying to control a large population.

What they needed was one highly placed chief to discuss matters with and make decisions.

Mackenzie was impressed with Quanah, as was the primary Indian agent, P. B. Hunt. Both men wasted no time deciding to appoint Quanah chief over the Comanche.

"He's a born leader," Mackenzie said. "With great influence over his people."

"And he's willing to work within our system and not buck us," Hunt added. "He's very intelligent, too, absorbing every word I say and how it impacts his people. But some of the older warriors are jealous of his young age and mixed white blood."

"How old is he?"

"I heard anywhere from twenty-five to twenty-nine."

"He seems much older," Mackenzie said.

"That's why he should be chief."

Without any debate, Quanah was made chief of the reservation Comanche. Then Hunt implemented the second prong of the master plan.

Initially, whenever rations or money were doled out, one chief took all the rations and money for hundreds of people and gave it out as he saw fit. This provided one chief with way too much power.

Hunt demanded chiefs or warriors come forward with no more than twenty to thirty people in their care. This fractured the tribes, giving no one male more power than a small group could command. The big idea was to force these small groups to accept farming and not be under chiefs who refused to assimilate.

Unfortunately, the plan would never work because Indians refused to farm. But it did diminish the chiefs' power.

One thing the Indians loved was gambling and whiskey. One chief remarked, "If we ever figure out a way to make money with cards and whiskey, we'll never work another day in our lives."[20]

With Indian Agent Hunt pressing smaller groups to take up the white man's way of farming and General Mackenzie funneling the significant decisions down to a few chiefs of the various tribes, the plan was in place. All they had to do now was keep them on the reservation long enough to forget their past.

Was that even possible?

After killing their former Apache buddies, Herman Lehmann's band remained free for six months. But skirmishes with the bluecoats and Texas Rangers took their toll. Every few weeks, the Apache were driven farther into the Wichita Mountains.

One day, Quanah Parker appeared with a band of Comanche. He met with the Apache chiefs and councils were held.

Quanah stayed there until he convinced them to give up. The chiefs said they planned to take their time getting to the fort.

With that done, Quanah returned to the field, looking for more Indians. He went to Cedar Lake in West Texas and found some Comanche he knew. Yet the army was right on their tail.

---

[20] Federal and state law prohibited gambling facilities. But amazingly, many tribes found exemptions in their treaties as their land was basically a separate nation. Eventually, these tribes set up lucrative casinos to make money off "cards and whiskey."

Quanah sent the Comanche north and raced toward the bluecoats, carrying a white flag. Riding up to the captain, Quanah handed him a large envelope.

"What's this?" the captain asked.

"It's a commission from General Mackenzie. It allows me to hunt up Indians and send them to Fort Sill."

The captain looked it over. It read,

> The Indians of various tribes desire to give themselves up but do not want to fall into the hands of the Texas authorities. Quanah Parker is authorized to offer them terms to report to Fort Sill. Do not mistreat Quanah Parker or delay him in his mission. Assist him in any way possible.

The captain slapped his hat over his horse's head, letting loose an angry curse.

"So you find them first and deny us the glory of bringing in the Indians. We have no way to distinguish ourselves now, no way forward for promotions."

Quanah shook his head. "No, Captain, you are wrong. You can bring them in. The group you are chasing has taken off southeast toward Mustang Spring. Our mounts are tired and we need to rest. You can have a head start and capture them. It will save me the trouble."

The captain calmed down and smiled. "Thank you."

Quanah's group dismounted and settled into the bluecoat's camp. Shortly after his arrival, though, army scouts came racing in, saying they had found fresh Indian tracks headed west onto the Llano Estacado. It was a bigger group than the ones they'd been chasing.

Quanah knew his people were headed north, so these had to be other Indians.

"Mount up, men, we ride now!" the captain barked loudly.

In their haste to leave, most soldiers failed to fully fill their canteens with water. Instead, they raced west after their prey, quickly scaling the escarpment and reaching the flat, endless Llano Estacado.

The tracks were plainly visible. All they had to do was follow them.

It was hot and dry—scorching, in fact. By the second day of the chase, the soldiers had given up hope of catching any Indians. Instead, they desperately searched for water before they died of thirst.

Days dissolved, one after another. Eventually, they crossed into New Mexico but were no closer to water.

Just when they were almost dead, they collected the urine from the horses and themselves, sprinkling it with sugar and drinking it. When that failed to quench their thirst, they killed a horse and drank its blood. Nothing worked.

Near death, the company stumbled onto a lake and survived. But it was a costly lesson. Four men were dead or missing. Twenty-five horses and four pack mules were dead.

Later, they learned the eastern newspapers had reported the captain's men dead. That put a mark on his reputation and stopped him from ever collecting the glory he craved.

At least he never craved water again. For the rest of his days, the captain always made sure he had plenty of cool, clear water on hand.

Herman and his Apache band arrived at Fort Sill only to discover the men were treated like cattle. After enduring the Ice House, the warriors were given land to settle on.

Herman continually hid from the white men since he would be sent back to his family.

Hundreds of Texans rode north to Fort Sill to inspect their horses and claim any stolen ones. It was humiliating for the Apache warriors to parade their stock in front of the men to see if anyone raised their hand.

More than one warrior suspected the Texans were lying, but they could do nothing. They were captives now.

The white children were exchanged for captured Apache squaws and children.

Carnoviste told Herman, "I have not lost a squaw to the white man, but I am still not giving you up."

Post Oak

Herman was in camp when the bluecoats came to inspect.

"We've heard a white boy is here. We must look around," a lieutenant announced.

The Indians saw the men coming and made Herman lay flat down on his face. They tossed blankets over him and sat on the boy during the inspection.

The lead lieutenant stayed and smoked a pipe, talking and carrying on. The chief finally grew mad and the soldier took the hint and left.

As Herman had seen before, reservation life was destructive to the Apache. Many of the warriors sought solace in bottles of whiskey.

The evil spirits inside each bottle set loose old feuds and disputes. Fights and killings were commonplace, but no one seemed to care. After all, it was just one Indian killing another.

One evening, Herman walked around the camp and found Chief Bull Bear deep in a bottle. Herman had heard he'd been worthless ever since his son, Presleano, was taken away.

Whether by profit or some cruel design by the white man, local traders continued to bring in large quantities of whiskey in exchange for furs, trinkets, and any money the government had given them. It was so plentiful that each Apache had their own bottle.

The whiskey not only caused men to fight and kill each other but women too. Many of the squaws were cut to pieces.

One woman slept with another man she had been interested in and soon found a knife slicing off her nose. She was forced at knifepoint by her husband to go to the lover's tent and stay there with him.

Eventually, the new couple moved to a spot at the very edge of the sprawling camp and remained there, shunned by their community.

"We're leaving," Carnoviste told Herman one day. "I've had enough of this prison life. Grab your things and horse. I'll round up the others and the firewater. Meet me at the large post oak west of here."

Herman did as he was told, and soon, the small band was off the reservation.

Carnoviste's men and squaws rode day and night before finding a cool spot to rest. They had plenty of water and liquor to quench their thirst. With no one having any quarrels in this group, the men set up camp and relaxed.

The escapees sipped on whiskey and discussed where to go next. Suddenly, another group of Apache from their own band back on the reservation charged into camp and surprised them. In seconds, it was hand-to-hand combat. Caught off guard, Herman's group was losing.

Herman stabbed a warrior but the man fell and pushed Herman back. From a seated position, Herman forced the man off him just in time to see another warrior about to thrust a lance into Herman's chest. It was over for the German boy, now a man. There was nothing he could do.

He prepared to travel to the Indian's Happy Hunting Ground when a spear hit the back of the attacking warrior and came out the other side. Herman twisted to the right as the soon-to-be-dead warrior made one last thrust with his own lance but missed Herman's chest. Then the man's spirit left him.

Carnoviste came over and tried to jerk the lance out. He had been the one throwing the spear at Herman but knew he'd hit the attacker.

Carnoviste had just saved Herman's life. But the lance was stuck, so he stepped on the warrior's back to free it, spraying blood everywhere while pulling out skin and intestines intertwined with the spearhead.

Herman nodded at his father and smiled. Carnoviste smiled back briefly, then frowned as a spearhead protruded from his chest.

Behind Carnoviste was the hated medicine man holding the other end of the shaft. Carnoviste slumped over next to the warrior he'd just killed.

Like Carnoviste, the medicine man tried to retrieve his lance, but it refused to come loose. So he gave up and shifted to his Winchester rifle.

Herman had bare seconds to move his shield into place and deflect the first shot.

"This is your last day," the medicine man pronounced, "for now you must die!"

He fired again, but Herman's shield held.

Herman sprang to a nearby rock, collecting his bow and arrows along the way. The medicine man was behind him, chasing Herman around the large rock and firing his rifle.

The other attackers were killing the rest of Herman's band and left the medicine man to finish off Herman. It would be easy since every good Apache knew a medicine man could not be killed unless he ate swine.

Herman made one lap around the big rock, deflecting several shots with his shield. By the end of the second lap, he was still alive.

On the third lap, Herman grew calm and cool. He started thinking of a way to survive this fight. Then it came to him.

Just as the pair finished a fourth lap, Herman dropped his shield, nocked an arrow, and let it fly just below the medicine man's shield into his stomach. The stunned attacker dropped the rifle and shield and threw up his hands.

"I give up," the medicine man said.

Herman sent another arrow into his side and the medicine man fell to the hard ground.

"I'm dead," he cried. "You don't have to shoot me anymore."

"Why take the chance," Herman said as he stood over his long tormentor and sent an arrow straight through his heart.

The medicine man's eyes rolled and fluttered. With a long exhale, he groaned and died.

Herman stood there collecting himself. He picked up the rifle and removed the man's belt, fastening it to his waist.

Herman climbed up to a flat part of the hill and stared back down at the camp. He saw the squaws wailing as the attackers finished off the rest of his group. He watched as a few warriors went to the medicine man and found him dead. Herman knew he'd be chased forever and killed. He had to flee.

The German boy took off on a hard run back to the reservation. Along the way, he decided to leave the Apache and join the Comanche.

Even though there was a treaty between the two tribes, there had been recent friction on the reservation. It wasn't ideal, but he had no choice. His Apache father and friends were dead. Since he'd killed the medicine man, he'd be killed too. It had to be this way.

Herman slipped back to the reservation near Fort Sill, confident the attackers were drinking all the liquor left behind. They wouldn't be here for several days.

He found Carnoviste's sister, Ete. Herman loved Ete dearly and wanted to let her know her brother was dead.

Ete thanked Herman for avenging Carnoviste's death and agreed he had to flee. She gave him blankets and provisions and urged him to steal a gray horse Herman had won many races on.

Among tears and sobs, Herman left Ete and collected his arms and other tools from his teepee before spending a long hour sorting the large herd to find his horse. It was past midnight when Herman sent the gray mare flying eastward. It was fly or die.

The next morning, he noticed he was on sandy ground. This would make finding his tracks easy.

Among the cactus and sagebrush, he was alone. Without water, he grew thirsty. But in the evening, he came to a creek, and he and his horse quenched their thirst.

After a brief rest, Herman mounted up and rode to a secluded bluff where his horse grazed on fresh grass. He set up on a rock and squinted back to the west to see if he'd been followed.

By late morning, he spotted the riders as specks on the western horizon. They were coming for him. He'd have to ride harder. This was going to be tough.

Henry Kohfeld looked at the clothes laid across his bed.

"Why do we have to pack?" he asked.

"Because we are leaving this place," Katharina said. "It's too difficult to think about what would happen if we stay. And I'm not sending you to another country to fight his wars. You know we abhor violence."

Henry stared at his bed. This was really happening.

Once the Kohfelds loaded up their buggy, they took off, though there were no sad farewells or people wailing. This wasn't because the Kohfelds were unloved or disrespected. There were no people left. In many Mennonite villages, each neighbor left at the same time.

It was 1877, six years into Russia's revocation of the eternal promises. No one knew that Czar Alexander II and his staff were close to panic. The hardworking and productive Mennonites were melting away. Already, the country was feeling the pinch of reduced crops and production.

Post Oak

To stop the Mennonites from leaving, the Czar tried several tactics. He sent a general to seize and hold their passports. However, upon assessing the situation, the general deduced that this trick would cause panic and many more would flee.

The next trick was making it hard to leave. The Czar prohibited shipping companies from transporting the Mennonites, forcing them to travel to other countries and making the journey longer and harder.

Still, at least one-third of the Mennonite population abandoned their factories and fields—so far. This had to stop.

The Czar then promised that Mennonites could choose the forestry service instead of military conscription. However, with the continued Russification of their educational system, the Mennonites' Low German heritage was disappearing. So, the exodus continued.

Henry's family wasn't waiting around to see what other tricks the Czar had up his sleeve. They had had enough.

On a clear, pleasant day, they began the long journey to the United States.

First, they traveled by boat down the Dnieper River to the Black Sea. Then they took a cart north to Odessa.

From there, they picked up the train and traveled through Balta, Ternopil, Lemberg, Krakow, Berlin, and Hamburg before reaching Bremen. At this port city, they boarded the three-masted steamship SS *Vaderland* and sailed to the United States. So long, South Russia.

Henry was told that the first 10,000 Mennonites to leave went to Minnesota, Kansas, Nebraska, and Dakota. Another 8,000 went to Manitoba, Canada.

"We shall see how well the Czar fares without the Mennonites working the land and running the factories," August remarked.

"Where are we going?" fourteen-year-old Henry finally asked.

"We are traveling to Kansas," his father said. "We have some relatives there. They say land is available."

"Is Kansas near the Indians?"

"Yes, but I understand almost all of them have been subdued."

That night, Henry put thoughts of Indians out of his mind and dreamed about being a teacher. He could only hope.

The two-week journey on the SS *Vaderland* was rough. The Kohfelds were in steerage, the lowest class on the ship. In steerage, each passenger brought their own food for the entire voyage.

His father constantly worried about the winds because the weather could stretch the trip to fourteen weeks. If that happened, their food would be long gone.

According to Henry's father, some captains made a lot of money by selling food to starving passengers. This "food" was mostly spoiled bread, which was ground up and mixed with fresh flour, sugar, and baking soda and then re-baked.

Water was another issue. The ship provided it, but the casks used to store the water were often poorly cleaned after transporting oil, turpentine, vinegar, or wine on previous journeys. Thus, a rancid smell was often present when the water was dished out.

Mix in the darkness and lack of fresh air on the lower decks as well as diseases, fires, collisions, stormy weather, and icebergs, traveling to the New Country was not only an unpleasant venture but risky and dangerous.

To survive the voyage, Henry's mother had packed plenty of smoked ham and toasted zwiebacks.

Zwiebacks are a Mennonite specialty, basically a large yeast roll topped by another smaller yeast roll. The rolls are served fresh and hot, then pulled apart and dipped in jams and jellies.

Of course, most became seasick, Henry included. Being seasick curtailed appetites and extended food supplies for those who could still eat.

When would they get there? he wondered constantly.

At the end of two weeks, Henry felt like he'd been on this ship for a year.

He closed his eyes and sighed. After saying a quick prayer, Henry heard a man yelling from deep in the steerage section.

"Land ho! We've arrived!"

Chapter Forty~Two

The Comanche have always hated the Tonkawas. The Tonkawas have always hated the Comanche.

From this hatred, the U.S. Army took advantage and recruited the Tonkawas to find the Comanche and kill them. The army supplied the Tonkawas with superior weapons, and the Tonkawas took full advantage of this arrangement.

Many times, the Tonkawas went out on their own, hunting Comanche without the army in tow. Herman learned this the hard way one day after joining the Comanche and a scout came running into the camp.

"The Tonkawas!" he shouted. "They killed our other scouts. I barely made it out alive!"

Herman and his new companions grabbed their weapons and jumped up.

"Revenge!" they all shouted.

The chiefs immediately huddled. The Tonkawas had repeating rifles and could do plenty of damage to any attacker. They were dangerous foes.

"Those criminals are probably relaxing around a campfire and not guarding themselves. We must attack!" the war chief said.

The band agreed.

Sure enough, the chief was right. Herman's band surprised the Tonkawas. In seconds, it was fierce hand-to-hand combat.

Herman squared up with a younger man and the two jabbed spears at each other, using their shields effectively. It became a battle to see who would make a mistake.

The Tonkawa warrior shifted to the side but slid on some loose dirt. His legs splayed slightly as he tried to recover.

Herman saw a tiny opening and thrust his lance at his opponent's left shoulder. The warrior screamed as the spearhead sliced muscles and tendons.

The Tonkawa shifted the shield to his right hand and tried to lift his lance but couldn't. Herman charged, using his shield to push the warrior back.

The Tonkawa dropped his shield for a brief moment, giving Herman time to thrust the spearhead through his neck. The warrior collapsed and grabbed his throat, trying desperately to hold in the blood and flesh.

When Herman jerked the spear back, the warrior held his neck with his left hand before gasping and dying on the spot. Herman went to the next fighter and started all over again.

Each time he killed a man, Herman looked around and saw his men dying. It would be a close call.

"Hi-yah!" a Comanche chief yelled as Herman stabbed his last opponent.

The fight was over. Each Tonkawa fighter was dead or wounded. None of the wounded were able to fight.

The Comanche organized their men and counted eight dead and fifty wounded. It was clear that many of the injured would soon die.

The wounded Tonkawas were collected near the campfire. Herman and the others collected the dead Comanche scouts and gave them a proper burial with the other dead.

When he collected his shield, Herman found three metal arrowheads and one bullet embedded in the rawhide exterior. It was hard to kill him if he used his shield properly.

The next morning, the Comanche had more dead. This meant more burials. Their fighting numbers had dwindled. It was no surprise that when Quanah Parker showed up, the chiefs had to listen to him.

"You must go to the reservation," Quanah said. "Our wild life is over. It's useless to keep fighting, as the white men will kill you all. But if you go to the reservation, the Great White Father in Washington will feed you and give you homes. In time, you will become like the white man with lots of good horses and cattle and pretty things to wear."

"We can beat them!" one of the chiefs cried out.

Quanah shook his head. "No, you can't. The white man has us all surrounded. When you kill one, seven more take his place. You know this. They are more numerous than the buffalo ever were."

The warriors and chiefs argued for three days. Quanah stayed put, working each objector to his side.

By the start of the fourth day, the Comanche decided to come in. They trusted Quanah and believed they wouldn't be killed.

"I don't want to go back to my family," a panicked Herman told Quanah.

"I understand. You go to my camp and avoid the Ice House. I will hide you there and take care of you."

Herman thought it over. There was no way to survive on the plains alone. If his Comanche brothers were going in, he'd have to go, too.

Quanah led the Comanche band toward Fort Sill. Fifteen miles out, a large dust cloud appeared ahead. It was the soldiers coming toward the Comanche.

Once again, Herman panicked. He rode a strong black mare and immediately wheeled the horse over, racing away from the cloud.

Quanah pursued the boy and caught up to him after a vigorous four-mile ride.

"What are you doing!?" Quanah yelled, grabbing Herman's reins and slowing his horse down.

"I'm scared!" Herman cried. "I don't want to go."

The horses slowed to a trot.

"Don't be afraid," Quanah said. "I will protect you. Just go to my camp. You will be safe there."

Herman agreed and turned around. Their horses exhausted, the pair took their time getting back.

By now, the other Comanche had been disarmed and the men taken to the Ice House. Because Herman fled, the soldiers had already disappeared with their prisoners, allowing him to slip unnoticed into Quanah's camp. He hid there until Quanah appeared and showed him where to sleep.

Over the next several months, Herman guarded Quanah's herd and occasionally hunted with the chief. While he was alone with the herd, a Comanche rode up.

"Herman, you must be careful," the warrior said.

"Why?"

"The Apache north of here have heard you are on the reservation. Some want to avenge the medicine man you killed. Watch yourself. They will try to kill you."

Herman felt for his small knife and considered this news. He needed more weapons, but a knife was all he could have. He thanked the man and watched him ride away.

Maybe time will cool their hearts, he thought.

Maybe not.

Henry Kohfeld stood on the dock, surveying this new land—America. He had survived the journey and was ready to get moving. Fortunately, the next part of the Kohfelds' journey went fast and was relatively pleasant.

After clearing Immigration and Customs in Philadelphia, they boarded a train and headed west to Kansas. There, they located relatives near Lehigh and stayed with them until they could inspect the available land and make a purchase. This gave Henry's father time to catch up on events.

"So, what's it like here?" August asked his cousin.

"In South Russia, we were fearful that if we stayed, our freedom would be taken," Cornelius said. "But here, the opportunities seem endless if we keep working. Some of the railroads are offering Mennonites cheap land and temporary shelter. A few railroads are talking about chartering steamships to transport more Mennonites and our tools across the Atlantic Ocean."

"Why would they do that?" August said in disbelief.

"Because they know we will be shipping crops and cattle on their railroads, not to mention our extensive families traveling, too. We are money to them."

August smiled. "Ah, I see. It's nice to be appreciated again."

"Until we aren't," Cornelius said glumly.

"How are the villages going?" August asked, changing the subject.

"We've had less success with that. The local and state laws prevent us from combining our tracts, so we can't have common pastureland and church property. But we are trying to work around it."

The typical Mennonite village had been perfected in Prussia and South Russia. Usually, fifteen to thirty families joined their land to create a master plan. The layout had a focal point where they met for church and discussed current issues.

A substantial tract of land was also set aside as a common pasture where each family grazed their animals. The men and children rotated supervision of these animals while controlling the breeding; it was an efficient use of time and resources.

"How is the quality of the land?" August asked.

"Excellent. The prairie sod is easy to plow the first time and takes seed well. Our Turkey Red wheat produces many bushels per acre, although others plant sorghum."

"How hard is it to get lumber?"

"It's available," Cornelius said, "but because this country is so large, it must be transported a great distance unless you buy land near a sawmill. But that land is usually expensive. That's why most of us first built sod dugouts with thatching for the roof, though rain often seeped through it. To stay dry, we had to cover the bedding with an oilcloth. Then there were the skunks that snuck in and found cool spots. Same with the spiders, tarantulas, scorpions, and fleas."

August rubbed his forehead. "That sounds challenging."

"Not half as challenging as the poisonous rattlesnakes and copperheads that slither into your bed. Plenty of Mennonites have been bitten, with a few enduring a painful death. But as you know, hardships and suffering are something we are used to."

"Amen, brother. I'll set out tomorrow and see what land is available."

"I'll come too and show you where I would buy."

"You are too kind," August said. "I owe you a great debt."

"Just bring me some of your wife's apricot jam when you get set up," Cornelius said. "That will be plenty of payment."

August grinned. "Count on it."

Just over the southern horizon, the massive herd appeared, slowly ambling its way north. Quanah, Herman, and five other Comanche sat atop fine horses, waiting for the herd's arrival.

"Why are we doing this?" Herman asked as he shifted in his saddle. "Seems to me we're gonna get run over by them cattle."

Quanah pulled out his six-shooter and checked the load. Satisfied, he put it back in his holster. He looked like any other cowboy, with a wide-brim hat, collared shirt, and pants.

"The Big Pasture," he proclaimed.

"What about it?" Herman asked. "Last time I checked, the Big Pasture wasn't going anywhere. Why don't we hide and stampede their cattle like before?"

Herman was referring to the trick Quanah had been pulling for a while. At night, he and several warriors would ride around the cattle, yelling and making loud noises to stampede them. Once the cattle ran in every direction, Quanah and his men peeled off a few and added them to their growing herd.

"Because the cattlemen came to talk. They promised to pay me for the right to cross our reservation and eat the fresh grass of the Big Pasture. They don't want me to stampede their herd, so they will pay before crossing it."

Herman arched his eyebrows and said only, "Oh."

Soon, a trail boss rode up to Quanah's party and stopped. "Howdy," he said. "I have Little Jimmy cutting you out a yearling or two. He'll be along soon."

"Agreed," Quanah said.

Sure enough, Little Jimmy led two yearlings to Quanah and helped the men get started back to their camp. When Quanah's group was free of the cowboys, Herman had more questions.

"Why don't the cattlemen drive farther west so they don't have to pay anything?"

"Because the grass west of here is less," Quanah replied. "The Big Pasture is untouched by white men and Indians. No one lives on it, so the grass is fresh. The trail boss slows the herd so they can eat more grass and grow fat. Once they are off the reservation, they will move faster."

Quanah didn't tell Herman that a consortium of cattlemen was already paying him $50 a month to help preserve the Big Pasture for their cattle. Quanah had also demanded four other Comanche be paid $25 per month. The cattlemen even agreed to hire some of the best Comanche riders to help drive their herds to market.

It was a smart move, as Quanah made sure to spread the wealth around to his people.

The horses took their time getting back to camp. This gave Quanah and Herman a chance to talk more.

"What happened to your knee?" Quanah asked.

Herman chuckled. "Topay."

"She shot you?"

"No," Herman replied. "Her father did."

Herman proceeded to tell Quanah the story. He had fallen for Topay, a beautiful young maiden. Her father did not like this and warned Herman off, but love finds a way.

One night, Herman waited until her parents were asleep. Topay was with them in the same teepee and agreed to sneak Herman in after they were out. He eased through the entrance, slipped under her buffalo robe, and coupled with the young maiden.

Soon, Herman was speaking sweet nothings into her ear when he felt a strong kick. It was Topay's father.

Cautiously, Herman peeked out from the buffalo robe and saw her father getting up and filling the entrance. The jig was up.

Left with no choice, he slithered under the teepee like a snake. But he wasn't free yet as he had to pick a direction to run.

He chose poorly and ran into Topay's father, who held a bow. Before Herman could react, an arrow struck his knee. The boy fell to the ground, incapacitated.

Topay emerged from the teepee and covered Herman. She rebuked her father for shooting him.

The old man weakened and pulled the arrow out. Then he told Herman that for only two ponies, he could have her as his squaw.

As Herman tried to stop the bleeding, his love for Topay drained away. After that incident, Herman left Topay alone and was content with staying single.

"Two ponies for Topay?" Quanah said.

"Yeah. Someone will get a good deal because she's beautiful. But only if her old man agrees."

Quanah nodded, turning the idea over. "Say, Herman, is it true the Apache women go on raids?"

"Yes. They even have babies on raids. But the men leave the new mother behind to care for herself and the child as best she can. If there's another squaw on the raid who wants to stay and help, they will. Sometimes, they don't make it back."

"What else is different between the two tribes?"

"The Apache never laugh or have a good time. The squaws provide so little affection to the children, that's probably why. My mother, Laughing Eyes, was the exception."

Quanah considered all this. Leaving healthy squaws behind to fend for themselves? No wonder the Apache had such a hard time growing their tribe. They failed to value the lives of their own people.

"Take these cattle to the others," Quanah ordered Herman. "I'm going to ride over and check on Topay."

Herman smirked. He knew what that meant. Quanah was going to add a new wife to his others.

Good luck, he thought. *You're going to need it.*

Chapter Forty-Three

August Kohfeld searched for weeks before finding suitable land south of Lehigh, Kansas. He was both excited and relieved that everything he'd been told back in South Russia was true.

One year after their arrival, the Kohfelds erected a typical house with an attached barn, shop, stable, and retail space to sell their goods. The rest of the 160 acres were used for orchards, gardens, and crops. And just like he had been told, the land was highly productive.

As for Henry, he grew up fast after arriving in Kansas. At twenty-one, he was baptized by the Mennonite Brethren Church in Gnadenfeld, Kansas.[21]

He attended school at Halstead, Kansas, and met Henry Miles, an Arapaho Indian from the Oklahoma Territory. This was Henry's first glimpse up close of a real Indian. Both boys were devout followers of Jesus, and they became good friends.

Henry then attended school in Florence, Kansas. He hoped to become a teacher or preacher and eventually trained as a teacher before teaching at the Gnadenau School District, located south of Hillsboro, Kansas.

Henry met Elizabeth Unruh, a Mennonite from Prussia, and married her. Soon, they had a daughter, Emma, and Henry's life would change forever.

In 1879, the Mennonite Brethren Church of North America held a conference. The leaders were determined to create a mission somewhere, and they sent missionaries to China and India. Some church leaders visited tribes in Arizona and New Mexico but decided against them. They even

---

[21] Gnadenfeld is Low German for "Field of Grace." The village of Gnadenfeld was later renamed Goessel after the German Captain Kurt von Goessel, who went down with his steamship *Elbe* in the English Channel.

selected a missionary who got sick and couldn't travel anywhere, so they needed a replacement.

"What about me?" Henry Kohfeld said, stepping forward.

"What about you?" a church leader asked. "Do you have any references?"

He did, and they were all excellent. He also had a solid background as a teacher. By the end of the 1894 conference that was held in Hamilton, Nebraska, they told Henry he would be the one.

"You must search the Oklahoma Territory for a suitable mission location," they told him. "Can you do that?"

"I can," Henry replied, "God willing."

By this time, his relationship with Henry Miles had greatly diminished his fear of Indians but hadn't disappeared completely.

As he traveled south into Oklahoma Territory, he stopped at various missions and sought advice. Several missionaries directed him to the southeastern area of the massive reservation system. He collected all the advice and returned to Kansas to report his findings.

A delegation of Mennonite leaders was assembled to assist Henry in finding the right spot to preach the Good News to the Indians.

After being adequately provisioned, the delegation headed south from Kansas to Shelly, a town on the Washita River. Henry had left earlier and was already there.

The men arrived and sat down with a local missionary.

"Right here," the man said, pointing to a map. "This is the western portion of the Kiowa-Comanche Reservation. The Baptists tried to start a mission there, but Quanah Parker refused permission."

Henry's heart skipped a beat.

Quanah Parker? Is this where God is leading me?

Henry swallowed hard.

"I suggest you men travel to a Kiowa mission where the American Baptists are holding a meeting. It's forty miles away, but perhaps the men there can give you some guidance."

Henry studied the expressions on his delegation. Reverend Abraham Schellenberg only looked down at the ground while Reverend John F. Harms fidgeted with his fingers.

Post Oak

Abraham Richert, a Washita Mennonite Brethren Church elder, seemed okay with the plan. Then, all eyes went to Henry.

"Let us go there and hear what they have to say," Henry said boldly.

Whatever his future, he was confident it was in God's hands and not Quanah Parker's.

As always, Fort Sill was busy with activity. Billy was hobbling around when he saw Jennie. He hustled over so he could block her path.

"Hey, Jennie, how are you doing?" he asked cheerfully.

"I'm good, William, thank you for asking. I didn't know if you'd heard I'm getting married next week."

"Yes, I heard, and I'm happy for you. You deserve the best. Is he a good man?"

"Oh yes, he is, William. I feel very protected. Are you doing okay?"

"Doing fine," he replied. He didn't want to mention that he'd just celebrated his thirty-seventh birthday alone.

"Well, I have to be going," Jennie said. "Take care, William."

"You too," Billy said, feeling better having seen her.

It was strange how fast life could change on the Western frontier. He'd read the reports of families setting up a house and life going fine. Then, out of nowhere, Indians appeared and killed everyone.

Billy vowed to move quickly with the next woman who showed any interest in him. Now, he just had to find such a person.

Herman led the horses to Quanah's camp, the frosty breath of the ponies fogging the air as he rode through it. March had just arrived, so it was still cold on the open plains.

He wrapped a buffalo robe around his thin frame and pulled his cowboy hat down tighter to stay warm.

Herman was filling out and eating more, especially after Quanah adopted him as a son. The Indian agent worked with the chief and gave him extra rations for the teenager.

By now, Herman loved and respected his new father. And he was in no way jealous that Quanah had taken Topay as one of his wives. He knew Topay's old man would never challenge Quanah and was likely celebrating the match. Good for them.

When he arrived at Quanah's camp, hundreds of Indians were already mounted, some of them riding to a large post oak in the western part of the reservation. General Mackenzie and the Indian agents had agreed to allow the men to experience one last buffalo hunt.

By now, Quanah and his people had been on the reservation for almost two years. The other bands and tribes had reached four, five, and some ten years. It had been so long since any of them had hunted buffalo that malaise and depression now infected these once proud warriors.

With this one last hunt, government officials hoped to restore their morale and pride, if not their manhood. At least the weeks of practice and preparation had severely reduced their consumption of distilled spirits. That was something to be happy about.

Only the Kiowas and Comanche would participate in this hunt. The Apache were either not allowed or uninterested in hunting beside their old foes.

Herman rode up to Quanah and watched as the chief easily hopped on his horse. For this trip, Quanah wore Indian skins and moccasins with a thick buffalo robe, looking ever the fierce warrior he had been years earlier.

Quanah was the unofficial leader of the hunt. He led his group of Comanche to the post oak tree and rendezvoused with the Kiowas and other Comanche who lived north of Quanah's people. With a wave of his hand, the mass of horses and warriors took off, heading west for the old stomping grounds of the buffalo.

By the end of the second day, the group had left Oklahoma and crossed into the panhandle of Texas. Yet they hadn't seen a single buffalo. Instead, they saw something else that disturbed them.

That night, Herman sat with Quanah around a campfire, listening to several warriors complain.

"Did you see those piles of bleached bones?" one of them said.

"Yes," the other replied. "Are all the buffalo dead?"

"No!" Quanah said with a thundering voice. "We are heading to our old camp in the canyon. From the beginning of time, buffalo have wintered there because good grass is available under the fragrant cedar trees. The cold, clear water quenches their thirst, and the beasts are sheltered from the harsh winds. You'll see. Then we'll have a proper hunt, and each of you will eat some liver with gall. It will be like we never left."

The warriors frowned, unsure what Quanah said would be true. After all, he wasn't a medicine man. How could he know?

Herman caught Quanah right before bed and said, "Are you sure about the buffalo?"

"They are there. I can feel it."

The Indians rode for three more days. All along the snow-covered plains were piles of bleached bones. Occasionally, they found decaying corpses preserved by both the frigid weather and the already fattened predators, as there was only so much they could eat at one time.

When the warriors reached the opening of the Palo Duro Canyon, he divided the men. The Kiowas went one direction, a Comanche band went another, and Quanah led his Comanche warriors a third way.

The chief hoped one of the three groups would intercept the buffalo and drive them toward the others. This way, they could corral the beasts and take turns killing one.

The warriors had waited so long to return to their youth, to feel a wooden lance in their hand, and to hear the zing of the arrow as it pierced the hairy hide. They would be men again.

A small cedar outpost sat on the outskirts of the canyon. Before the Indians came close, a white man inside spotted them first. He dispatched a rider deeper into the canyon.

The man rode hard and dismounted at a sprawling structure named the Old Home Ranch. He didn't bother tying up his mount and instead raced inside to his boss.

"Indians coming!" he blurted out. "Hundreds of them."

"How can that be?" Charles Goodnight said, getting up from his desk. "They should all be on the reservations."

"Well, Indians are coming regardless of where they came from. They just crossed the canyon entrance and don't seem to be coming to pay respects."

Goodnight strapped on his guns, grabbed his coat, rifle, and provisions, and hurried outside. He mounted his best horse and took off, knowing his best chance of staying alive was to meet them head-on and talk.

He and his men rode for half a day, receiving more reports from his outposts. The men were on edge.

It was their job to watch for stray cattle and rustlers. At no point did any of them sign on to fight Indians. To them and Goodnight, that matter had been decided years ago.

Yet, apparently, that was not the case.

Goodnight found their trails and realized they had split into three columns. He followed one and found dead cattle along the way, counting at least forty carcasses. When he finally reached the Kiowas, they were in an angry mood.

"Be ready for anything," Goodnight told his men. "And don't shoot until I do."

The men nodded. Goodnight didn't mention that he felt this might be their last day alive.

From the mass of Kiowas, a Mexican renegade stepped forward and spoke Spanish to Goodnight. This allowed Goodnight to calm the warriors while he learned their purpose.

They said Quanah was the unofficial captain, but he was with another group. Goodnight told them to proceed north to his ranch house and they would have a parley when Quanah arrived.

Everyone was relieved when they agreed.

Goodnight and his men took off, leaving a trail in the snow for the Kiowas to follow. It was sundown when Quanah and his last group arrived to set up camp.

Cautiously, Goodnight approached the Comanche chief and asked his name.

"Mr. Parker or Quanah," the chief replied. "Why are you here, Leopard Coat Man? This country belongs to The People."

Goodnight wore a unique coat, which now gave him his Indian name. He sat down across from Quanah and tried to relax.

Post Oak

"Mr. Parker, I keep cattle here and sell them to the U.S. government. This land is called Prairie Dog, and The Great Captain of Texas claims it. So the dispute is between Texas and The People—*your* people. I promise to settle with The People if you are found to own it."

He wisely decided to leave out the part about how he had killed his father and helped capture Quanah's mother, Cynthia Ann. That information could come later, if ever.

Quanah stared into space. Comanchería had now been sectioned and quartered like a buffalo, and different white men appeared to own various parts of it. This greatly disturbed him.

Several Comanche warriors surrounded Goodnight and put some serious questions to him. Quanah stood up and joined them.

"Are you a Tejano?" Quanah asked

Goodnight flinched. He was a Tejano—a Texan—and knew they hated Texans more than anything except Tonkawas. But perhaps they knew very little about the rest of the United States.

"I'm from Colorado," Goodnight lied.

Two warriors moved closer and began quizzing the rancher about some specific features in Colorado.

The cattleman was an expert tracker and had traveled all through Colorado, so he knew most of its features. After correctly answering at least ten questions, the warriors nodded and agreed Goodnight was from Colorado. He had dodged a sharp arrow but was not fully out of the woods.

Quanah appeared to be either angry or confused at all this. Goodnight still wasn't sure how this would go. That's why he had already sent a rider to Fort Elliott, begging soldiers to come to keep or make the peace. He had to believe they would be there shortly. He just needed to delay any problems from erupting.

Goodnight finally decided to take a chance.

"Mr. Parker, I've got plenty of guns and plenty of bullets. Good men and good shots. But I don't want to fight unless you force me."

He pointed directly at the Comanche chief. "You keep order and protect my property and let it alone, and I'll give you two beeves every other day until you can find out where the buffalo are."

Goodnight dared not tell Quanah there were no buffalo around as the species had pretty much been exterminated. He wasn't about to steal the hope from so many angry Indians and risk the likely terrible consequences.

"I accept your treaty," Quanah finally said.

Goodnight sighed. "Very well."

Two days later, soldiers from Fort Elliott arrived and put away all thoughts of fighting unless the Indians were prepared to travel back with far fewer companions.

Quanah and his warriors stayed and hunted in Palo Duro Canyon, now called Prairie Dog. They didn't see any buffalo or much game.

At the end of three weeks, Quanah received orders from Fort Sill to return immediately.

Goodnight watched the chief organize his men and ride away. Somehow, the cattleman had avoided a disaster.

On the ride back to Fort Sill, Herman stayed away from Quanah. It was clear the chief and his warriors had not only failed to restore their morale and pride but now realized the world had truly changed.

No matter what happened in the future, none of them would ever ride on a buffalo hunt again. They needed to convert to the white man's ways or stay in their teepees and die. The choices were simple but painful.

Chapter Forty-Four

Henry Kohfeld was determined to succeed. He knew God was on his side. All he had to do was obey.

He and his Mennonite delegation journeyed to the Kiowa mission at Elk Creek and met with two Baptist missionaries. They confirmed what Henry had previously heard from others: "The western section of the Kiowa-Comanche Reservation has been untouched by Christians. Quanah Parker will not give permission to start a mission. You should give it a try."

Henry and his group thanked the missionaries and went some distance to read scripture and pray for guidance.

After this, they returned to Shelly, Kansas, where they made plans to send Henry to Fort Sill. It was hoped that the officials there would help him gain some land to build a mission. But again, Henry needed help.

Two leaders in the Washita Mennonite Church, Reverend Isaak Harms and Peter Bergman, volunteered to take Henry by wagon to Fort Sill. The three men made the trip and located the Indian Agency head. The agent listened to Henry's request.

"We can give you a quarter section of land if you can get the signature of Chief Quanah Parker and other tribal leaders approving it," he said. "But good luck with that."

"Hold on there," Henry said. "I have a lot of questions for you."

Reverend Harms interrupted Henry. "The light is falling. Peter and I will take the wagon to that grove of trees we saw coming in and begin setting up camp. You can join us when you're done."

Henry agreed, and the two men left. Henry and the Indian agent continued their discussions.

When Henry finished, he left the agent and found it completely dark. He had lost track of time.

Henry hurried to the grove to join his companions but found hundreds of oxen relaxing under the trees where the camp was supposed to be. He panicked.

As the blackness of the night descended all around, crazy thoughts of Indians running wild raced through his mind. He was in Indian country, and anything could happen.

Every night since his arrival in Oklahoma, Henry heard the drumbeats from unseen Indians. This caused him to believe the worst. Left with no choice, Henry raced back to Fort Sill and found a safe place to sleep. Thanks to God, he had survived another day in Indian country.

The next morning, the young missionary awoke refreshed. He thanked the Lord and prayed for wisdom before setting off to find his friends. It didn't take long.

"Oh, Henry!" they cried. "We feared the worst had happened to you last night."

"Where were you?" he asked.

"A quarter mile from the oxen. The creatures had taken our spot, and we had to move farther west."

The three men talked briefly before Harms and Bergman loaded up and took off. They had sixty miles to go, and it would take them more than a full day to reach home.

Henry could see from their expressions that they would be grateful to leave Indian country. He would have to get permission from the Comanche chief on his own, a daunting task.

Now by himself, Henry spent the next two and a half months traveling over the designated territory, trying to convince the Comanche and Kiowa leaders to give him some land for a mission.

He stayed at the nearby Baptist mission run by E. C. Deyo. Deyo knew perseverance and provided endless encouragement to Henry.

Deyo explained how it had taken two years of hard work before he'd gained his first convert. Both men realized it would be tougher for Henry as he was a German. He wore a black beard and spoke English with a thick accent. And he was a European (paleface), the kind of person the Indians hated. In total, he didn't fit in.

Post Oak

Each day, Henry walked or rode five to ten miles northwest of the Deyo Mission, which itself was five miles from Fort Sill. He went to Quanah Parker's home, but he was never there.

The first time he found it, Henry marveled at the two-story clapboard structure on the prairie. It had ten rooms and ten-foot ceilings, and its roof was painted with four giant white stars to signify Quanah's special status. Everyone called it the Star House.

Henry learned that Quanah had initially asked the government for financial assistance to build it, but the government refused. Cattleman Burk Burnett and four others stepped up to pay $2,000 for everything, including a wallpapered dining room and a wood-burning stove.

Aside from Fort Sill, the Star House was the center of business on the reservation. Poor and hungry Indians camped around it, and Quanah fed them.

Each time Henry showed up, he found Quanah's wives and numerous children running the place, yet Quanah was not there. Henry met with other Kiowa and Comanche leaders, but no one gave him the time of day.

As he left one of the camps, a chief told Henry, "You are a Jesus man looking to start a Jesus house. That may be a good thing, but it should not be on our land or even too close to us."

Needless to say, Henry struggled to find his place, or any place, among Indians who did not share and were not open to his belief system.

To get the land for the mission, Henry had been given $150 for expenses. By now, it was running low.

One morning, he woke up frustrated and sad. He was ready to give up. But before he did, he fell to his knees on the hot, dry prairie and prayed to God for permission to give up.

Incredibly, a voice came to Henry and said, "Do not flee like Jonah. Instead, put your trust in Me and I will give you victory."

Henry lifted his head and wiped away the tears.

Full of vigor, Henry jumped up and headed back to Fort Sill. There, he begged the Indian agent to provide an interpreter. Howard Whitewolf was chosen.

Known as White Wolf, he had been converted to Christianity by the Dutch Reformed Mission located five miles east of Deyo's Mission. As an additional answer to prayers, the Indian agent provided a wagon with a team to take Henry out west.

Along the journey, Henry told White Wolf, "I will give you my prized watch if you can talk Quanah into giving us land for a mission."

White Wolf nodded and grew excited. He'd like to have a white man's watch.

The pair arrived at the Star House. Henry and White Wolf went to the porch and explained their purpose to Quanah's family and friends.

Like before, they said Quanah was gone. Henry could leave or stay and wait. With a wagon, a team, and an interpreter, he may never get another chance.

"I'll wait," he told them.

Quanah eventually arrived. Seeing Henry, one of his wives, Topay, hurried to the chief and said, "My dear husband, we have lived together twenty years and have been happy. Here is the Jesus man, sent from God to build a Jesus House and teach us the way to heaven. If you hinder him, I shall never be happy again."

Quanah put his hands on his hips and looked at his wife. He could tell she was serious. And he'd never hear the end of it.

Quanah left and summoned ten other tribal leaders to the Star House. The men arrived and discussed the issue. Henry could barely breathe, waiting for an answer.

Eventually, Quanah came out with hatchet in hand and said, "Mount a horse and follow me."

Henry reluctantly climbed a horse Quanah provided and White Wolf did the same. Several of the leaders also mounted up. Being last, Quanah skipped onto the back of his horse and took off at full speed.

The terrain was uneven and treacherous. Unhindered and uncontrolled, Henry's horse raced after Quanah's mount, trying hard to keep up. Henry could only hold on for dear life. Visions of his life tumbled through his mind. Could he fall to his death?

The group rode southwest from the Star House. When they dangerously crossed a creek at breakneck speed, Henry decided this probably was his time to meet God.

Quanah pulled up before a prominent post oak tree and took out his tomahawk. He cut several branches and hung them from other branches. Finally, he made a prominent notch on the trunk.

"Here build Jesus House," he said loudly.

Henry, still shaking from the ride, produced a paper and pen. "Could you sign this?" he asked the chief, his voice and hands shaking.

White Wolf told the Comanche leader what it was, and Quanah and the other leaders signed the paper.

Henry was dumbstruck. Even though he was certain God had given him this victory, he removed his watch and handed it to White Wolf.

"He want you to join him for supper at the Star House," White Wolf translated.

"I would be honored," a stunned Henry replied.

That night, the food and company were wonderful. After the dishes were taken away, Henry dared to preach a sermon to Quanah and the other leaders.

Quanah listened but seemed indifferent. He still trusted in the medicine man. Henry could have his land, but he wasn't getting the famous chief's spirit.

Quanah offered the missionary a room, and Henry slept well.

The next morning, he said goodbye and returned to Fort Sill to deliver the document to the Indian subagency representative. Formal authorization would have to come from the commissioner of Indian Affairs in Washington, but that was almost guaranteed.

With his task accomplished, Henry loaded up and headed back north to report to the Mennonite Brethren Church. They finally had their first "foreign" mission. And what a great victory it was!

Chapter Forty-Five

Herman Lehmann had been living with Quanah for over three years. Yet each day, he awoke with a fear that by sundown, his former Apache buddies would seek revenge.

Late one night, he took Quanah's horse to eat fresh grass. As Herman sat atop his horse, bullets zinged around him. Muzzle flashes in the darkness pinpointed their location.

Herman dropped out of his saddle and hit the dirt, unloading his six-shooter. Sure enough, he heard someone moan.

Unwilling to wait and see what happened next, he ran all the way back to Quanah.

"I've been shot at!" he yelled.

"Calm down," Quanah said. "Tell me what happened."

Herman explained the gunshots and urged Quanah to investigate. The chief called up his men.

They soon learned that five Indians were missing. A wide search was conducted and the wounded assassin was found.

Quanah examined the horse they used. It was Apache. The wounded man quickly gave up his accomplices and admitted they'd been hired by the Apache to kill Herman.

Now Quanah had a problem. Herman's life was truly in danger.

He took the boy to Fort Sill and tried to convince him to return home to his family, but Herman refused.

"The Indians are my people," Herman insisted. "I will not go live with the whites."

Quanah stayed with him until General Mackenzie returned. The general had some news.

Post Oak

"I met your mother in Fredericksburg. She and your siblings are very much alive. They want you to come home."

The eighteen-year-old boy resisted until Quanah put his arm around him. "I will keep your horses safe. If you find your family is dead or they don't want you, you are always welcome to stay with me."

Herman's lips quivered. He could not see living with white people anymore. It would be a hard change.

Still, Quanah soothed and comforted the boy until Herman gathered his things.

"I'll go now. But I know I'll be back."

"I know you will," Quanah said. "You're my son, and I will see you again."

In reality, Quanah felt this was the last time the two would be together. At least Herman was going home to his people and would be out of reach of the Apache.

Billy grabbed his crutches and hobbled to the door. "Come in, Mr. Parker."

"You have an office now," Quanah remarked.

"Yes. The government decided to keep me longer."

By now, the entire reservation knew Billy Tyler worked to eliminate fraud.

"My people thank you for your work," Quanah said. "For too long, the people working for the Great White Father have cheated us. Now we receive our full rations. And they have stopped putting us in the Ice House."

"Yes, Mr. Parker. That's a good thing."

Quanah reached into his pouch and produced several slips of paper. "Here, these are reports from the Comanche and Kiowa."

Billy studied the papers. Each one detailed the possible capers to cheat the Indians. He knew Quanah couldn't read or write; the chief was not shy about making that known. He had assistants read everything to him and take his dictation.

"I will get on this right away," Billy promised. "Thank you."

"If they are true, I hope you can catch them. We'd love to scalp the criminals, but I know we can't do that any longer."

Billy chuckled nervously, unsure if it was a joke.

Quanah had been on the reservation for ten years and had become an incredible leader for his people. He constantly negotiated to get more.

"I'm headed to Fort Worth with Yellow Bear and will return in two or three weeks," Quanah said. "I will stop in and see how you are doing."

Yellow Bear was Quanah's father-in-law. His daughter Weckeah had married the chief a long time ago.

"I should have some progress for you, Mr. Parker," Billy promised.

Quanah studied Billy. "How old are you?"

"Forty-five. Why?"

"And you are still unmarried?"

"I had someone but let her slip through my fingers. Now she's married with kids."

"Do you need more horses to buy her?" Quanah said.

Billy laughed. "I wish. Of course, you and I are opposites. I have no wife, and you have what? Six or seven?"

Quanah grinned. "I have the right number of wives I should have. I love them and they love me. Maybe I find one for you."

"That's okay," Billy said. "I'll just keep on looking."

The two men shook hands.

"Have a safe trip to Fort Worth, Mr. Parker. I'll see you when you get back."

Billy watched him leave and thought of Jennie again. At least one of them was happy.

Quanah went back to the Star House and loaded up. Then he and Yellow Wolf climbed up in the buggy and took off to the train station. Soon, the men were comfortably seated in first class and enjoying a drink.

The cattlemen paid for this trip because Quanah had been instrumental in keeping the Big Pasture open for grazing.

Post Oak

There had been an ongoing contest between the cattlemen and the settlers. The white men wanted to dole out parcels to break up the prairie sod and plant crops. This would close the last open range in the west.

Instead, Quanah had used his connections and persuasiveness to hold off the settlers for a little while longer.

To compensate the chief for his work, the cattlemen paid Quanah and his people six cents an acre to lease the Big Pasture. This money fed and clothed the Indians, though many considered Quanah a sellout and a fraud. Old jealousies and disputes still lingered among the reservation Indians. With Quanah being half-white, many warriors spoke ill of him. Still, they couldn't deny his financial acumen. He had a knack for out-negotiating the white man.

The men arrived on the Fort Worth & Denver City Railway train. They were there to meet Captain Lee Hall, a federal agent for the Kiowa, Comanche, and Wichita tribes, and discuss continued payments to lease reservation lands for grazing.

A local Fort Worth reporter met Quanah and wrote,

> Parker is by far the most influential man in the Comanche nation, well-to-do, intelligent, and liberal and a fast friend of the whites.

George Briggs, a foreman on the Waggoner Ranch, accompanied the two Comanche. The medicine man, Isatai, and his son had also merited an invitation.

At first arrival, Briggs convinced everyone to pose before photographer Augustus R. Mignon.[22]

After an expensive dinner, Quanah and Yellow Bear checked into the Pickwick Hotel at Main and 4th Street. The pair were given Room 78 over the Taylor & Barr Dry Goods store.

---

[22] That photograph is available on the internet.

To get there, they had to walk to 405 Houston Street, an annex to the hotel. No one ever found out whether the hotel didn't take Indians or was booked.

Yellow Bear was tired, so he went straight to bed. Quanah saw it was only 10 p.m. and decided to go out on the town with Briggs.

Around midnight, Quanah returned to Room 78 and crawled into bed.

The next morning, the two men failed to appear for breakfast. An employee of the Taylor & Barr Dry Goods store smelled gas. Hotel workers hurried to Room 78 and knocked. When they received no answer, they forced the door open.

Yellow Bear was purple and bloated on the floor, clearly dead. But Quanah was struggling to breathe.

The employees turned off the gas and opened the windows. Quanah was sick but still alive.

Once he could talk, the employees learned Yellow Bear had blown out the gas lamp without turning off the gas. This was a common problem for people who had never seen gas lamps or stayed in modern hotels as they had no idea how it worked.

Quanah had come in later and lit the lamp, somehow not exploding the entire upper floor. He undressed, blew out the lamp, and turned the valve, but not all the way off.

He awoke during the night and smelled gas but pulled the bedcover over his nose and went back to sleep.

In the morning, Quanah felt sick. He shook Yellow Bear, who also said he was sick.

Quanah got his father-in-law out of bed, and the two men crawled along the wood floor to the door but couldn't make it. Yellow Bear died while Quanah passed out next to an open window. The fresh air from the window saved him.

Three days later, Quanah was well enough to travel. He took Yellow Bear's body back to Oklahoma, where 50 women and 100 men waited, their bodies cut and bleeding, as a great man was buried.

The *Fort Worth Daily Gazette* ran a headline and subheadings that read,

He Blew Out the Gas—And on That Breath the Soul of Yellow Bear Flew to Its Happy Hunting Grounds. Another Instance in Which the Noble Red Man Succumbs to the Influences of Civilization.

Though Quanah survived the gas disaster, he clung to his way of life. Isatai, the medicine man, was still alive, having also traveled to Fort Worth on the fateful trip. But Henry Kohfeld couldn't worry about any of that. He had Quanah's permission to build a church, and it was time to move forward.

Bureaucratic red tape in Washington delayed the commissioner's final approval until late April 1896.

Finally free to start the mission, the Mennonite Brethren Church provided $800 to build a chapel and residence and another $500 per year for Henry's salary. He was over-the-top excited.

In May, Henry loaded up a wagon with his wife, Elizabeth, and his daughter Emma, and headed south.

The first stop was at Marlow, where he spent a week finalizing the arrangements for constructing the buildings. He also hired freighters to carry the lumber to the mission site.

Through providence, he found volunteer construction workers from Korn, Oklahoma. Korn was a fast-growing Mennonite town that had been established three years earlier by refugees fleeing South Russia.[23] And the Korn Mennonite Brethren Church would soon be a big supporter of the new Post Oak Mission.

Henry found another prominent Mennonite from Fairview, Abraham Becker, who volunteered his carpentry skills.

With everything coming together, Henry took his family to the mission site and set up a tent.

"This will give us a taste of what it feels to live like the Indians," an excited Henry told Elizabeth.

---

[23] Korn would be renamed Corn after World War I, when anti-German sentiments were high.

By early December 1896, Henry reported to his church that the buildings were almost finished. Then he stood on a rise and surveyed the rocky and rough terrain. He was beginning to understand why no other tribe had chosen to occupy this land.

"It's time to spread the Good News of Jesus Christ," Henry finally said as he roamed the territory in search of willing converts.

At one of his stops, an Indian approached and listened to the Good News. Henry wasn't sure if the man was ready to put his trust in Jesus Christ, so he pushed the matter.

The Indian folded his arms and said, "White man heap cheat and no good. Maybe Jesus Man no good."

It was a strong rebuke for Henry but a common reaction. During his travels over the reservation, he found suspicion and mild hostility toward him and whites in general. Sometimes, the Indians were just annoyed at his intrusions. One thing was for sure: all of them were indifferent.

Quanah was firmly indifferent and unsupportive of this venture. At least he wasn't hostile.

Henry soon learned that the Indians, including Quanah, participated in peyote ceremonies as part of their religion. This drug caused visions, hallucinations, and dreams.

Another Indian told Henry, "Ta-a'pah gave you whites the Bible to hear His words but He talks to us through peyote." [24]

In other words, "You aren't taking away our drug."

The only people who showed up to Henry's church on Sunday were a few white cowboys. If Indians did appear, they couldn't understand his words as there was no interpreter. Henry had barely enough money to care for his family, much less pay for another worker.

Henry tried to learn Comanche, and the result was a few common phrases that helped with simple conversations. He did find a volunteer interpreter to convert the Lord's Prayer, the Ten Commandments, and some Bible stories into Comanche. But that was it.

Water was another huge problem for the mission. It had to be hauled in from four miles away.

---

[24] Ta-a'pah in Comanche means God.

In 1898, a dry summer wreaked havoc with the mission's water supply. Determined to solve this issue, Henry locked himself in a closet and prayed to God for an answer.

Eventually, God said to him, "Today you shall find water."

A knock at his closet door startled Henry. He opened it to find his interpreter.

"What are you doing?" the man asked.

"I'm praying to God for guidance in finding water for the mission."

The Indian grinned. "Coming here, I noticed a green spot of grass in the field north of the chapel."

Henry knew the entire field was dry, so this was odd. How could it be green unless it was getting water?

"Grab some shovels and let's check it out."

The pair walked 200 yards and found the spot. Sure enough, the grass was green.

They started digging, and within fifteen minutes, a shovel hit a spring. Water dribbled, then gushed forth. Henry was amazed.

"This will supply at least a hundred head of cattle."

Eventually, a windmill was added, and never again was water an issue.

Over time, Henry learned that the Indians gathered at certain spots to receive their government payments. This immediately led to rampant gambling on card games.

Henry and Elizabeth visited the Indians during this time, forcing their way into the gambling tents while singing, praying, and preaching the Good News. However, the Indians were not moved, and most were offended by this aggressive behavior.

Then one day, a crack appeared.

Hughes, a young Indian, came down with tuberculosis. He met with Henry and Elizabeth and became attached to them. They insisted he move in so they could take care of him. This allowed them to fill the young man with Jesus.

Before Hughes died, he accepted the "Jesus Way" and wanted a Christian burial. The man's family consented, and he was buried in a grave near the chapel.

In the summer of 1898, Hughes was the first member of what would become the Post Oak Mission Cemetery.

Next came an elderly woman related to one of Quanah's wives. She went to Henry and said, "I had a dream where I died and faced Ta-a'pah. It was my time to be judged, yet I am a very sinful person. Then I awoke screaming because I understood how bad it was about to be. Can you help me?"

Henry ministered to her and soon she accepted the Jesus Way.

When she fell ill, she told the medicine man to go away. "I am ready to die and go to heaven."

She was the second person buried at the Post Oak Mission Cemetery.

Henry was starting to see God's work in the Indians. But a health issue had hindered his work. If he ate meat or fatty foods, he came down with severe indigestion.

One day, some Kiowas invited him to join them for a meal. When he arrived at their camp, he saw meat hanging in the sun, rotting and stinking the area.

He spotted fry bread crackling in a skillet next to dirty coffee. His stomach turned. He couldn't eat any of this, yet he would offend them if he refused.

As he rubbed his lips, deciding how to handle this, an Indian said, "Henry, can you say grace over the food?"

"Sure," he replied. "Dear Father, we thank You for the hospitality of these hosts and for the food they have prepared. Please bless us as we spend time together and share this meal. In Jesus's name, Amen."

Henry received a plate of everything he couldn't eat. It looked disgusting. Still, he chewed the food slowly and prayed they wouldn't offer seconds.

They didn't.

Later, a miracle happened when Henry didn't get sick. In fact, after that meal, his stomach problems completely disappeared and he enjoyed plenty of beef for the rest of his life.

The Rainy Mountain Mission was located thirty miles north of the Post Oak Mission. It was started by the Baptists in January 1894 and called Immanuel Mission before its name changed. The mission reached out to the Kiowa, who occupied that part of Oklahoma.

Sanco, a Kiowa warrior, had come to the Rainy Mountain Mission and heard several sermons. It wasn't long before he chose to follow "God's Road."

Shortly after this conversion, the medicine man approached Sanco and chastised him. A big peyote ceremony was being held that night, and Sanco was a prominent singer during such events.

"Do not join the mission church," the medicine man said. "I'm warning you. If you do not give up the Jesus Road and participate in the peyote ceremony, I will pray to The Great Spirit to strike you with a fatal illness."

"I will not abandon God's Road," Sanco said firmly. "And I will not participate in the peyote ceremony either."

The medicine man smirked and nodded. "Goodbye, Sanco."

That night, Sanco lay in bed with his wife, listening to the drums and singing of the Indians. The old stories of the powerful medicine men spun through his mind. He could not sleep and rolled over several times, trying to get comfortable.

"Sanco, you are not sleeping," his wife said. "Are you sick?"

"No!" he yelled.

However, he soon felt ill and considered the fact that he might die. But then he remembered what would happen to him, *For I am on the road to heaven.*

Reassured, he fell into a deep sleep.

At sunrise, he stretched his arms and got out of bed. The sun was barely peeking over the horizon and he felt refreshed.

One hundred feet away, the medicine man also awoke and left his tent. He, too, faced the sun and stretched his arms wide.

"Great Spirit!" he yelled. "Destroy Sanco for leaving the peyote road."

Several witnesses watched the medicine man pray for Sanco's death.

After a few minutes, more men and women gathered around. When the medicine man prayed again for Sanco's death, a trickle of blood left his lips.

Several onlookers nervously stepped back. The trickle turned into a gusher, and the Indians became afraid.

In seconds, the medicine man bent over, struggling to breathe. In great pain, he fell face forward to the prairie.

Two warriors ran to Sanco's tent. It was known he kept a good-sized water supply.

The warriors filled two gourds and returned to the medicine man. When they rolled him over, everyone could see he was dead.

Sanco stood there, shocked and amazed. He took off fast to find the preacher and was baptized that very day.

Sometime later, Sanco traveled to Henry's Post Oak Mission and repeated that story. From the pulpit, he told the listeners, "You Comanche are holding back. What are you afraid of?"

No one changed their minds, though they continued to think about Sanco's testimony.

Years later, the seeds Sanco had sown would bear fruit.

I am an old woman now. The buffalo and black-tail deer are gone, and our Indian ways are almost gone. Sometimes, I find it hard to believe that I ever lived them.

My little son grew up in the white man's school. He can read books. He owns cattle and has a farm. He is a leader among our Hidatsa people, helping teach them to follow the white man's road. He is kind to me.

We no longer live in an earth lodge but in a house with chimneys, and my son's wife cooks by a stove. But I cannot forget our old ways.

Often in summer, I rise at daybreak and steal out to the corn fields, and as I hoe the corn, I sing to it, as we did when I was young. No one cares for our corn songs now.

Sometimes in the evening I sit, looking out on the big Missouri. The sun sets and dusk steals over the water. In the shadows, I can still see our Indian village, with smoke curling upward from the earth lodges; in the river's roar, I hear the yells of the warriors and the laughter of little children of old. It is just an old woman's dream. Then I see only shadows and hear only the roar of the river, and tears come into my eyes. Our Indian life, I know, is gone forever.

~Waheenee or Buffalo Bird Woman
Hidatsa Tribe

Post Oak Mission

Chapter Forty-Six

With frost on the grass each morning and a cold wind blowing at night, Christmas arrived on the plains of Oklahoma. For the Indians, it was just another day; they had no understanding of holidays or the birth of Christ.

Celebrations with food were ingrained in both the Comanche and Mennonites. Henry Kohfeld would use this common denominator to full advantage and show the Indians the importance of Christmas by putting on a big feast at the Post Oak Mission. It would take a lot of work, and they would need more people to help out, but fortunately, Henry had other willing hands to pitch in.

Three years earlier, Maria Regier arrived from Ebenezer Mennonite Brethren Church in Kansas. She hopped out of the wagon, put her belongings away, and started working after barely saying hello.

Maria's daily chores involved teaching the Indian women how to sew the white people's clothing and visiting them in their teepees.

Two years after Maria's arrival came Katharina Penner. She was from the same church as Maria and had the same hardworking attitude. With Katharina's arrival, the mission began a new program of serving meals after each Sunday service. Hot food brought in more Indians.

Still, they didn't understand Henry's words. Often, they snored or talked, ignoring what was happening at the pulpit.

Despite this behavior, Henry, his wife, Elizabeth, Maria, and Katharina were determined to make this Christmas special.

Before the day started, the missionaries were up, preparing meals for upward of 120 people. By 10 a.m., Indians streamed in from all directions, some on horseback and others in wagons.

When Henry started his sermon, at least 170 packed the small church. It was clear they wouldn't have enough to feed everyone. Left with no choice, the women stoked the fires and put more food in the kettles and skillets.

From the pulpit, Henry noticed the problem and dragged out his sermon. It was about the "Sin Way" versus the "Jesus Way."

For the first time, not one Indian spoke or disrupted the service. To Henry, this was extremely promising. These unbelievers were finally getting it.

After the service, the missionary women, concerned about the food supply, nervously rubbed their hands together. Henry said a prayer and the food was served.

In a report back to her church, Maria wrote about an event similar to the Bible story of five loaves of bread and two fishes: "The Lord blessed the food so that there was enough for all, and some left over."

Henry felt relieved. Sending Indians away hungry would have been terrible for the mission's reputation.

After the meal, he pushed everyone back to the chapel so he could explain the meaning of Christmas for the very first time. With that done, he handed out gifts to the Indians. Mennonite churches in Oklahoma and Kansas had raised money for this surprise.

The Indians were impressed when they unwrapped the paper and saw the gifts. The food and gifts did wonders for their enthusiasm. Henry and the others patiently waited for the first convert to approach them.

One woman asked Maria about the Jesus Way, but she didn't fully understand the concept due to language barriers. With no one willing to accept the Jesus Way, Henry stood there, astonished and saddened.

He whispered a silent prayer in High German: "Herr Hilfe Uns." *Lord, help Us.*

Henry watched the Indians mount up and take off with their presents tucked close to their full bellies. After years of hard work, it was another disheartening moment.

Will this mission ever show progress with these headstrong Indians? Henry wondered. But still he continued to sow the seed and prayed that God would give the increase.

Herman Lehmann could only stand there and watch the soldiers organize the wagon. Two of them loaded it with provisions while two more hitched a team of four mules. A driver sat in the box, waiting for the reins. This was really happening.

Herman was about to leave the only life he'd ever known. His adopted father, Quanah, would fade into a memory.

For a nineteen-year-old boy, this moment was both emotional and frightening as he hated all palefaces. He had no idea how or if he'd ever adjust.

Once the five soldiers signaled everything was ready, the driver grabbed the reins and started the mules for the large gate at the fort's entrance. Wiping tears away, Herman meekly waved at Quanah and began his long journey home—350 miles due south straight to Texas Hill Country.

At that time, Herman understood only two languages: Apache and Comanche. He had no memory of his first language, German, or his second, English.

With no interpreter on this trip, the soldiers and Herman communicated only by hand signals. It wasn't ideal, but there was no choice.

That first day, the team made a good twenty miles. They did a little better over the next three days.

By then, Herman and the five soldiers had consumed the fresh meat they'd packed in their wagon, but the soldiers wanted more. One evening, they placed a rifle in Herman's hands, made the sign of the antelope, and pointed for him to go hunting. Sure enough, Herman brought back an antelope.

The men roasted it over a roaring fire and patted their bellies. That night, everyone went to bed happy and satisfied.

The next day, the sergeant sent a soldier with Herman to hunt. Herman decided to kill the man and run away.

Out in the woods, Herman wondered where he would go. Back to Quanah Parker? The soldiers at Fort Sill might kill him for murdering one of their own.

Could he make it to Comanchería? The white man seemed to own it all now. They also had outposts guarding every square inch. He'd seen that on the last buffalo hunt.

What should he do?

When they were out of sight of the wagon, Herman turned his rifle on the soldier and pointed for him to drop his gun. The soldier hesitated, knowing he'd likely die on the spot.

Finally, he dropped the gun and raised his hands.

Herman pointed his rifle at the man's chest and yelled, "Vamos!"

The panicked soldier took off running.

When Herman dragged himself back into camp carrying both rifles, the other soldiers made endless fun of the poor man. He'd been tricked out of his weapon by an Indian boy. For them, that was pathetic.

A few days later, Herman awoke before the soldiers and took his blanket to a stump. As the sunlight erased the night, Herman stood on the stump and screamed war whoops, waving his blanket at some unseen force in the woods.

The soldiers knew, from training and perhaps experience, that this signaled other Indians to attack. Each one ran in different directions. Even the mules scattered.

It took half a day to reorganize everything. Herman was having a good time making sport of these bluecoats. For the soldiers, the end couldn't come fast enough.

The group arrived at Fort Griffin, 130 miles west of Fort Worth, marking the halfway point in their journey. At the fort, the soldiers and driver celebrated by getting rip-roaring drunk.

The following day, they were in no shape to go anywhere. The commanding officer sent them to the stockade and assigned five more soldiers and a driver. This new group took off and continued south.

Like the first group of soldiers, Herman was allowed to hunt for game. These soldiers also helped by catching giant bullfrogs.

The frogs were fried in lard, which Herman refused to eat because lard was made from swine. He was so disgusted that he stopped eating with the soldiers for the rest of the journey.

Post Oak

On the second day after reaching Fort Griffin, Herman spotted an antelope and hopped out of the wagon to shoot it. One of the soldiers collected the carcass and loaded it into the bed. But as he climbed up, his foot slipped and the mules jumped, sending a wagon wheel over his leg and snapping it.

The soldier howled in pain.

With no choice but to continue, they set him in the wagon and listened to his moans for the rest of the trip.

Herman and his escorts finally reached Loyal Valley at night. Though it was raining, he saw hundreds of people waiting to see the white Indian boy.

The scene scared him so much he wanted to run away. Since he hated all palefaces, he couldn't imagine staying here, much less ever being happy.

Herman let the rain soak him to the bone. He sat in the wagon, hardly moving, staring at all the people holding lanterns and gawking at him.

He remained silent and focused on formulating a plan of escape. He just needed to find the right time to slip away and leave the white man's world. Herman would then ride day and night until he came up with a plan that made sense.

Billy Tyler pulled the Indian blanket up to his neck. The night had been cold but not bitterly so. Dawn was minutes away and he wanted just a few more moments of sleep.

It was quiet around his camp. Since the sounds of the animals on the Oklahoma plains had ceased, he could hear his own breathing.

Most of the beasts had smartly bedded down until sunset. That's when they would emerge from their hiding places and begin searching for food or fighting to stay alive until the next dawn.

Finally, Billy had had enough sleep. It was time to get up.

Free of the blanket, his warm breath created tiny clouds. He studied the dead campfire and looked for coal to blow on.

Collecting a few twigs, he set it on the coal. He was about to start blowing when a noise distracted him.

"Please, this is all we have," a man said.

"Shut up!" another man barked. "I know you have more."

"What are you doing?!" a woman cried.

Blam!

The sound of gunfire set Billy's heart racing. He was now fully awake.

Grabbing his rifle, he crawled to a nearby bush and quietly peered through its leaves. Just before him was the main road to the Post Oak Mission. Billy was heading there to celebrate Thanksgiving.

Because he'd gotten a late start, he camped just off the road, hoping to get up early and arrive in time. But that wouldn't happen now.

"No!" the woman screamed after the gunshot. "Oh no!" she cried.

Billy raised up on his good leg and kneeled over the bush. Expertly sighting the rifle, he slowly pulled the trigger.

Blam!

A man with a bandana over his face crumpled forward and fell off the wagon. The other bandit panicked and pushed the dead man off, forcing the woman out. He moved to the driver's box and started the two mules westward.

Billy limped back to his horse and mounted up. In seconds, he was studying the crime scene.

The bandit he'd killed lay on his back, a mask still covering his face. The man who owned the wagon was also dead. A woman huddled over him, wailing, ignoring Billy.

He was about to speak to her when another wagon came racing down the road from the east. The man held a rifle aimed at Billy. He threw up his hands.

"What is going on here?!" the man yelled.

"Highwaymen!" Billy shouted back. "I shot one and another is getting away with this woman's wagon. I'll ride after him if you take care of the lady."

"I will do that, sir," the man replied, pulling back on the reins and bringing his wagon to a halt.

His face seemed familiar.

"I'll be back," Billy said as he raced in the direction of the stolen wagon.

It didn't take long at full gallop to catch sight of the stolen wagon. The bandit had the mules running hard, but pulling a full load was no match for Billy's sturdy mare.

As he drew closer, Billy ripped his rifle out of the scabbard and calmly aimed at the man, trying to time the gallops of his mare. The gun fired.

The man pushed forward before jerking back. As he released the reins, he slumped to the right side and fell over.

Billy rode alongside the wagon and slowed it down. Sheathing his rifle, he hopped into the wagon and tied off his horse's reins.

With his pistol out, he crawled to the driver's box and made sure the second bandit was dead. Billy removed the man's guns and turned the wagon around.

Fifteen minutes later, he arrived back at the scene.

"Is this your wagon, ma'am?" Billy asked.

"Yes, it is," she said, still cradling her man's head. "I'm grateful to you, sir. It's all the belongings we had left."

Billy looked at the other man. "Do I know you, sir?"

"My name is Bruno de la Huerta," he replied, bowing his head. "I am at your service."

"Yes," Billy said. "I met you years ago at Fort Belknap with Captain Robinson. You sell swords and knives, right?"

"Ah yes, Senõr William," Bruno replied. "I remember you. And you are correct. I used to sell swords and knives. But now I am leaving the business to my family as my days are growing short. I am returning to Mexico after making my final delivery."

Billy did the math. Bruno had to be in his eighties, yet he appeared to be in excellent shape. It was an extraordinary age for someone who'd plied his trade along the frontier.

"Let us help this woman into the wagon," Bruno said. "Where are you heading?"

"I'm off to the Post Oak Mission to celebrate Thanksgiving," Billy replied, "but I think I should take her back to Fort Sill."

"I agree. I will join you and ride ahead. There are many highwaymen and these two might be part of a larger gang."

Bruno pulled out his rifle, checking to see if it was loaded.

"I thought you used only swords?" Billy said.

"Those days are gone, Senõr William. I find it hard to stab an enemy who stands a hundred feet away holding a firearm. By the time I get close to him, he has pulled the trigger, and, well, as these two outlaws discovered, a bullet will get to you before you even know it has been fired."

Billy gave a quick nod.

"If there are more highwaymen, I will be the first to encounter them," Bruno continued. "You can protect the woman and back me up, Senõr William."

"Will do, Bruno," Billy said. "Lead on."

Billy sat next to the woman in the driver's box. She continued crying hysterically over her dead husband.

His body had been loaded in the back and needed to be buried soon. It was a horrifying new reality for this woman; one Billy had seen too many times to count.

He glanced at her face, covered with dirt and tears. Her dress was ripped in several places, likely from the bandits.

"Here's a handkerchief," Billy said. "I'm so sorry for your loss. My name is Billy. Billy Tyler."

The woman finally stopped crying. Then she blankly stared ahead. Billy wasn't sure, but he was concerned she had stopped breathing.

"William?" she said, turning to study his face. The sun was higher now, almost above the prairie bushes and trees.

Her strange expression took Billy aback. Did he know her?

He looked at the woman carefully. Her face was fuller and her hair streaked with gray, but the thin scar was unmistakable.

"Is it really you, Jennie?" he choked out.

She could only nod as a fresh set of tears streamed down her dirty face.

Suddenly, all the pain in Billy's heart returned. But there was another feeling, too—one of hope.

He yelled at the mules and pushed them forward. He needed to get Jennie to Fort Sill and have her checked out.

Chapter Forty-Seven

The day was clear and bright, making the view of the Oklahoma plains endless. Henry Kohfeld sat up high in the saddle, confident.

By now, the road to the Star House was easy; he knew the way in his sleep.

As he pulled into the front yard, several Indians milling about took his horse and tended to it.

"Thank you," he said as he dusted himself off and walked to the porch.

"I have been invited to see Harold," Henry announced to an assistant.

Harold was the son of Quanah Parker and his wife Cho-ny. He had been educated at the Indian school in Carlisle, Pennsylvania. Now, he handled his father's correspondence.

Since Quanah never learned to read or write, Harold read him the letters and wrote out Quanah's responses. Everyone around the big chief could see Harold was his pride and joy.

The assistant walked a ways off and announced, "Tia-cho-nika here."

Tia-cho-nika was Comanche for Little Hat. The Indians named Henry that since he often wore a derby hat.

The Indian returned and pointed to a large arbor in the sideyard. Henry went over and found thirty Indians surrounding a boy on a wooden lounge. One of them was Quanah.

"Sit here," Quanah said, patting a spot next to him.

Henry took a seat and studied the Comanche chief, who still looked strong and powerful.

"What can I do for you?" Henry asked.

By now, Quanah spoke English exceptionally well for an Indian.

"As you have heard, Harold has tuberculosis. We are told he will die, so we have questions about the Mennonite religion."

Henry noticed Quanah's eyes filling with tears before the chief controlled himself.

Henry shifted in his seat. He'd been waiting all these years for a moment like this but seeing the famous chief like this was unsettling.

"Of course," Henry said. "What would you like to know?"

"What happens when I die?" Harold asked bluntly.

Henry leaned closer. "There is life after death, young man. Our Lord has prepared a wonderful place for us to live forever. It is free of disease, violence, hunger, and strife."

Harold took this in. It sounded hopeful, but he wasn't sure about it. "Do all of us go there?"

"Each one of us, including me, is a sinner. We have sinned against God and done horrible things. We are not fit for heaven, so we must stand before God and face our judgment."

"So God will punish all of us?" Harold asked.

Quanah leaned closer.

"Each person deserves punishment and God's wrath," Henry responded. "However, God has made a way for us to be forgiven. His Son, Jesus, was sacrificed on the cross for our sins. Because I have repented of my sins, asked God's forgiveness, and accepted Jesus as my Lord and Savior, when I stand before God and face judgment, God will pronounce me guilty. Then Jesus will step forward and tell God that my punishment was taken by Him. He endures the sentence I deserve."

Harold pondered this. "Will *you* go to this wonderful place—heaven?"

"Yes. I will go there because of God's mercy and grace and Jesus's sacrifice, which I have accepted."

"Where do the others go?" Quanah asked.

"For those who reject Jesus and God's love, they will go to the other place that is prepared for them. It is filled with fires and pain and suffering with no water to drink. It will have the most difficult living conditions you can imagine. That place is called hell."

"Like being in a prairie fire?" Quanah said.

"No, much worse, because you will be in that fire forever."

"It never ends?" Harold asked.

"No. Neither does heaven."

A long silence enveloped them.

Quanah grabbed Henry's hand and squeezed it. "I see. I see now what I never could understand or grasp before."

Harold turned his head to Henry and closed his eyes. "I want to accept the Jesus Way. Will you pray for me?"

Henry nodded. But before he could say the words, Quanah's eyes filled with tears again, and he dropped to his knees next to Henry.

Finally, Henry spoke. "Please, dear Father, accept this young man, Harold Parker, and his belief in You. Save him as You have saved me and so many others. And thank Jesus for opening the eyes of Harold Parker to place his faith in You as his Lord and Savior. Amen."

Quanah again grasped the missionary's hand. "Thank you, Henry, for your prayers and concern."

The chief wiped his eyes as two men showed Henry back to his horse.

Harold's health continued declining.

Quanah's first wife, Ta-ho-yea, an Apache, came from the New Mexico Territory. She convinced Quanah to send Harold there for treatment.

Three days after Henry's visit, Harold was taken to Carrizozo, New Mexico. Sadly, he died shortly after his arrival. His body was returned to a devastated Quanah.

Henry learned from Quanah's men that Harold had often talked about how happy he was that he had found God's love. Quanah even spoke about how much Harold had mentioned Henry's words. Because of this, Quanah insisted his son be buried in the Post Oak Mission Cemetery.

A funeral was held, and Henry said to those gathered, "Do not despair, for Harold is now at peace. He is resting on God's bosom."

Several Indians nodded in agreement.

"As you all have heard, God's son, Jesus, died to bring salvation to the Indians. Harold's death could be the way to bring His people to the same eternal life Harold now enjoys."

After Harold was buried, Quanah asked everyone to go back inside the chapel. Once the mourners were settled, Quanah stepped to the pulpit and held a Bible up high.

"I have been to Washington many times. I have met presidents and senators. But I have never heard anything as comforting or inspiring as what I heard from the Bible and this dear missionary today."

He glanced at Henry.

"I urge my people to come to the mission every Sunday and listen to God's word. Here is the way to the heavenly home. Harold told me he loved Jesus and wanted to go home. Today, God granted his wish. He is there now."

Quanah wiped his eyes and prayed before leaving the chapel and a stunned Henry Kohfeld.

The following Sunday, Quanah arrived with twenty Indians. He sat through the entire service. Never again did he discourage his people from participating in mission activities.

Many years later, numerous members of the Parker family would be baptized and saved, becoming members of the church. The Post Oak Mission would finally bear some fruit from the Tree of Life, but Henry would not see it.

Mrs. Augusta Buchmeier knelt and put her hands together. "Please, God, I ask you for mercy and blessings by returning my son, Herman, to me. Before I die, please soothe a mother's heart. In Jesus's precious name, I pray. Amen."

From the moment her two boys had been stolen, she prayed several times a day. After Willie was brought back, she thanked God immensely but never stopped praying for Herman's return.

The entire town of Loyal Valley knew Augusta to be a faithful and God-fearing woman who was always there to help her neighbors, someone generous to a fault. Would it be too much for God to return her son?

"No, for He can do anything," she told her friends.

One day, a rider appeared on her porch and knocked on her door. Her daughter, Mina, took care of it.

"Can we help you?" Mina asked.

"I need to speak to Mrs. Buchmeier," the rider said, breathing hard. "It's urgent."

"She's away. Can I give her a message when she returns?"

"Sure, but it will be too late as General Mackenzie is coming through here tomorrow morning. He's from Fort Sill and has a white boy who's been returned. It might be Herman."

"Oh no!" Mina said. "She would want to talk to the general. I will tell her the second she returns."

Mina found three riders to race to places where her mother might be staying. The following morning, one of the riders reached her.

Augusta immediately jumped on her horse and sprinted home, only to find General Mackenzie had already passed through. Now, he was headed to Fredericksburg.

"Philip!" she shouted to her husband. "I need fresh horses. Help me with the carriage."

Philip hurried to the barn and hitched up the team. In minutes, the couple was off, flying down the road as fast as the animals could go.

By evening, they were within three miles of Fredericksburg when they found the general's camp. Augusta hopped out of the carriage and ran to the general's tent, surprising his aides.

"Come in," he said to the desperate mother, who was out of breath.

"I'm Augusta Buchmeier. I've heard there is a white boy at Fort Sill. I'm praying it is Herman."

She provided the details and date of his capture, along with a description and his current age.

"Ma'am," the general said, frowning, "I don't believe this boy is yours. However, I will telegraph the fort and have them send for the boy."

He pulled out a piece of paper, scribbled some lines, and handed it to his aide.

"Send this off now!" he ordered.

The aide left.

"Mrs. Buchmeier, I have ordered a detail of soldiers to bring the boy here for your inspection. If he is not yours, I will send him to San Antonio to learn a trade. He has no business living with the Indians. I should receive a response shortly saying that he is on the way. Why don't I have my men make you comfortable until we hear back sometime tonight?"

"Thank you, General. That would be fine."

The Buchmeiers were shown to a spot around the campfire and sat down, waiting nervously for what they hoped was good news.

Several hours later, a rider came into camp. He delivered the telegraph to General Mackenzie, who came to Augusta.

"Ma'am, the reply says the boy just left on a buffalo hunt. He will not return for three months. I will send another telegraph ordering my soldiers to bring him to you in Loyal Valley when he returns. By the time he returns, though, I will be finished with my inspection of the forts and be there to send him myself."

"Oh, thank you again, General Mackenzie," Augusta said. "I will try to wait with the patience of Job but probably be more like Peter—impatient and worrying."

He chuckled. "Good luck to you, ma'am. I hope it's your boy."

Weeks later, a telegram came to Augusta that the boy was on his way. A trembling, nervous mother spent every day on the road in front of her house, inquiring from every passerby if they had seen a military detail with a white Indian boy. Finally, a man said he had seen such a boy. The wagon would arrive that night.

Augusta decided to throw a big feast. She started working in the kitchen to create loaves of bread and dozens of rolls. Runners spread the word around town, and the women of Loyal Valley joined in with every oven stoked red hot.

The smell of fresh bread, cakes, beeves, mutton, and pies floated in the air. Not every citizen could generate this much activity, but the citizens of Loyal Valley loved Augusta Buchmeier. They wanted to give back for all she'd done for them. It would be a "Thanksgiving" to remember.

Then the rain came. The pitter-patter of drops on the roof and her beating heart were the only sounds Augusta heard.

The bread was baked and covered on the table. With nothing more to do, she paced the floor inside her house, staring out the window every few seconds. All she needed now was her lost son to enjoy this food.

Hours crawled by until the lamps swinging from a wagon were spotted. When the wagon pulled in front of the Buchmeier house, hundreds of people milled around, trying to stay dry and hoping to see the Indian boy.

Augusta ran outside, threw her arms around the boy, and wept. When a lamp moved close to his face, she realized this boy was not Herman.

"Oh no!" she wailed.

Mina grabbed the boy's right wrist and inspected it carefully. "Momma, it is Herman! See this scar? I gave it to him with that hatchet."

Augusta looked at the wrist and cried even harder. "Oh, sweet Lord! It is my boy! Herman, you're home."

Then she praised God, giving thanks for His mercy, for over the last nine years, the Lord had indeed heard her prayers and answered them.

All night long, tears and prayers flowed in both German and English. And there was the feasting.

It continued well into the next day, with visitors from miles away coming to see the white Indian boy who had returned from the wilderness.

Yet for all this happiness, Herman stood in a corner, emotionless and stoic. He could not speak the language. Instead, he watched for visual clues about what was happening around him.

Augusta provided the best feather bed for Herman to sleep in, but he refused. He insisted on making a pallet with his own blankets to sleep outside on the ground.

The next day, when the soldiers left, Herman tried to follow them but was held back by his brothers. After that, one of his brothers stayed beside him around the clock, watching the boy and teaching him English.

Augusta and her children celebrated Herman's return, but they fully understood how hard this would be. And Herman decided he wouldn't make it easy.

He wanted to like his family, but he hated whites. How would that ever change?

For Augusta, it was also frustrating. She felt in her soul Herman's longing to escape back to the Indians. How could she ever keep him from doing that?

Billy guided the wagon over the rough road with Jennie's head against his shoulder. All the feelings he thought were gone had come back. It was like they had never been apart.

He had no idea about the future, so he focused on right now, content with whatever might happen next.

The bandit fleeing in the wagon had damaged the wheels. Bruno and Billy inspected each one, unsure if they would make it back to Fort Sill. When they rolled through a sharp dip and crossed a narrow stream, the left rear wheel departed. The wagon came to an abrupt stop on an incline, the absolute worst place to make a repair.

"What happened?" Jennie said, waking from a nap.

"The back wheel came off," Billy said.

He applied the brake and hopped down.

Bruno was way ahead and turned around when he lost track of them.

"Which one is it?" Bruno asked, pulling his wagon to a stop.

"The left rear," Billy said, crawling underneath the wagon. He had a wrench and needed to loosen up the spare.

"Let me help," Bruno said, coming to his side. "I will grab some rocks and tree limbs to prop up the axle."

"What can I do, William?" Jennie asked.

"Sit in the box and make sure the brake stays engaged," Billy said. "Hold the reins so the mules don't get any ideas."

Billy untied his horse, and the two proceeded to install the spare. It took three hours of pounding and banging, but finally it was done.

"Let us ride to a clearing ahead and camp for the night," Bruno said. "No sense in pushing it and losing another wheel in the darkness."

Billy agreed and followed the sword salesman to a good campsite. Jennie helped get a fire going, and soon, Bruno had some beef sizzling in a cast-iron skillet. Billy provided a pile of beans and bread to go with the meat, which turned the event into a small feast.

As they dished out the food, it was hard to forget the body of Jennie's husband lying in the wagon.

"Senõr William," Bruno said. "Will you say grace?"

Billy did and the three ate their food in silence.

"I guess this is our Thanksgiving celebration," Billy said softly.

Jennie nodded. "I have so much to thank you both for. You saved my life."

"I am sorry we were too late for your husband," Bruno said. "Was he in the military?"

"He was, but he retired six years ago as a captain."

"What were you doing out here?" Billy asked.

"We had been in Arkansas, where he worked as a deputy sheriff. Last year, he invested all our money in railroad stock, but it was a scam. We lost everything, including his job. We were on the way to Colorado, where he still had some family left. All our belongings are in that wagon."

"I'm real sorry, Jennie," Billy said, holding her hand. "This is no way to spend a Thanksgiving."

"No, William, it's a perfect way," she said. "We are out here on God's creation only to be reminded how short life is."

The camp fell silent except for the pops and crackles of the firewood. By now, the cold had set in, turning their breaths into more tiny clouds.

Finally, Bruno broke the silence.

"You know, the first Thanksgiving in North America was held right here in Texas."

"What?" Billy said. "You're joking."

"No. It is true. In 1598, if I recall correctly, my Spanish forefathers went on an expedition to explore this land and find a city of great wealth. They stumbled into a deep canyon northwest of here in Comanchería, Palo Duro Canyon. It is now called Prairie Dog. Tired and hungry, they found Indians there who kindly offered them food and water. The Spaniards held a mass to celebrate this event, and it was like the first Thanksgiving in North America."

"The Comanche did that?" Billy asked.

"No, in 1598, the Comanche weren't the fierce bunch they eventually became. I believe it was the Teyas near what now is called El Paso. The Comanche came later, in 1758, and beheaded Father Santiesteban while he kneeled at the altar in prayer. That told us what they felt about our religion."

"Was that during Thanksgiving?" Jennie asked.

"Well, Father Santiesteban was giving thanks and praise to God, but it was not a celebration. Just a daily Mass."

The three took in his words and said very little else. Instead, they stoked the fire and crawled under their blankets.

Billy and Jennie were right next to each other. He felt for her hand and grabbed it tight.

As he stared at the dark sky above, he had two thoughts: he would never let go of her hand, and if he died tonight, he'd die a happy man.

Chapter Forty~Eight

Henry and his wife, Elizabeth, diligently continued spreading the Good News. Although they had seen some progress, not one Indian had been baptized and joined the church.

Sure, there was the young Indian Hughes, the elderly woman related to one of Quanah's wives, and Harold, Quanah's son, but that was it. They had all died before being baptized and joining the church.

Gaining church members was an important measuring stick for the Mennonite Brethren Conference. In fact, most missions at that time wanted to see increasing numbers of members as a reason to keep providing financial assistance.

With that not happening at the Post Oak Mission, the Mennonite Brethren Conference decided to double down and open a school there.[25]

Quanah Parker had long been upset with the lack of education for Comanche Indian children. Among all the promises not kept across all the Indian treaties, providing a schoolhouse and a teacher for every 30 Indian children was another one the federal government didn't honor, at least until many years later. To fill the gap, day schools and boarding schools run by religious organizations sprung up. The hope was that teaching and bringing the children to Christ might also bring their parents in.

To build and run the Mennonite school at Post Oak, Abraham Becker and his wife, Magdalena, were selected. The couple would build and run the school with adjoining dormitories for the students. Abraham would be the school's superintendent.

---

[25] This had been the requirement from Quanah Parker from the beginning when he gave permission to Henry Kohfeld to build his Jesus House. But the Post Oak School would not be started until 1948 and closed in 1959.

Post Oak

After some research into the costs, the Conference scrapped that idea. Instead, the Conference sent the Beckers to be missionaries and help Henry minister to the Indians.

Abraham Becker had a farm but decided to leave it all behind for the chance to work at the mission. One day, he and his family loaded everything up and started south. Unfortunately, they had hardly made any progress when an icy cold front ripped through the nation's midsection. The Beckers and their two sons, Daniel and William, were forced to sleep on the open prairie, risking their lives unprotected in the fierce cold.

The next morning, Abraham discovered one of the horses had gone lame. He had to help the other horse pull the wagon up steep inclines.

The rest of the trip was hard and harsh. But on March 7, 1902, the Beckers arrived at the Post Oak Mission, incredibly thankful to still be alive.

The Conference designated Abraham a salary of $400 per year plus funds to build a house. Due to Abraham's excellent carpentry skills, the church assumed he would perform the most work.

Abraham also asked his farmhand, David C. Peters, if he'd like to come and help build the house. Peters agreed and ended up staying at the mission for the next fourteen years.

All of a sudden, the mission was humming along nicely. Henry had his wife, Elizabeth, and two single women, Maria Regier and Katherina Penner, helping with everything. When you added in the Beckers and David Peters, the Post Oak Mission had turned into a small town.

Even though they weren't educating any of the Indian children, Henry could feel the progress. Soon, they would surely have their first church member.

David Peters, a white man, turned out to be the one. Henry held a big celebration as he baptized Peters.

The Indians watched with fascination as Peters was dunked in a pond that Peters himself had helped build. As Henry stood around waiting for his first Indian to ask to be baptized, several told him, "God's way is a good way."

Yet when the event ended, there were no takers.

Maria Regier, the woman who came in 1897 to help, was forced to return to Kansas in 1900 to care for her sick mother. Four years later, she married Dietrich D. Peters and became pregnant with their first child. The following year, Maria died in childbirth.

Katherina Penner was another story. Having arrived in 1898, she used her own money and purchased a two-wheel cart with a horse so she could travel to Indian residences and campsites. Through the hot, dry summers, she bounced along the rough roads, visiting Indians and spreading her love and joy.

The entire time Katharina was at the mission, she prayed for a chance to have a happy marriage. Besides Peters, few unmarried prospects existed on the remote patch of Comanche reservation.

One day, she received a letter from her home church in Kansas. Henry Suderman, a member of her church, wanted her as his wife.

Excitedly, she resigned from her position and raced home to get married. For the next twenty-eight years, she and her husband provided financial support for the mission until she died in 1933.

As for Henry Kohfeld, he worked well with Abraham Becker. Due to Abraham's short blond beard, the Indians called him White Beard.

Abraham's wife, Magdalena, was a powerhouse of work and energy. The Indians called her Our Older Sister.

People who met Magdelena said the light of God shone from her sparkling eyes and bright smile.

In 1903, the Foreign Mission Board approved Magdalena for the position of field matron in the Indian Service. This entailed training Indian women in basic homemaking skills as well as keeping tribal records.

By 1906, the Mennonite Brethren Conference realized it was paying five people at the Post Oak Mission. Henry made $700 annually and Abraham $400. Both wives received salaries for their work, and David Peters was also paid.

The Conference was sending missionaries to India and started questioning the costs and results of the Post Oak Mission. They needed to trim the staff there.

Henry learned about this and sent a letter to the elders listing his accomplishments. In addition to Hughes, Harold, and the old woman accepting the Jesus Way, he had obtained permission from Quanah Parker for the land, built the church and his house, found a sustainable water supply for the mission, and established the Post Oak Cemetery while changing the Indians' attitudes toward burying their dead in caves and killing their horses.

Henry also increased Sunday worship attendance with the meal program and established the extravagant Christmas celebration. Plus, the entire mission was debt-free.

Sure, he had no Indian church members. When he looked at his accomplishments over the past twelve years, he was confident the Conference would select him and cut the Beckers loose.

The letter with the decision arrived, and Henry excitedly tore it open. As he read the words, the brave missionary from South Russia was utterly stunned.

The Beckers had been chosen to run the Post Oak Mission, and the elders were releasing the Kohfelds from their mission service.

Twelve years of his life had been spent on the dusty Oklahoma prairie, and now he'd have to move on.

Though Henry understood that this was all part of God's plan, it still hurt deeply. He had no idea where he was going or what he'd do next.

One thing was certain: his time at the Post Oak Mission was over.

The transition from a wild Indian boy to a white citizen living in a small town was anything less than smooth. Herman Lehmann, back from the dead, was miserable.

He refused to wear a suit a local man had given to him. Instead, he wore breechclout, leggings, feathers, and war paint. It was a crazy sight in the conservative German town.

Before the soldiers headed back to Fort Sill, they explained to Mina how Herman liked his food cooked. She did her best to serve him the meals he wanted. Still, Herman resolved himself to sneak away and get back to Quanah, his adopted father.

To celebrate his homecoming, a huge feast was prepared. Herman sat at the table and spotted a large ham a few feet away. Instinctively, he kicked over the table and made for the door. There was no way a proper Indian would ever eat swine.

Tina Siemens

The locals stopped him and brought him back to the table, which had been repaired and the food cleaned off. Herman pointed to the ham, and they removed it from the table.

He tried to eat the other foods, but sitting at a table with the hated white man and knowing they were hog eaters made him choke on his food.

They offered him some tobacco, and he readily accepted it. That was the one thing white people were good for: cigarettes.

Feeling the smoke stick to his lungs and the tobacco infusing his body, he calmed down. As long as he had a cigarette in his mouth, he was able to put up with the palefaces.

His mother, Augusta, kept a hotel in Loyal Valley. Curiously, Herman liked dressing in his Indian garb and painting his body before running to the hotel and yelling war whoops.

The guests, sometimes still asleep, were scared out of their wits. Most of them were sure the Comanche had returned to kill them all.

During his alone time, Herman went to the nearby creek and fashioned a bow and arrows. He practiced every day and became proficient.

He found children going to or coming home from school and proceeded to scare the shine out of their eyes. Parents complained.

It didn't help when some local men brought him to the town square and urged him to perform. Herman shot arrows, threw tomahawks, and jumped on the wildest of horses, riding them around town.

A gambling industry sprung up as locals took bets on his abilities. Herman even earned candy treats for his feats.

One day, he went to the square and tried his usual tricks but found the place deserted. He heard some shouting down by the creek and went there, only to find a large tent with people inside. Peeking through the opening, he saw the townspeople sitting in chairs and listening to a man with long black tails.

Seemingly unprovoked, the man started yelling about something and gesturing angrily with his hands. Herman watched all this and realized it was some kind of war dance. He needed to act fast.

Herman ran to the front of the tent and raised his bow. Inserting an arrow, he yelled out war whoops.

Post Oak

In seconds, the frightened worshippers fled, along with the men running it. Finding himself alone, Herman stood at the pulpit and reigned supreme over the emptiness.

When he wasn't causing havoc with the local citizens, he terrorized passersby. Many times, he shot blunted arrows that left a painful deep blue mark on their targets.

He could easily pass a sharpened arrow through any hat. The local hatmaker became rich off Herman.

One time, he forgot to use a blunted arrow and sank a real one into a man's left shoulder. The town grew angry. Yet Herman was angry, too, especially since they loved showing off the wild Indian boy and making money from visitors.

Whenever the locals got mad at him, Herman tried to run away. Each time, he was brought back home, only to find his mother and sisters bawling.

Seeing those tears truly bothered Herman. He was hurting people, and he didn't like it.

It took a great deal of time and patience for things to change. As he wrote in his famous book,

> At last, the kindness, tenderness, and gentleness of my good Christian mother, the affectionate love of my sisters, and the vigilance of my brothers gradually wove a net of love around me that is as lasting as time itself.[26]

With Willie teaching him more English, Herman began to see a new way of life, one without killing, stealing, or war paint.

One night, he picked his pallet off the ground and came inside. Crawling into a feather bed, he relaxed and let sleep find him.

Finally, Herman Lehmann was home to stay.

---

[26] *Nine Years Among the Indians 1870–1879*, by Herman Lehmann

Jennie adjusted the scarf over her head, drawing a cocked eyebrow from Billy.

"What?" she said. "I don't like the sun on my delicate skin if I can help it."

"You still look young to me," Billy said, holding the reins of his two horses.

Jennie was comfortable now and watched as Henry steered the wagon. Fidgeting, she spun the gold band on her left hand.

It had been four and a half months since highwaymen killed her first husband. Officials from Fort Sill found the bodies where Billy and Bruno had left them and attributed several robberies and killings to the men. Billy and Bruno were cleared of any wrongdoing.

After that, Billy spent all his time nurturing Jennie's spirit back to life. Finally, he proposed.

The couple was married at the Post Oak Mission and befriended the Kohfelds and Beckers. They even helped out during the large Christmas celebrations. But Billy was always restless.

"I feel like I've missed so much life without you," he said. "I want to find a way to squeeze decades into a few years."

Jennie caressed his hand. "Oh, William, you'll live a long time."

"I'm sixty-five. How many more years do I have?"

"Enough to make me happy."

"That's easy for you to say. You're twelve years younger and look as beautiful as ever."

Jennie beamed, squeezing his hand. "Maybe we should go somewhere, take a big trip, do something unexpected to get back some of that time."

Billy nodded. "I like that idea. But I need to give you some background on our host before you meet him. Are you ready?"

"Sure, William," Jennie replied. "I have my thinking scarf on."

Billy told her about Quanah Parker, the attacks, violence, and killings in his early years. He knew so much since he'd read all the reports. But when Quanah surrendered, the Eagle accepted the white man's way.

On the reservation, Quanah started learning the ropes. He not only survived but thrived, especially when dealing with a big issue that festered from the early 1880s to 1900: the cattlemen versus the settlers.

Quanah discovered that the cattlemen paid tremendous fees for leasing the Big Pasture. These lease payments enriched his people for many years.

On the other side was Lone Wolf, the Kiowa chief. He didn't want the land leased and demanded it remain unused.

Later, Lone Wolf sided with the settlers, thinking that if Congress would divide up the reservation into 160-acre plots for each Indian, they would keep the land and money.

Quanah fought him, believing the sale of land would be a one-time payment while leasing fees would continue forever.

In 1900, after years of delaying the inevitable, Quanah gave in to the settlement of the land but gained something in return: $500,000 more than the $2 million originally offered to his people and the preservation of the Big Pasture (480,000 acres) for the younger generation.

Each Indian received 160 acres, and the rest was put out for settlement by the whites. Many Indians signed over their land for a pittance when they ran out of money or were hungry. It was in this way that the whites quickly devoured the land.

Despite the settlers winning, Quanah's opponents—the Indians and white men—did not rest. They forced an investigation of Quanah for fraud and theft.

Washington sent out one of their best investigators. He worked for weeks checking everything out, inspecting records, and talking to hundreds of Indians and whites, including Billy Tyler.

In his report to Congress, the investigator had a few interesting things to say:

> These cases and dozens of like tenor had nothing whatever behind them except falsehood…The choice by the Comanches of Quanah Parker as their chief dates back to the memory of any but the oldest members of the tribe, and if ever Nature stamped a man with the seal of headship, she did it in this case. Quanah would have been a leader and a governor in any circle where fate may have cast him—it is in his blood.

Quanah was cleared and free to continue negotiating deals with the government on behalf of his people.

"He sounds like quite a man," Jennie said. "Someone I'm glad to meet on this side of his life and not when you were shooting his brothers from the back of our wagon."

Billy grinned. "That's for sure."

Soon, the wagon pulled up to the Star House and stopped at a white picket fence ringing the large house.

Jennie marveled at the enormous white stars painted on the roof. The two-story structure was one of the largest she had ever seen outside a proper town like Fort Worth.

Billy helped her down, and the couple went to the front porch.

"Can I help you?" an Indian asked.

"We're here to see Quanah Parker. I'm Billy Tyler, and this is my wife, Jennie."

"He's not here but should be back soon. Care to come inside? I can show you around."

The couple agreed and walked into a large living room. Jennie took in the fancy surroundings.

"See, I told you it was something else," Billy said.

He used his crutches to move close to some photos in the living room, one of which was a steam locomotive.

"This engine is sitting on the Quanah, Acme, and Pacific Railway," Billy said. "It operates between the towns of Quanah and Floydada. Quanah told me he's invested $40,000 in it."

"Gosh, William, that's a lot of money," Jennie remarked.

He pulled his wife over to a photo of a badge. "If they steal his money, he can arrest them because he was elected deputy sheriff of Lawton, Oklahoma. They've even named a town after him: Quanah, Texas. It's just across the Red River. Look at the inscription on that plaque."

Quanah, Texas, formed on this day in 1884 in Hardeman County.

"Here's a speech he gave there on May 23, 1890."

> It is well, you have done a good thing in honor of a man who has tried to do right both to the people of his tribe and to his pale-faced friends. May the God of the white man bless the town of Quanah. May the sun shine and the rain fall upon the fields and the granaries be filled. May the lightning and the tempest shun the homes of her people, and may they increase and dwell forever. God bless Quanah. I have spoken.

"Who are these women?" Jennie asked.

"They're his wives," Billy replied. "This one is To-pay and Chony. And here's Mah-cheeta-wookey, Au-uh-wuth-takum, Coby, and Weckeah. The only one missing is his first wife, Ta-ho-yea. She was Apache and returned to New Mexico to live with her people."

"Is this one of his wives?"

"That's Tonarcy, his favorite. He takes her everywhere and dresses her like an American woman. He told me she keeps all the silverware in her room. Oh, and each wife has their own room."

"What do they do?" Jennie asked.

"Fine beadwork on fabric and leather. They also keep their rooms clean."

"They are all such good-looking women," Jennie said.

"Yeah, he has an eye for the ladies. I'm almost worried about him meeting you. Years ago, when I told him I'd let you slip through my hands, he offered to give me some horses to buy you back."

Jennie laughed.

"He told me he was in Washington when an official gave him a hard time and demanded he have only one wife. Quanah told the man that he loved them all and asked the man to decide which ones would have to leave, as well as telling them himself because Quanah couldn't do it. The man let the matter drop, and Quanah has never heard another word about it."

"Would you like to see his room?" the Indian offered.

"Sure," Billy said.

The three went to a spacious room and stepped a few feet inside. Next to the chief's bed hung a picture of Cynthia Ann Parker with her child, Prairie Flower, nursing.

"That was sent to me by Sul Ross," a booming voice said.

Startled, Billy and Jennie spun around to see Quanah Parker standing in ranching attire—pants, a long-sleeved shirt, and a bandana around his neck.

"Ross was the soldier who captured my mother, Naduah," Quanah said.

Billy noticed a nearby portrait of Jesus and another one with a halo.

"Do you know Henry Kohfeld at the Post Oak Mission?" Billy asked.

"Yes. Little Hat helped my son Harold find the Jesus Way."

Another man interrupted the group. It was Dummy, Quanah's deaf and dumb driver.

Every day, Dummy made a buggy trip into Cache to collect anything for Quanah. He quietly handed the mail and newspapers to his boss and disappeared.

"Billy, I must leave again," Quanah said. "I'm sorry, but the president is coming here to hunt on the Big Pasture. I have so much to do. Still, I am glad to have met your wife."

He turned to face Jennie. "I want you to know how important Billy has been here on the reservation. Many white men and some Indians steal from us. He has smoked out many of their schemes, and we owe him a great deal."

Jennie squeezed Billy's arm. "Thank you, Chief Quanah. William has been a very important man in my life, too. I lost him once, and I'm not losing him again."

Billy beamed with pride as he shook Quanah's hand and left the Star House. He was stirred up with excitement after learning that the president of the United States was coming to Oklahoma. He knew Jennie would have to listen to him talk about it all the way back home, though. Somehow, though, that was okay.

Chapter Forty-Nine

Henry Kohfeld sat in his church for the last time. The official word was that the Kohfelds had planted and watered the seeds. It was time for the Beckers to bring in God's crop of believers.

No one could find out the truth, but speculation started with the clear fact that Magdalena Becker was like an additional hired missionary. She was fluent in Comanche and worked alongside the Indian women while teaching them childcare, housekeeping, healthcare, cooking, and sewing.

The Indian women grew close to Magdalena and were more willing to listen to her message of salvation and the Jesus Way.

Abraham Becker was an industrious man. His carpentry skills were always needed. While he and his wife treated sick Indians, he built the coffins when they passed.

At the burials, Abraham was good about using the opportunity to preach the Good News. And because the Beckers were fierce advocates for the rights of all Indians, Quanah Parker trusted them.

Then there was Henry. He had built the mission from nothing, setting the table for the Beckers to continue the work. Without him, none of them would be there.

It was difficult for Henry to swallow the news of his own apparent demotion in the church. For a while, he felt betrayed by David Peters, a man Becker had brought with him. He also blamed the Beckers, believing they forced him out.

The likely truth was the limited funds of the Mennonite Brethren Conference. With the Beckers, they got two for the price of one. The elders probably considered the foolishness of kicking out someone who spoke excellent Comanche like Magdalena.

Regardless of the reason, it was time for the Kohfelds to move on. In March 1907, they packed up and said goodbye. Quanah came to see them off.

"Henry, you have told me your people were pushed off your land and forced to relocate like us. I have always wondered why you did not fight them."

"Jesus teaches us violence is not the way, Quanah. Peace and love for our enemies is what we must give. Sure, we were forced out, and yes, like you, the government broke its promises. And even though I disapprove of your peyote ceremonies and medicine man religion, like us, we were persecuted for our different beliefs. So I guess it's ironic that you and I find ourselves on the exact same piece of ground. No matter what our past, though, we all need forgiveness, and that comes only through the grace of God."

Quanah frowned, thinking this over. "So your God will punish me and not you?"

"No, my God punishes everyone—you and me alike, unless we are covered in the blood of his Son, Jesus Christ."

"That's right," Quanah said, folding his arms. "It always comes back to the shedding of someone's blood."

"It does," Henry said. "The difference is if we physically murder or hate a brother, we are murderers. The Bible teaches that if we hate, we are like a murderer: 1 John 3:15 says that if we kill someone, that's shedding of someone's blood, and it dooms us to the fires of hell unless we repent, while the blood of Jesus washes us clean of our sins."

"You have picked the right God, then."

"I have, and Quanah, the best part is that you can choose the same God and be washed clean of your sins."

"No matter how bad?"

"No matter how bad," Henry replied.

Quanah pulled at something on his collar before hugging the missionary.

"Goodbye, Henry. And thank you for everything you did for Harold and the others."

"Goodbye, Quanah," Henry said with watery eyes. "It has been a great pleasure of my life to meet you and your family. Please think about what I have said."

Quanah nodded as Henry shook the reins and urged the mules forward. That was the last time the two men ever saw each other.

With the Kohfelds gone, Abraham and Magdalena Becker made a promise to themselves. They would stay for six months but no longer unless God provided them two things: an interpreter and souls.

During the first week on their own, they prayed for these two needs several times daily. On the first Sunday, Reverend Becker had a man approach him.

"You and your wife have been so kind to me," Herman Asenap said. "Last night, I could not sleep. So now I want to interpret for you."

Tears streamed down Reverend Becker's face.

"And I want no money," Asenap added.

Abraham hugged the man and said, "You're an answer to my prayers."

Herman Asenap was nineteen. His father was Mexican but had been kidnapped by the Comanche as a child and grew up as an Indian. He was named Grayfoot (Asenap) after coming out of a creek with gray mud on his feet. Later, he became a great and feared medicine man.

Asenap had an eighth-grade education, a rarity. He had served as an interpreter for the Indian Office and worked in a bank.

Though Asenap wasn't a Christian, he was the perfect man for the job. With the first prayer fulfilled, the Beckers needed souls.

They discussed the matter and prayed before coming up with a big idea. It had to do with the Red Store just outside of Cache.

The Red Store was the location of government disbursements. When the money hit the Indians' hands, the gambling and drinking started.

Shrewd businessmen set up tents for these activities, hoping to liberate the money from the Indians' pouches. The Beckers decided to set up their own large tent for revivals and positioned it right next to the biggest gambling tent. A second tent was set up for the Beckers' living quarters.

After receiving their money, Indians came by to watch the Beckers sing, pray, and preach. Despite over 500 Indians camped out around the Red Store, no one converted.

Two weeks of tent revivals had come and gone. The Beckers had left their children with a housekeeper, and Magdalena missed them terribly. One evening, she walked to a nearby stand of trees and wailed inconsolably.

A Comanche squaw, Wi-e-puh, came over and put her arms around Magdalena. "Why do you cry so?" she asked.

"I do not care about how we suffer," Magdalena replied. "But your Indian people are trampling my God with their feet. They do not want to be saved."

That night, after Reverend Becker's sermon and a call for believers to come up front, Wi-e-puh presented herself and said she wanted to follow the Jesus Way. Five more women and a man followed Wi-e-puh's example.

Suddenly, the Beckers had their souls.

The seed for Teddy Roosevelt's trip to Oklahoma was planted by Quanah at the president's inauguration three months earlier. He had ridden on a horse in full Comanche regalia with five other chiefs.[27] It was during one of these trips that Quanah Parker became so impressed with the Washington Monument that he requested that a similar monument be set up at his grave.

At some point, Quanah talked to Roosevelt about coming to Oklahoma and hunting in the Big Pasture. Roosevelt loved hunting and the outdoors, so the offer was impossible to pass up.[28]

Roosevelt traveled on a special train to Wichita Falls, Texas, and gave a speech. The train then traveled northwest to Frederick, Oklahoma, where the president gave a second speech. Quanah was there to meet him and the president invited him to speak too.

"I got bigger cheers than Teddy," Quanah later told his friends.

---

[27] The other five chiefs were Geronimo of the Apache, Little Plume of the Blackfeet, Hollow Horn Bear and American Horse of the Sioux, and Buckskin Charlie of the Ute.
[28] President Theodore Roosevelt truly loved the outdoors as one of his proudest achievements was creating the Forest Service and the National Parks system.

Also hosting the presidential hunt were cattlemen W. T. Waggoner and Burk Burnett.[29] These men provided the dogs, horses, and buggies, with Burnett going out in front to find the animals.

Since it was April, the oppressive heat had not yet arrived. Instead, the weather was good, and the temperatures were cool.

They hunted for five days. When it was over, the group had killed seventeen wolves and coyotes. Roosevelt even killed a five-foot rattlesnake with his quirt.

The big event was dinner at the "Comanche White House," as Quanah called his Star House. He wanted everything to be perfect.

The table was set for thirty people, and each woman was assigned a specific task. The wine was served in huge goblets after Quanah had seen it served in small glasses at the White House. Even though he didn't drink wine, he told his fellow Comanche he was determined to be more generous than the president.

The president noticed that the Comanche chief ran a peaceful and orderly household. Each morning, Quanah arose and listed all the activities and chores for the day. He had duties for the upstairs wife, the downstairs wife, another wife who tended to outdoor tasks, and other helpers. He was efficient and in charge, and Roosevelt did not chastise him for his many wives.

Eventually, President Roosevelt boarded his train and traveled back to Washington and the cauldron of politics.

For all the excitement and prestige of having the president visit the Indians on their reservation, something permanent came out of it besides the stories Quanah told for years. Two months after Roosevelt's visit, he designated the land north of Quanah's home as the Wichita Forest Reserve. Later, it was changed to the Wichita Mountains Wildlife Refuge and declared a national forest by another president named President Franklin Roosevelt.[30]

---

[29] President Roosevelt renamed the Texas town of Gilbert to Burkburnett after he met the rancher on this hunt.

[30] In 1905, the New York Zoological Park (later called the Bronx Zoo) offered the refuge fifteen buffalo to start a herd. In 1907, an American Indian contingent led by Quanah Parker, greeted the newly arrived bison and many of the elderly Comanche related stories of their experience with the wild animals prior to their near extermination, their emotions on full display.

"Did you pack the blankets?" Billy asked.

"Yes, William. All your favorites from the hands of Leaping Deer," Jennie said.

"She weaves the best," Billy declared.

A horse came riding up. It was Chief Quanah Parker.

"So you are leaving us for good?" he said.

"Yes," Billy said. "When Jennie and I first met, we had a big adventure thanks to your Comanche brothers. Now she wants to see the heart of Comanchería—the Palo Duro Canyon."

"Prairie Dog," Quanah said. "Charles Goodnight owns all that. Give him my greetings if you see the man."

"I will."

"Did you sell everything?" Quanah asked after inspecting the fully loaded wagon.

"We did," Billy said.

"So you are not coming back here?"

"No," Billy replied. "I promised Jennie we'd start a life in a new town out west, at least as much life as I have left."

Quanah reached down and shook Billy's hand. "I will miss you, Four Legs, even though you are a paleface."

Billy chuckled. "And I'm glad we're all friends now, as I wouldn't want to see how I'd fare against you on the warpath."

"The warpath is gone," Quanah said. "I'm on the white man's path now."

Billy stowed his two crutches and climbed into the driver's box. "We're traveling the Comanche's path to your favorite hideout. It's quite a reversal."

Quanah adjusted his cowboy hat. "With Little Hat gone and Teddy back in Washington, I am saying goodbye a lot."

"I hope it's not goodbye, but until we meet again, perhaps in heaven."

"Perhaps," Quanah said, his eyes scanning the horizon. "Be careful out there. The wolves and coyotes and snakes don't know we're all friends now."

"I will, especially since I have her to protect now." Billy noticed Jennie blushing. "Goodbye, Chief Parker."

Quanah tipped his hat and galloped off, disappearing through a cloud of dust.

"Now it's our turn," Billy said, patting the passenger's seat. "Climb up and let's get to gettin'."

Jennie stepped up and took the seat beside her husband. As she clutched his hand, Billy knew all was right in the world.

Chapter Fifty

After the Beckers' big tent gamble at the Red Store, the missionaries harvested the fish. Sam No Hand was the first Comanche baptized and admitted as a member of Post Oak Mission Church.

His name came from a childhood incident when he tried to save a pet bear that fell into a kettle of boiling water. As a result, Sam burned and deformed his hand. Despite this, he grew up and learned to use a bow and arrow, going on buffalo hunts and fighting with his fellow warriors.

Once the Comanche came to the reservation, he accepted work at the Burnett Ranch and was given the first name of Sam.

Before his conversion, Sam spent many years rejecting the Jesus Way. Once baptized, he was all in, serving as an usher and pushing out yapping dogs who tried to interrupt the service.

Sam also told vivid stories, making sounds of waterfalls, horse hoofs, animals, birds, thunder, and lightning. People loved to hear him talk.

The Beckers gathered in even more souls when they finally realized that the Comanche received religious information best when presented in their own language. Unfortunately, the government mandated that everything be taught in English.

Reverend Becker struggled with Comanche since his first language was Plautdietsch or Low German. His second language was High German, then English. Adding Comanche was tough since he had to think in Low German, translate to English, and then to Comanche. That's why having Herman Asenap translate was so important.

It was ironic that one of the reasons families like the Beckers and Kohfelds left Prussia and South Russia was the requirement that they start using the local language—yet another thing the Mennonites and Comanche now had in common.

Another vital service the missionaries provided was taking care of sick people. When a young Indian boy became ill, Magdalena provided loving care.

"There you go," she said as she dabbed the forehead of Clarence Lost Wolf. "Let's get you feeling better."

Magdalena dipped a cotton cloth into cool water and dabbed him again, but the boy did not improve.

A doctor from Cache had examined him and said he had typhoid fever.[31]

Clarence had no family or friends around to help him. His father, Chief Crooked Nose of Daring, Montana, was not in Oklahoma.

How the boy ended up near the Post Oak Mission was anyone's guess. Before he could tell them, he died.

For eighteen days, Magdalena had been with him day and night, talking to him about the Good News while hoping he understood and believed. It was all she could do.

For Magdalena, she knew death. After arriving at the Post Oak Mission, she gave birth to her third daughter, Augusta, who died two days later.

Then there were all the deaths of the babies on the reservation. Sometimes, she witnessed it firsthand while helping a mother in labor. But she never stopped working.

In the first few years, Magdalena traveled at least 100 miles each month in her buggy. Later, she pushed it to 250. This meant slogging through bad, muddy, or nonexistent roads while often getting caught in Oklahoma's sudden weather changes.

Her reward was helping people with infectious diseases, picking lice out of squaws' hair, and teaching them how to clean a house, bathe, or cook tasty foods. She also convinced the women not to go barefoot in the winter.

When an Indian fell sick, she showed the women how to wash their clothes and disinfect the bed and surroundings so the disease didn't spread.

Magdalena didn't just work on the women. She lovingly explained to the men how they should chop wood and not make the women, especially

---

[31] Typhoid fever is a life-threatening bacteria spread through contaminated water or food. It was very common in the 1800s and into the early 1900s until proper sanitation laws and waste disposal methods improved.

pregnant ones, do it. She did so much to improve their lives, all while explaining in Comanche how Jesus was the way, the truth, and the life.

Over time, it worked. The women came around and joined the church.

Another issue the Beckers worked hard on was eliminating the Indians' reliance on the medicine men. It hurt their cause that white doctors were so scarce. In fact, there was only one in the area.

When trying to find a way to encourage the Indians to visit the doctors, one warrior told Reverend Becker, "All white doctors do to us is say, 'Stick out tongue. Stick back in. Three dollars, please.'"

That's why many of the sick came to Magdalena instead of the white doctor. She provided loving care, which they craved, and the missionary never asked for three dollars.

The U.S. government readily supported the Christian missionaries, believing that the best way to Americanize the Indians was to Christianize them. Government officials were always on the lookout for the needs of certain missionaries.

The Beckers were frugal people too, as were most Mennonites. Eventually, they convinced the Indians to bring all the food for Sunday services.

The Indians loved eating and getting together for big meals as the Comanche are naturally gregarious and friendly. With Sundays becoming a special time, more and more people came to experience the meals and hear the sermons.

Before long, Reverend Becker looked out at the congregation and saw not only Comanche but Kiowas, Mexicans, blacks, and whites.

Over time, the Indians learned about the Mennonites' special time every afternoon at roughly 4 p.m. It was called "faspa."

Back in South Russia and Prussia, the men worked until sunset. Then they'd come in for supper. From breakfast around 9 a.m. to supper at 7 or 8 p.m., it was hard not to be hungry.

To solve this problem, the Mennonites created faspa. Around 4 p.m., the women would set out buns, tea, cheese, cold meats, and other foods so everyone could take a fifteen-minute break and be satisfied until supper. If necessary, the women carried the food and drink to the fields to save the workers time.

On Sunday, faspas turned into elaborate social gatherings with zweiback, coffee, and jelly added to the selections. For special meals, the woman made pluma mos—a thick fruit soup with raisins, prunes, and dried fruits like apples and apricots. They also cooked wareneki—perogies stuffed with cottage cheese or ground beef, boiled and served with gravy.

For New Year's celebrations, portzelke were served. These cookies were deep-fried raisin fritters rolled in powdered sugar. Also, pfeffernusse—small, spiced cookies the size of a quarter—were given at Christmas.

In addition to these dishes, the Mennonites mastered cheeses and jellies. While they might have been heavy on white flour and sugar products, the Mennonite women were excellent cooks.

Births on the reservation became big events. It seemed like Magdalena was there for each one of them.

Over time, she named the newborn Indian babies, selecting ones like Lizzie, Edith, Troy, Eli, and Gilbert. Many Comanche born in that area owe their names to these Mennonite missionaries who fled South Russia and settled in Kansas.

As for their priceless interpreter, Herman Asenap, he married Two-Va-Bitty and had five children. When Two-Va-Bitty died, he married Bessie Parker, Quanah's daughter. The new couple got busy and produced four children.

In later years, when Asenap's eyesight failed, he memorized Bible passages. This allowed him to pretend to read the words from a Bible on the pulpit.

Then, another important volunteer arrived at the mission: Anna Hiebert. She stayed for many years and was almost as crucial as Magdalena in helping the Comanche women.

Anna noticed that many of the Indians left their wives for no reason at all. When she talked to a man who had left his wife, he said, "Before we come to reservation, man not desert wife unless she with another man."

"Why do it now?" Anna asked.

"When we came to the reservation, we learned two things from the white man we never know before: deserting wife and getting drunk."

Anna shook her head and walked away. There wasn't much she could say to that.

The townspeople of Loyal Valley finally got back to normal. Herman Lehmann relearned English and German and was restored as a citizen in his community. He learned to work, too, and was often hired by ranchers and farmers.

Fannie Light, a woman in Loyal Valley, caught his eye. They married and had two boys and three girls.

During parties and events in town, local citizens often asked Herman to tell some Indian stories. Two stories he told many times concerned new inventions.

Herman and some fellow Apache went on a raid near Fort Concho in San Angelo, Texas. It was daytime, and they were moving to a spot from which they would conduct another raid on the Texas settlers.

As they rode up a hill, they found a tall pole with a wire running horizontally to another pole. Looking down the line, they saw many poles, all with wire strung across them.

The Indians stopped and studied the pole. Each warrior offered his own opinion about this new thing.

Finally, the chief spoke.

"It is a fence built very high to keep out the Indians. We must tear it down."

They did and continued on with their raid.

After stealing a bunch of horses and returning the same way, the pole and wire had been repaired. Seeing that, they rode away fast, greatly disturbed at this strange thing, the telegraph line.

The second story had to do with a raid near Austin. Herman and his fellow warriors were hidden in a ravine, waiting for the moon to appear so they could raid some farms.

Out of nowhere, an angry beast with glowing eyes approached, belching steam from both sides of its mouth. It made a loud noise and screamed when it spotted them near its intended path.

Herman and the raiders scrambled to their horses and rode as fast as they could to get away from the giant beast. But it still came after them. It was only when they made a sharp turn north that the beast went on, obviously looking for more Indians to devour.

Once free from danger, the warriors were confused and upset. They had never seen anything like it. They decided right there to leave that area and never return as the monster might catch them next time.

Back at camp, they told everyone what had happened. Their fellow Apache were greatly disturbed.

The medicine man listened carefully and said it was an evil spirit. "You must avoid that area forever."

They did.

The Loyal Valley citizens loved hearing Herman's stories, especially since the threat of being killed by him was long gone.

Herman grew to love the attention he received as a celebrity among these Texas Hill Country residents. He continued exhibiting his skills.

Later, he met the Texas Rangers and soldiers he'd fought against so many times. They swapped even more stories.

Though he was blessed to be restored to his people, it wasn't all perfect. His first marriage to N.E. Burke ended in divorce; his oldest boy died during World War I in a U.S. Army camp in Houston.

Years later, Herman took his family from Texas and moved back to Indian Territory to be closer to his friends. He did see Quanah Parker again and obtained a legal affidavit from the chief stating he was Quanah's adopted son. This required the U.S. government to give Herman his allotment of land, some of which he later deeded to a school.

Herman died on February 2, 1932, at the age of 72. He was buried next to his mother and stepfather in a cemetery next to the Loyal Valley one-room schoolhouse.

Known as En Da with the Apache and Montechena with the Comanche, Herman Lehmann lived a life that sounded like it came from a dime novel. But it was all true.

West Texas was having a peaceful day. As evening approached, two horses trudged slowly forward, their stomachs needing quality oats and their bodies a long rest. Billy intended to provide them with just that, so long as they made the final mile to the town that lay before them.

"I can't believe we did all that," Jennie said. "What an incredible adventure, William."

"It was, dear. I feel like I have just spent ten years with you in the wilderness."

"We'll have stories for the rest of our years, especially with your shooting."

She was right. Billy had been forced to shoot at predators at least eight times. From mountain lions to cougars, coyotes, and wolves, the animals came around whenever they started a fire and cooked meat.

Billy explained that with all the buffalo gone, the overpopulated predators were always hungry. Anything or anyone was fair game.

"How many buffalo are left?" Jennie asked one night after Billy shot his rifle from their campsite deep in the Palo Duro Canyon.

"I've heard that in 1840, more than thirty-six million buffalo lived in North America. Now, there are less than three hundred confirmed."

Jennie couldn't believe it.

"It's true," Billy said. "First, the buffalo were killed to feed the railroad workers. After the tracks were all laid, railroad companies advertised hunting trips. Passengers sat up in the windows with rifles and shot any buffalo they saw as the train rolled on. Plus, buffalo were safety hazards as just one animal could derail an engine."

"So that's where they all went," Jennie said despondently.

"People like Buffalo Bill Cody also did their part. He was hired just to kill buffalo, and that he did. Within two years of employment, he had killed over 4,000."

"What did they do with the meat, William?"

"Traders and trappers removed the hides and tongues. The rest was left to rot. Hides sold for about $2.00 to $3.50 each. The bones were ground down and sold for use in bone china, fertilizer, and sugar processing. A ton of buffalo bones sold for about $8.00."

"That's too bad," she said. "So much waste."

Post Oak

"It looks like we're almost here," he said, seeing the buildings come into view.

"Why this town?" Jennie asked.

"I read about it in the reports. The Indians used some nearby springs hidden in a draw to stay alive. Without it, they would've died up here on the Llano Estacado. When the soldiers eventually found the springs, the water saved many of their lives, too. In one of the reports, a soldier wrote that he had a second chance at life with this water. I want a chance at a second life with you, my darling."

"That's not only romantic, William, but it reminds me of the last sermon we attended at the Post Oak Mission. Do you remember when the preacher said that whoever drinks the water Jesus gives him, that person will never thirst and have everlasting life? Maybe our chance at a second life is after we die."

"Yes, you are right. I'm sure of it."

They were almost at the main square when Jennie said, "What's the name of this town? You kept it from me all this time."

"I did. It's called Seminole."

"After the Indians?"

"That's right. It seemed only right."

Jennie squeezed Billy's hand again, and all was right in the world.

Chapter Fifty-One

In October 1910, the State Fair of Texas held an event to honor Quanah Parker. He traveled with his entourage in a special car on his Quanah Line to Dallas and put on a show.

Dressed in his full war regalia with feathered headdresses, buckskin clothes, moccasins, and beads, paying attendees came from several states to see the great Comanche chief.

When the time arrived, Quanah gave a speech to the curious fans:

Ladies and gentlemen. I say a few words to you… I used to be a bad man. Now I am a citizen of the United States. I pay taxes the same way you do. We are the same people now.

He told the audience it was important to clear up some Texas history. Sul Ross did not kill his father. Peta Nocona died years later of a wound he suffered on the raid on Parker's Fort back in 1836.

With that said, Quanah moved on to a sensitive subject. He wanted the remains of his mother, Cynthia Ann Parker, to be moved from Poynor, Texas, to the Post Oak Mission Cemetery. But Texas was objecting even though Congress had passed a bill giving him $800 to help with the costs.

"Why is this so important to you?" the reporter asked.

"I want to be buried there, and I want my mother right next to me," Quanah replied. "I have picked a spot on a hill that faces east."

East and the rising sun have always symbolized reviving life for the Comanche.

He said, "Like I have been a leader to my people during life, I want to continue being their leader after death. For that reason, you shall bury me at the head of the Comanches who have died and lie buried there."

Post Oak

Texas released its objections. Cynthia Ann Parker or Naduah would be headed back to Comanchería and her people.

Quanah finished up at the State Fair and returned to Cache, Oklahoma, and his precious Star House.

Two months later, he stood at the Post Oak Mission Cemetery, watching the men put the finishing touches on a marble monument. It was something he wanted to do for his mother.

With that in place, Quanah asked Magdalena to put on a big feast for his mother's reburial. He expected 200 people. She agreed to help.

Quanah had four beeves and a wagonload of every available delicacy delivered to the mission. Magdalena and a few Indian women started early the day before and produced everything Quanah wanted.

On December 4, 1910, his mother, Cynthia Ann Parker, was finally lowered to her new resting place.

Quanah told the attendees to follow the white way, get educated, learn how to work and grow crops before the government payments stop and "know white man's God… when the end comes… then I want to see my mother again… Perhaps in a year—possibly ten—I will be lying next to my mother."

The reburial was more of a celebration than a sad funeral. Quanah seemed both happy and relieved to have his mother finally close to him.

He told the attendees how after he came to the reservation, General Mackenzie wrote a letter to the Parker family in Weatherford, Texas, hoping to gain some information about Cynthia Ann's whereabouts.

Later, Quanah learned a picture had been taken of his mother in Fort Worth. He placed ads in the city's newspaper looking for any information about Naduah.

Sul Ross saw the advertisement and sent the photo to Quanah. Eventually, the chief learned she had died and was buried in East Texas.

Now that she was home, the big chief could focus on another matter. Recently, he'd learned that the U.S. Army was recruiting warriors from Quanah's band. He told them to stop.

"The white missionaries teach us fighting in wars is bad, so the whites should not try to get us to fight their wars."

Somehow, his words found their mark, and the recruiting stopped.

Two and half months after they'd buried Quanah's mother, on the morning of February 23, 1911, Abraham Becker heard a rider coming fast up the road. He met the man outside and received a telegram requesting he meet Quanah in Indiahoma. The chief was sick and returning home on the train.

Quanah had traveled to visit the Cheyenne at Hammon, Oklahoma when he became ill. He had been suffering from asthma and rheumatism, and his health was failing. This telegram wasn't a total surprise to Abraham.

Studying the words again, the missionary could tell Quanah summoned him to hear about the Jesus Way before he died. This was the moment the preacher had been waiting for. God had allowed him to cast the net, and Quanah was about to be caught and taken to heaven.

Abraham hurried to the barn and mounted his best and favorite horse. Then he pushed the horse at full speed to the train station at Indiahoma.

Reaching the depot, he found the train with Quanah had already left for Cache. Once again, Abraham raced his horse there.

After flying into Cache, Abraham learned he had missed Quanah again. The chief was now headed to the Star House in a car driven by his son-in-law Emmet Cox.

Frustrated, Abraham aimed his horse in that direction and took off.

Quanah arrived at the Star House before Abraham. His wife, To-pay, asked if the chief wanted to see the white doctor who'd just arrived. Quanah agreed and the doctor gave him a heart stimulant. It didn't work.

Quanah allowed Quas-e-aye, a medicine man, to work on him. First, he gave Quanah the Cotes-E-Wyne: the Comanche's last rites.

"Father in heaven," the medicine man said, "this our brother is coming."

He placed his arm around Quanah and flapped his hands, imitating the call of the Great Eagle, the messenger of the Great Father.

The medicine man then lodged an eagle bone in Quanah's throat to clear a passage for his wife, To-nar-cy, to squirt in some medicine. As the

Post Oak

liquid went down, Quanah coughed, gasped, and died. He had not been home for twenty minutes and he was gone.

Abraham arrived and rushed upstairs. He was too late.

He slammed a fist into his palm several times.

Suppressing his anger and frustration, the missionary tended to Quanah's distraught family. Three of Quanah's daughters fainted and needed help reviving.

When he'd done all he could do, Abraham went outside and discovered his favorite horse had sat down, rolled over, and died. The race from the Post Oak Mission to Indiahoma, Cache, and the Star House was too much.

He rode a borrowed horse home and collected Magdalena. They proceeded to notify Quanah's children, who were not living at the Star House.

When that was done, the Mennonite couple prepared for a burial that would be held the very next day.

On February 24, 1911, mourners gathered at the Star House to pay their final respects to the Eagle, the famous Chief of the Comanche.

At just after noon, Quanah's body was placed in a spring wagon and started for the Post Oak Mission Cemetery. The procession stretched a mile and a half.

To-nar-cy, said to have been a favorite wife, rode in the car while To-pay and fifteen children rode in the bed of a farm wagon.

Over 1,200 people attended, far too many to fit into the chapel.

"It was the largest crowd our mission has ever seen or will ever see," Magdalena said.[32]

Reverend Becker spoke clearly about God and how Quanah had urged the Indians to accept Him. Reverend Deyo of the nearby Baptist mission said some words, too.

When the service was over, Quanah's body was taken to the gravesite. He was dressed in his best buckskin suit and surrounded by feathers, a war bonnet, and Indian relics. A silver dollar was placed on each eye, and his favorite diamond stick pin from Burk Burnett was fastened to his buckskin.

---

[32] She was wrong. When she died twenty-seven years later, over 1,500 people came from all over. A tent city of Indians was set up around the now-famous Post Oak Mission to hold everyone.

His casket was lowered to the ground, and his wives spread Quanah's best blankets over the top. Then, the wailing began.

"There was not a dry eye among the Comanche," Magdalena later said.

Quanah was believed to be between fifty-nine and sixty-five. No records of his date or place of birth existed, although his mother said he was born in the Wichita Mountains. Quanah himself indicated he was born near Cedar Lake in Gaines County.[33]

Regardless of when or where he was born, he now rested in the white man's cemetery, which happened to be in his precious Comanchería. He was truly a man stretched between two worlds.

At one time, Quanah had been considered the richest Indian in the country. Before that, he and the Comanche ruled the plains, with buffalo everywhere and the world at their feet.

But at his death, his family discovered how generous he had been. He hated seeing anyone hungry, so he fed his fellow Comanche whenever they were in need.

To confirm this, all one had to do was look at all the teepees around the Star House. The people in those tents depended on him. That's why the great chief was broke when he died.

So now the buffalo were all gone. The remaining Comanche were confined to small plots of land, waiting for government disbursements. And the wealth of a once-great Comanche nation died with him. In death, Quanah had nothing more to give.

Four years later, that last statement proved incorrect when some lanterns were seen over Quanah's grave one night.

The following morning, the Beckers and Parkers discovered someone had dug up the chief's body and stolen the two silver dollars from his eyes. Due to the decomposition of the bones, the criminals missed the diamond stick pin from Burk Burnett, as it was hidden under a rib bone.

Devastated at this terrible act, the two families lovingly collected the scattered bones and washed and reburied them in a baby's casket.

---

[33] Walter Posey, a prominent Lubbock, Texas, citizen, ran into Quanah when he came through Lubbock in a new touring car. The chief told Posey he was headed to Cedar Lake since it was a tradition for Comanche to visit their birthplace before they died.

It was a sad indictment of the sins of lust and greed.

But finally, the world of white men had taken every last thing from Quanah Parker.

Except his legacy.

Epilogue

With a story this big, there was so much I had to leave out. I want to add some of that here while also providing more information on certain characters. In thinking about how to do it, I decided to go by sections, roughly starting at the end and working back to the beginning. First up is the Post Oak Mission.

After Henry Kohfeld's excellent start, the Beckers carried on the Lord's work for decades. Then Abraham's precious wife, Magdelena, died in 1938. Abraham worked hard for three more years before retiring in 1941. Yet the Mission continued to flourish.

Quanah Parker had always wanted a school for the Indian children as he believed they were poorly treated in the white schools. In September 1948, the Post Oak Mission School opened its doors to the Comanche children as well as the children of the missionaries.

The first class consisted of 28 pupils and their teacher was Ruth Wiens. Only the first four grades were taught. By 1951, a school building and apartments for the teachers were completed, and eight grades were taught.

The missionaries located six Indian children deemed wards of the state and took them in so they could have a better home and proper schooling. The staff even purchased a nearby home to turn into an orphanage for these children.

There have been several books written about the formation of the Post Oak Mission and all that was done by the Mennonites that I have not included here. Ron Parker continually expressed his appreciation for the Mennonite Brethren Church and his upbringing at the Post Oak Mission Church and School. So did Ron Parker's siblings and many other Comanche brothers and sisters. Most had tears in their eyes as they recalled their experiences at the Post Oak Mission School and Church. The church even received a letter from President Theodore Roosevelt in 1907.

I also wanted to note here that Henry Kohfeld and his wife, Elizabeth, had six children: Bertha, Emma, Henry Jr., Sarah, Gus, and Kathryn. Abraham Becker and his wife, Magdalena, had seven children, with one dying in infancy. Their names were Daniel, William, Augusta (who died young), Peter, Herwanna, Samuel, and Glenn. After Magdalena died, Abraham eventually remarried. He died on January 15, 1953, in Lawton, Oklahoma.

Sadly, after numerous Comanche protests, the Mission and cemetery were relocated to Indiahoma to make room for a missile range. In 1959, the status of Post Oak changed from a mission church to a self-administering congregation. The fact that the Post Oak Mennonite Brethren Church still exists to this day testifies to the success of the Mission.

As for Henry Kohfeld, after being dismissed from the Post Oak Mission, he and his family traveled 30 miles north to Gotebo, Oklahoma. They stayed there for three years before moving to California, where they remained active in various Mennonite Brethren churches.

Henry died in 1932, and his wife Elizabeth died in 1933. Although he left Post Oak Mission in a tough way, his work set up the Beckers for success, and many Comanche men and women were saved and became active in both the church and school.

What happened to Comanchería?

In early 1912, land in Comanchería was sold "dirt cheap" by the U.S. and state governments. Two years later, sales were accelerated by a war in Ukraine. This war was a precursor to World War I.

After the czar set in motion policies that forced the Mennonites out of the country from 1871 to 1881, it took a long time for normal crop production to return to Ukraine, but it finally recovered. The land was too fertile not to be productive.

In 1914, once again, Ukraine became a massive producer of wheat and other important crops to the world. However, the 1914 war cut these crops off from being shipped. This forced the United States to provide financial incentives to farmers to buy cheap land and plant wheat. And they did.

Farmers quickly plowed up more and more of the virgin prairie and planted seeds. Even suitcase farmers got into the act.

A suitcase farmer traveled by train from another part of the country to the Midwest, bought low-priced land, and either plowed and planted it himself or hired locals to do it. Then he'd get back on the train and go home. When it was time for harvest, he'd ride the train back and pay men to cut the wheat or other crops and take it to market. He'd pocket a sizable profit and then do it all over again.

This worked out very well until prices were depressed due to wheat growing on every square inch of arable Comanchería. With prices down, it made no sense to plant anything else. So these suitcase farmers (and other locals) left the land bare, refusing to tend to it or even plant another crop.

Dust storms soon blew the loose, untethered dirt to the southwest, eliminating the topsoil. With no topsoil, nothing could be planted.

We now know there was a delicate balance of moisture stored in the thick prairie sod. But all the plowing interrupted that balance, and soon, the rain stopped. With no rain, the land was utterly destroyed.

In 1935, Hugh Bennett was head of the Soil Erosion Service, a temporary agency that administered unemployment relief funds for erosion control in the United States. Bennett was a pioneer in soil conservation and wanted to teach farmers how to preserve the land. Yet his funding was almost gone, much like the topsoil in Comanchería.

Bennett made one final attempt to get a bill through Congress to continue funding his service. Without this bill, there was literally no hope of restoring the topsoil to Midwest farms. Yet congressmen yawned, tired of hearing the endless doom and gloom Bennett laid out. As he ran out of time allotted for his hearing, something straight from the Bible happened: a massive dust storm rolled into Washington, D.C., unheard of before this.

Willington Brink wrote about this scene in his 1950 biography of Bennett, *Big Hugh: The Father of Soil Conservation*.

The group [of congressmen] gathered at a window. The dust storm for which Hugh Bennett had been waiting rolled in like a vast steel-town pall, thick and repulsive. The skies took on a copper color. The sun went into hiding. The air became heavy with grit. Government's most spectacular showman had laid the stage well. All day, step by step, he had built his drama, paced it slowly, risked possible failure with his interminable reports, while he prayed for Nature to hurry up a proper denouement. For once, Nature cooperated generously.

The congressmen were shocked. A few weeks later, Black Sunday happened in the Midwest. Throughout Oklahoma and Texas, the Sunday afternoon sun was completely blotted out with 60 mph winds pushing a biblically high wall of dust and sand. Congress saw photos in the newspapers, and after their own experience in the nation's capital, Bennett's agency was saved.

These dust storms and the destruction of land heavily affected Native Americans. After all, they lived right where this was happening. It was not a coincidence that with the devastating dust bowls of the 1930s, the white man's destruction of Comanchería was finally complete. Gone were the buffalo, the fighting Comanche, and the land. The whites had consumed and destroyed everything while moving on to the next way to make a buck.

Though it took many years and lots of money, the government implemented new farming techniques and the rains eventually returned. Using rainwater to break down the remaining layer of earth, the topsoil also returned. Since then, the government has willingly funded soil conservation and outreach services. The consequences of not doing so are cataclysmic.

In Henry Kohfeld's section, I mentioned a big oak tree. That tree actually existed and was famous. It was called the Chortitza Oak and lived to be 700 years old. Henry's parents and everyone in the region knew about it.

It is true that Mennonites held important meetings under the Chortitza Oak. YouTube videos still show that special tree and some of its history, including the fact that these trees existed in Ukraine's oldest Mennonite settlement. After the tree died, acorns were collected from it and planted all over the United States—a reminder of the connection between America and Ukraine.

General Ranald Mackenzie is credited for finally figuring out how to defeat the Comanche. Though he didn't use many of the tactics pioneered by Jack Coffee Hays and his Texas Rangers (mainly because he didn't know about them), he quickly learned to find his own way.

One of his vital tactics was killing captured horses. General Mackenzie saw that he and his scouts could never hold the animals or prevent the Comanche from stealing them back. Once that was clear, the only solution, as gruesome as it was, was to kill them.

The extraordinary range of the weapons that were able to hit the Comanche also tipped the advantage to the military. Quanah saw that at the second Battle of Adobe Walls.

The last and perhaps most devastating tactic was the chase. Using three generals, including himself, Mackenzie not only squeezed the Indians into a smaller area but forced the tribe to dump years of hard work and stores of food to make their escape. Each successful escape meant starting all over again. In fact, the numerous victories Quanah racked up in escaping Mackenzie eventually led to Quanah's surrender. He simply ran out of food.

Yet Quanah was too smart. He knew he was beaten by a stronger foe with more troops and better technology. Once he surrendered, Quanah set out to beat this foe at their own game. And that he did.

The first meeting between General Mackenzie and Quanah was documented and brief. I used that account for the scene of this monumental meeting.

Though Quanah was defeated, his captor did not live a comfortable life afterward. General Mackenzie suffered tremendous wounds in the Civil War while being severely concussed from explosions. He also fell from a wagon at Fort Sill and injured his head, barely conscious for three days.

After that, he started acting strangely. His handwriting grew unreadable. Though he didn't consume alcohol, at 43, Mackenzie started drinking heavily. The quartermaster at the fort considered Mackenzie to be insane.

The general became engaged to a woman nine years his junior. Then he got drunk and started a fight with two local citizens who didn't recognize him. They beat Mackenzie to within an inch of his life and tied him to a cart. He was found the next day and loaded on a train, supposedly to see Sheridan. Instead, he was taken to New York City and placed in an insane asylum.

The Army knew there was something seriously wrong, so it retired Mackenzie against his protests in March 1884. He stayed there for six months before being taken to his sister's home in New Jersey. There, he essentially behaved like a baby, with no one understanding his words. He couldn't do anything or take care of himself. This went on for years.

On January 18, 1889, Ranald Mackenzie died. He was 48. He had a brief obituary and was soon lost to history.

Today, doctors who evaluated his symptoms and past injuries believe that he was likely suffering from chronic traumatic encephalopathy (CTE), which has no cure. It was a tough way to go for such a successful officer and a favorite of both General and President Grant.

People

Sam Houston – The winning general in the war for independence against Mexico, Houston became the new country's first elected president in 1836 after beating Stephen F. Austin. The Texas Constitution prevented Houston from running for a consecutive term. Instead, he ran and won in 1841.

Texas became a U.S. state in 1845, and Houston was selected as one of its U.S. senators—the only former head of a foreign state to serve in Congress. Houston ran for governor in 1857 but lost. In 1859, he ran again and won this time.

He was closely aligned with the Cherokees and advocated peace with Native Americans. Eventually, he realized peace was not possible with the

Comanche, and he joined with other governors and legislators in taking the fight to the Indians.

When the South seceded, Houston refused to allow Texas to join the Confederacy and declared Texas an independent republic. He was removed from office and urged citizens not to join the war. However, he received no support for his viewpoint and eventually agreed to stand with the South.

Out of office, his military skills were not used by the Confederacy. At 70 years of age, Sam Houston died on July 26, 1863.

Luther Thomas Martin Plummer – There is evidence that Luther was deeply distraught when his wife, Rachel, was captured. He was mad at himself for bringing her to such a wild frontier. But after Rachel's death, he married Sarah Elizabeth Lauderdale, who produced seven children. Sarah was half-Cherokee Indian on her mother's side. When she died, Luther married Angeline Glenn Plummer and had eleven more children. Including all his wives, Luther produced 21 children, obviously an active fellow. He died around 1875 and was about 64 years old.

Jack Coffee Hays – The legendary Indian fighter who developed excellent tactics against the Comanche and Apache left Texas for the California gold rush in 1849. The next year, Hays was elected sheriff of San Francisco. In 1853, he was appointed U. S. Surveyor General for California and was one of the developers of Oakland, holding interests in land, banking, and utilities. In 1876, Hays was selected to be a delegate to the Democratic National Convention. He died on April 21, 1883, and was buried in the Mountain View Cemetery in Oakland, California.

Captain Mathew "Old Paint" Caldwell – Another legendary Indian fighter, Caldwell was present at the Council House Fight in San Antonio and barely survived. He continued fighting Indians and died in his home on December 28, 1842. He was just 42. Later, Texas named Caldwell County after Old Paint.

Buffalo Hump – After being attacked by Van Dorn and Sul Ross, Buffalo Hump again brought his people into the reservation and ended his traditional Comanche life. He asked for a house and farmland so that he could set an example for his people. He most likely died before 1867 while trying to live out his life as a rancher and farmer. It was a sad ending for a proud chief.

Sul Ross – After fighting the Comanche, Ross resigned from the rangers due to a miscommunication in orders from Sam Houston. He later joined the Confederacy and scouted for the South. He even fought under Earl Van Dorn, who lost the Battle of Pea Ridge. Ross blamed Van Dorn for the loss and turned against him.

When the Civil War ended, Sul Ross was just 26 years old. He'd seen a lot of action. Ross settled down west of Waco and bought land to farm. He and his wife had eight children.

He became the sheriff of McLennan County and later a state senator and governor of Texas, serving two terms. Finally, he became president of Texas A&M University.

Sul Ross lived three lifetimes in one life and accomplished many more things than I can list here. On January 3, 1898, he died at home. He was 59.

Isatai'i – Not much is known about this medicine man, but supposedly, he died in 1916 and is buried in a family cemetery in Stephens County, Oklahoma. After the Adobe Walls disaster, he had little influence except perhaps with Quanah Parker. Nothing else is known about him.

Juliet Watts – She survived Buffalo Hump's raid on Linnville, Texas, when her whalebone corset stopped an arrow from killing her. She returned to the Linnville area (although the town was gone) and married Dr. J. M. Stanton. He opened the Stanton House, the first hotel in Port Lavaca.

Charles Goodnight – He was a Texas Ranger before creating the Goodnight-Loving trail to drive cattle north through Texas, Colorado, and Wyoming. Goodnight also invented the first chuckwagon. In 1870, he married Mary Ann "Molly" Dyer, a teacher from Weatherford. Six years later, he established a bison herd to preserve the species.

After seeing America completely change from a wild frontier to a settled and populated land, Charles Goodnight died on December 12, 1929, in Tucson, Arizona. He was 93.

Lorenzo Dow Nixon Jr. – Lorenzo played a large role in Rachel's return. His wife, Sarah Parker, escaped the 1836 attack but died ten years later. Yet that's all we know about Lorenzo—no date of death or location of burial.

Antonio López de Santa Anna – Santa Anna lived an unbelievable life, often resurrecting himself from terrible defeats. He started his military career fighting to preserve Mexico's sovereignty as part of Spain. But when the Mexican rebels managed a stalemate, a superior switched sides and fought for Mexico's independence. Santa Anna joined him and was placed in an important military position.

Yet Santa Anna soon rebelled against his superior and began making a name for himself with his own military. He then attempted to place himself at the head of any government that ruled Mexico. He was unsuccessful until he managed to win enough battles, which placed another man as president of Mexico.

Santa Anna was given a prominent position and soon worked hard at promoting himself as "the Napolean of the West." When his boss was captured and executed, Santa Anna fought and, again, did enough damage to force free elections. He was elected president, a title he coveted.

Santa Anna loved the prestige and power but hated governing. He let his vice president govern while he retired to a seaside resort to enjoy the good life.

When Texas revolted, it gave him something to do. He went to Texas and lost the war, signing away the territory. Sometime after this loss, he was made president for the fifth time. This time, his poor governing led to his capture and exile to Cuba.

Like Napolean, he made a comeback from exile. After one year in Cuba, America was at war with Mexico. President Polk made an agreement with Santa Anna that Polk would break up the blockade if Santa Anna returned to the presidency and brokered a deal to sell more land to the United States. Polk then restored Santa Anna, who took control of his troops, reneged on his deal, and turned them on the Americans.

Like many times before, Santa Anna lost and the U.S. captured Mexico City. He fled to Jamaica and later Columbia. Incredibly, after yet another revolt, he was made president again in 1853, when he declared himself a "dictator for life" and took the title of his Most Serene Highness.

Short of cash, he finally sold more territory to the U.S. and was soon overthrown. In 1855, he was exiled a second time (like Napolean), this time to St. Thomas.

Santa Anna was married twice but didn't show up for the weddings. Apparently, they were arranged affairs that paid him handsomely for the marriage.

In 1874, he accepted a general amnesty issued by the current president and returned to Mexico. By now, he was crippled and almost blind from cataracts. This incredible self-promoter and political climber died on June 21, 1876, in Mexico City, Mexico. He was 82. Of course, Santa Anna was buried with full military honors in a glass coffin in Panteón del Tepeyac Cemetery.

John Richard Parker – John's father, Silas, was killed in the attack on Parker's Fort. His mother, Lucy, escaped with two children, leaving behind Cynthia Ann and himself. John Richard was 12 when he was ransomed back to the Parkers. Unable to fully reintegrate into his past life, he ran back to the Comanche.

On one of his raids, John Richard contracted the deadly smallpox. The Comanche had captives, horses, and other goods but stopped when he became too ill to ride. When the Comanche saw he had smallpox, they were terrified and left him just north of the Rio Grande in West Texas.

To help him, they left a girl captive behind. As the story goes, she stayed and nursed John Richard back to health rather than trying to return to her family. Apparently, he returned to Mexico with the girl and her family and married her.

Later, John Richard returned to the United States and fought for the Confederacy in Texas. After the war, he returned to Mexico and lived until 1915, when he died on his ranch.

Martha Parker – Wife of James Parker, the Searcher, Martha was fed up with his wanderings throughout Comanchería while looking for his niece and nephew. She died on October 30, 1846, in Houston County, Texas. She was 48.

James Pratt Plummer – Son of Rachel and Luther Plummer, he was ransomed back when he was eight years old. Because his uncle, James Parker, refused to return him to his natural father, Luther Plummer, Pratt grew up in Rachel's family. Later, Pratt married twice and fought in the Civil War in Arkansas, where he died of pneumonia on November 17, 1862. He was 27 years old.

Quanah's Wives – Here is what I think is the complete list, though it may not be fully accurate or thorough.
    First – Aer-wuth-tak-um
    Second – Wec-Keah
    Third – Coby
    Fourth – Chony
    Fifth – Mah-cheet-to-wook-ky
    Sixth – To-Pay
    Seventh – Tonarcy
    Genealogy of the late Ron Parker (who wrote the Foreword):
    Great-grandparents – Quanah and Chony Parker
    Grandparents – Balwin Parker Sr. and Nora
    Parents – Balwin Parker Jr. and Marguerite
Harold Parker was born in 1890 and died on August 2, 1902. Harold's parents were Quanah and Chony Parker. Harold's older brother was Balwin Parker Sr.

Others – Many of the people in this story entered and exited with nothing more ever written about them. Thus, history keeps silent about their fate. In the future, perhaps we will learn a little more about their lives and be able to add more here. But for now…

Places

Parker's Fort – The fort was abandoned after the attack and disintegrated with age. A replica of the fort was built on the site in 1930, and another rebuild was made in 1967. It is still there today.

Fort Sill – Located in Comanchería and later Oklahoma, the fort is still in operation. It has been a training facility and used as artillery headquarters and flight schools with airfields on the land. It is still being used today.

Adobe Walls – After Quanah's attack on Adobe Walls in 1874, the U.S. Army arrived and evacuated the buffalo hunters and civilians from the area. The hunters attempted to repair the forts, but Native Americans attacked and burned them in late September, leaving only the adobe walls behind. Adobe Walls is now a historical site with monuments, including one erected by the Panhandle–Plains Historical Society in 1924. Some say that the site is unchanged from 1874, aside from a few fences, an electrical line, and some gas tanks.

Star House – Quanah built this house with help from cattlemen. It quickly became a de facto headquarters for the Comanche Nation. It even held a dinner for a sitting U.S. president. The house was purchased by one of Quanah's daughters after he died. Even though it was originally located near the Wichita Mountains north of Cache on Fort Sill's West Range, she moved the house to Cache and sold it to Herbert Woesner in 1958.

The white stars painted on the roof have two explanations. The first is that Quanah had seen the stars on the U.S. generals and wanted to display his rank and importance. Quanah's descendants offered a second explanation. They said that Quanah had been to Washington, D.C., to speak with Theodore Roosevelt and stayed in a "five-star hotel." So Quanah had *ten* stars painted on his roof to explain to Roosevelt upon his arrival that he would have better accommodations than Washington, D.C. This makes more sense since we know Quanah ordered large glasses filled to the brim with wine instead of the tiny glasses at the White House.

Over time, the Star House has deteriorated and is listed by the Preservation Oklahoma organization as endangered. It is still privately owned and sits on the back lot of an amusement park. It appears the house is destined to join Quanah.

I have always loved history. So, from a very young age, I asked questions.

In 2016, John, my husband, and I booked our first Mennonite history tour to Poland, where our ancestors had lived from the 1530s. This is where I really started connecting the Mennonite migration timeline.

I read every book I could find on our history. In January 2020, I was browsing online for new books and came across a book titled *From Russia to Oklahoma: Mennonite Pioneers Lena and Agatha Funk* by Maureen Galloway. I purchased this book because my maternal grandma's maiden name is Funk—Elizabeth Funk Friesen.

Upon receiving the book, I discovered it had a picture of Cynthia Ann Parker, Prairie Flower, and Chief Quanah Parker. This was so surreal that I frantically looked for more material.

I soon came across a book by the late Marvin L. Kroeker titled *Comanche and Mennonites on the Oklahoma Plains*. This was the connecting point not only for my Mennonite background but also for the history of my hometown, Seminole, here in West Texas. Unbelievably, one of Chief Quanah Parker's favorite camping grounds was in the Seminole Draw, located just south of the city.

As I read through both books, I checked with the Genealogical Registry and Database of Mennonite Ancestry or GRanDMA. I wanted to see if there were any family connections to missionaries who served the Comanche Nation in Oklahoma. The day I discovered that Henry Kohfeld was my blood relative, I immediately knelt and praised the Lord for this personal connection with the Post Oak Mission.

Henry Kohfeld was my third cousin, who was three times removed from my paternal grandmother Katharina Giesbrecht Rempel. Henry immigrated from Ukraine to Kansas at the age of 14 with his parents. This was almost exactly 100 years earlier from when I, at age eight, immigrated to Texas with my family.

Excitedly, I contacted Mrs. Marg Gerbrant in California. She attended Post Oak School while her parents were missionaries there. Mrs. Gerbrant told me about Ron Parker, a descendant of Quanah Parker. She said if I could locate Ron in Oklahoma, then I could get the details about Post Oak Mission.

On May 28, 2021, I traveled to the Lawton, Oklahoma, area looking for Mr. Ron Parker. As the evening grew late, I assumed my trip would be unsuccessful. Then my phone rang.

The caller explained that he had missed a call from my number and introduced himself as Ron Parker. Holding my breath, I asked if he had attended Post Oak Mission Church and the school. Sure enough, he had. At that moment, I knew this story was just beginning to unfold in front of me.

Ron came to the hotel lobby, where my granddaughter and I were staying. There was an immediate connection between us, just knowing my ancestors had been there for him growing up. We quickly became close friends, and he felt like a father figure to me.

Soon, Ron traveled to Seminole, Texas, and I had the privilege of taking him to Cedar Lake, just one of several places claiming to be the birthplace of his great-grandfather, Chief Quanah Parker.

As you read in the Foreword, the late Ron Parker played a major role in the formation of this book. Not only Ron Parker but all his siblings, too, including the community at Post Oak Mission in Indiahoma, Oklahoma. I am also grateful to the Pete Coffey Mennonite Church in Cache, Oklahoma. These communities carry on the Mission to the next generation after their forefather, Chief Quanah Parker, gave permission to start it all. Today, I consider each of them my Comanche brothers and sisters in Christ. I even got a Comanche name PU?E?AITU POSA?KANI

God, who is the Orchestrator and the One who connects history with the present, will continue the work that was started in 1896. I am forever grateful for this opportunity to continue the work that my cousin started that year, spreading the gospel of salvation!

Go therefore and make disciples of all the nations, baptizing them in the name of the Father and of the Son and of the Holy Spirit, teaching them to observe all things that I have commanded you; and lo, I am with you always, even to the end of the age. Amen.

Matthew 28:19–20

Post Oak Photos

Exterior view of Fort Parker in Groesbeck, Texas. Notice how the blockhouse hangs over the lower block to allow shooting at the enemy below. Also, see the double gate next to the blockhouse that was left open on May 19, 1836.

Interior view of Fort Parker.

Native American teepees (illustration).

View from inside a teepee.

Post Oak

General Sam Houston fighting for the freedom of Texas.

The crafty, political, and vain General Antonio Lopez de Santa Anna.

Texas Ranger Jack Coffee Hays. His hair tells the story of a man constantly on the move.

Cynthia Ann Parker, after being rescued or captured (depending on your point of view). She is nursing her third child, Prairie Flower. Notice the large hands from years of working hides.

Post Oak

Chief Yellow Bear, Weckeah's father. Weckeah was one of the many wives of Quanah Parker.

Isatai'i, the charismatic medicine man who lost the respect of many Comanche warriors after the Second Battle of Adobe Walls.

General William Tecumseh Sherman, the famous Civil War general, was sent to settle the west and thus subdue the Comanche. Interestingly, at birth, his middle name celebrated the great chief of the Shawnees.

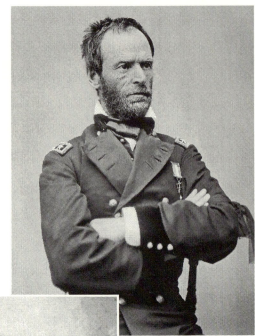

Quanah Parker with his wife Tonarcy, right after his surrender in 1875.

Colonel Ranald Slidell Mackenzie no earlier than Oct. 19, 1864, when he was promoted to brigadier general.

Comanche woman with child. (Courtesy of the Mennonite Library & Archives, Fresno Pacific University Collection.)

Tina Siemens

Texas President and then Governor Sam Houston.

A Native American teepee with exterior lodgepoles (illustration).

Texas Governor Lawrence Sullivan "Sul" Ross, long after his ambush of Chief Buffalo Hump with Major Earl Van Dorn.

Quanah Parker, Chief of the Comanche.

A Comanche village. (Courtesy of the Mennonite Library & Archives, Fresno Pacific University Collection.)

The famous Star House, from which Chief Quanah Parker managed the Comanche tribe and entertained a popular president.
(Courtesy of the Oklahoma Historical Society.)

Current ruins of Chief Quanah Parker's Star House. (Courtesy of the Mennonite Library & Archives, Fresno Pacific University Collection.)

(Back row, left-right) David C. Peters, A. J. Becker, George Koweno, unidentified. (Front row center) Magdalena Becker. (Courtesy of the Mennonite Library & Archives, Fresno Pacific University Collection.)

Tina Siemens

Post Oak Mission main residence in the 1900s. (Courtesy of the Mennonite Library & Archives, Fresno Pacific University Collection.)

Chief Quanah Parker, posing for a portrait in a full Comanche outfit in 1909.

Magdalena Becker (left) with part of her serving, canning, and flower-making club. (Courtesy of the Mennonite Library & Archives, Fresno Pacific University Collection.)

Post Oak missionary residence in the foreground with the church in the background. (Courtesy of the Mennonite Library & Archives, Fresno Pacific University Collection.)

Tina Siemens

Herman Asenap, translator for the Post Oak Mission. (Courtesy of the Mennonite Library & Archives, Fresno Pacific University Collection.)

Camp meeting at the Post Oak Mission in the 1900s. (Courtesy of the Mennonite Library & Archives, Fresno Pacific University Collection.)

Post Oak

Chief Quanah Parker with two of his wives. The wife on the right is Chony Parker, as identified by Ardith Leming, great-granddaughter of Quanah Parker and also sister to Ron Parker. (Courtesy of the Oklahoma Historical Society.)

A Comanche baby named George Washington was born July 4, 1911, and happy in a cradleboard. (Courtesy of the Mennonite Library & Archives, Fresno Pacific University Collection.)

Wanada Parker, daughter of Weckeah and Quanah Parker in 1904. (Courtesy of the Mennonite Library & Archives, Fresno Pacific University Collection.)

Quanah Parker on horseback in Lawton, Oklahoma. (Courtesy of the Mennonite Library & Archives, Fresno Pacific University Collection.)

Post Oak

Magdalena Becker (front center) with women at Post Oak Mission. (Courtesy of the Mennonite Library & Archives, Fresno Pacific University Collection.)

Chief Quanah Parker standing next to his mother's casket (Cynthia Ann Parker) prior to reburial in Post Oak Cemetery. (Courtesy of Fort Parker.)

Chief Quanah Parker's funeral at Post Oak Cemetery on February 24, 1911. (Courtesy of the Mennonite Library & Archives, Fresno Pacific University Collection.)

Chief Quanah Parker's burial at Post Oak Cemetery on February 24, 1911. (Courtesy of the Mennonite Library & Archives, Fresno Pacific University Collection.)

Post Oak

The Quanah Parker Memorial at Post Oak Cemetery. (Courtesy of the Mennonite Library & Archives, Fresno Pacific University Collection.)

Post Oak Mission in the 1920s. (Courtesy of the Mennonite Library & Archives, Fresno Pacific University Collection.)

Sarah Grunau with orphans at Post Oak in 1949. (Courtesy of the Mennonite Library & Archives, Fresno Pacific University Collection.)

D. J. Gerbrandt and Ruth Wiens with students at Post Oak School. (Courtesy of the Mennonite Library & Archives, Fresno Pacific University Collection.)

The children of Post Oak Mission School. (Courtesy of the Mennonite Library & Archives, Fresno Pacific University Collection.)

Production of *How the Gospel Came to the Comanches* at Post Oak Mission School in 1948. (Courtesy of the Mennonite Library & Archives, Fresno Pacific University Collection.)

Missionaries at Post Oak Mission from 1949-1952. (Adults left-right) Anna Gomez, Joe Gomez, Eva Nickel, D. J. Gerbrandt, Linda Gerbrandt, Herman J. Neufeld, Anna Neufeld, Sarah Grunau, Ruth Wiens. (Courtesy of the Mennonite Library & Archives, Fresno Pacific University Collection.)

Buffalo herd in Oklahoma in 1954. (Courtesy of the Mennonite Library & Archives, Fresno Pacific University Collection.)

Post Oak

Post Oak Mission School in February 1957. Also, the site of the new church building is in the foreground. (Courtesy of the Mennonite Library & Archives, Fresno Pacific University Collection.)

Herman Asenap's family at his funeral in 1959. (Courtesy of the Mennonite Library & Archives, Fresno Pacific University Collection.)

Tina Siemens

Post Oak Cemetery on July Fourth. (Courtesy of the Mennonite Library & Archives, Fresno Pacific University Collection.)

Oklahoma land transfer from the United States of America to the American Mennonite Brethren Mission Union signed by President Theodore Roosevelt. (Courtesy of Post Oak Mission, Indiahoma, Oklahoma.)

Post Oak

THE UNITED STATES OF AMERICA,

To all to whom these presents shall come, Greeting:

Whereas, There has been deposited in the General Land Office of the United States an order of the Secretary of the Interior directing that in accordance with the act of Congress approved June 21, 1906, (34 Stat. L. 325.) a fee simple Patent issue to "The American Mennonite Brethren Mission Union, a Corporation, organized in accordance with the laws of the State of Kansas" for the North West fractional quarter of Section seven, in Township two North of Range fourteen West of Indian Meridian, in Oklahoma, containing one hundred and fifty eight acres and sixty hundredths of an acre

NOW KNOW YE, THAT THE UNITED STATES OF AMERICA, In consideration of the premises, have given and granted, and by these presents do give and grant unto the said The American Mennonite Brethren Mission Union, and to its successors, the lands above described: TO HAVE AND TO HOLD the same, together with all the rights, privileges, immunities, and appurtenances, of whatsoever nature thereunto belonging, unto the said The American Mennonite Brethren Mission Union, and to its successors and assigns forever. ~~And there is reserved, from the lands hereby granted, a right of way thereon for ditches or canals constructed by authority of the United States.~~

IN TESTIMONY WHEREOF, I, Theodore Roosevelt, President of the United States of America, have caused these letters to be made patent, and the seal of the General Land Office to be hereunto affixed.

GIVEN under my hand, at the City of Washington, the twenty first day of June, in the year of our Lord one thousand nine hundred and seven, and of the Independence of the United States the one hundred and thirty first.

By the President: Theodore Roosevelt

By F. M. Kean, Secretary.

H. W. Sanford, Recorder of the General Land Office.

Recorded, Miscellaneous Vol. _____ page _____

REV. HENRY KOHFELD
Jan. 24, 1863 - Jan. 1, 1932
At Post Oak, 1894 to 1907

Henry Kohfeld – (Courtesy of Center for Mennonite Brethren Studies, Tabor College, Hillsboro, Kansas.)

Author Tina Siemens with Ron Parker at Cedar Lake, in Gaines County east of Seminole, Texas. It's the possible birthplace of Quanah Parker.

Author Tina Siemens, with her husband John Siemens and Ron Parker, at the Quanah Parker Center in Quanah, Texas.

Johann Johann Krahn

Jacob Krahn	Nicholas Krahn
Helena Krahn	Helena Krahn
Katharina Janzen	Helena Wiens
Heinrich Kohfeld	Maria Heinrichs
	Katharina Giesbrecht
	David G. Rempel
	Katherina Rempel

Katherina Rempel
is the third cousin, thrice removed of
Heinrich Kohfeld

This genealogy chart shows the connection between Heinrich (Henry) Kohfeld and Author Katherina "Tina" (Rempel) Siemens.

Bibliography

Published Materials

Brice, Donaly E. *The Great Comanche Raid: Boldest Indian Attack in the Texas Republic.* Austin: Eakin Press, 1987.

Carlson, Paul. "Caprock Chronicles: Competing Claims for Quanah's Birthplace." *Lubbock Avalanche-Journal*, January 14, 2017.

Crum, Tom, and Paul Carlson. *Myth, Memory, and Massacre: The Pease River Capture of Cynthia Ann Parker.* Lubbock: Texas Tech University Press, 2010.

Deshields, James T. *Cynthia Ann Parker: The Story of Her Capture.* St. Louis: Nixon-Jones Printing, 1886.

Esau, Mrs. H. T. *First Sixty Years of M. B. Missions.* Hillsboro, KS: Mennonite Brethren Publishing House, 1954.

Galloway, Maureen. "From Russia to Oklahoma: Mennonite Pioneers Lean on Agatha Funk." *Mennonite Life*. Accessed October 19, 2024.

Gwynne, S.C. *Empire of the Summer Moon.* New York: Scribner, 2010.

Hagan, William T. *Comanches and Mennonites on the Oklahoma Plains.* Norman: University of Oklahoma Press, 2004.

Hagan, William T. *Quanah Parker, Comanche Chief.* Norman: University of Oklahoma Press, 1995.

Hamalainen, Pekka. *The Comanche Empire.* New Haven: Yale University Press, 2008.

Kohfeld, Henry. Photo provided courtesy of Center for Mennonite Brethren Studies, Tabor College, located in Hillsboro, Kansas.

Kroger, Marvin E. *Comanches and Mennonites on the Oklahoma Plains.* Norman: University of Oklahoma Press, 2016.

Lanehart, Chuck. "America's first Thanksgiving was celebrated on Texas Plains." *Lubbock Avalanche-Journal*, November 27, 2022.

Lehmann, Herman, and J. Marvin Hunter. *Nine Years among the Indians 1870-1879: The Story of the Captivity and Life of a Texan Among the Indians*. Reprint ed. Albuquerque: University of New Mexico Press, 1993.

Lofton, Rachel, Susie Hendrix, and Jane Kennedy. *The Rachel Plummer Narrative.* Copyright 1926.

Miller, David, and Joe Hays. *In Citizen's Garb: Images of Native Americans on the Southern Plains, 1889-1891*. Photographs by William J. Lenny and William J. Sawyers. Lawton, OK: Museum of the Great Plains, n.d.

Natives and Settlers: The Mennonite Invasion of Indian Territory. PDF.

Neeley, Bill. *Quanah Parker and His People*. El Paso: Texas Western Press, 1986.

Neeley, Bill. *The Last Comanche Chief: The Life and Times of Quanah Parker*. New York: Wiley, 1995.

Parker Genealogy Chart. No publisher. No date.

Post Oak Mission Centennial Binder. Manuscript.

Robinson, Lila Wistrand, and James Armagost. *Comanche Dictionary and Grammar*. 2nd ed. Dallas, TX: SIL International, Global Publishing, 2012.

Smithwick, Noah. *The Evolution of a State or Recollections of Old Texas Days.* Austin: University of Texas Press, 1900.

Websites and Links

1945 Post Oak Mission Video. YouTube video, 17:49. Posted by *Red Oak Productions*, 2020. Accessed October 19, 2024. [https://www.youtube.com/watch?v=zdaXOw-IZDk&feature=youtu.be].

Ancestry.com. "Sarah Elizabeth Plummer." Accessed October 19, 2024. [https://www.ancestry.com/genealogy/records/sarah-elizabeth-plummer-24-2n0vgp5].

Anderson, H. Allen. "Blanco Canyon, Battle of." *Texas State Historical Association*, Handbook of Texas Online. Accessed October 19, 2024. [https://www.tshaonline.org/handbook/entries/blanco-canyon-battle-of].

Anderson, H. Allen. "Camp Radziminski." *Texas State Historical Association*, Handbook of Texas Online. Accessed October 19, 2024. [https://www.tshaonline.org/handbook/entries/camp-radziminski].

Anderson, H. Allen. "Comanche Indian Reservation." *Texas State Historical Association*, Handbook of Texas Online. Accessed October 19, 2024. [https://www.tshaonline.org/handbook/entries/comanche-indian-reservation].

Anderson, H. Allen. "Parker, Isaac." *Texas State Historical Association*, Handbook of Texas Online. Accessed October 19, 2024. [https://www.tshaonline.org/handbook/entries/parker-isaac].

Anderson, H. Allen. "Puhtocnocony (Nocona)." *Texas State Historical Association*, Handbook of Texas Online. Accessed October 19, 2024. [https://www.tshaonline.org/handbook/entries/Puhtocnocony-nocona].

Anderson, H. Allen. "Walker's Creek, Battle of." *Texas State Historical Association*, Handbook of Texas Online. Accessed October 19, 2024. [https://www.tshaonline.org/handbook/entries/walkers-creek-battle-of].

Anderson, H. Allen. "Wichita Indians." *Texas State Historical Association*, Handbook of Texas Online. Accessed October 19, 2024. [https://www.tshaonline.org/handbook/entries/wichita-indians].

"Antietam on the Web: Lawrence Sullivan Ross." Accessed October 19, 2024. [https://antietam.aotw.org/officers.php?officer_id=1766].

"Big Old Oak Tree in Chortitza." *Mennonite Heritage Archives*. Accessed October 19, 2024. [https://archives.mhsc.ca/index.php/big-old-oak-tree-in-chortitza].

Brown, J. Willard, ed. *The Army and Navy in the Civil War*. Washington, DC: U.S. Army Center of Military History, 1895. [https://history.army.mil/books/r&h/R&H-5CV.htm].

"Cavalry Tactics: Wichita Village." *Little Bighorn Associates Forums*. Accessed October 19, 2024. [https://lbha.proboards.com/thread/1154/cavalry-tactics-wichita-village?page=1].

"Chortitza Oak Sapling to Be Planted at AMBS." *Anabaptist Mennonite Biblical Seminary*. Accessed October 19, 2024. [https://www.ambs.edu/news/chortitza-oak-sapling-to-be-planted-at-ambs/].

Collins, Dan. "Hugh Bennett and the Perfect Storm." *Boundary Stones*, WETA. Last modified November 19, 2012. [https://boundarystones.weta.org/2012/11/19/hugh-bennett-and-perfect-storm].

"Comanche Divisions and Bands." *AAA Native Arts*. Accessed October 19, 2024. [https://www.aaanativearts.com/comanche-divisions-bands#:~:text=Before%20the%201750s%2C%20there%20were,away%20Kotsotekas%2C%20the%20eastern%20Comanches].

"Comanche Marker Tree." *The Historical Marker Database*. Accessed October 19, 2024. [https://www.hmdb.org/m.asp?m=53056].

Council Meeting Notes. Accessed October 19, 2024. [https://jack0204.tripod.com/gen/Heskew/council.htm].

Cox, Mike. "Nocona's Raid and Cynthia Ann Parker's Recapture." *HistoryNet*, March 1, 2012. [https://www.historynet.com/noconas-raid-and-cynthia-ann-parkers-recapture/].

Cox, Mike. "Sarah's Story." *TexasScapes*, March 12, 2013. [https://www.texasscapes.com].

"Daniel Webster Lehman, Indian Pioneer," *Texas State Genealogical Society*. Accessed October 19, 2024. [https://txsgs.org/TXSGS_DNA/showmedia.php?mediaID=42].

Dulaney, Josh. "Comanche Quanah Parker Star House in Oklahoma Crumbling but Restoration on Horizon." *The Oklahoman*, October 18, 2023. [https://www.oklahoman.com/story/news/2023/10/18/comanche-quanah-parker-star-house-oklahoma-crumbling-but-restoration-on-horizon/71219961007/].

Eddleman, Michael. "Pochontas." *Oklahoma Historical Society*, The Encyclopedia of Oklahoma History and Culture. Accessed October 19, 2024. [https://www.okhistory.org/publications/enc/entry.php?entry=PO020].

"Elm Grove." *City of Willow Park, Texas*. Accessed October 19, 2024. [https://www.willowparktx.gov/residents/pages/elm-grove].

Find a Grave. "James Pratt Plummer." Accessed October 19, 2024. [https://www.findagrave.com/memorial/51713733/james-pratt-plummer].

Find a Grave. "Luther Thomas Martin Plummer." Accessed October 19, 2024. [https://www.findagrave.com/memorial/14057015/luther-thomas_martin-plummer].

"Fort Parker History." *Genealogy Trails: Limestone County, Texas.* Accessed October 19, 2024. [http://genealogytrails.com/tex/prairieslakes/limestone/fortparker.html].

"Fort Worth's Schools Close so Children Can Visit the Zoo." *Durango Texas*, April 13, 2012. [https://durangotexas.blogspot.com/2012/04/fort-worths-schools-close-so-children.html?m=0].

Mennonite Brethren Oklahoma Photo Album. Accessed December 7, 2024. [https://fresno.canto.com/v/MennoniteBrethrenMissions/album/QICQC?display=thumbnail&viewIndex=2].

Fretwell, Charles. "James C. Ewing Genealogy." *The Fretwells: Family History*. Accessed October 19, 2024. [http://www.thefretwells.com/research/jcewing.aspx].

Frost and Gilchrist Family Tree. Accessed October 19, 2024. [https://frostandgilchrist.com/getperson.php?personID=I40192&tree=frostinaz01].

Gameo. "Becker, Abraham J. (1872-1953)." Accessed October 19, 2024. [https://gameo.org/index.php?title=Becker,_Abraham_J._(1872-1953)].

Geni.com. "Martha Patsy Duty Parker." Accessed October 19, 2024. [https://www.geni.com/people/Martha-Patsy-Duty-Parker/6000000040517595660].

"Grandchild of the 700-Year-Old Chortitza Oak, Located in Ukraine, Finds Home at Henderson Mennonite Heritage Park in Nebraska, USA." *RISU Religious Information Service of Ukraine*, November 2, 2018. [https://risu.ua/en/grandchild-of-the-700-year-old-chortitza-oak-located-in-ukraine-finds-home-at-henderson-mennonite-heritage-park-in-nebraska-usa_n93867].

"Greatest Challenge." *Quanah Parker Day*. Accessed October 19, 2024. [https://quanahparkerday.com/history/greatest_challenge.html].

Gwynne, S.C. *Killing Cynthia Ann*. New York: Scribner, 2010. [https://epdf.pub/killing-cynthia-ann.html].

Harrigan, Stephen. "Big Wonderful Thing Excerpt: Savage Warfare." *Texas Monthly*. Last modified October 24, 2019. [https://www.texasmonthly.com/being-texan/big-wonderful-thing-excerpt-savage-ware-fare/].

Hayes, Lisa. "Have You Ever Seen Trees Like This in Texas? They Have a Special Meaning." *Wide Open Country*. Accessed October 19,

2024. [https://www.wideopencountry.com/ever-seen-trees-like-texas-special-meaning/].

"Hill, Citizen of Tarrant County." *Tarrant County RootsWeb*. Accessed October 19, 2024. [http://www.rootsweb.ancestry.com/~txtarran/citizens/c_hill.htm].

"History of the Star House." *Save Star House*. Accessed October 19, 2024. [https://savestarhouse.com/history/index.html].

"History of the Texas Rangers." *Texas Ranger Hall of Fame and Museum*. Accessed October 19, 2024. [https://www.texasranger.org/texas-ranger-museum/history/].

James Parker. Geni. Accessed October 19, 2024. [https://www.geni.com/people/James-Parker/6000000010055641477].

Kroeker, D. E. *The First Sixty Years of Mennonite Brethren Missions*. Kansas: Mennonite Brethren Historical Society, 1952. [https://ia601904.us.archive.org/16/items/FirstSixtyYearsOfMBMissionsOCRopt/FirstSixtyYearsOfMBMissionsOCRopt.pdf].

Legends of America. "Adobe Walls." Accessed October 19, 2024. [https://www.legendsofamerica.com/tx-adobewalls/].

Limestone County, Texas Cemeteries. "Luther Thomas Martin Plummer." Accessed October 19, 2024. [https://www.txgenwebcounties.org/limestone/cemeteries/plummer.htm].

MacNeill, Andrea. "Ukraine Oak Grandchild Planted at MEI." *Canadian Mennonite*, April 19, 2018. [https://canadianmennonite.org/articles/ukraine-oak-grandchild-planted-mei].

"Mary Ann Brown Crawford Memorial." *Find a Grave*. Last modified November 6, 2014. [https://www.findagrave.com/memorial/19423736/mary-ann-brown-crawford].

May, Jon D. "Wichita." *Oklahoma Historical Society*, The Encyclopedia of Oklahoma History and Culture. Accessed October 19, 2024. [https://www.okhistory.org/publications/enc/entry?entry=WI004].

Mennonite Heritage Archives. "The Hup Airplane." Accessed October 19, 2024. [https://www.mharchives.ca/stories/the-hup-airplane/].

Montgomery, Dr. Robin. "Dr. Robin Montgomery: James W. Parker, a Hero or Villain?" *Conroe News*, May 20, 2021. [https://www.yourconroenews

.com/neighborhood/moco/opinion/article/Dr-Robin-Montgomery-James-W-Parker-a-hero-or-16194802.php].

Moore, Ruth S. "Peveler, Francis Marion." *Granbury Depot*, Hood County Genealogical Society. Accessed October 19, 2024. [https://www.granburydepot.org/z/biog2/PevelerFrancisMarion.htm].

"Muddled Comanche Command at Wichita." *Mary's Musings*, November 17, 2011. [https://mary-theoc.blogspot.com/2011/11/muddled-comanche-command-at-wichita.html].

National Weather Service. "April 14, 1935: The Black Sunday Dust Storm." Accessed October 19, 2024. [https://www.weather.gov/oun/events-19350414].

"NTI Database." *Show Me the Bitticks*. Accessed October 19, 2024. [http://www.showmethebitticks.com/html-f/nti/nti01277.htm].

Oklahoma Historical Society. "Alamo and the Texas Revolution." Accessed October 19, 2024. [https://www.okhistory.org/publications/enc/entry?entry=AM012]

"Old Fort Parker." *The Clio*. Accessed October 19, 2024. [https://theclio.com/entry/44135].

Orr, Susan, and H. D. Orr. "Howard, Sarah Creath." *Texas State Historical Association*, Handbook of Texas Online. Accessed July 2, 2022. [https://www.tshaonline.org/handbook/entries/howard-sarah-creath].

"Palo Duro Canyon Topographic Map." *Map Store*. Accessed October 19, 2024. [https://mapstore.mytopo.com/products/explore_351].

Parker, Rachel. *Rachel Plummer Narrative*. Internet Archive. [https://archive.org/stream/rachelplummernar00park/rachelplummernar00park_djvu.txt].

"Peta Nocona." *Fort Tours*. Accessed October 19, 2024. [https://www.forttours.com/pages/nocona.asp].

"Quanah Parker's Star House." *Hometown by Handlebar*. Last modified August 12, 2021. [https://hometownbyhandlebar.com/?p=2622].

"Ranald S. Mackenzie." *Oklahoma Historical Society*, The Encyclopedia of Oklahoma History and Culture. Accessed October 19, 2024. [https://www.okhistory.org/publications/enc/entry?entry=RA006].

Schmidly, David J. "Buffalo Hunting." *Texas State Historical Association*, Handbook of Texas Online. Accessed October 19, 2024. [https://www.tshaonline.org/handbook/entries/buffalo-hunting].

Smithsonian Magazine. "Who Were the Six Indian Chiefs in Teddy Roosevelt's Inaugural Parade?" Last modified October 10, 2018. [https://www.smithsonianmag.com/smithsonian-institution/photos-who-were-the-six-indian-chiefs-in-teddy-roosevelts-inaugural-parade-1976255/].

Tanner, Ogden. "How They Killed the Buffalo." *American Heritage*, March/April 1976. [https://www.americanheritage.com/how-they-killed-buffalo].

Texas Monthly. "Showdown at Waggoner Ranch." Last modified February 1, 2020. [https://www.texasmonthly.com/being-texan/showdown-at-waggoner-ranch/].

Texas Ranger Hall of Fame and Museum. "Hays, John." Accessed October 19, 2024. [https://www.texasranger.org/Hall-of-Fame/Hays-John].

Texas State Historical Association. "Fort Parker." Accessed October 19, 2024. [https://www.tshaonline.org/handbook/entries/fort-parker].

Texas State Historical Association. "Isa-tai." Accessed October 19, 2024. [https://www.tshaonline.org/handbook/entries/isa-tai].

Texas State Historical Association. "Lehmann, Herman." Accessed October 19, 2024. [https://www.tshaonline.org/handbook/entries/lehmann-herman].

Texas State Historical Association. "Parker, Silas M." Accessed October 19, 2024. [https://www.tshaonline.org/handbook/entries/parker-silas-m].

Texas State Historical Association. "Williams, Leonard G." Accessed October 19, 2024. [https://www.tshaonline.org/handbook/entries/williams-leonard-g].

Texas Time Travel. "Old Fort Parker." Accessed October 19, 2024. [https://texastimetravel.com/directory/old-fort-parker/].

"The Elusive Wichita Village." *Stories from the Road*. Last modified July 15, 2018. [https://storiesfromtheroad.net/2018/07/15/the-elusive-wichita-village/].

The First Sixty Years of MB Missions. Archive.org. Accessed October 19, 2024.[https://archive.org/stream/FirstSixtyYearsOfMBMissionsOCRopt/FirstSixtyYearsOfMBMissionsOCRopt_djvu.txt].

"The Salt Creek Massacre." *City of Mansfield, Texas*. Accessed October 19, 2024. [https://www.mansfieldtexas.gov/1370/The-Salt-Creek-Massacre].

Travels of James Parker. Scribble Maps. Accessed October 19, 2024. [https://www.scribblemaps.com/maps/view/Travels-of-James-Parker/James_Parker_Travels].

"Turkey Red Wheat." *Historical Marker Project.* Accessed October 19, 2024. [https://historicalmarkerproject.com/markers/HMZUL_turkey-red-wheat_Walton-KS.html].

TXSGS DNA Project. Accessed October 19, 2024. [https://txsgs.org/TXSGS_DNA/showmedia.php?mediaID=92&tngpage=50].

"Ukrainian Acorns, Canadian Oaks." *MCC Centennial.* Accessed October 19, 2024. [https://mcc.org/centennial/100-stories/ukrainian-acorns-canadian-oaks].

Wikipedia contributors. "Adobe Walls, Texas." *Wikipedia, The Free Encyclopedia.* Last modified August 12, 2023. [https://en.wikipedia.org/wiki/Adobe_Walls,_Texas].

Wikipedia contributors. "Antelope Hills Expedition." *Wikipedia, The Free Encyclopedia.* Last modified May 3, 2023. [https://en.wikipedia.org/wiki/Antelope_Hills_expedition].

Wikipedia contributors. "Antonio López de Santa Anna." *Wikipedia, The Free Encyclopedia.* Last modified October 18, 2023. [https://en.wikipedia.org/wiki/Antonio_L%C3%B3pez_de_Santa_Anna].

Wikipedia contributors. "Battle of Blanco Canyon." *Wikipedia, The Free Encyclopedia.* Last modified October 13, 2023. [https://en.wikipedia.org/wiki/Battle_of_Blanco_Canyon].

Wikipedia contributors. "Battle of Pease River." *Wikipedia, The Free Encyclopedia.* Last modified October 10, 2023. [https://en.wikipedia.org/wiki/Battle_of_Pease_River].

Wikipedia contributors. "Battle of the Washita River." *Wikipedia, The Free Encyclopedia.* Last modified October 13, 2023. [https://en.wikipedia.org/wiki/Battle_of_the_Washita_River].

Wikipedia contributors. "Big Tree (Kiowa leader)." *Wikipedia, The Free Encyclopedia.* Last modified October 12, 2023. [https://en.wikipedia.org/wiki/Big_Tree_(Kiowa_leader)].

Wikipedia contributors. "Bison Hunting." *Wikipedia, The Free Encyclopedia.* Last modified October 5, 2023. [https://en.wikipedia.org/wiki/Bison_hunting].

Wikipedia contributors. "Blanco Canyon." *Wikipedia, The Free Encyclopedia*. Last modified October 5, 2023. [https://en.wikipedia.org/wiki/Blanco_Canyon].

Wikipedia contributors. "Buffalo Hump." *Wikipedia, The Free Encyclopedia*. Last modified September 4, 2023. [https://en.wikipedia.org/wiki/Buffalo_Hump].

Wikipedia contributors. "Burkburnett, Texas." *Wikipedia, The Free Encyclopedia*. Last modified August 3, 2023. [https://en.wikipedia.org/wiki/Burkburnett,_Texas].

Wikipedia contributors. "Earl Van Dorn." *Wikipedia, The Free Encyclopedia*. Last modified October 10, 2023. [https://en.wikipedia.org/wiki/Earl_Van_Dorn].

Wikipedia contributors. "Fort Belknap (Texas)." *Wikipedia, The Free Encyclopedia*. Last modified October 9, 2023. [https://en.wikipedia.org/wiki/Fort_Belknap_(Texas)].

Wikipedia contributors. "Fort Parker Massacre." *Wikipedia, The Free Encyclopedia*. Accessed October 19, 2024. [https://en.wikipedia.org/wiki/Fort_Parker_massacre].

Wikipedia contributors. "Fort Sill." *Wikipedia, The Free Encyclopedia*. Last modified July 21, 2023. [https://en.wikipedia.org/wiki/Fort_Sill].

Wikipedia contributors. "George Armstrong Custer." *Wikipedia, The Free Encyclopedia*. Last modified October 15, 2023. [https://en.wikipedia.org/wiki/George_Armstrong_Custer].

Wikipedia contributors. "Goessel, Kansas." *Wikipedia, The Free Encyclopedia*. Last modified August 5, 2023. [https://en.wikipedia.org/wiki/Goessel,_Kansas].

Wikipedia contributors. "Great Raid of 1840." *Wikipedia, The Free Encyclopedia*. Last modified July 29, 2023. [https://en.wikipedia.org/wiki/Great_Raid_of_1840].

Wikipedia contributors. "Herman Lehmann." *Wikipedia, The Free Encyclopedia*. Last modified October 8, 2023. [https://en.wikipedia.org/wiki/Herman_Lehmann].

Wikipedia contributors. "History of Fort Worth, Texas." *Wikipedia, The Free Encyclopedia*. Last modified October 15, 2023. [https://en.wikipedia.org/wiki/History_of_Fort_Worth,_Texas].

Wikipedia contributors. "Isatai'i." *Wikipedia, The Free Encyclopedia.* Last modified September 29, 2023. [https://en.wikipedia.org/wiki/Isatai%27i].

Wikipedia contributors. "John Richard Parker." *Wikipedia, The Free Encyclopedia.* Last modified January 15, 2023. [https://en.wikipedia.org/wiki/John_Richard_Parker].

Wikipedia contributors. "Land Run of 1892." *Wikipedia, The Free Encyclopedia.* Last modified May 1, 2023. [https://en.wikipedia.org/wiki/Land_Run_of_1892].

Wikipedia contributors. "Lawrence Sullivan Ross." *Wikipedia, The Free Encyclopedia.* Last modified June 6, 2023. [https://en.wikipedia.org/wiki/Lawrence_Sullivan_Ross#Civil_War_service].

Wikipedia contributors. "Magdalena Hergert Becker." *Wikipedia, The Free Encyclopedia.* Last modified May 9, 2023. [https://en.wikipedia.org/wiki/Magdalena_Hergert_Becker].

Wikipedia contributors. "Mathew Caldwell." *Wikipedia, The Free Encyclopedia.* Last modified April 15, 2023. [https://en.wikipedia.org/wiki/Mathew_Caldwell#Legacy].

Wikipedia contributors. "North Fork Red River." *Wikipedia, The Free Encyclopedia.* Accessed October 19, 2024. [https://en.wikipedia.org/wiki/North_Fork_Red_River#/media/File:Redrivermap1.jpg].

Wikipedia contributors. "Quanah Parker Star House." *Wikipedia, The Free Encyclopedia.* Last modified June 29, 2023. [https://en.wikipedia.org/wiki/Quanah_Parker_Star_House].

Wikipedia contributors. "Sam Houston." *Wikipedia, The Free Encyclopedia.* Last modified September 7, 2023. [https://en.wikipedia.org/wiki/Sam_Houston#President_of_Texas].

Wikipedia contributors. "Satanta." *Wikipedia, The Free Encyclopedia.* Last modified October 7, 2023. [https://en.wikipedia.org/wiki/Satanta].

Wikipedia contributors. "Texas–Indian Wars." *Wikipedia, The Free Encyclopedia.* Last modified October 14, 2023. [https://en.wikipedia.org/wiki/Texas%E2%80%93Indian_wars].

Wikipedia contributors. "Theodore Roosevelt." *Wikipedia, The Free Encyclopedia.* Last modified August 27, 2023. [https://en.wikipedia.org/wiki/Theodore_Roosevelt#Presidency_(1901%E2%80%931909)].

Tina Siemens

WikiTree. "Sarah Elizabeth Parker." Accessed October 19, 2024. [https://www.wikitree.com/wiki/Parker-360].

YouTube. "Quanah Parker's Star House." Last modified September 6, 2023. [https://www.youtube.com/watch?v=zdaXOw-IZDk&feature=youtu.be].

Biography of Tina (Katharina) Siemens

Tina (Katharina) Siemens immigrated from Chihuahua, Mexico to Seminole, Texas, on March 26, 1977. She came with her parents, Anna and David Rempel, and her siblings. On October 31, 1986, Tina became a U.S. citizen. She considers it an absolute privilege to integrate and become a thread in the fabric of this great country.

On April 17, 1988, Tina married her best friend and now husband of 36 years, John Siemens. She and John are the proud parents of two sons, Jonathan and Christopher. Jonathan and his wife Tina, and Christopher and his wife Christy, have produced four "grandloves" for Tina and John, who call their grandparents Oma and Opa.

John and Tina own JW&T Inc., which specializes in residential and commercial construction. Tina considers it an honor to give back to her community while being a liaison between the different cultures of the area.

Tina was named the Citizen of the Year in 2015 in Gaines County.

On June 18, 2023, she received a Comanche name, PU?E?AITU POSA?KANI (translation: Bridge), and considers it an honor beyond words.

Tina's first book was *Seminole: Some People Never Give Up*. It tells the story of perseverance, survival, and faith.

Her second book, *The Little Sandals That Could,* detailed her migration story through the eyes of an eight-year-old child—Tina.

Post Oak: Quanah Parker, the Comanches and the Mission, is her third book. An important part of that story is Henry Kohfeld, Tina's third cousin three times removed. Henry was the first missionary at Post Oak and established the Mennonite Brethren Church.

Tina Siemens

Tina also owns the West Texas Living Heritage Museum, which had its grand opening on June 16-17, 2023.

All the glory to God…

For no one can lay any foundation other than the one already laid, which is Jesus Christ. 1 Corinthians 3:11 NKJ

Tina can be reached at:
- Personal Email: K.Siemens@yahoo.com
- Book Website: SeminoleTheBook.com
- Book Email: SeminoleTheBook@gmail.com
- Museum Website: WTLHM.com
- Museum Email: Info@WTLHM.com